THE CHINESE QUESTION IN CENTRAL ASIA

MARLÈNE LARUELLE AND SÉBASTIEN PEYROUSE

The Chinese Question in Central Asia

Domestic Order, Social Change and the Chinese Factor

Columbia University Press
New York

Columbia University Press
Publishers Since 1893
New York
cup.columbia.edu

Library of Congress Cataloging-in-Publication Data

Laruelle, Marlène.
The "Chinese question" in Central Asia : domestic order, social change and the Chinese factor / Marlène Laruelle and Sébastien Peyrouse.
p. cm.
Includes bibliographical references and index.
ISBN: 978-0-231-70304-8 (alk. paper)
ISBN: 978-0-231-80083-9
1. Asia, Central—Relations—China. 2. China—Relations—Asia, Central.
3. Social change—Asia, Central. 4. Asia, Central—Civilization—Chinese influences.
I. Peyrouse, Sébastien. II. Title.

DK857.75.C6L37 2012
303.48'251058—dc23

2012003969

♾

Columbia University Press books are printed on permanent and durable acid-free paper. This book is printed on paper with recycled content.
Printed in India

c 10 9 8 7 6 5 4 3 2 1

CONTENTS

INTRODUCTION

Of all the countries in the world, China is the one that probably arouses the most debate, ranging from the serious to the most provocative. Controversies over its probable ascension to superpower status in the coming decades are prevalent: China is a demographic power that conjures up, directly or indirectly, the myth of the "Yellow Peril," while India, which is expected to surpass China in terms of population by 2030, has not given birth to an "Indian peril;" it is an economic power hungry for raw materials, consuming the subsoil riches of its neighbors, and now those of sub-Saharan Africa and even Latin America; it is a growing financial power through its foreign exchange reserves in dollars, potentially capable of one day bringing the United States to its knees; it is a hybrid political system where the institutionalized generational change signals a recognition of pluralism, but there remains a single-party system based on a well-developed repressive apparatus. Finally, Chinese society is torn by its own internal transformation, with its middle-class consumers of entertainment, leisure activities and technology, and its hundreds of millions of peasants seeking to escape poverty and gain access to urban well-being, not to mention the resistance of the Tibetan and Uyghur minorities to Sinicization.

In this context, the Central Asian countries born of the collapse of the Soviet Union seem to occupy a very modest role. The media attention they receive is limited either to their proximity to Afghanistan and the internal destabilization of the weakest states among them, Kyrgyzstan and Tajikistan; or to the return of the alleged "Great Game" between the major powers, primarily the former colonial authority, Russia, and the United States, a newcomer seeking to gain a foothold on the Eurasian continent and now posing as successor of the British Empire, to use what in reality is an irrelevant historical metaphor from the nineteenth century.[1] Since independence in 1991, the five states—Kazakhstan, Kyrgyzstan, Uzbekistan, Tajikistan, and Turkmenistan—have taken increasingly divergent political, social, and geopolitical courses that undermine the regional concept of "Central Asia." Indeed, it tends to erase diversity in order to enhance unity. Although there are many similarities, the differences between them are just as important. To these five states one could also add, with caveats, Azerbaijan, the second oil power of the Caspian Basin after Kazakhstan. Afghanistan can also be included, not only because of its cultural proximity, but also because it drives a large part of the geopolitical orientations of the region; Xinjiang, too, on account of its being a crossroads between independent Central Asia and China, whose current evolution indirectly illuminates Beijing's new inroads into the region.

Accordingly, what place does Central Asia occupy in China's foreign policy strategies? The latter are driven by dynamics far removed from the region: they favor stability of relations with the United States and maximum delay to frameworks of opposition to Washington, which will probably arise first in financial and commercial terms[2]; the improvement of China's still difficult relations with Japan and other Asian neighbors; the maintenance of China's right of influence on the North Korean issue; and, lastly, the development of a partnership with the European Union and improved relations with India.[3] In this foreign policy framework, establishing relations with the new post-Soviet neighbors occupies a relatively minor place. For the Chinese elite, it was initially necessary to take in the demise of the Soviet regime, which remained an unacknowledged "big brother" despite the high level of tensions in the 1960s and 1970s. The evolution of the USSR under Mikhail Gorbachev aroused doubt and misunderstandings on the part of Chinese political elites, who viewed the developments in Moscow negatively and wished to avoid the Soviet path of collapse.[4] Once the Soviet Union disappeared, the primary objective of China was to maintain stability on its northern and northwestern border by addressing the issue of territorial boundaries with Russia, Kazakhstan, Kyrgyzstan, and Tajikistan, and seeking confirmation that they would respect the "One China" discourse.

Yet in China's perception of its environment, Central Asia is not only a part of the post-Soviet world, but also a part of West Asia. In neighboring Afghanistan, Beijing is investing more and more heavily: to ensure its influence in the country, it has placed its bets on establishing close political relations with Kabul, and developing trade and economic relations. China's role is particularly noteworthy in the Afghan extraction and export of raw materials, and Beijing has become one of Afghanistan's main economic partners.[5] Central Asia is also a space that embodies the competition between India and Pakistan, as each of the two rivals hopes to make allies out of the region. India wants to contain the expansion of Pakistan, curb potential terrorist destabilization that would affect Central Asia and also Afghanistan and Kashmir, access their economic wealth, and prevent China from entrenching itself and thus become the dominant power in the region. For its part, Pakistan tries, largely unsuccessfully, to acquire strategic depth by playing the card of Islamic solidarity, and to create economic inroads by presenting itself as the main transit country between Central Asia and the southern seas.[6] Finally, Central Asia affords China an opening to Russia, Iran and Turkey. In 2009, the combined gross domestic product (GDP) of the five Central Asian countries did not exceed US$160 billion—less than Malaysia or Pakistan—representing a population of about 60 million.[7] The market is therefore modest compared to the dynamics of Chinese production, but it is a central link in the conquest of the Russian market of 140 million people, and those of Turkey and Iran with about 75 million each, seen as gateways to the Persian Gulf.[8] Chinese revalorization of continental routes must thus be understood as part of a long-term historical evolution.

Moreover, Central Asia is unique for Beijing in terms of its significance with regard to Chinese domestic issues. The cultural, linguistic, and religious similarities between the Central Asian and Uyghur populations are not only important, they are also regularly revived. The Soviet Union was a key political and economic partner of Xinjiang in the 1930s and 1940s, before the founding of the People's Republic of China. The world as seen from Urumqi was oriented toward Moscow more than Beijing.[9] In the 1950s and 1960s, tens of thousands of Chinese citizens from Xinjiang migrated to the Soviet Union; the Uyghur intelligentsia mainly moved to Kazakhstan and to a lesser extent to Kyrgyzstan and Russia.[10] In 1991, the sudden appearance on the international stage of five new states reinforced Chinese concerns about the political aspirations of Uyghurs, who can be likened to the "sixth people of Central Asia," still waiting for independence.[11] The multiplication of contacts across the border and the growing support of part of the diaspora in campaigning for the rights of their fellow Uyghurs led Beijing to focus on "regulating" this issue. Although very different in scope, the Chinese policy pursued in Central Asia is a double-edged sword, as it also is in Xinjiang. It is repressive in political terms when it comes to pressuring the Central Asian governments to eliminate Uyghur associations, and constructive in economic terms when it comes to offering development aid on the principle that the improvement of living standards defuses political conflict. Central Asia is also conceived of as a key engine for Xinjiang's current economic development: Beijing's "open door policy" and "Far West Development Program" have indeed helped to transform this landlocked region into a place of major subsoil resource exploitation and an outpost for the advancement of Chinese trade in Central Asia, Afghanistan, and Pakistan.[12]

Finally, Central Asia has come to position itself on the Chinese radar as a partial solution to two concerns: securing continental energy supplies that are not subject to global geopolitical complications; and appearing as a peacefully rising power able to play the card of multilateralism.[13] In Chinese energy strategies, Kazakhstan is emerging as an exporter of oil and uranium, and Turkmenistan as an exporter of gas, while Tajikistan and Kyrgyzstan have the potential, still unrealized, to export hydroelectricity. As for the second concern, through the Shanghai Cooperation Organization (SCO), China is experimenting with new platforms for discussion between powers and promotes the image of its "peaceful rise" (*heping jueqi*) so as to allay international disquiet.[14] However, these two most publicized elements should not be overestimated. Central Asia represents less than 1 percent (0.89 percent in 2009) of the foreign trade of the People's Republic of China,[15] and will not replace the Middle East in terms of hydrocarbon supplies. The SCO is a preferred venue for Beijing on the international stage, but its potential failure, or at least weakening, would have no direct consequences for Beijing, as it can support other multilateral mechanisms to enhance its strategy of peaceful rise.

Even if energy and multilateralism remain important components of Chinese international positioning, Beijing's interest in Central Asia is primarily driven by the duality of domestic stability in Xinjiang and good neighborly relations with local governments, and the transformation of Xinjiang and Central Asia into areas of transit trade for the conquest of new markets.[16] Central Asia is therefore, paradoxically, fundamental in terms of domestic stability because of the Uyghur issue and marginal to the preoccupations of Chinese foreign policy as a whole. It is not related to Japan or North Korea, or even to Taiwan, since the Central Asian governments have not sought to challenge the "One China" policy. Even if the importance of the region stems partly from relations with the United States because of the US military base in Kyrgyzstan, it remains a trivial problem compared to the issues of trade, currency, and human rights that occupy everyday US China relations. It seems thus that tensions do exist between Chinese global foreign policy strategies and its specific interest in Central Asia. For some experts such as Zhao Huasheng, the marginality of Central Asia in Chinese foreign policy is confirmed by the lack of strategy, in the full sense of the term, toward the region.[17]

This simultaneously overrepresented and underrepresented place of Central Asia is not specific to Chinese foreign policy. The region occupies the same paradoxical niches for Moscow and Washington since it is a space where Russia, China, and the United States act out their triangular relations. Each wants to have a privileged relationship with each of the other partners, since any alliance between two of the actors will weaken the position of the third. Hence Washington does not want to see any fundamental strategic alliance emerge between Moscow and Beijing, as this would block its advances into the Eurasian space and its progress on major international issues like Iran and North Korea. Russia is concerned by Sino-American rapprochement and the growing economic and financial interdependence between those two countries that could see the emergence of a Sino-American twenty-first century in which Moscow is only a second-rate actor. Finally China takes no delight in improvements in Russian-American relations or in the positive functioning of the US-Europe-Russia trio. In Central Asia, the United States tends to perceive Russia as its main rival in terms of influence: Russia's strategies to defend its interests in the post-Soviet space are criticized, and yet Chinese obstructions to US influence, regarding the closing of the military base in Kyrgyzstan for example, are often passed over in silence.[18] Russia, for its part, also continues to work within the schemas inherited from the Cold War by focusing on US containment strategies, and so fails to measure China's pace of advancement. As for China, it unambiguously prefers Russian control in Central Asia to American domination, and can only be glad about the mutual Russian-American "neutralization," which leaves the field open to it for economic investments.

For the Central Asian states, the arrival of China on their agenda, both domestic and international, has been sudden. Although human contacts were never broken entirely, China was considered at worst a dangerous neighbor, responsible for the 1969 clashes along the border with Kazakhstan, or at best a nonexistent one. The southern border of the Soviet Union was effectively sealed—albeit less than the frontier with Europe—and Moscow perceived Central Asia as its southern *cul-de-sac*. Political, economic, and cultural relations oriented the Central Asian societies entirely to the north, with the exception of a few dissidents who turned to the Islamic umma. Chinese, Afghan, and Iranian neighbors were either completely hidden or minimized, being of relevance only for the population living in militarized border areas, or during specific events, such as the Soviet intervention in Afghanistan. With the disappearance of the Iron Curtain and the "discovery" of its new neighbors, Central Asia changed its geographical self-representation. The region is no longer just the south of Russia, but also the north of Afghanistan and India, the west of China, and the north-east of Iran. The prevailing feeling is that an historical chapter has been definitively closed, ensuring that regardless of future developments in Central Asia, the region will never again be entirely dependent on a single power.

In the first half of the 1990s, the attention of the Central Asian elite focused on the reaffirmation of belonging to the umma. The presidents made pilgrimages to Mecca, increased contacts with Turkey, Iran, the Gulf monarchies, Egypt, and Pakistan, and rebuilt mosques with funds mainly from Turkey, Saudi Arabia, and Kuwait. Soon, however, the trend toward integration in the Islamic world slowed. Economic partnerships have proved to be disappointing, and only Turkey succeeded in becoming a major player in terms of trade and investment. The Central Asian governments were concerned about the uncontrolled spread of radical Islam from abroad and quickly put an end to Islamic aid. Proselytizers were surprised to discover largely Sovietized Central Asian populations who were weak in religious practice and lacking in theological knowledge; while many of the Central Asians who went to Muslim countries were shocked by the version of Islam that did not conform to their vision of faith as a primarily cultural element.[19] Although mostly underground, the slow process of re-Islamization of Central Asian societies is no less decisive, and will reappear in one form or another in the years to come.

In the second half of the 1990s, while the relationship with the umma declined in importance, Russia returned to the Central Asian scene, at first timidly, then more assuredly with Vladimir Putin's coming to power. Moscow still controls the major hydrocarbon export routes, invests in the Central Asian economies, reinforces its military relations with the countries' armies, maintains its close links in political circles, remains a cultural reference for the Central Asian societies, and draws millions of Uzbeks, Tajiks, and Kyrgyz for labor migration.[20] The United States also increasingly asserts itself in the region, but its influence has been subject to numerous ebbs and flows. Washington imposed itself rapidly in the 1990s only to lose influence markedly around 2003, remain at an historical low in 2007 and 2008, and regain some stature since 2009.[21] The dynamics of the so-called Russian-American "Great

Game" combine geopolitical strategies (sphere of influence in the Near Abroad for Moscow and control of the heart of the Eurasian continent for global influence for Washington), economic logics (managing the energy resources of the Caspian Basin and reorienting export routes), and political issues (continuing the Russian model of consensual authoritarianism versus promoting democracy, civil society, and good governance on the US side). In the second half of the 1990s, China was a modest player in this Central Asian "Great Game": it succeeded in settling border disputes, put pressure on Central Asian governments to hamper the politicization of the Uyghur diaspora, and had a very modest economic presence.[22]

In the 2000s, developments that had so far proceeded quietly accelerated sharply. Economically, in less than ten years, China has positioned itself as one of the top three trading partners for each of the Central Asian states. It controls a quarter of Kazakh[23] oil and has built a pipeline going from the Caspian Sea to Xinjiang; has become the preferred client of Turkmenistan for its gas exports; has transformed Kyrgyzstan into an economic quasi-protectorate that survives mainly on the re-export of Chinese products, and Tajikistan into a privileged gateway to its presence in Afghanistan. Kazakhstan enjoys a particular status. The China-Kazakhstan partnership is termed "strategic"—the highest of diplomatic modifiers—confirming that Astana is one of Beijing's major political allies not only in the post-Soviet space, where one day it may even be ahead of Russia if Sino-Russian relations deteriorate, but also more globally in Asia and the Middle East. Strategically, China is second to Russia, conducting annual military exercises with Kazakhstan, Kyrgyzstan, and Tajikistan, and openly displays support for the Central Asian regimes, which it sees as the only bulwark against Islamism or a form of "democratic chaos." Less visible but no less structural, China is also deeply transforming the local social fabric by creating new economic and cultural niches, and through timid strategies of cooptation of certain segments of the population.

The self-perception of Central Asian societies has therefore drastically changed. In the 1990s, the opening to China was widely perceived as a way to get rid of Russian rule and to avoid being trapped in competition for influence between Moscow and Washington. The balance is now inverse: after becoming the west of China—that is, once proximity to China becomes the primary driver of economic and geopolitical status in Central Asia—how does the region achieve a positive balance between an array of international actors and competing interests? For Central Asia, China rises as an immutable neighbor while the relationship with Russia is seen as evolutionary, dependent on domestic and international, geopolitical, economic, and cultural factors, which may affect Moscow's influence in the region. Other actors are even more in flux. The Central Asian states feel that they have no influence on Washington's involvement; Europe remains too modest a partner; Turkey and Iran have already yielded their interests in the region; and Japan's involvement has not had the expected effect. China is therefore the only power whose weight in Central Asia is seen as a given with which one must learn to live, regardless of future regime changes and geopolitical developments vis-à-vis Russia and the West.

The question follows of whether ties with China should then be formulated in terms of a "vassal relationship,"[24] similar to the way in which Imperial China maintained relations with buffer areas on the outskirts of its empire. Like the reference to the "Great Game," the historical metaphor can illuminate long-term processes but also tends to obscure reality. The Central Asian states are not shifting political configurations like the khanates of the eighteenth century but are now independent actors, recognized and protected as such by the international community. Contemporary and Imperial China are not one and the same: China's vision of its own territory, borders, and the unity of its population has changed, the nation-state has become the standard reference, and strategies of influence over neighbors have evolved dramatically. The contemporary situation is closer to a kind of "soft hegemony"[25] with China seemingly able to hold the upper hands in Central Asia by virtue of the absence of real competitors. Indeed Beijing plays multiple hands in the region: it insists on its equality with the Central Asian states in diplomatic terms and in the framework of the SCO, but, at the same time, displays a more threatening face when the Uyghur issue is at stake, employs resource diplomacy with formidable efficacy,[26] presents itself as a key partner in matters of development aid,[27] and yet moves timidly in the arena of cultural affairs. Therefore the arsenal used is mainly that of soft power, but in this *soft* form, there exists such an asymmetry in power relations that even this can sometimes seem *hard* to the governments and societies of Central Asia. The power differential is even deeper because the five states have poor relations among themselves and logics of regionalization have failed. None of the regional fora where they could potentially find themselves together, without much great power to lead, has managed to come to life, and they only participate in regional activities in venues where Russia dominates, or in the SCO.[28]

Relations to China are therefore complex—full of ambivalences, hopes, fears, and opportunities, as well as logics of having no other choices.[29] Beijing brings the diversity of Central Asia spectacularly to light. Each of the five states has to work alone in managing its power differential with Beijing, and has its own specific "Chinese question." By this term one does not imply a "Chinese problem," but a large tangle of debates and stakes that have gripped Central Asian societies and for which China has become, voluntarily or not, the catalyst. One does not think of China in the same way in Astana, where Kazakh elites pursue multi-vectoral policies and great power ambitions, as in Dushanbe, where the dominant feeling is that the Chinese neighborhood represents the last chance to avoid a spread of the Afghan scenario. Kyrgyz petty traders competing for Chinese products and high-level officials in Ashgabat overseeing the Sino-Turkmen gas pipeline see different faces of the Chinese world. There are shared perceptions, however, particularly in the economic domain. Since the global downturn in 2008, all the Central Asian states have become even more convinced of the essential role that Beijing plays. Whereas European countries were forced to reduce their investments and were weakened by domestic economic crises, China quickly got back on its feet and was the only country able to invest large sums in the region, taking advantage of the discrediting of international organizations and Western powers.

Existing publications on relations between China and Central Asia generally limit themselves to discussing energy issues and security questions. The purpose of this book is to go beyond such geopolitical analysis by articulating the role of an external influential factor, namely China, and domestic societal changes in neighboring Central Asia. China's rise to power constitutes one of the driving forces behind the domestic order that was established in the region during the last decade. It has become part of the various national narratives on numerous internal challenges, and the rise of both Sinophilia and Sinophobia has a significant impact on Central Asian societies over the short, medium, and long terms. Through this analysis, we hope to highlight the complex interplay between domestic issues, social change, and globalization. The cultural concerns, although difficult to measure, form a central part of the post-Cold War world: the transformation of the global system is shaped by perceptions and world views that require the researcher to conduct his or her observations at the intersection of the internal and external.

The objective of this work is thus to discuss the multifaceted impact of the China factor on Central Asian domestic orders. A multidisciplinary approach is needed: the discipline of international relations for studying diplomatic contacts between the two sides, economics for the impact of the Chinese presence in Central Asia, sociology for the political, social, and cultural components that affect the change emanating from China, and analysis of discourse to understand the diversity of the perceptions and arguments put forward by the Central Asian elites in thinking about their own situation. This book is not devoted to studying Chinese foreign policy: it does not therefore detail the multiplicity of Chinese actors in Central Asia (diplomats, intelligence services, and businessmen), or the internal debates of the Chinese elites on which strategies to pursue in the region, both of which will be topics for subsequent research. The inclusion of Afghanistan would have been merited. However, as this study is based primarily on fieldwork, interviews on the ground and the analysis of discourse, it could seriously be carried out only if limited to post-Soviet states and sources available in Russia,[30] as such an in-depth analysis was impossible for Afghanistan. Fieldwork was organized in the five Central Asian states and China over the course of several months, mainly in 2008, and more briefly in 2009 and 2010.[31] The Smith Richardson Foundation funded much of this research in 2008, and the Swedish Foundation for International Cooperation in 2009, both of whom we are very grateful to. We are very much indebted to all those who have helped us to realize this project, Christophe Jaffrelot, Michelle Smith, Steve Corcoran, Alec Forss, and Irina Vauday.

PART I

CHINA AS A GLOBALIZED ACTOR IN THE CENTRAL ASIAN STATES

At the collapse of the Soviet Union, China arrived in Central Asia with few assets. Prior to this date, the generally bad state of Sino-Soviet relations had impeded the development of direct relations between the two regions. Central Asia was also perceived by Beijing as a space reserved for Moscow. With a few exceptions, the federated Central Asian republics were without any access to the outside world. Such access by Uzbekistan alone—as a symbol of the alliance between Islam and socialism—was championed by the Soviet regime, which sought support from Third World countries, many of them Muslim. For the new Central Asian states, establishing direct bilateral relations with Beijing has thus required overcoming the extremely negative clichés of China put about by Soviet propaganda; clichés that reinforced Central Asian societies' already longstanding apprehensions of their large neighbor. The Chinese authorities, aware of their negative image in Central Asia, immediately recognized the independence of the new states, welcomed their diplomatic delegations with full honors, and decided to implement a "good neighborhood" policy.

Chinese interests in Central Asia have been structured in phases. In the first half of the 1990s, Beijing's concern was to sign demarcation treaties, demilitarize the borders, and prevent the strengthening of Uyghur separatism. In the second half of the 1990s and early 2000s, China aimed to create a platform for discussion and mutual discovery, and to elaborate a collective security framework through the Shanghai Cooperation Organization. In the first half of the 2000s, it moved to establish itself vigorously on the Central Asian market, mainly in hydrocarbons, extractive industries, infrastructures and communications. Finally, since 2005, Beijing has been trying—still timidly—to establish ways to promote its language and culture and to train Central Asian elites according to the Chinese model. For China, Central Asia is a buffer zone. The Soviet Union's collapse, instability in Afghanistan, and strengthened US presence in Eurasia offer both opportunities and dangers. China's geographical proximity and ethnic contiguity with Central Asia, though an asset from some perspectives, is also perceived as a danger. Despite these challenges and China's initially negative overall image in Central Asia, the Middle Kingdom has succeeded in improving its reputation through the exercise of soft-power diplomacy.

Over the long term, China's presence in Central Asia must be compared with that of Russia, since both involve not only state-to-state relations, but also societal implications of great magnitude. The US presence is limited to geopolitical questions, Iran's and Turkey's influence did not have the impact that had been expected in the early 1990s, and the European Union is taking a long time to establish itself as a key part of the Central Asian agenda. China, by contrast, is having an impact on all aspects of Central Asian societies. It is therefore a globalized actor in the same way as Russia: a diplomatic neighbor, a geopolitical ally, an economic partner, and a bearer of what is simultaneously an attractive and alarming societal and cultural model. After having resolved the nascent problems—mainly border demarcation and the Uyghur diaspora—that came with the unexpected independence of Central Asia in 1991, China imposed itself through the SCO. It very quickly made successful economic inroads into the region, to the point that, in less than a decade, it has become one of the main trading partners of the five states, "flooding" the markets with its products. It is also one of the principal actors of the so-called energy Great Game, and one of the main investors in the local economies.

1

BORDERS AND DIASPORAS

SOLVING THE PROBLEMS ARISING FROM CENTRAL ASIAN INDEPENDENCE

With the collapse of the Soviet Union, China was quick to become aware of the unique opportunities that arose with this new geopolitical situation, which was not however without new risks, particularly in relation to its north and north-west borders. In 1991, Chinese economic power was still a shadow of what it was to become two decades later, and the idea that the post-Soviet states were new markets to be conquered had yet to play a major role in Chinese strategies. What dominated were elements of anxiety: despite the satisfaction of seeing a superpower state like the Soviet Union disappear, and with it the historical Sino-Soviet conflict, Beijing was above all concerned about the impact of Central Asia's independence on the situation in Xinjiang, in particular due to the significant Uyghur diaspora present in the new states, and the risks of conflict linked to the non-resolution of territorial borders.

The border treaties between China, Kazakhstan, Kyrgyzstan, and Tajikistan

In December 1991, three states of Central Asia, namely Kazakhstan, Kyrgyzstan, and Tajikistan, found themselves in a situation of having to patrol their new international borders, whose demarcation China disputed. Despite the decade of Sino-Soviet friendship, which started with the proclaiming of the People's Republic of China in October 1949 and ended with the demise in relations between Moscow and Beijing in 1959, the two Communist states had been unable to settle their border disputes inherited from the late nineteenth century. China presented itself as a colonized country, and accused Soviet Moscow of having validated the colonial borders of the Tsarist Empire.[1] The ideological conflict that pitted Mao and the Soviet leaders against each other came to light with frequent border tensions and, in 1969, the quasi-war that occurred between the two countries on the island of Damanski/Zhenbao, on the Ussuri River in the Russian Far East, and at the Alatau pass in Kazakhstan.[2] Despite new meetings between the authorities of the two countries in 1969 and 1978, no demarcation agreement was signed. Instead the conflicting parties were able to agree only on a declaration of intent to manifest their goodwill to settle this dispute in a peaceful way.

It was not until Mikhail Gorbachev took up the position of First Secretary of the Communist Party of the Soviet Union that the question of the border disputes was revisited. In 1988, a warming in bilateral relations made possible the creation of a working group whose mission was to prepare for negotiations over the western sector of the Sino-Soviet border. In May 1991, only a few months before the Central Asian states achieved independence, Jiang Zemin and Gorbachev claimed that they had reached agreement on the eastern sector of the Sino-Soviet border, but not on the western one. Upon independence, the three Central Asian republics thus inherited an unresolved situation that the Soviet Union had failed to settle and began negotiations with Beijing. More distinctly cordial relations contributed to giving fresh impetus to finding a solution to this thorny question.

According to Mao, the "unequal treaties" excised some 1,500,000 km^2 of territory from China to the advantage of Tsarist and then Soviet Russia. Close to two-thirds of this surface area, or 910,000 km^2, were situated in Central Asia, while the other third under dispute was located in Siberia and the Russian Far East.[3] Chinese documents questioned 22 percent of the total surface area of Central Asia: Beijing laid claim to a territory stretching from Semirechie to Lake Balkhash in Kazakhstan, almost all of Kyrgyzstan, and some 28,000 km^2 in the Pamir region of Tajikistan. However, with the opening of negotiations, the Chinese authorities toned down their claims and opted for a "good neighborhood" strategy with the new independent states. Still under international sanction for the violent repression in Tiananmen Square in June 1989, the Chinese authorities agreed to reduce their territorial claims to "only" 34,000 km^2, chiefly out of a desire to secure allies in Central Asia. Kazakhstan, Kyrgyzstan and Tajikistan also announced their desire to negotiate with China on the basis of the various agreements made between Moscow and Beijing prior to 1991 as well as on the principles of international law.[4]

The new post-Soviet balance of forces afforded China advantages as well as inconveniences: whereas previously it had to negotiate with a single country, the particularly powerful Soviet Union, now it had to negotiate with several weak partners, a fact that enabled it to use a "divide and conquer" policy but which prevented any mutual exchanges of territory. Beijing laid claim to a total of 2,235 km^2 in Kazakhstan, distributed across 11 zones (some parts of which were just 10 km^2 in size), and 3,728 km^2 in Kyrgyzstan spread across five zones; however, it stuck to almost all of its original demands of Tajikistan, from which it wanted a large part of the Pamirs (28,430 km^2), equivalent to one fifth of the country's area. In 1992, a working group of the four Commonwealth of Independent States (CIS) countries and China was created so that the Central Asian states would not find themselves alone and in a position of weakness vis-à-vis China. These first multiparty meetings helped the Central Asian states, with Moscow's support, to start their negotiations with Beijing—as did the creation of the Shanghai Five group in 1996—but the actual agreements were signed within bilateral frameworks.[5]

The Kazakh President, Nursultan Nazarbayev, made every effort to achieve rapid progress on this issue during a visit to Beijing in 1993.[6] A first agreement was reached on the delimitation of nine of the eleven contested border zones. The negotiations were made easier by the absence of mountainous terrain between the two countries, making the demarcation less complex, in contrast to the mountainous zones separating China from Kyrgyzstan and Tajikistan. The territorial demarcation treaty concerning these nine zones, amounting to 1,700 km^2 of borders, was signed in March 1994. The status of the two unresolved border regions, namely the districts of Sardy-Cheldy and the Chagan-Obo Valley, which comprised a surface area of 946 km^2 and a non-delimited border of about 120 kilometers, was settled in 1998 and the treaty ratified a few months later.[7] Although the opposition criticized this decision, the Kazakh authorities were satisfied with it, as they were still left with 57 percent of those territories that China had coveted.[8] Astana at last felt liberated from Chinese threats over Lake Balkhash.

The negotiations with Bishkek lasted longer, for several reasons: Beijing was more distrustful toward the regime of Askar Akayev, who presented himself as resolutely pro-Western; it exerted more direct pressure on the small Kyrgyz state, whereas it had sought to accommodate the Kazakh neighbor; and the negotiations led to domestic problems which thwarted the ability of the Kyrgyz regime to ratify the agreements it had made.[9] During the 1994 CIS-China meetings, the Chinese and Kyrgyz authorities made public an initial document detailing the border sections on which they had already agreed. In 1996, a first Sino-Kyrgyz border treaty was signed (and ratified in 1998), which detailed the demarcation of about 900 kilometers of the 1,011 kilometers of common borders, and both countries agreed to begin the process of demarcation within the already shared zones. In 1999, the Chinese President, Jiang Zemin, and his Kyrgyz counterpart signed a second agreement in which China was granted 90,000 hectares in the Uzengi-Kuush region in exchange for control by Bishkek of two-thirds of the Khan Tengri peak (the second highest point in the country, which rises to an altitude of 7,000 meters) and of the Victory Peak.[10]

In ceding Uzengi-Kuush, however, Kyrgyzstan, already short of agricultural land, lost a valuable arable area. In addition, border security was partly undermined as the territory transferred to China contained the one and only road link between the three Kyrgyz border posts. Through the treaty, China gained control of the Sarydzhaz and Uzengi-Kuush Rivers, as well as some of the glaciers that make up an important part of Kyrgyzstan's water resources, and mineral resources such as tungsten. Despite the massive protests organized by the opposition and the subsequent crackdown that resulted in the deaths of several demonstrators,[11] President Akayev managed to secure the ratification of the treaty in 2002. But settling the border disputes with China created an upheaval in domestic Kyrgyz politics and began the process of undermining Askar Akayev's legitimacy, eventually leading to the "Tulip Revolution" of March 2005.

The negotiations between China and Tajikistan over their 400 kilometers of common borders turned out to be the longest and most difficult to settle. They began in 1993 under the auspices of the CIS-China joint group. In the middle of a civil war at the time, Tajikistan was hardly in a position to make progress on resolving the issue. Not until 1999 did the negotiations result in the signing of a first border agreement on the Karazak Pass region and the Markansu River, which had already been mentioned in the Tsarist protocol of Novyi Margelan, signed in 1884. The entire section stretching from the Uz-Bel pass to the Afghan border, however, still had to be negotiated. On the occasion of a Shanghai group meeting in Dushanbe in 2000, a treaty was signed on the three-way zone between China, Kyrgyzstan, and Tajikistan, while the status of the remainder of the Pamir region was left hanging. Only in May 2002 did China and Tajikistan finally manage to reach agreement on all their border disputes. The Tajik authorities ceded to China 1,000 km^2 of mountainous zones situated east of Murghab, whose transfer Parliament ratified only at the start of 2011.[12] The territory Beijing obtained represented only 3 percent of that claimed under the Soviet regime: Tajikistan managed to hold onto 97 percent of the 28,000 km^2 under dispute.

The unresolved water issue with Kazakhstan

Settling border issues did not lead Kazakhstan and China to reach any agreement on the thorny question of water and cross-border river management, an issue that today remains one of the main stumbling blocks between both countries. Two of Kazakhstan's main rivers, the Ili and the Irtysh, originate in China, the former in the Tian-Shan Mountains and the latter in the Chinese Altay Mountains. The Chinese authorities regularly draw water off upstream from both rivers, without seeking agreement from Kazakhstan, a situation that became worse after the implementation of the "Far West development programs" (*xibu dakaifa*).[13]

These programs aim to foster the rapid expansion of Xinjiang's agricultural industry, particularly for cotton and wheat, two water-intensive crops. Similarly, the development of oil reserves and Han Chinese colonization strategies of rural and urban areas are accelerating population growth throughout Xinjiang, leading to greater water consumption. In order to successfully complete these projects, Beijing has decided to increase the amount of water it extracts from the Ili and Irtysh Rivers. In the 1990s, it announced the construction of the 300-kilometer-long and the 22-meter-wide Kara Irtysh-Karamay Canal, intended to redirect between 10 and 40 percent of the Irtysh to Ulungur Lake. The objective was two-fold: first, to irrigate 140,000 new hectares of agricultural fields; and second, to transport water to the Karamay oil fields, situated about 400 kilometers from Urumqi, with confirmed reserves of 1.7 billion tons of oil.[14] Currently, the canal diverts around 500 million cubic meters of water per year, but the figure is projected to exceed one billion cubic meters when it reaches full operational capacity in 2020. This has adversely affected Kazakhstan's agricultural and industrial development, and could even influence regions as far away as Siberia, since the Irtysh is the main tributary of the Ob River, which flows through the Omsk region.[15]

Kazakhstan is concerned about the falling level of these rivers on its territory, since it also requires a large amount of water to support its economic development. According to the Kazakh government, the Irtysh is the main source of water for around four million out of the country's total population of 16 million people.[16] Important towns of the northeast, such as Karaganda, Semei and Pavlodar, all draw some of their supply of fresh water directly from the Irtysh. Developing the capital, Astana, also requires greater provision of water. In order to meet the demands of this bourgeoning city, the authorities need to divert part of the Irtysh-Karaganda Canal to supplement the Ishim, the Irtysh's main tributary, which supplies Astana directly. In addition to threatening urban development in Kazakhstan, the fall in river levels also impairs industrial potential. Three hydroelectric stations in the northeast—in Bukhtarma on Lake Zaysan, in Ust-Kamenogorsk, and in Shulbinsk—depend on Soviet-age reservoirs that rely on the water flows from the Irtysh. The river is also navigable during the summer months and is one of the drivers behind commercial exchange between this part of Kazakhstan and the Russian town of Omsk.[17] As the Ili, it feeds into the Kapchagay hydroelectric station, which supplies energy to the south of Kazakhstan, where energy shortfalls are still prevalent. Between the Chinese border and Lake Balkhash, the Ili is the chief source of irrigation for the fields lining the length of the Grand Almaty Canal and is crucial to rice growing in the Akdalinsk region.[18]

In addition to these economic arguments, Kazakhstan—with the backing of international environmental organizations—is concerned about potential ecological risks accruing from China's upstream diverting of water. A reduction in the flow of the Irtysh would result in the degradation of the entire region's already fragile ecosystem, since the river also carries nitrates and petroleum products in addition to several heavy metals.[19] If this situation worsens, it could cause significant damage to Lake Zaysan, which, according to some sources, would be threatened with extinction.[20] A reduction in the effluence of the Ili would have even more serious consequences: it provides Lake Balkhash with more than 50 percent of its water supply, but by the time it reaches that lake, the river already carries many agricultural chemical pollutants. Lake Balkhash was ecologically damaged in the 1960s and 1970s due to the construction of the Kapchagay reservoir. The fifteenth-largest in the world, the lake plays a key role in maintaining the climatic balance of southeast and central Kazakhstan. Regular increases in the lake's salinity, however, adversely affect its fresh water levels.[21] Moreover, with the combination of dropping water levels, a deteriorating ecosystem, a reduction in the number of fish species, and declining fishing yields, the living conditions of the local population have been detrimentally affected. The United Nations Development Program has raised the alarm, warning that the fall in the water supply from the Ili to the lake "could become an environmental tragedy comparable to the Aral Sea disaster."[22] If river levels continue to drop, the ensuing climatic transformation of the region could become irreversible.

International treaties do not adequately regulate the use of cross-border water resources and Kazakhstan has had difficulties given the power differential that favors its Chinese neighbor.[23] The first Kazakh Ambassador to Beijing, Murat Auezov, raised the problem though he did not succeed in bringing it to the attention of the Chinese authorities.[24] Kazakhstan then attempted to convince Russia to become interested in the problem, pointing to the dangers that exploiting the two rivers would have for the Omsk region, since the Ob River depends on the Irtysh. Yet Moscow has preferred not to get involved in tripartite negotiations. With alarmist articles being published in the Kazakh press about the Kara Irtysh-Karamay Canal, the threat of the souring of diplomatic relations between the two countries eventually compelled Beijing to consent to some superficial negotiations with Astana. Five rounds of discussions at various levels were organized in 1999, 2000, and 2001.[25] Both countries finally signed a framework agreement for the protection and utilization of cross-border rivers in September 2001.[26]

Nevertheless, the document does not stipulate any rules for the specific treatment of the Ili or the Irtysh, going no further than calling for a "measured" utilization of common waters. Beijing has systematically refused to set up a joint authority for managing the Irtysh, accepting only the creation of a Sino-Kazakh consultative commission, which has met only on a few occasions. In 2006, the commission completed a draft agreement concerning information about water quality that each party was to disseminate, and submitted it to Beijing for approval. In 2011 an intergovernmental agreement on the protection of water quality of cross-border rivers was signed, according to which both parties are taking on strict obligations to monitor water quality, but Beijing and Astana have failed to develop a unified position with respect to water intake limits.[27] The problem has therefore yet to be properly addressed. As long as the negotiations remain bilateral, Kazakhstan will have difficulties in making itself heard, while China's attitude reinforces already prevalent concerns within Kazakh society about its intentions in the region.[28] The problem of diverting water is bound to be a recurrent one, to the extent that China draws off more water and the ecological situation worsens on the Kazakh side.

Quelling the Uyghur diaspora's support for Xinjiang autonomy

Relations between Central Asia and China have not been built solely on the peaceful resolution of their border issues; an important component has also been managing the difficult Uyghur question. In the Deng Xiaoping's era the Uyghur population in Xinjiang came to benefit from a partial liberalization both culturally and economically. This period saw the reopening of mosques and Uyghur-speaking schools.[29] However, with the fall of the Soviet Union, political stakes rapidly came to the fore and halted any prospect of increasing autonomy. Bolstered by the independence of the neighboring Central Asian states, the dream of an independent Uyghur state was revived. However, this led to new political tensions, since Beijing objected to all autonomist ideas and to any undermining of its territorial integrity. Uyghur activism peaked in the 1990s, with growing numbers of skirmishes, bomb attacks, and several bloody popular riots including the Yining (Khuldja) riots in February 1997.[30]

Anxious about the political radicalization of sections of Uyghur society, about the structuring of an autonomist narrative with Islamic connotations, and about the ambiguous role of the Central Asian diaspora, China bluntly demanded that the Central Asian states prevent any anti-Chinese movement from emerging on their territories.[31] Between 1993 and 1997, Beijing exerted immense but discreet pressure on the Central Asian governments, in particular Kazakhstan and Kyrgyzstan, over their Uyghur diaspora. In 1995, the Friendship Declaration between Kazakhstan and the PRC spoke of their common struggle against separatism. Each state committed itself to refusing access to its territory to any forces that threatened to undermine the territorial integrity of its partner. These tensions persisted in the 2000s in the international context of the "War on Terror," which allowed Beijing to play on the alleged threat of Islamist Uyghur terrorism.

The Uyghur diaspora in Central Asia includes about 300,000 people, although it is impossible to obtain exact figures due to processes of interethnic assimilation, but also due to the coercive pressures that some Central Asian states, like Uzbekistan, have put on minorities to assimilate into the national majority. Only a few hundred Uyghurs live in Turkmenistan, and there are about 2,000 of them in Tajikistan.[32] In Uzbekistan, according to the 1989 census, as many as 23,000 people claimed to be Uyghurs. They are divided between the Tashkent and Ferghana Valley regions, including several relatively densely packed villages in the Pakhabad district close to Andijan.[33] In contrast to the Uyghurs in Kazakhstan and Kyrgyzstan, those in Uzbekistan are largely integrated: their linguistic and cultural proximity to the Uzbek majority, the many mixed marriages, the absence of Uyghur-speaking primary schools and active cultural centers, and the national policy of giving preference to ethnic Uzbeks are all factors that have contributed to reducing Uyghur national sentiment. In Kyrgyzstan, there are about 46,000 Uyghurs dispersed among the regions of Chui, Bishkek, and Issyk-Kul in the north of the country, while one-third of them are situated in Osh and Jalalabad in the south, where they are largely assimilated with the Uzbek population. Kazakhstan, with a total population of around 223,000 (according to a 2009 census)[34], actually has the largest Uyghur diaspora of any Central Asian country. The Uyghurs there form the country's seventh-largest ethnic group, and live in relatively dense groupings: 95 percent of them have settled in the Almaty region, where they constitute 9 percent of the population, and have fifteen Uyghur-speaking primary schools available to them. They make up a majority of the Uyghur autonomous district, and are also numerous in that of Panfilov, situated close to the Khorgos border post with China, and in that of Enbenshikazakh.[35]

To speak of the existence of an "Uyghur diaspora" in Central Asia raises several problems. First, the term Uyghur appeared in the region only with the Soviet census of 1926 and only thereafter did it gradually come to replace the terms commonly in use—*Kashgari* (those originating from the Kashgar region) and *Taranchi* (all the Turkic-speaking Muslims originating from the Ili Valley)—that have now altogether disappeared.[36] During the decades of Soviet rule, persons identified as Uyghurs were able to benefit from minority rights (cultural centers, primary schools, publications, television and radio programs in their native language) and an Uyghur intellectual elite took shape, which maintained very few links with Xinjiang. In Kazakhstan, the community is divided into two groups each with its own strong identity: the *yerliklär* (locals), who were born in Kazakhstan and whose parents, or indeed grandparents, first settled in Semirechie in the late nineteenth and early twentieth centuries; and the *kegänlär* (new arrivals), who arrived during the last waves of migration from China in the 1950s and1960s, and who often still have family links with Xinjiang.[37] The *yerliklär* consider themselves to be indigenous Kazakhstanis, no longer have any family links with Xinjiang, and in the 1970s often dreamed of obtaining an autonomous republic in the Kazakh Soviet Republic. This feeling of belonging to Semirechie, of autochthonism and autonomy, has provoked fierce reactions among ethnic Kazakhs. The symbolic rivalry that developed between the Uyghur and Kazakh Soviet elites in the 1970s and 1980s still stamps attitudes today, underscoring their mistrust of one another.[38]

The largely russified Uyghurs of Central Asia are mostly secular and Europe-oriented, and hence are very distant from the Uyghurs of Xinjiang. For many decades, they regarded themselves as rightful members of the Soviet space and had no desire to play the role of a diaspora in exile. The *yerliklär*, who had their sights set on the fatherland, were an exception to this, but were marginalized. Not until the 1991 declarations of independence and the resumption of relations with China did the idea that they were not only a Soviet people like any other, but also a diaspora with links to Xinjiang, become widespread and serve to fracture the community. Even today, many Central Asian Uyghurs are not preoccupied with the situation in Xinjiang and, in fact, look condescendingly upon the Chinese Uyghurs, who they see as rural and backward, and are disdainful of their strong religious practices and Chinese-influenced culture.[39] In a similar way, the Xinjiang Uyghurs who come to Central Asia for trade-related reasons are shocked by the Westernized lifestyles of the post-Soviet Uyghurs, whom they call *sovietlik* (the Soviets), and who are in turn called *kitailik* (the Chinese).[40] Both groups are largely hampered from understanding one another's written language, since Chinese Uyghurs use the Arabic alphabet, the post-Soviet ones the Cyrillic, and others the Latin alphabet. Even more significant, the widespread entry of Russian and Chinese terms into daily language contributes to underlining their differences and acts as a reminder to the ideologists of the "great Uyghur nation dispersed throughout the world" that the Uyghur populations are largely integrated into their respective environments.

Lastly, many fraught political divisions have long worked to impede the emergence of a unified diasporic scene.[41] The Chinese Uyghurs are often suspected of working for Beijing, those settled in Arab countries or who support Saudi Arabia are considered too Islamized, while the community based in Turkey is often accused of being too pan-Turkist. Hence all these groups are scarcely followed in Central Asia, where local Uyghurs have preferred to focus on nationalist, not pan-Turkist, even less Islamic, issues. These divisions were reflected in the 2004 debates surrounding the creation of a World Uyghur Congress led first by Erkin Alptekin and subsequently by Rebiya Kadeer. Wheareas some wanted to call it the East Turkestan World Congress, thereby including territorial belonging in the definition and according a place to the other minorities, the majority pushed for a definition expressed in ethnic terms without any territorial reference.[42] Despite the attempts at centralization undertaken by the Congress and its most eminent members, in Munich and Washington, the Uyghur diaspora remains divided on issues concerning its geopolitical alliance, its relation to Islam, and its difficulties in establishing contact with the Xinjiang-based autonomists.

In Central Asia the political pressures that the authorities exert in their efforts to respond to Beijing's demands have intensified the multiple political divisions among the Uyghur community. In Uzbekistan, there is no functioning Uyghur association, and the Uyghur-Dungan Cultural Center only organizes occasional non-politicized events promoting folklore. In Kyrgyzstan, Uyghurs are divided between the Union of the Uyghurs of Kyrgyzstan, and the Committee of Human Rights of Bishkek. In Kazakhstan, a CIS-International Uyghur Union was set up in early 1992 with the objective of protecting human rights and seeking self-determination for Uyghurs in Xinjiang. Several newspapers in the Uyghur language such as *Uyghur Awazi* (The Voice of Uyghurs) were published, and many rival associations coexisted: the Organization for the Liberation of Uyghurstan (OLU), led by Hashir Wahidi, included some thousands of members, while the Yusupbeg Mukhlissi-led United Revolutionary Front of East Turkestan was less well known in the region, as was the Regional Organization of Uyghur people, whose aim was to unify the entire diaspora of Central Asia. In the second half of the 1990s, Beijing compelled Kazakhstan to dissolve the Uyghur associations, and forced closure of the Institute of Uyghur Studies, which had been created within the Institute of Oriental Studies.[43] Today some underground groups still survive and are financed by businessmen who support the cause of Uyghur independence.[44] The others have been encouraged to gather in official associations, such as the Cultural Center of the Uyghurs of Kazakhstan, which rallied to Nursultan Nazarbayev and engages in depoliticized activities (publications, financing of cultural operations, the translation of the Koran into Uyghur, etc.), and the Society for the Uyghur Culture.[45]

* * *

In the early years after bilateral relations had been established, the Central Asian states and China first learned to understand each other as well as to gauge the state of their relations. Though the territories that Beijing had obtained were far smaller than those stipulated in its original claims, it had got what it wanted: a recognition of the inequality of the Tsarist treaties, and a gesture of goodwill on the part of the new Central Asian states, which promoted the establishment of pragmatic, good neighborly relations, and the avoidance of conflict. Trust was therefore successfully created. Moreover, the territorial areas Beijing acquired, in Kazakhstan, Kyrgyzstan, and Tajikistan, have real economic and strategic viability, and include access to rivers, subsoil resources, and high-mountain passes.

The Central Asian states, for their part, learned several lessons. First and foremost, as the border disputes threatened the very existence of Kazakhstan, Kyrgyzstan, and Tajikistan, the relationship to China was understood to be vital for the survival of the nation as an independent state. The obtaining of a peaceful settlement within a decade of independence—indeed within only a few years for Kazakhstan—is something that the Central Asians, in their overwhelming majority, credited to China. If the Chinese authorities had wanted to deliver a fatal blow to the young states, which were negotiating for their survival after the collapse of the Soviet Union, they would not have been able to withstand it. However, the sentiment that this peaceful solution might only be provisional remains very present. Not one of the territorial treaties has been published, a fact that fuels assumptions about the existence of possible secret clauses. Legal imprecision is rife: are the treaties definitive, or have they been established only for a period of twenty years, like, for example, some of the Sino-Russian treaties signed in the 2000s?[46] The possibility of having to renegotiate some territories in the years to come, when the power differential in favor of China will be even greater, is a legitimate public concern in Kazakhstan, Kyrgyzstan, and Tajikistan. In addition, China does not hesitate to violate with regularity, in the name of its security in Xinjiang, the demilitarization agreements that are supposed to limit the conducting of exercises in border regions.[47]

Second, the settling of the borders demonstrated the absence of any post-Soviet unity in the face of China, a bitter lesson for the Central Asian governments, which had hoped that Russia would weigh in on their side. Despite the meetings of the CIS-China group in 1992–94, all technical negotiations were conducted bilaterally, without any post-Soviet state obtaining support from its neighbor. Accordingly, Kazakhstan and Russia failed to present a common front on the question of the key Sino-Kazakh-Russian river, the Irtysh. Neither were Kazakhstan and Kyrgyzstan able to negotiate together in the showdown with Beijing over balanced water exchanges between states situated upstream and downstream.

Lastly, the Central Asian governments were under no illusions as to Beijing's determination regarding the Uyghur issue and of course that of Taiwan.[48] Although no official proof can confirm this type of information, the Chinese authorities exerted pressure at the highest state level, which is to say directly on the presidents themselves, threatening to undermine the very foundations of the new states in case they refused to adhere to the "One China" discourse or to solve the Uyghur problem in its favor. Thus, Beijing's reduced territorial claims seem to have been directly linked to the settling of the Uyghur question in Kazakhstan and Kyrgyzstan. Other elements were also in play: Kazakhstan was able to point in its own favor to its denuclearization, which was made official in 1994, and which reassured China, while Kyrgyzstan and Tajikistan for their part ceded territory in exchange for promises of Chinese control over some subsoil resources. The political pressure placed on the Kazakh and Kyrgyz governments over the Uyghur issue spread a negative image of China throughout the region. The Central Asian societies came out of this experience with a paradoxical feeling that Beijing could simultaneously show itself to be a pragmatic economic and diplomatic partner, ready to aid regional development, but also a neighbor with whom certain limits related to territorial integrity could not be crossed. The governments thus readily subscribed to the Chinese narrative on the need to combat the three evils (*san gu shili*) of separatism, extremism, and fundamentalism. The Shanghai Group, born from the CIS-China group, thus reinforces their own quest for political legitimacy founded on the definition of external and internal enemies.

2

THE SHANGHAI COOPERATION ORGANIZATION

SUCCESSES AND CHALLENGES

With the border issues resolved and the Uyghur question—at least temporarily—buried, China then reinforced its presence in Central Asia by investing massively in the Shanghai Cooperation Organization (SCO). Created on the basis of a structure first established in 1996, called the Group of Five or the Shanghai Group, the SCO has not gone unnoticed in the international community. It is probably one of the most discussed and most studied international organizations, a fact that stands in total disproportion to its real levels of activism. All the debates on the state of Chinese and Russian relations, on China's rise to power on the international scene, on the emergence of a new world order stamped by anti-American alliances, feel obliged to mention the SCO. This can be explained for the most part by the fundamentally new character of the organization: it is the only multilateral organization that has been set up by China; it brings together countries that were practically in open conflict only a few decades ago; it encompasses three-fifths of the Eurasian continent and a quarter of the world's population; and it gives off the image—whether true or false—of being an anti-Western organization, challenging US supremacy in the heart of the Eurasian continent.[1] Granting associated member status to Mongolia, Iran, India, and Pakistan in 2004–2005 thrust the SCO even more into the media spotlight. However, beyond its rhetoric of cooperation and declarations of good intentions, the young organization faces many difficulties. Its member states often have very divergent interests, some of which bring into question its mid to long-term credibility.

The security paradigm: the effectiveness of the SCO and of China

Created to settle border tensions peacefully and progressively demilitarize borders, the Shanghai Group rapidly transformed into a more global platform for discussion between Russia, China, Kazakhstan, Kyrgyzstan and Tajikistan. The series of destabilizations during the summer of 1999 and that of 2000, which saw incursions from the Islamic Movement of Uzbekistan across the Tajik and Kyrgyz borders, and the incapacity of the Kyrgyz army to regain control of its territory, gave renewed impetus to the Shanghai Group, which then decided to go a step further in terms of institutionalization and became the Shanghai Cooperation Organization. The decision by Uzbekistan, without any common border with China, to join the SCO in 2001 confirmed that the organization was no longer limited to settling border disputes, but was now concentrated on regional security stakes. Whereas until that point Uzbekistan had been very reluctant to enter a regional organization, even more so one in which Russia was a key power, and whereas it made no secret of its support for growing US involvement in the region, the Islamist incursions changed the situation profoundly, and highlighted the need for all the state actors to create a new multilateral platform.[2] The US-led "War on Terror," which made it possible to add the East Turkestan Islamic Movement to the list of international terrorist movements, also partly legitimized the SCO's turn toward counterterrorism.

Security cooperation is conceived of as being at the very core of SCO activity. The first joint military exercises began in 2003, and they are conducted on an annual basis in one of the member countries.[3] The main participants in them are the Russian, Chinese, and Kazakh forces. The participating troops sent by Kyrgyzstan and Tajikistan are minimal due to lack of means, while Uzbekistan remains reluctant to embark on any large-scale involvement. Simulations of terrorist attacks—like those that took place in 1999 and 2000—are carried out, including exercises in mountainous terrain and hostage scenarios. Since an agreement between the SCO and the Moscow-led Collective Security Treaty Organization (CSTO) in 2005, some exercises, called Peace Missions, now include both organizations (with Armenia being a member of the latter but not of the former).[4] These exercises have an impact upon national and international public opinion, giving the impression of collective actions in sensitive domains linked to national sovereignty. However, they remain superficial: they can be described as being more parallel maneuvers rather than joint ones as such. While the general staffs may decide on a common strategy together, the battalions involved often remain without any contact with their foreign counterparts. During the "Peace Mission 2010" exercises held at the Kazakh firing range of Matybulak, the only combats necessitating real interaction between troops were those carried out by the Russian and Kazakh forces, whereas the Chinese forces lead their own demonstration in parallel.[5] Operations organized in a bilateral manner, such as the Sino-Kazakh border drug-seizing operations, which have been ongoing since 2008,[6] are more effective than the SCO exercises in terms of interaction between Central Asian and Chinese soldiers.

The second element of SCO security cooperation is linked to a larger, less militarized conception of security. The organization is particularly committed to fighting against non-traditional threats, the latter being where the interests of all member states converge, with only relatively minor divergences of opinion.[7] This security focus is embodied in the Regional Anti-Terrorist Structure (RATS). Originally planned to be opened in Bishkek, it was ultimately "offered" to Tashkent as a gesture for its joining and because the issue of terrorism is of particular concern to the regime of Islam Karimov. Active since 2004, RATS, because of the sensitive nature of its activities, is opaque to external analysis with very little information available about its activities.[8] The Structure was set up to promote common methods to combat terrorist movements and to exchange information on suspect individuals. Its greatest successes are probably the extradition treaty between member states and the formation of a 'black list' of about one thousand people and forty organizations.[9] It seems that on several occasions the Chinese authorities have requested their Central Asian partners to arrest and deport some Uyghur opponents, and when alleged Islamists cross the border, they are followed by the RATS joint procedures set up to monitor them. However, it is difficult to say whether this type of information exchange has been made possible thanks to RATS, or rather whether it took place in a bilateral framework. Truly sensitive matters, such as the expulsion of Uyghur opponents to China, are generally managed at the highest levels of bilateral relations.[10]

Even if the RATS and the SCO multilateral exercises enable doctrinal dialogue to take place, and promote better understanding between the security structures and the armies of member states, the organization's multilateral security dynamic remains embryonic.[11] Not having any mission to become a supranational organization that would infringe on its members' sovereignty, the SCO does not have a military structure like the CSTO, which in addition involves the sale of technological material to member states. It does not project itself as a military defense alliance in the image of NATO, nor does it seek to create multilateral or police military units, and RATS cannot be considered a sort of Interpol for the SCO. Moreover, the hesitation of member states to embark on closer collaboration is apparent. All extol their right to sovereignty and criticize supranational logics. Russia has refused to participate in several exercises in which China has taken part and seems less and less committed to promoting the military aspect of the organization. Neither Moscow nor Beijing is inclined to disclose sensitive information about new technologies and their respective nuclear complexes. While the two capitals do not officially see themselves as potential enemies, traditional distrust and a sense of inevitable rivalry dominate.[12]

Despite its emphasis on security, the SCO has been helpless to react to any of the crises that have impacted upon the Central Asian region, such as "the Tulip Revolution" in Kyrgyzstan in March 2005, the overthrow of the Bakiyev government in April 2010, the interethnic violence of Osh in June 2010, the regular clashes between the security services and alleged Islamist groups in the mountainous regions of Tajikistan (for the most part in the Rasht Valley), and so on. For the SCO, the worsening situation in two of its member states, Kyrgyzstan and Tajikistan, is not only disquieting at the level of security, but also revealing of the ineffectiveness of its mechanisms and its inability to undertake concerted collective actions on subjects that significantly affect state sovereignty.

Afghanistan is also an indicator of the difficulties that the SCO has in advancing any collective management of global security. While there is a great disappointment among the Central Asian states about the West's handling of the Afghan question—they all criticize NATO's focus on military solutions and, by contrast, endorse political solutions and economic reconstruction—the SCO has not come up with any solution to end the stalemate of the international coalition. Afghanistan has already become a symbol of one of its first defeats in terms of image. In 2001, the US intervention, launched only a few weeks after the attack of September 11, demonstrated the capacities of the world's premier superpower and its European allies to engage rapidly and massively in a new war theater that the SCO deemed to be more or less part of its "sphere of influence." In addition, the organization's members reacted in their own separate ways to this event: Moscow's rapprochement with Washington and the opening of two US military bases in Kyrgyzstan and Uzbekistan displeased the Chinese authorities and weakened political confidence among member states.[13]

The SCO began to feel the need to develop a common policy on Afghanistan in 2004, and a few years later the organization's name started cropping up regularly among the international protagonists of the Afghan theater. In 2004, the SCO created a first contact group with Afghanistan, which was institutionalized in 2005. In 2006, Hamid Karzai declared that his country "belonged to the region in which the SCO was situated. Afghanistan has no other solutions and cannot exist outside of this region."[14] In 2007, the Afghan Vice-President, Ahmad Zia Masood, stated that he expected far greater cooperation with the organization, in particular in the economic sector. Ever since, the Afghan issue has become one of the major SCO discussion topics. In 2008, a conference devoted to this issue was held on the shores of Lake Issyk-Kul, for the purpose of increasing the organization's profile as well as making Iran a fully-fledged member. In 2009, it was made clear at the SCO meeting in Moscow, which included representatives from the G8 and other international organizations, that Russia as well as China wished to be seen as essential partners in any Afghan solution.[15]

Nonetheless, despite its declarations of intention, the SCO has few means to be able to influence Afghan realities.[16] Its financial capacities as a multilateral organization are minimal. The idea of creating collective military forces is not included among its members' objectives. Even collective actions in the domain of reconstruction seem difficult to make a reality. While all the SCO member states play a role in Afghanistan—Russia due to its Soviet past,[17] China due to its massive investments in the exploitation of resources,[18] Kazakhstan thanks to its humanitarian aid and its cereal sales, and Uzbekistan and Tajikistan due to their co-ethnics in the northern Afghan provinces and their electricity exports—there exists no attempt to unify these individual approaches into a collective action. In addition, Kabul clearly gives its priority to bilateral relations. Nikolai Bordiuzha, the CSTO General Secretary, acknowledged for instance that the CSTO-Afghanistan working group was only minimally effective and that the Karzai government had asked Moscow for bilateral and not multilateral cooperation.[19]

In the ten years of Western initiatives in Afghanistan the SCO, therefore, has often found itself on the margins: it has had no solutions to offer to the stalemate, unless this has been to criticize the International Security Assistance Force's lack of success, and none of its members want to send its troops to Afghanistan; despite its insistence on the need for reconstructing the country and finding a political solution, no collective action has been organized in this regard; all its members engage bilaterally with Kabul without any coordination between them. This stands in stark contrast to the Northern Distribution Network.[20] Established by the United States, this has managed to create networks for negotiations with the Central Asian governments, and enables a modest level of regional coordination related to transit to and from Afghanistan, something that the SCO has never succeeded in doing.

Even in a bilateral framework, China is unable to rival Russia's major role in military cooperation with the Central Asian states. Its aid is limited to electronic material, automobiles and military clothing, but includes almost no military sales properly speaking. Since 2000, Kazakhstan and China have signed multiple agreements under which Astana buys Chinese technical equipment.[21] In total, between 1997 and 2003, Astana has received US$4.5 million in technological aid, and communications and transportation equipment from China. It has expressed its intention to obtain military materiel from the People's Liberation Army (PLA) and hopes to take advantage of free transfers of decommissioned military assets when the Chinese army modernizes its equipment.[22] Under the joint counterterrorism operations, Kazakhstan also wants to take advantage of the expertise and experience of China, which has strengthened its special forces in this area.[23] The 2007 Kazakhstan military doctrine attaches special importance to the bilateral security relationship with China, but not at the expense of Russia's prominent role.

Chinese aid to the other states is more modest. During a meeting between the defense ministers of China and Turkmenistan in 2007, it was decided that Beijing would equip the Turkmen army with precision equipment and uniforms for officers and soldiers, offering a US$3 million loan for its military needs.[24] China is also trying to expand its military cooperation with its two immediate neighbors, Kyrgyzstan and Tajikistan. In 2005, an official visit of the Chinese Minister of Defense to Dushanbe led to the signing of several military cooperation documents, although limited in scope and mostly rhetorical, such as sharing of intelligence on terrorism, drug trafficking, and organized crime.[25] Between 1993 and 2008, Beijing has provided US$15 million in aid to Tajikistan,[26] and in 2009 it pledged $1.5 million to the Tajik military, the latest in a series of financial aid packages for the region's armed forces. Under an agreement signed in 2002 in Bishkek, China has also provided technical military assistance to Kyrgyzstan worth $1.2 million.[27] With Uzbekistan, relations are more complex. In 2000, China took a first step on to the Central Asian arms market, delivering sniper rifles to Tashkent. In 2009, the two countries signed a new agreement whereby Beijing will provide $3.7 million to the Uzbek authorities to equip its border crossings with mobile scanning systems.[28]

Finally, joint training is being developed, however modestly. Exchanges have been organized to train military cadres, but the language barrier hinders prospects. Courses for Central Asian officers in Chinese military academies are taught in Russian, as Chinese instructors are unable to speak Central Asian languages or Central Asian officers, Chinese. Between 1990 and 2005, only fifteen Kazakh officers were sent to China for training. Yet this cooperation is growing: between 2003 and 2009, sixty-five members of the Kazakh military took courses in Chinese institutions.[29] Further negotiations in this area were organized between the two countries at the beginning of 2009. About thirty Kyrgyz officers also received training in China, and in 2008, thirty members of the Tajik army were trained in Chinese military academies. For the Central Asian governments, equipment and training from the People's Liberation Army is a— albeit still mainly theoretical—welcome balance to the supplies of outdated Soviet hardware that are sometimes offloaded by Moscow, but for the time being aid remains focused on non-military material and involves little training.

The SCO's search for some "Shanghai Spirit"

Whereas it originally focused on security questions, the SCO has quickly formed many commissions and fora devoted to not only economic, financial, and investment questions, but also environmental and cultural exchanges. This activism has earned it increased visibility, but has also worked to accelerate the dissolution of its security objectives while failing to yield any new, well-defined priorities.[30] Each member state therefore tries to promote its own interests, which are often very divergent from those of its neighbors. The differences in prospects for economic development, in domestic fragility, and divergences in geopolitical strategies broadly influence the perceptions harbored by each of the states and their expectations of the SCO. For Russia, the organization obliges China to play the card of multilateralism and allows Moscow to curb Beijing's ambitions without directly confronting its growing influence in the Central Asian region. For China, the SCO has made it possible to institutionalize its legitimacy in the region. With this done, it can set about playing on the contradictions between member states and lobby groups without the risk of being accused of expansionism. For the Central Asians, the organization serves as a buffer: it can mediate disagreements peacefully and channel competition between the two dominant powers for more advantageous solutions.

An implicit hierarchy has therefore taken shape, despite discourses about equality among member states. At the first level, Russia and China dominate the SCO's international visibility: through it both powers negotiate their relations to Central Asia but also their international positioning in favor of a multipolar world, and the organization's relations with other regional and international institutions. At a second level, Kazakhstan joins this duo to form a dominant trio. The Moscow-Astana-Beijing trio is in charge of promoting the organization among the observer states, as well as the other parts of the post-Soviet space (through their overlapping membership in several regional organizations, such as the CSTO or the Eurasian Economic Community). It is also pushing the SCO to adopt a more economic focus, since Kazakhstan is one of the region's energy leaders and constitutes the territorial link between Russia and China. Astana is at an advantage whenever the SCO seeks to promote a nuclear weapons-free world. While Russia and China appeal for the world to avoid nuclear proliferation, neither country is ready to call its atomic status into question and the issue is a sticking point for the three main observer countries (Iran, Pakistan, and India). In Kazakhstan, on the contrary, denuclearization was a complete success. Astana plays this hand to its fullest, as it did, for example, during the nuclear security summit in Washington in April 2010, or with Nursultan Nazarbayev's proposal to elaborate a universal declaration for a denuclearized world.[31]

Uzbekistan, Kyrgyzstan, and Tajikistan occupy a third tier—Uzbekistan as a rebellous member opposed to any collective activities, the latter two undermined by their internal weaknesses. The leaders of these three countries participate much less in the high-profile SCO activities or in the large-scale energy projects; instead they appeal to the organization to return to its initial aims, namely regional stability, and the fight against terrorist threats.

China constitutes the main driver behind the SCO's economic orientation, in which it sees, among other things, an opportunity for the development of the "Far West" and the conquest of new markets. Since 2002, Beijing has proposed to make the SCO a free trade zone that would be the largest in the world, encompassing more than 1.5 billion people. At a 2003 summit, the SCO prime ministers signed an agreement for multilateral trade and economic cooperation. In 2004, four working groups were formed for electronic commerce, customs, inspection of goods and harmonization of standards, and cooperation in investment. However, this Chinese dynamic toward a common market is far from being unanimously accepted. Moscow, as well as the Central Asian states, fear that they will pass under a kind of Chinese economic protectorate given the development and growth differential. In the post-Soviet space, where transformative industries have never recovered from the collapse of the USSR, those that still exist cannot compete with the profitability of their Chinese competitors. Russia and Central Asia are thus not interested in forming a free market with China, but they privilege the energy sector and Chinese investment capacities, in which they see an alternative to their more demanding Western partners. The setting up of a transportation corridor between China and Europe via Russia and Central Asia, export agreements for electricity, and the transit of hydrocarbons thus elicit the interest of all member states,[32] even if Sino-Russian competition for Central Asian gas in particular is also growing.

Uzbekistan occupies its own specific position since it is the only member state to have declared its reluctance to engage in any multilateral cooperation and its refusal to envisage, even symbolically, any loss of sovereignty. Islam Karimov's regime regularly refuses to participate in SCO joint military exercises, often only sending observers or a few representatives from the security services, but not its regular army. Tashkent does not conceal its discontent at the SCO's caution: Moscow and Beijing are criticized for refusing to tackle basic problems, such as the question of water management, and for not expressing support for the Uzbek stance. Only the activities of RATS, as they are based in the Uzbek capital city and focus on questions of anti-terrorism, seem to meet with Tashkent's approval. Uzbekistan's strategy is thus to use the SCO as a multilateral platform to seek advancement of its own issues: the anti-terrorist struggle, and the settling of tensions related to hydroelectricity. The other SCO components are laid aside—such as the debates on economic integration—as they go directly against Uzbek isolationist logics. Lastly, the Uzbek regime interprets the declarations presenting the SCO as a "rampart" against Western influence in accordance with its geopolitical strategy of the moment: either such pronouncements are deemed to be in line with its own anti-Western stance, or else they are denounced as Russian interference and American interest is solicited.[33]

Kyrgyzstan and Tajikistan have similar positions when it comes to their expectations of the SCO. During official meetings, Dushanbe and Bishkek complain of the decreasing interest in security questions, despite the centrality of these matters for both of them given their domestic weaknesses. The Tajik and Kyrgyz governments, also, could barely hide their disappointment during their wrestling with Tashkent over water management, since neither Moscow nor Beijing openly took their side. The SCO anti-Western rhetoric has sometimes caused Bishkek difficulties, notably over pressures to close the US base at Manas, but this does not prevent the Kyrgyz government from negotiating directly with the United States or the European Union. Thanks to American and Russian presence on its territory, financial blackmail (the annual rent paid for the two bases) and symbolic blackmail (the change in status of the Manas "base," which since 2009 has officially become a "transit center") now form part of Kyrgyz foreign policy and guarantee it some room for maneuver. Dushanbe is more restricted than Bishkek since the United States has no presence there, Russia dominates on the security level, and neighboring Iran makes debates on strategic evolutions even more complex. On the economic level, Kyrgyzstan and Tajikistan are enthusiastic SCO participants: they were the grateful beneficiaries of US$900 million in credit, offered to them by Beijing, and are able to take plenty of advantage of developments in cooperation over banking and finance, investments for large projects, and SCO scholarships and training—all essentially at China's initiative. Lastly, on the military level, the supervision provided by the organization, even if it is more limited than that of the CSTO, offers unique possibilities for the weak Tajik and Kyrgyz armies.

Kazakhstan, for its part, can allow itself to be both a key actor of the SCO and an autonomous, demanding partner. The organization is pointed up in Kazakh official discourse, since it is part of its logic of promoting all the regional and international organizations, but Astana does not consider that this membership restricts its own foreign policy choices.[34] The partnership with Russia under the auspices of the CSTO is the more privileged one, and Kazakhstan makes no secret of its preference for this institutional framework, which guarantees it low-price Russian military material, Russian investments in its military-industrial complex, the training of hundreds of officers, and so on.[35] Kazakhstan is also the most advanced Central Asian country in terms of cooperation with NATO, thanks to its Individual Plan of Action for the Partnership (IPAP).[36] It is, furthermore, the only Central Asian state to have created a peacekeeping force—the Kazbat battalion, which has been elevated to the status of a brigade, Kazbrig, and was deployed in Iraq from 2003 to 2008—which it has done in collaboration with NATO under UN mandate. In the years to come, Astana thus hopes to obtain interoperability status with NATO, and this is in spite of its privileged partnership with Russia and its official enthusiasm for the SCO.

On the economic level, Kazakhstan, like Russia, is pushing for the establishment of collective rationales in terms of hydrocarbons, electricity, and transit corridors, but rejects Chinese projects for a common market that would abolish customs barriers. Astana is also anxious about the possibility of the yuan becoming the common currency for intra-SCO exchanges.[37] As a result, Kazakhstan has joined forces with Russia and Belarus to request joint entry to the World Trade Organization. This was to the great displeasure of China, which had been hoping for rapid, individual entry for Kazakhstan in order to boost economic exchanges without having to go through Kyrgyzstan, a member of the WTO since 1998. The new Russia-Belarus-Kazakhstan Customs Union which came into effect in July 2010 confirms that Astana's economic orientation privileges Moscow over Beijing, and that the SCO is not seen as the main engine of economic cooperation in the region.

The SCO political alliance: an "Axis of Convenience"

Since its inception, the SCO has announced that it does not oppose any other organization or foreign state. However, it quickly emerged as a virtually anti-Western organization. It was founded during the NATO attacks against Serbia and the bombing of the Chinese Embassy in Belgrade, which raised the ire of Moscow and Beijing. In 2000, the Dushanbe Declaration asserted that the organization was opposed to any intervention undertaken without UN approval and interference in internal affairs under the pretext of defending human rights, a direct reference to US policy in the region. This anti-Western orientation became clearer at the Astana summit in July 2005, when the SCO demanded that the United States limit the duration of its military presence in Central Asia. After Andijan, Tashkent insisted that Washington close the base at Karshi-Khanabad, which Washington did in November of that year.[38] Though Russia is often accused, by the West, of wanting to see the US Manas base in Kyrgyzstan closed, the Chinese authorities seem just as intent on ending the American presence on their borders. They are said to have offered financial compensation to the Kyrgyz state for any revenue loss incurred by the base's closure.[39]

China and Russia both share a similar commitment to combating Western influence in Eurasia and claim that they are victims of a containment policy pursued by Washington through establishment of friendly regimes via "color revolutions."[40] They also have the same view of the dangers that they face in Central Asia, deemed a potentially unstable area with risks of Islamism, state failure, and drug trafficking. For this reason, Beijing, like Moscow, gives its support to local authoritarian regimes, arguing that they are the last guarantors of stability and secularism. They have all adopted similar interpretations of the Chechen issue in Russia, the Tibetan and Uyghur issues in China, and the Islamist risk in Central Asia. Nevertheless there have been several SCO policy fits and starts. After September 11, 2001, China was displeased when Moscow and the Central Asian regimes agreed to cooperate with the United States in Afghanistan. Nonetheless, since 2003, the atmosphere once deemed conducive to cooperating with the West has come to an end. Although SCO statutes formally prohibit any interference in the internal affairs of members, the shock waves that rolled across the post-Soviet space as a result of the "color revolutions" and the Andijan events in May 2005[41] helped to revive political ties between the SCO member states. However, Moscow's recognition of the independence of South Ossetia and Abkhazia in August 2008 caused confusion in China, and angered Central Asian authorities, which made calls for former Soviet borders to be preserved and for the propagation of secessionist movements to be limited. China and Central Asia's refusal to recognize the new states disappointed Moscow, which had sought the unwavering support of its SCO allies.[42]

The question of Chinese influence on the Central Asian political regimes ought to be discussed. Western observers often tend to overestimate Beijing's ability to direct Central Asian political choices. With the exception of the Uyghur diaspora, over which, indeed, the Chinese authorities bring their full weight to bear, the Central Asian regimes remain as impermeable as possible to Chinese political influence. The authoritarian hardening of their regimes, even if evidently influenced by the regional situation, cannot be explained by this proximity; in other words, it cannot be assumed that Kazakhstan, Tajikistan, Uzbekistan, and Turkmenistan are inherently more democratic but have become "victims" of Russian and Chinese authoritarian pressures. The proof of this is Kyrgyzstan, a country which has managed to uphold a greater ideological liberty and where freedom of expression is less curtailed, regardless of Beijing's being able or wanting to prevent this. Even Moscow's influence, although much more manifest in this domain than China's, is unable to explain the choices of the Central Asian regimes; choices which are driven by domestic issues and local political culture. Though the SCO is to all extents and purposes an alliance of authoritarian regimes, with the partial exception of Kyrgyzstan, it is an axis of convenience rather than a coercive organization used by Russia and China to bully and influence its weaker member states.

Moreover, although the SCO undeniably attempts to counter Western influence in Eurasia, no member state wishes to pursue an aggressive policy aimed directly against US interests or a slowdown of its integration into the international community.[43] China cannot afford to be declared a "rogue state" by Washington, as its economy is now too dependent on its relations with the United States. The Central Asian states seek to maintain contacts with the West in order to weaken both Moscow and Beijing. Despite the rise of anti-American sentiment among Central Asian elites, all consider Western presence in the region to guarantee stability and agree that the exclusive, dual grip of Russia and China is dangerous.[44] For its part, Russia seeks to signal to the West that it has geopolitical alternatives if the European Union and the United States oppose its objectives, without calling for a rupture of its partnership with the West. For Moscow, the SCO can be seen as an extension of the "Primakov doctrine," which sought to reorient Russian foreign policy toward Asia, and to strike a balance between East and West. Given this state of affairs and the interests of its members, the Shanghai Cooperation Organization does not pose a direct threat to the West, despite the refusal of the US request to be granted the status of associated member.[45]

The issue of enlarging the SCO to include new states has come up as well, but for now is a subject of contradictory discussions related to the internal balance between member states and to the organization's international image. While four states were granted associate member status in 2004–2005, the SCO's terms of membership were not defined until 2010.[46] They prohibit entry into the organization of countries not signatory to the Nuclear Non-proliferation Treaty or countries that are subject to UN sanctions, which makes it possible to refuse membership to India and Pakistan, on the one hand, and to Iran, on the other. In the short term, the six members appear reluctant to make any wide overtures. Observer status is not considered to be a door leading to membership, and the two states that currently lack any formal status, Turkmenistan and Afghanistan, could potentially enter the organization before the observer states. In 2009, Belarus and Sri Lanka, the former advanced by Russia and the latter by China, have become "discussion partners," which is a more informal status than that of associate member.

For the three main observer states—India, Pakistan, and Iran—the question of SCO membership constitutes part of a broader range of geopolitical issues. New Delhi and Islamabad want to find a new institutional framework to negotiate their competition in Central Asia.[47] The agreement reached between India and the International Atomic Energy Agency in 2008 helped Delhi escape from its "nuclear apartheid," which in principle could be used as a positive argument in case of a membership request. However, the border tensions between India and China have not been settled and could therefore cast a shadow over the SCO's main success, namely the peaceful resolution of the Sino-Soviet border disputes and the border demilitarization, a gain that no member wishes to see undermined, not even symbolically. The state of Indian-Pakistani relations, in particular the situation in Kashmir, can also only disquiet the SCO member states, which do not want to have to manage "hot conflicts." The prospects for entry are thus limited so long as the SCO sees itself as a non-conflictual, regional platform. However, Russia has confirmed that it supports India's possible membership, probably in order to weaken China, and the strategic partnership signed between India and Kazakhstan in 2009 works to strengthen Indian ambitions toward the SCO.

Under the weight of international sanctions and US embargo, Iran is on the search for new allies and means to enter the international arena as a regional power, rather than as an Islamic revolutionary state as such. Tehran has therefore been trying for several years to break out of its international isolation by emphasizing its Asian identity and turning in the main toward China. The SCO is especially appealing given its repeatedly stated principle of non-interference in internal affairs. Iran is also seeking cooperation in the energy sector. In 2006, President Mahmoud Ahmadinejad hosted the SCO leaders to discuss possible joint energy development.[48] However, Russia and China have already conveyed that they do not intend to share their influence over Central Asian oil and gas with other regional Asian powers, some of which, like Iran, are also energy producers. Moreover, the prospect of working closely with the Iranian regime would not be without consequences for the relations between member states and the West, particularly the United States.[49] Such cooperation would distinctly paint the SCO as an anti-American grouping, which is not desired by either Moscow, Beijing or the Central Asian regimes.

More globally, the Sino-Russian partnership in Central Asia, supposed to be embodied in the SCO, remains ambivalent: not founded on a "values base," it lacks resilience to political, strategic, or economic downturns, and could be tested by a change in the geopolitics of either actor. China has positioned itself as a faithful second fiddle to Russia and tacitly recognizes Central Asia as still being in the Russian "sphere of influence." Beijing in actual fact wishes to preserve Russian strategic domination, preferring to let Moscow pay the heavy costs of military security and of guaranteeing the survival of unsustainable regimes, while it focuses on economic involvement.[50] Russian military presence in the region does not raise any problems for China, which actually needs the Kremlin's support both to nip its own separatist movements in the bud and to act as a check on Western influence and growing competition with Washington. For Russia, the situation is more complex and ambivalent.[51] Russian policymakers are indeed increasingly concerned at the speed with which China is narrowing the strategic gap, and the Middle Kingdom awakens old identity fears (what Bobo Lo rightly called the "Mongol syndrome"),[52] raising concerns about the territorial unity of the Russian Federation in the future. In Central Asia, economic competition between Moscow and Beijing is already palpable and will become increasingly important in the years to come.[53] Any change in the overall balance between Moscow and Beijing may upset the Kremlin, which is unprepared to accept China as a pre-eminent political or cultural power. The Sino-Russian "axis of convenience"[54] is all the more paradoxical as both Russian and Chinese elites are in reality geared toward the West, but geopolitical and economic imperatives call them to order in Central Asia.

* * *

In its fifteen years of existence, the SCO has allowed the Central Asian governments to familiarize themselves with their Chinese neighbor, a neighbor with which historical relations were partially ruptured in the twentieth century. This improved mutual knowledge has materialized in the framework of bilateral exchanges, but the SCO continues to be important in this regard: the proliferation of commissions, fora and working groups, has given rise to an intense diplomatic ballet throughout all sectors, from the more political to the more cultural. Thus, in addition to the official summits at which heads of state and ministers gather, and the military exercises for which officers come together, thousands of Central Asian state employees, experts, and academics have had the occasion to visit China, to be welcomed there with full honors, and to host their Chinese counterparts in return. With the numerous partnerships signed under SCO auspices, the Central Asians' degree of institutional, not to mention personal, familiarity, with the Chinese world has grown exponentially within the space of a few years. It can thus be said that SCO positives include the gaining of knowledge about the "Other," person-to-person relations, and the forming of—at least partial—relations of confidence with China.

The SCO and its precursor, the Shanghai Group, have undeniably been successful. They have helped to ease long-standing tensions between the Russian and Chinese worlds, to put in place cooperative mechanisms for border management, and to establish a collective narrative on the common threats they allegedly face. But now that this threshold of development and institutionalization has been reached, the organization faces new challenges. Despite its security rhetoric, it is relatively inactive in practice and unable to compete with Russian influence in strategic terms. It cannot be compared to the CSTO structure, which offers real interactions between the general staffs and army corps, along with the training of soldiers, arms sales, technological and logistical interoperability, and so on.[55] SCO activities largely remain at the stage of declarations of intent. A lack of coordination between member states is evident, the desire to exchange information is restrained, the financial resources are far too few, and bureaucratic structures remain too weak. Furthermore, the absence of actual common jurisdiction in most areas and the lack of relay on important and related matters weaken considerably the scope for potential action. In economic terms, the SCO has failed to compete with the Eurasian Economic Community or the Customs Union, has been unsuccessful in guiding the development of trade relations between member states—which remain primarily bilateral—and has not dispelled Russian and Central Asian fears of the impending "invasion" of Chinese products. In the coming years, a growing Sino-Russian competition for Central Asian resources—mainly hydrocarbons and potentially uranium, but probably not electricity—could also impede SCO energy-related cooperation.

If the SCO is viewed as a mechanism to reinforce confidence, it has been an historical success. But if it is viewed as an organization that attempts to influence Central Asian security realities, for the time being at least it appears to be no more than a "paper tiger."[56] The gap between the organization's narrative about the fight against non-traditional threats and its mechanisms to enable collective, or at least concerted, action is immense. The SCO provides neither military guarantees in cases of domestic crisis nor does it offer any such structure as a "rapid intervention force" or a collective troop force like that of the Ministry of Emergency Situations in Russia, able to intervene in situations such as natural and ecological catastrophes, sudden population displacements, and so on. The SCO has never managed to react to a large-scale crisis within one of its member states: its silence during the Kyrgyz events of 2010 confirmed this, as does its incapacity to offer anything collective to a state that, albeit a non-member, is as strategic as Afghanistan.

The obsession with consensus and maintaining the status quo has in fact hampered the effectiveness of the SCO, and risks delegitimizing it in the future. Since 2008, the organization seems to have entered into a growth crisis. It has not defined any positive long-term goals, has no well-defined priorities, and refuses to discuss divergences in its members' priorities. The SCO seems therefore primarily to be a reflection of Chinese willingness to support the so-called "healthy Central Asian order," free from any of the three evils[57] and devoid of pro-Western forces that might act to destabilize China. Even if the organization partially limits the room in which the Central Asian states have to maneuver, in particular relative to the West, it provides the established regimes with an ideological framework by which to shore up their legitimacy on both the domestic and international fronts.

3

CHINESE ECONOMIC INROADS IN LANDLOCKED CENTRAL ASIA

Growing Chinese power does not affect only the political and geopolitical situation of Central Asia; it has also profoundly changed the economic status quo in the region. Whereas Central Asia is often seen as a space of geopolitical competition between Russia and the United States, in economic terms the peaceful competition is actually being played out between China and the European Union, with Russia an increasingly less powerful economic actor. As in the other regions of the world where Beijing is establishing itself, its settlement strategies respond to many objectives, seen by the Chinese authorities as intrinsically related. First, China is seeking to consolidate its geopolitical influence in Central Asia by creating economically-based "good neighborhood" relations that work to diffuse potential political tensions. Secondly, it wishes to contribute to regional development in order to avoid political and social destabilization, which could have domestic consequences in Xinjiang and slow down Chinese economic growth. Lastly, the Central Asian states provide new markets for Chinese products that could open up to the whole of Russia, Iran, and Turkey. Thus, they are part of China's rediscovery of its continental ambitions after many decades of being exclusively turned toward its maritime coast. For landlocked Central Asia, the Chinese economic engine opens up the prospect of new trans-Eurasian corridors and is thus seen as a unique historical opportunity.

Exponential growth in trade relations

Developing trade relations between China and Central Asia has involved overcoming many obstacles. The first are geographical: the Tian-Shan and Pamir mountains, as well as the Taklamakan desert, hardly facilitate the development of economic relations in a world in which trade is no longer carried out by camel caravans as it was during the time of the Silk Roads. On both sides of the border, the population is relatively sparse; about 60 million inhabitants for the five post-Soviet states and 20 million inhabitants in Xinjiang. Moreover, the distances required to reach major urban centers, whether situated in Eastern China, European Russia or in Siberia, are particularly long. The second issue that curbs development has its roots in the history of the twentieth century: the Sino-Soviet border has always been one of the most secure in the world. The heavily militarized border towns were considered strategic zones: special permits were required for them, the inhabitants were subject to rigorous controls, and both central powers, Moscow and Beijing, regarded them as likely to be disloyal.

Economic relations between Central Asia and Xinjiang were extremely limited: the Soviet republics imported livestock and raw materials from Xinjiang, and exported industrial products and equipment. A few border posts closed to individuals were opened, such as those at Khorgos, Bakhty and Maikapchagay, while the Ili and Irtysh rivers were used for commercial transport. The construction of a railway linking Urumqi and Alma-Ata had begun during the period of Sino-Soviet friendship, but was interrupted by the conflict between the two communist powers.[1] Nonetheless, despite the fact that the borders were officially closed, small-scale relations between the local populations were maintained through familial, clan, and regional networks.[2] In 1988, even before the visit of Mikhail Gorbachev to Beijing, the Soviet Union and the PRC signed an agreement permitting citizens of their border regions to cross the border without a visa. The Kazakh and Kyrgyz Soviet Socialist Republics were then linked with Xinjiang, and the first cross-border movement of people and goods occurred, primarily among small traders of Kazakh, Kyrgyz, Dungan, and Uyghur nationalities.[3] In December 1991, a Chinese delegation led by the Minister of Trade and Foreign Economic Relations undertook the first official visit to the newly independent republics of Central Asia, a trip that foreshadowed China's grand return to the region.

Since the fall of the Soviet Union, China-Central Asia trade has gone through three principal phases. The first period, spanning the years 1992–1996, was marked by the opening of the first Sino-Kazakh border post at

Dostyk-Alashankou and the signing of multiple friendship treaties and agreements for cooperation. The volume of trade exchanges at that time ranged between US$350 million and $700 million per year, much less than Central Asia's trade—albeit in free fall—with Russia, or its growing trade with Turkey and Iran.[4] During the second period, between 1997 and 2001, exchanges doubled. After a first phase of promises and hopes, the setting up of Chinese firms was somewhat hindered by the global crisis that affected the Central Asian economies, which was further exacerbated by the Russian crash in the summer of 1998.[5] Despite the success of the border negotiations, renewed separatist claims in Xinjiang have also negated the desire of the Central Asian and Chinese authorities to simplify clearance through customs.

The third phase began in 2002: with the two main problems either resolved (border issues) or obviated (Uyghur separatism), dealings henceforth became much more pragmatic, based on mutually advantageous economic cooperation. The trade boom was accompanied by the first Chinese economic ventures into Central Asia in key sectors such as hydrocarbons and infrastructure; profound economic changes in Xinjiang thanks to the "Far West development program," and strengthening of the role of the SCO. Between 2002 and 2003, trade increased about 300 percent, going from about a billion dollars per year to more than three billion. An increase of 150 percent followed between 2004 and 2006, with trade reaching more than US$10 billion according to Central Asian figures,[6] or US$13 billion according to Chinese figures.[7] In 2008, before the world economic downturn, trade between China and Central Asia exceeded US$25 billion, while trade between Russia and Central Asia was at US$27 billion.[8] Since then, China has clearly gained the upper hand while Russia has decreased, with US$28 billion for Beijing compared to less than 15 billion for Moscow in 2010.[9]

Compared with the countries of South-East Asia, medium-sized Chinese enterprises are still relatively thin on the ground, leaving the Central Asian market open primarily either to small individual traders or to large state companies.[10] In Kazakhstan, the number of Chinese companies settling grew on paper in the 2000s, but the majority of accredited joint ventures are empty structures. There were reported to be about 300 Chinese-Kazakh joint ventures in 1995, 4,000 in 2007,[11] and 3,000 in 2010, but only about 200 or 300 of them are really active.[12] Today trade between China and Central Asia can be divided into three categories: border trade, which is dominated by shuttle trade; trade organized by the Xinjiang Production and Constructions Corps or the XPCC (*Xinjiang Shengchan Jianshe Bingtuan*), one of Beijing's main

The growth of China-Central Asia trade in billion dollars 1992–2010

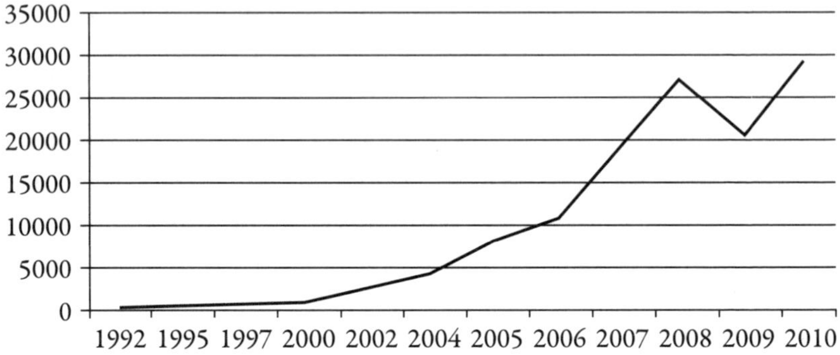

Source: Graph constituted from V. Paramonov V., and A. Strokov, *Ekonomicheskoe prisutstvie Rossii i Kitaia v Tsentral'noi Azii*; and European Union's statistics for 2007, 2008, 2009, 2010, http://ec.europa.eu/trade/trade-statistics/ (December 11, 2011).

political instruments in Xinjiang; and private entrepreneurs, formerly Uyghurs, now mainly Han Chinese. However, each Central Asian state occupies a quite distinct position in trade with China.

With GDP per capita estimated at US$12,800 in 2010, Kazakhstan is placed just behind Russia ($15,900), but far ahead of the other countries of Central Asia ($2,000 in Tajikistan, $2,200 in Kyrgyzstan, $3,100 in Uzbekistan and the improbable figure of $7,400 in Turkmenistan).[13] Kazakhstan constitutes the majority of Central Asia's economic dynamism, since its GDP represents 70 percent of that of the region, which is more than that of its four neighbors put together. Unsurprisingly, therefore, its share of the Sino-Central Asian trade total is more than 65 percent, most of which is with Xinjiang. Indeed Kazakhstan quickly rose to become the second largest of China's trading partners in the Commonwealth of Independent States (CIS) after Russia and has held the mantle of Xinjiang's largest foreign trading partner for quite some time. While the volume of Kazakhstan-Xinjiang cross-border trade reached a little more than US$1 billion between 1990 and 1993, it exceeded US$10 billion between 2000 and 2004.[14] In 2007, trade was reported to be at almost US$12 billion,[15] and reached record levels at the beginning of 2008, before the world economic downturn.[16] This trade is particularly effective in the northern part of Xinjiang, which accounts for only 23 percent of the territory and half the population, but 70 percent of regional production due to its considerable resources, including the Karamay deposits, the Koktagay mines, and fertile agricultural areas.[17] For Astana, the partnership with China has been mostly focused on the extractive industries (hydrocarbons, uranium, and precious metals), communications technologies, and trade in consumer staples.

For Kyrgyzstan, the stakes are different: China accounts for about two-thirds of its imports and largely overshadows trade with Russia or the EU. Despite its intrinsic economic weakness, Kyrgyzstan is the second-largest country of Central Asia in terms of trade exchanges with China, as it serves as a platform for the re-export of Chinese products. According to World Bank calculations, Bishkek re-exports close to three quarters of incoming Chinese products, mainly to Kazakhstan and Uzbekistan, enabling it to generate substantial revenues. The value of these re-exports is allegedly equivalent to the country's GDP, and today constitutes the Kyrgyz state's main source of foreign currency, ahead of the gold mine of Kumtor.[18] Kyrgyzstan offers a very advantageous system for the payment of customs taxes, which are calculated on the basis of product volume and not value. Chinese traders, preferring to negotiate with the easily corruptible Kyrgyz customs officers rather than with the Kazakh authorities, who are much stricter on imports, thus see the country as a particularly attractive albeit unstable option.[19] However, this changed abruptly in 2011 with the entry into force of the Customs Union, of which Kyrgyzstan is not a part yet, which holds back its role as a platform for the re-export of goods to Kazakhstan.

On paper, trade between China and Uzbekistan, the most populated country of Central Asia with 27 million inhabitants, remains at an abnormally low level of total Sino-Central Asian trade. The absence of shared borders and Uzbekistan's isolationist stance are the primary reasons for this. However, Chinese products reach the Uzbek market via neighboring Kyrgyzstan (mainly via the Karasuu bazaar), and often by clandestine means, in order to escape Uzbek customs.[20] As direct calculations are impossible, an idea of the significance of this trade, which is bound to grow in scope in the coming years, can only be made through the approximate figures of Kyrgyz re-exports.

Tajikistan was obliged to wait until the opening of the border post at Kulma-Kalasu in 2004 before it could try and emulate Kyrgyzstan's success in re-exporting Chinese goods. Today, the wholesale Chinese bazaars that have opened on Tajik territory serve not just the national market but also the neighboring Uzbek and Afghan ones. The Chinese credit institutions have been particularly supportive of Tajikistan, in part because it is seen by Beijing as the missing link in its access to Afghanistan. Accordingly, Dushanbe consumes two-thirds of the Chinese loans offered to Central Asia as a whole. Tajikistan's largest creditor is China and its indebtedness toward its neighbor has reached dramatic proportions: more than a third of Tajik debt is tied to Chinese credits, amounting to more than US$700 million at the end of 2010.[21] More than 80 percent of Chinese investments in the country are in fact offered in the form of credit, which one day Tajikistan will be liable to have to pay back in some way.

Turkmenistan was the last to come onto the Chinese radar, but has rapidly developed in scale: almost absent from the trade figures at the time of the visit of President Saparmurat Niyazov to Beijing in 2006, the most closed country in the post-Soviet space has since opened itself up to trade with China. However, with no common border, both countries exchange mainly gas and raw materials, while petty trade is still very weak. Turkmenistan is now the only remaining Central Asian country whose food products and basic goods come mostly from Turkey and Iran instead of from China.[22]

Chinese imports, exports and total trade with Central Asian states in 2010 in millions of dollars[23]

	Imports from China	*Rank*	*Exports to China*	*Rank*	*Trade total*	*Rank*
Kazakhstan	9,839.8 (34.1%)	1	9,655.6 (21.1%)	2	19,495.6 (26.1%)	2
Kyrgyzstan	4,320 (62.7%)	1	61.1 (5.7%)	4	4,381.2 (55%)	1
Tajikistan	230 (9%)	4	427.3 (37.3%)	1	657.4 (17.8%)	2
Turkmenistan	553.6 (10.2%)	4	920.2 (28.4%)	1	1,474 (17%)	2
Uzbekistan	1,247 (15.2%)	4	1,133.3 (20.5%)	2	2,380.3 (17.3%)	2

Structure of Sino-Central Asian trade

It remains somewhat difficult to assess the trade figures between China and Central Asia as official statistics take little account of the realities of border trade, and even less of contraband networks. Following the Soviet tradition of secrecy, the Kazakh, Kyrgyz, and Tajik governments do not publish detailed information on cross-border trade, and the Chinese authorities are quite comfortable with this lack of transparency. In addition, the information China provides, on the one hand, and that provided by the Central Asian states, on the other, often do not correspond. For 2006 for instance, China announced trade figures of US$13 billion, that is, 23 percent more than the official figures given by the Central Asian republics. For the two countries with which China's border trade is the greatest, Kazakhstan and Kyrgyzstan, the figures are especially divergent. Thus in 2005, Kazakhstan is, according to Astana, supposed to have imported goods worth US$1.2 billion from China, but Beijing puts the figure at close to 4 billion.[24] In 2008, Kazakh customs statistics recorded 3,000 trucks passing through Khorgos, while Chinese data put the figure at 36,000 trucks that year.[25] With Kyrgyzstan, the divergences are also very visible: for 2005, Chinese figures are ten times Kyrgyz ones (US$30 million in exports and 100 million in imports according to Bishkek, 300 million and 1 billion respectively according to Beijing).[26] Chinese statistics are more reliable: as customs duties are practically non-existent, Chinese exporters have very little incentive to undervalue their sales to Central Asia. On the Central Asian side, the bias in the calculations is twofold: the customs services obstruct the flow of some goods in exchange for bribes, and the authorities attempt to doctor the figures so as not to make visible their trade deficit with China. The divergences in calculation are smaller with Uzbekistan and Turkmenistan because most trade is organized at state level, includes big energy projects, and involves few petty traders, a result of their lack of borders with China.

In order to facilitate trade, Beijing has vigorously supported the applications of Kazakhstan, Uzbekistan, and Tajikistan to join the World Trade Organization,[27] and would like to see all the members of the Eurasian Economic Community admitted to the WTO so that its ballooning trade can be subjected to consistent regulations. While Uzbekistan and Turkmenistan have high levels of protectionism, the customs duties that Kazakhstan, Kyrgyzstan, and Tajikistan impose on goods are relatively low, which is favorable to developing trade, but they often subject the most common Chinese products (textiles, toys, shoes, small electrical, and electronic goods) to special regulations.[28] Furthermore, Chinese traders complain that the legal environments are not conducive to investment and in particular denounce corruption levels and the recurrent absence of contracts. However, in a difficult environment, the Chinese companies find themselves in a privileged position, since they have the diplomatic backing of their government, as well as financial and credit terms granted by their national banks.

China is indeed one of the few investors present in Central Asia that attaches such importance to the frequently neglected banking sector, which enables the Central Asian states to pursue large-scale projects. With the exception of Kazakhstan, local banking systems are particularly weak. Chinese banks offer higher lines of credits than those extended by the Islamic or the European banks, and at lower interest rates than those of the main international lenders.[29] Kyrgyzstan and Tajikistan were among the first to receive Chinese assistance, mainly to finance infrastructure projects: in 2004, China announced a loan of US$900 million to Central Asia, most of which was given to Dushanbe; and in 2009, a few weeks before the SCO summit in Yekaterinburg, China extended to Kazakhstan US$10 billion, half of the sum being made up by a loan from the Eximbank to its counterpart, the Development Bank of Kazakhstan.[30] Chinese aid for development is granted either by subsidies, which are generally paid in kind in order to reduce the risks of corruption, or by preferential or concessional credit paid by the Chinese Export-Import Bank (Eximbank), the Development Bank, or the State Bank. The Ministry of Commerce subsidizes the differences in interest rates.[31] Though the money from loans is, on paper, granted to the recipient country, it is generally transferred to the company or enterprise in charge of the project, which makes it possible to keep the money inside the Chinese system.[32] China also uses offshore vehicles to organize transactions in Central Asia and its energy-backed loans have helped it expand its footprint in the region. These multiple tools give China a certain advantage over other external actors.

The Central Asian states as well as China have every interest in developing mutual relations as their economies are more complementary than in direct competition with one another. China, for example, has the capacity to export consumer products to Central Asia at low prices, which suit the low living standards of the Central Asian populations, whereas Russian, Turkish and Iranian, not to mention Western, products remain too expensive. It is also able to provide technological goods to the middle classes, whose consumption patterns are very developed, in particular in Kazakhstan. Between 80 and 90 percent of Chinese exports to Central Asia consist of finished, diversified goods: consumer products, machinery, processed foodstuffs, textiles, shoes, electronic goods, pharmaceutical products, automobile parts, etc.[33] Conversely, more than 85 percent of Central Asian exports to China consist of raw materials, petrol, and ferrous and non-ferrous metals.[34] As Hsiu-Ling Wu and Chien-Hsun Chen have shown for the beginning of the 2000s, the lack of diversification in Central Asian exports is striking: a quarter of Kazakhstan's exports to China consist of petrol, a quarter of nonferrous metals, and a quarter of iron, steel and other metals. Kyrgyzstan's exports to

China consist one-third of metals, 20 percent chemical products and one quarter non-ferrous metals.[35] This distribution of exports has not altered much over the years and so today remains broadly similar. It is not specific to the relation to China, but to the global structures of Central Asian exports, focused on raw materials.[36]

Trade with China has become so large in scale that it is now a key aspect of the Central Asian economies. Competition between states and between regions has therefore ballooned. Tajikistan is seeking wrest from Kyrgyzstan its role as a re-export platform for Chinese products at the regional level. Dushanbe actually has one major geopolitical card up its sleeve that Bishkek does not: its proximity to Afghanistan. To enable them to shave off a share of the manna crossing through the Sino-Kyrgyz Irkeshtam border post, the Tajik authorities have put a three-pronged, long-term strategy into place: first, to provide Chinese bazaars with better, more secure conditions than those that currently exist in Kyrgyzstan; second, to become one of the transit points for products heading to Uzbekistan, in particular to the regions of Samarkand, Bukhara, and Karshi; and third, to acquire special partnership status with China by transforming the country into the obligatory point of passage for Chinese commodities bound for northern Afghanistan.[37] For instance, the Sogd region, in the north of Tajikistan, has implemented market-capture strategies to win over the large Chinese markets situated on the Kyrgyz side of the border at Osh and Karasuu.[38] For its part, Kazakhstan has sought for some years to strangle the Kyrgyz bazaar of Dordoy, situated in the periphery of Bishkek near the Kyrgyz-Kazakh border, and to relocate it onto its territory.[39] Astana thus regularly closes its borders to trade in order to asphyxiate its Kyrgyz neighbor. It hopes that Bishkek will be forced to join the Customs Union, or that Chinese products will be redirected toward its own market, thus doing away with Kyrgyzstan's role as intermediary.[40]

Uzbekistan, for its part, would like to have a railway link between its very populated Ferghana Valley and Kashgar. Launched in the mid-1990s, the idea of building a railroad from China to Uzbekistan via Kyrgyz territory has run up against multiple political tensions, divergences of opinion, and technical difficulties. As of 2008, there have been some more positive developments, however. A tripartite commission reached agreement on a winding route of close to 570 kilometers, which will start in Kashgar, link up to Torugart border post, the Naryn region, and then bifurcate via the Arpa Valley and the Ferghana Mountains on its way to Uzgen and Karasuu in the Osh region, before crossing the Uzbek border in the direction of Andijan. Once operational, the line is bound to play a key role not only in the development of Sino-Uzbek trade relations, but also in the opening up of Kyrgyzstan.[41] However the regular tensions on the Uzbek-Kyrgyz borders will not help with the simplification of border-crossing procedures, and making the railroad a reality is likely to take a while. Upon completion, Tashkent hopes that this railway will not only obviate the need to pay commission levied by Kyrgyz businessmen for the transit of commodities, but also avoid Russia by opening up to the south. This will enable a more effective distribution of its own industrial products, in particular the cars constructed in the small village of Asaka near Andijan by the former Uzbek-South Korean joint venture Daewoo. Kazakhstan was, for its part, discreetly opposed to this rail project and has done everything it can to improve its own network so as to maintain control over rail transit between China and Central Asia.[42]

Borderposts: Local theaters for large continental strategies

The globalization of the economy has made a significant impact on the transportation of goods as well as passengers. At a 2006 SCO meeting, the Central Asian countries and China launched a proposal for an East-West air corridor, with the aim of using the central geographical location of Xinjiang and Central Asia to create an "aerial Silk Road."[43] Following in the footsteps of other aerial hubs of world commerce, such as Shanghai, and Guangzhou, the Chinese government has plans to transform Urumqi into a crossroads for trade with Europe, the post-Soviet space, and the Indian subcontinent. To this end, it has ordered renovation works on the international airport of Urumqi, so that, by 2015, it will be able to process annually over 16 million passengers (tourists and foreign businessmen) and handle 150,000 takeoffs and landings.[44]

Indeed, Sino-Central Asian trade is in part carried out by air freight: flights to Beijing, Shanghai, and Guangzhou, but even more so to Urumqi, grew in number throughout the 2000s and have now made Chinese towns, above all those of Xinjiang, accessible from all the Central Asian capitals. To strengthen this trend, the Chinese authorities have allowed visas to be issued at Urumqi airport. More than 70 percent of the commercial air cargo in Urumqi is so-called "return" freight purchased locally by Central Asian and Russian businessmen.[45] Finally, Central Asia and China hope to invest in the opportunities linked to the opening up of the Arctic. Indeed the opening of Arctic airspace will reconfigure the map of flights worldwide in coming years to the advantage of the former Soviet space; new routes will shorten existing ones that link the

Eurasian and American continents. Tashkent, Astana, and Urumqi therefore will have a vested interest in positioning themselves as quickly as possible in this rapidly evolving transportation market.

Land-based trade is also developing rapidly. Of the eight border posts between China and Central Asia currently in operation, only four—Dostyk, Khorgos, Irkeshtam, and Torugart—have actually succeeded in making an impact on global regional trade, while the others serve mainly as points of passage for the local populations and small-scale trade. In a bid to counter the geographical isolation of the border posts and their distance from large urban centers, the Chinese authorities have opened free trade zones in Xinjiang and granted special status to Shihezi, 150 kilometers from Urumqi, in the hope of turning the city into a crossroads on the Urumqi-Almaty route. The Urumqi-based regional government has opened its own free trade zones, whose main function is to serve as hosts to large industrial exhibition parks, as is also the case with Urumqi (3,000 m^2 of exhibition space), the town of Yining, and the small railroad town of Kuytun.[46] In addition, simplified visa procedures have been established. Some Chinese border posts can issue one-day visas without the authorization of the embassy in the capital. Free trade zones situated in the border areas can also be accessed without the need for customs formalities.

In terms of being a platform for trade with Central Asia, Urumqi quickly gained the upper hand over Kashgar. At the beginning of the 1990s, Bianjiang, the first Central Asian neighborhood of Urumqi, took shape in the heart of the Uyghur part of the old city. With its "Russian-speaking" hotels and stores and its "Muslim" restaurants, it attested to the Uyghurs' role as mediators in this emerging trade with Central Asia. It was nevertheless quickly taken over by Han sellers, often students, practicing their Russian language skills, who in turn were superseded by the setting up of the Center for Foreign Trade and several commercial malls in the new town, which are completely dominated by Han Chinese.[47] In Kashgar, the bazaar still largely remains controlled by the Uyghurs, but it now plays only a minor role as a commercial crossroads for Kashgaria. The basic consumer goods for sale are destined for a few Central Asian, mainly Kyrgyz, but also Pakistani businessmen; however the entire household appliance and technology market is restricted to the industrial parks of Urumqi and of border zones. Even the Pakistani businessmen now tend to avoid Kashgar and go directly to the Chinese maritime regions to replenish their stocks, while their Central Asian counterparts mainly go to Urumqi to negotiate with Han wholesalers.[48]

The border posts between China and Central Asia

These developments have served to sideline Kashgar's famed bazaar, now limited to small-scale cross-border trade flows.

The first Sino-Kazakh border post, at Dostyk-Alashankou at the Alatau Pass, was opened in 1992. Located in the Almaty region close to the town of Zharkent and the regional capital of Taldy-Kurgan, it quickly became the main transit point between the two countries: in 2003, it was already handling 50 percent of the total trade between Kazakhstan and Xinjiang and 90 percent of border and petty trade.[49] The checkpoint mainly manages rail trade and the Atasu-Alashankou oil pipeline, which has freed up rail freight to make room for other types of commodities. The first free trade zone at Dostyk, with the support of Hong Kong-based companies, was slated for as early as 1993, but the city's retrocession to China in 1997 and fears of a "flood" of Chinese products onto the Kazakh market put an end to the project.[50] However it was revived in the 2000s, when Beijing and Astana sought to transform the Dostyk-Alashankou post into a veritable transit point of international proportions, mainly but not exclusively for rail transportation.

In 2012, the Dostyk-Alashankou line was still the only rail link between Kazakhstan and China, indeed the only one between Central Asia and China. Using that link, opened in 1990, the journey between Almaty and Urumqi lasts forty hours, eight of which are spent at the border crossing due to customs formalities and the need to change train wheels given the differences in Chinese and Soviet gauge-widths. For goods, the wait at customs and manual offloading can take several days.[51] To increase the passenger and freight traffic and reduce transit time, simplified customs procedures have been introduced.[52] The trade via rail through Dostyk is increasing exponentially: it reached 7 million tons in 2004, around 15 million in 2009, and is forecast to reach as high as 25 million by 2015.[53] In 2008, the daily throughput at Dostyk-Alashankou was 520–550 rail cars, but it is estimated that it could transit about 306,000 TEU (foot equivalent units) annually.[54] This rail development is part of Kazakhstan's strategy to become one of the transport links of the Eurasian continent, a wish that will be realized by a transcontinental line joining the Lianyungang port on the Pacific to Lanzhou, Urumqi, Dostyk, Chelyabinsk, Moscow, Kiev, and Chop. Thanks to the Trans-Asian Trunk Railway project launched by the United Nations Economic and Social Commission for Asia and the Pacific (UNESCAP), Kazakhstan hopes to reduce the journey between China and Europe to about ten days, turning this route into the shortest between Europe and Asia, by constructing railroads with the same standard gauge as Chinese and European tracks.[55]

The second Sino-Kazakh border post was opened in 2004 at Khorgos, located further south on the Khorgos River (a tributary of the Ili), not far from the Chinese town of Yining and around 90 kilometers from Khuldja. In contrast with Dostyk, the road joining Khorgos to Zharkent and to Almaty is in good condition. For this reason Khorgos has quickly become the main Sino-Kazakh road transit point, far outstripping Dostyk,[56] and since 2010 it has been in operation twenty-four hours a day. With a current annual transit capacity of three million people and two million tons of cargo, it could become the main gateway to western China. Once the Shihezi-Yining-Khorgos route is rehabilitated, the trip between Urumqi and Almaty will be reduced by 200 kilometers, improving its profitability. In 2003, the Kazakh and Chinese authorities announced the creation of a free trade zone in order to boost trade: becoming operational in 2011, Khorgos is the first free trade zone in Xinjiang and China's main cross-border free trade zone.[57] It includes a commercial and industrial zone that straddles both states—the Panfilov district in Kazakhstan, and the autonomous Kazakh region of Ili in China. A system of thirty-day, visa-free travel has been implemented. On the Chinese side, it is said that more than 200 companies, including China's largest leather company, are going to settle there; a number of them specialize in new technologies and manufactured products.[58]

In 2006, the two countries signed an agreement with a provision to link their respective railroads at the Khorgos Pass, creating a new route—Urumqi-Khuldja-Khorgos-Sary-Ozek, this last town being situated halfway between Almaty and Taldy-Kurgan. When finished, this electrified line of nearly 300 kilometers will run, on Kazakh territory, parallel to the existing highway and will have a capacity of 25 million tons per year.[59] It will connect to the main network that passes through Almaty and therefore enable a second Sino-Central Asian rail line to be opened in order to free up capacity in Dostyk. As at Dostyk, this connecting section is accompanied by the construction of a dry port which will host a logistical center for redistribution, significant storage facilities, communications services, enterprises for product certification, insurance companies, and so on.[60] Of all the Central Asian states, Kazakhstan is the most involved in transit strategies: it is part of the CATIC project (Development of Uniform Transport and Logistical System of Central Asian Transport and Industrial Corridor) and envisages developing three large border-logistics centers, one each in Khorgos, Taskal (on the border with Russia), and the Caspian port of Aktau.[61]

With the Customs Union between Russia, Belarus, and Kazakhstan, Dostyk and Khorgos are now in the process of becoming the main gateways for Chinese goods to a market of 170 million people, and their competition with the border posts of the Russian Far East may grow in the years to come.[62] In addition to these two main posts, which are open all the year round, Kazakhstan and China share three other border posts, which are currently limited to small-scale border trade and are not always open to foreigners. However, the Kolzhat-Dulart border post, located further to the south between Narynkol and Khorgos, seems to have a promising future ahead of it. The Aksay-Chundzha-Kolzhat section of road, which is currently being reconstructed, passes through several small towns in the autonomous Uyghur region, all of which are well placed to benefit from this trade. Moreover, once it is completed, the former capital Almaty, only 340 kilometers away, will be reachable in less than five hours.[63] Further to the north, two posts have been opened, Bakhty-Tacheng and Maikapchagay-Zheminay, both close to Lake Zaysan. They have the capacity to service all of northeastern Kazakhstan, as well as the Altay region (capital Barnaul) on the Russian side of the border. The Kazakh authorities are financing the reconstruction of the Tasken-Bakhty highway to augment its freight transportation capacity, while on the Chinese side at the Tacheng post, a small airport has been opened with facilities for commercial flights. The Maikapchagay-Jeminay post, a free trade zone since 2006, is likewise being fully developed.[64] A sixth post at Narynkol-Muzart, near the Kyrgyz border about 320 kilometers away from Almaty, opened in 1992 but was later closed. A seventh point of passage might be opened at Alekseevka-Aheytubiek, which is located more than 800 kilometers from Urumqi.

Kyrgyzstan and China share two border posts. The first one at the Torugart Pass, is situated on the Bishkek-Naryn-Kashgar route. At an altitude of 3,900 meters, the post is not easy to access and is often closed due to springtime floods. Between Torugart and Naryn, the highway is not even asphalted; it takes trucks around sixteen hours to complete a journey of only 190 kilometers.[65] The border checkpoint is only ever open in one direction at a time: in the morning, the traffic is authorized to flow from Kyrgyzstan to China, and in the afternoon from China to Kyrgyzstan. It is closed at weekends and public holidays, and private automobiles are rarely given authorization to use it. Kyrgyz trucks are not allowed into China, which means that all commodities must be unloaded and then reloaded onto Chinese trucks.[66] Neither the geographical nor the technical conditions at the Torugart Pass, then, are particularly conducive to the development of Sino-Kyrgyz trade; however this route serves the Dordoy bazaar in Bishkek and has been continually growing in significance.

A second post at Irkeshtam in the south of the country opened only in 1997. China and Kyrgyzstan had wanted it to be operational much earlier, but at the time Russian troops were patrolling the Sino-Kyrgyz border as part of CIS agreements and were not favorable to the idea. Until 2002, Irkeshtam was opened solely for commodity transit and not for passengers, and even then only for a few months a year. Situated 240 kilometers from Osh and 250 kilometers from Kashgar, the Irkeshtam post is the most direct road between the Ferghana Valley and Xinjiang. It is not, however, the quickest, since the road is not asphalted throughout and it winds through a particularly mountainous region. It takes four hours on average to get to the town of Sarytash, located only 45 kilometers away, and a whole day to get to Osh.[67] Irkeshtam's strategic position, however, has roused the interest of the international community and the road is being completely renovated. Once the works are finished, travel time between the border post and the markets of Osh and Karasuu will be cut by half. Irkeshtam seems poised to enjoy a substantial economic boom: whereas the Torugart Pass supplies Bishkek and the northern regions of Kyrgyzstan, Irkeshtam provides Chinese products with access to the rich Ferghana Valley, the Tajik provinces, and a large Uzbek market.

Tajikistan and China share only one border post, which was opened at Kulma-Kalasu in 2004. Access to the post, located in the Eastern Pamirs at an altitude of 4,300 meters, is technically challenging. Until 2010 the border was closed in winter and opened for only fifteen days per month;[68] the Tajik authorities have since decided to keep it open all year round. Only 140 kilometers from the border, the city of Murghab, with a mostly Kyrgyz population, has enjoyed something of a nascent commercial revival over recent years, and now benefits from improved transportation infrastructures. A customs terminal is being built and a cargo terminal already hosts dozens of trucks from China and Kyrgyzstan.[69] Chinese companies are renovating the Pamir Highway that the Soviet regime built in the early 1930s, connecting the capital of the Gorno-Badakhshan Autonomous Region (GBAO), Khorog, to Osh in Kyrgyzstan via Murghab. For the time being, the Pamir Highway is the only Tajik direct route for the import of Chinese products, but Dushanbe hopes to increase traffic through the Rasht or Karategin Valley so that the Chinese goods entering from Kyrgyzstan at Irkeshtam can go directly to Dushanbe.[70]

* * *

The economic development of Central Asia systematically stumbles on the transportation question. In Tsarist times, the construction of the region's first railway, the Trans-Caspian, to some extent opened up the region and integrated it with the flows of people and commodities arriving from Russia. The Soviet regime also invested considerable amounts in the railway network, one of the flagships of the national industry, as well as in roads and the development of air links. Nevertheless, the transportation issue continued to add to the cost of Central Asian products, even within the unified Soviet economic system. With independence, the situation became worse: traffic within the Central Asian region reduced significantly and the governments were reluctant to maintain their public transport networks. Nevertheless, as China became the European Union's largest trading partner, Central Asia dreamed of becoming a crossroads between the two areas and sought to elevate its status as a transit region. The prospect of collecting considerable transit rights motivates the local governments: in 2007, Kazakhstan was reported to have collected about US$500 million in transit fees, and it could see this figure double by 2015 if continental transit reaches US$1,000 billion.[71]

Central Asia, however, captures much less trade from the China-EU route than its geographical position would seem to entail. Until now, 99 percent of the commodities circulating between Asia and Europe have been transported by maritime routes, leaving only about 1 percent of this trade to the continental routes.[72] The development of continental trade must contend with geographical realities that political will cannot modify. Though the Siberian and Kazakh steppes are without any mountainous obstacles and open to transit, Kyrgyzstan and Tajikistan have terrains that do not lend themselves well to the development of major roads or railroads: the technological feats required to build tunnels and bridges entail skyrocketing construction costs; landslides occur regularly; the high altitude requires a particularly heavy treatment of surfacing in order to cope with the climatic conditions; and the routes are not sufficiently wide to take large-size trucks or high-speed trains. These geographical realities are not insurmountable from the technological viewpoint, but they reduce the profitability of the continental routes.

Geography is not the sole source of problems. Logistics always comprised one of the weak components of Soviet infrastructures, and this situation remains unchanged in present day Central Asia. The old age of the infrastructures, the lack of storage sites and terminals able to manage large flows, the dearth of modern trucks or refrigerated containers, the incapacity of computerized systems to enable the monitoring of flows—all these elements combine to make continental transit unreliable in the short and medium term. Moreover, the administrative problems have multiplied: visa regimes that demand that trucks change drivers upon entering a new country; overly complex customs formalities; great disparities in transit tariffs; excessive taxation on imports into Uzbekistan and Turkmenistan; a refusal to unify the opening hours of border posts; a lack of posts open to international traffic;[73] and of course corruption, which undermines the advantages of continental trade, increases transit costs and the unpredictability of waiting times, and slows down trade flows.[74]

Continental trade is therefore by no means likely to overtake maritime trade. The Central Asian Regional Economic Cooperation (CAREC)[75] program's hopes are that about 5 percent of Europe-Asia trade will transit along continental routes by 2020, and that the transit time along the corridors will reduce by a third.[76] To control the transit of 5 percent of Europe-Asia trade flows would already constitute a great economic feat for the states of Central Asia, since in addition to the transit fees, the international community hopes to see a revival of regional trade, and potentially also a greater circulation of people. In addition, continental trade is not merely commercial in its vocation; it also implies strategies of economic and social development whose primary objective is not profitability. Making local trade flows dynamic can help to solve social problems by alleviating poverty and providing work to landlocked populations. In this way, the Karakoram Highway between the Pakistani port of Gwadar and Chinese Xinjiang does not at all modify trans-Eurasian commerce, since the flows remain minimal, but it facilitates access to the products of remote Pakistani mountain regions. The pattern of development is similar for Sino-Tajik trade, as well as some border connections between Central Asia and Xinjiang. The aim is not to influence large international trade flows, which would be unrealistic, but to provide isolated populations with tools for development.

4

ENERGY-THIRSTY CHINA'S RESOURCE DIPLOMACY

The Chinese appetite for energy contributes to strengthening of relations with the Central Asian states, which are in search of new export markets for their hydrocarbons to dilute their reliance on Russia. Although production costs for Central Asian hydrocarbons prove higher than those in the Middle East, they hold two advantages: they are not subject to global geopolitical hazards, since they arrive via a continental route without passing through any intermediary country or ocean, and Beijing considers them reliable long-term investments, since they go hand-in-hand with political alliances and solid coordination of interests with Central Asian governments. The construction of gas and oil pipelines connecting Central Asian fields to Chinese markets is a technically and financially complex affair. With pipelines having to span distances ranging from 3,000 to 10,000 kilometers, their construction requires several billion dollars. In addition, China arrived several years after the big international majors had already established themselves on the most promising sites. Despite these challenging conditions, China's breakthrough, accomplished in less than a decade, is very visible and entails many geopolitical developments. Even so, Chinese influence over the Central Asian hydrocarbon market must not be overestimated. While Beijing has become an increasingly important player, one that can be counted on to offer alternative strategies, it will neither replace the large international majors in terms of exploitation, nor replace the Russian pipelines to Europe in terms of export paths.

The continued expansion of Chinese demand

Until 1993, the People's Republic of China was oil self-sufficient, even becoming a net exporter of oil in the 1980s. But its exponential economic development, with growth rates surpassing 10 percent per year, suddenly made China dependent on foreign suppliers. Within a few years, it became the world's second largest consumer of energy after the United States. It also overtook Japan as the world's second largest importer of energy, again after the United States. Though the country still consumes massive amounts of coal, oil represents a quarter of current energy consumption.[1] In 2010, China consumed 4.1 million barrels of oil per day, 52 percent of which were imported, mainly from the Persian Gulf and Africa, a figure that could rise to 70 percent by 2020.[2] Natural gas remains scarcely used, at around 3 percent, but the Chinese authorities hope to expand its use to 10 percent of national energy consumption.[3] Though gas imports are quite lower in proportion (only 11 percent of current consumption is imported), they are bound to grow considerably in line with China's industrial development and its will to replace coal with gas.[4] According to the US Department of State, Chinese demand for oil will double by 2020, reaching 13 million barrels per day (mbd), while that for natural gas will triple to 100 billion cubic meters (bcm) per year.[5]

To address this increasing demand for energy, in 1997 the Chinese authorities decided to pursue offensive strategies which mainly involved the purchase of oil fields abroad. The primary actors included the China National Petroleum Corporation (CNPC) and its affiliates, the China National Offshore Oil Corporation (CNOOC), which specializes in foreign investment, the National Oil and Gas Exploration and Development Corporation (CNODC), and the firm Sinopec (China National Petrochemical Corporation), which invests mainly in refineries. These actors benefited from the new resources they were allotted as well as from the support of the authorities to secure provisions for the country. The war in Iraq, which was perceived as a threat to energy security, reinforced Beijing's energy decisions. China's priorities, both domestically and abroad, are thus defined clearly.

The authorities want to continue to develop domestic oil and gas production, a policy that has been pursued since the 1980s. Indeed, China has proven oil reserves that were estimated in 2009 by BP at 14.8 billion barrels, or 1.1 percent of world reserves.[6] They are located mainly in the north and west of the country, far from the centers of consumption in the east and south. The fields that have been in production since the 1960s and 1970s, mainly Daqing and Shengli, are slowly being exhausted or at least becoming increasingly expensive to operate. Beijing has thus decided to develop new fields in Tibet and notably in Xinjiang, which may contain up to one-third of the country's oil and gas reserves. The Tarim Basin, which is considered the most promising, was opened for investment in 1993. Numerous multinational companies speculated, but its actual reserves proved somewhat disappointing.[7] However, Xinjiang quickly became the third largest oil-producing province, with about 30 million tons per year, and the second largest one in 2009. Beijing hopes to make it the country's energy center by 2012–2015.[8] The authorities also expanded offshore oil exploration, in particular in the East China Sea, but these sites are difficult to exploit and the object of territorial disputes with Vietnam, the Philippines, and Japan.

In terms of imports, China wants not only to diversify them, but also to secure them by directly acquiring foreign oil fields.[9] In less than one year—in 1997–1998—it spent more than US$8 billion on purchasing oil fields in the Sudan, Venezuela, and Kazakhstan.[10] The aim of the strategy is to decrease dependence on the Persian Gulf states (Saudi Arabia, Iran, Oman, Yemen, Kuwait, and Iraq), which currently supply more than half of China's petroleum imports. The authorities worry about the volatility of the Middle Eastern market and the risks of political destabilization. Moreover, bad relations with some producer countries of South Asia, such as Vietnam, make it difficult to imagine large imports, whereas the projected pipeline between Burma and China could suffer from Burma's domestic political changes. For this reason, Chinese firms sought to establish themselves in areas such as the former Soviet Union, sub-Saharan Africa (especially the Sudan), and Latin America. However, these new markets cannot replace the dominance of the Middle East.[11]

China is also seeking to reduce its dependence on energy imported by tanker (which comprise 80 percent of its oil imports),[12] since this is far too much at risk from the geopolitical hazards of the market. The country is concerned about the risks of "energy containment" by the United States, in particular by the latter's control of the Strait of Malacca, through which 60 percent of Chinese oil exports pass.[13] The Chinese strategy is therefore to avoid tanker transportation as much as possible and give priority to continental oil and gas pipelines. This includes the expansion of gas consumption, as Chinese authorities see gas as less dependent on geopolitical stakes. At the same time, the full realization of this policy is hampered by the fact that China does not have the ability to build the dozens of pipelines that would be necessary to satisfy its consumption demands.

China's thirst for energy obliges the country to develop paradoxical commercial logics. As large Western companies already control the majority of exploitable oil fields, Chinese firms must specialize in old or difficult-to-exploit fields, or settle in countries that are seen as unstable or are subjected to sanctions by the international community. In addition, they do not yet possess the same technical skills as the large majors, and prefer to minimize the risks of exploration by utilizing already-known extraction sites. However, Chinese firms have Beijing's full diplomatic and financial support, which enables them to outbid competitors during negotiations and put forward complementary "good neighborhood" measures. These strategies elicit angry reactions from competitors, who often perceive Chinese energy policy as overly aggressive.

Targeting a promising Central Asian market

Central Asian hydrocarbons have great potential, but it is costly to realize. The deposits can sometimes be difficult to access, such as those on the Ustyurt Plateau and in the Aral Sea. Some are also sensitive on the environmental level, like the Kashagan deposit in the Caspian Sea, and still others involve unresolved legal conflicts, like Turkmen offshore deposits, which are disputed with Azerbaijan and Iran. Moreover, the extraction conditions are technically complex: on most sites the gas is associated with oil; the sites contain a large volume of sulfur and carbon dioxide; and the deposits are deep and have high pressure levels. Without cutting-edge technology, the Central Asian state-run companies cannot perform the work alone, and Russian and Chinese companies are less qualified than the large international majors. Lacking capital and know-how, the Central Asian states are reliant on foreign countries to develop their hydrocarbon reserves and so have to contend with the geopolitical games that go along with the control of resources.

With close to forty billion barrels in proven reserves, Kazakhstan possesses 3.2 percent of total world oil reserves.[14] In a few years, with the exploitation of the gigantic Kashagan field, it will come to dominate oil production in the Caspian Basin area.[15] This Caspian production is by no means going to replace the Middle East in its role as the world's largest oil supplier, but it will play an important role outside of the Organization of Petroleum Exporting Countries (OPEC), in particular for neighboring powers such as Russia and China, and potentially also for Japan and the Indian subcontinent. Close to three-quarters of the oil from Kazakhstan is situated in the western regions, which are dominated by three large deposits, Kashagan, Tengiz, and Karachaganak. The other Central Asian states are distinctly less blessed. Uzbekistan is reported to have close to 600 million barrels of proven reserves, mainly concentrated in the regions of Bukhara and Khiva. Turkmenistan is said to have similar amounts of reserves as its neighbor, a little less than 600 million proven barrels, but has greater chances of discovering new offshore deposits, perhaps amounting to as many as 1.5 billion barrels.

In the natural gas sector, the show has been stolen from Kazakhstan by Turkmenistan. The latter's most promising deposits are not offshore, as they are in Azerbaijan or Kazakhstan (even though deposits are also being explored in the Turkmen part of the Caspian Sea), but onshore, in the Amu Darya Basin in the country's east. While the reserves of Dauletabat-Donmez in the south east are known and already under exploitation, the new site of Yolotan-Osman, situated in the Mary region and explored since 2006, is said to contain reserves exceeding the size of one of Russia's largest deposits, Shtokman: with between 4,000 and 14,000 bcm, it could be the fourth- or fifth-largest deposit in the world.[16] Uzbekistan, for its part, has estimated reserves of 1.8 trillion m^3, a figure that does not take into account the still unknown deposits of the Ustyurt Plateau and the Aral Sea. Kazakhstan has about 1.9 trillion m^3 of proven reserves according to BP, and 2.5 trillion m^3 according to the Kazakh authorities, half of which are contained in the Karachaganak deposit.[17]

For the Central Asian states, the exploitation of new gas and oil deposits constitutes only one plank of their energy policies. The second plank is more complex and necessitates finding profitable export routes that do not result in skyrocketing costs. Moreover, the state of the reserves does not provide an exact idea of the volumes available for export, which depends on domestic consumption. The Kazakh oil sector seems set for exponential growth, with its production doubling between 2000 and 2008. In 2009, Kazakhstan extracted 78 million tons of oil, and should produce more than 90 million in 2013 thanks to the Tengiz and Karachaganak sites.[18] Thereafter, the figures should skyrocket as the exploitation of Kashagan begins (scheduled for about 2018). If projections are borne out, the country will produce 2 million barrels per day (mbd) in 2015 and 3 million in 2020.[19] Particularly well endowed in terms of oil reserves, Kazakhstan is placed only sixteenth among world exporters, but envisages becoming one of the world's top ten exporters by 2050.[20] In 2007, Kazakh oil exports amounted to 1.2 mbd and distributed as follows: half of it, an amount of 620,000 bpd, transited through Russia via the Caspian Pipeline Consortium, 408,000 via the Russian pipelines and railways, 80,000 via Iran and 85,000 to China.[21] Transit via Russia, then, continues to make up the overwhelming majority of Kazakh oil exports.

In the gas sector, the export capacities of the Central Asian states are more diversified.[22] Turkmenistan has the greatest potential, with a production of 65 bcm in 2008 for only 20 billion used in domestic consumption, but it collapsed to only 42 bcm in 2009.[23] It hopes to sell 125 bcm per year by 2015, which is equal to twice current production, and close to 200 bcm by 2020, a prospect that seems somewhat unrealistic given the current conditions of deposit exploitation.[24] In contrast to its Turkmen neighbor, Uzbekistan consumes 80 percent of its gas production, which is about 80 bcm, leaving only 15 billion m^3 for export: a small share is earmarked for Central Asian neighbors and the remainder is bought by Russia. Until exploitation of the Aral and Ustyurt deposits is begun, Tashkent cannot hope to export more than 20 billion m^3, and has little room in terms of distribution routes. For its part, Kazakhstan is only just embarking on its future as a gas power. In 2008, its production was 33 bcm, but it is supposed to increase rapidly to about 70 bcm by 2015 and to twice that by 2020 once both Tengiz and Karachaganak have attained full production. In 2008, Kazakhstan exported about 15 bcm to Russia and Ukraine, and predicts that about 30 bcm will be available until 2020, with the remainder going to meet the rise in domestic consumption. Out of this figure, 15 bcm will go to the refinery of Orenburg, leaving a modest amount left for China.[25] Central Asian gas remains very largely under Moscow's control, even though Russia is losing influence, especially in Turkmenistan.

Maximal exploitation of Central Asian hydrocarbons is impeded by multiple problems stretching from the weak mastery of new technologies to the opaque functioning of state-run companies that control the oil and gas sectors.[26] The national extractive industries depend on equipment that is often outdated, and they lack qualified personnel. Kazakhstan has been able to take advantage of some technology transfers, whereas the more isolated countries of Uzbekistan and Turkmenistan have to contend with significant technological and human resource-related difficulties. However, it is precisely the transformation of primary resources into finished products, the development of alternative systems to pipelines, and a mastery of new CNG (compressed natural gas), GTL (gas to liquid), and LNG (liquefied natural gas) technologies that will enable the Central Asian states to maximize the profitability of their resources to their own advantage.

Chinese strategy toward Kazakh oil

Sino-Kazakh negotiations over petroleum began in 1994, during the visit of Chinese Prime Minister Li Peng to Almaty. Some preliminary discussions with the China National Offshore Oil Corporation took place about the joint exploitation of offshore fields in the Caspian Sea. The real beginning of oil cooperation dates back to 1997, with the signing of a general agreement between the two countries, under which the CNPC and its subsidiaries were invited to invest in Kazakh fields. The CNPC proposed to invest US$9 billion to buy Aktobe Munay Gas, the Uzen field's license, and to build two pipelines, one toward Xinjiang, the other toward Iran via Turkmenistan—a financial promise that proved impossible to keep.[27] The second pipeline project immediately ran afoul of US embargoes against Iran (the 1996 Iran and Libya Sanctions Act, renewed in 2001). The first project was sidelined when the low price of hydrocarbons in the second half of the 1990s made its construction unprofitable.[28] In 1999, Chinese authorities officially abandoned the idea and the CNPC ended up withdrawing from the Uzen project, but not from Aktobe Munay Gas.[29]

A second turning point in Sino-Kazakh energy relations occurred in 2003 with the start of the Atasu-Alashankou pipeline project and the purchase of new fields. But in this year the CNPC and Sinopec also experienced their most resounding failures. They attempted to acquire 16.67 percent of shares in the Agip KCO international consortium, which exploits several Caspian sites, mainly Kashagan. British Gas had accepted China's offer, which also enjoyed the support of the Kazakh government. However, the other members of the consortium, Shell, Exxon-Mobil, Total, Conoco Phillips, and Agip, declined Chinese participation and exercised their right of pre-emption over British Gas' shares.[30] The rejection of Chinese participation created a conflict with Shell that threatened to block the investments of that company in China.[31] Eventually, Beijing was forced to sell its British Gas shares to the other consortium members and to the Kazakh state-run company KazMunayGas. China then failed to establish itself directly within the Kashagan structure, the most promising Caspian field, in spite of support from Astana.

However, since this date, China has not suffered any further failures in its Kazakh strategy and has secured most of the acquisitions that it targeted. In less than one decade, Chinese companies have succeeded in making a grand entrance onto the Kazakh market, mainly by accepting Astana's stipulation that all oil consortiums involve KazMunayGas in their activities. The Chinese strategy for the purchase of oil and gas fields is influenced by the fact that Beijing arrived late on the Kazakh market, and is thus able to acquire sites of only relatively marginal importance. In spite of this negative initial condition, China has sought to follow a specific rationale in its acquisitions. It has invested in fields located in the Aktobe region and near the Caspian Sea in order not to be absent from the energy center of Central Asia/Caspian Basin, and is also involved in more isolated fields that have the advantage of being located along the route of the Sino-Kazakh pipeline.

In 1997, the CNPC surprised everyone by winning a tender from the Kazakh government. It acquired 60 percent of shares in the oil company Aktobe Munay Gas, based in the Aktobe region, which has a twenty-year user license for the Zhanazhol and the Kenkiyak oil and gas sites. In 2003, the CNPC reinforced its presence in Aktobe Munay Gas by acquiring an additional 25 percent of formerly government-owned shares in the company.[32] Aktobe Munay Gas currently controls one-seventh of oil production in Kazakhstan, and is essentially Chinese property, as the CNPC owns more than 85 percent of it. In 2009, it produced nearly 6.5 million tons of oil and 3.3 bcm of gas.[33] The CNPC functions in an autonomous way, as all of its extractive equipment comes from China. It manages the entire cycle (extraction, production, and infrastructure) and has built or renovated several gas processing plants (GPP). To date the oil and gas extracted by Aktobe Munay Gas is

Chinese involvement in the Kazakh oil sector

exported to Europe via Russian gas pipelines or is consumed locally, but with very little being freed up for distribution to China.[34]

In 2003, the CPNC launched a new wave of acquisitions in Kazakhstan and decided to invest massively in onshore fields in order to prepare for the future filling of the Sino-Kazakh pipeline. It repurchased 100 percent of the shares in the North Buzachi field, which is located in the Mangystau region north of Aktau and has estimated reserves of between 40 and 70 million tons. It also acquired the Bars exploration site (5,600 km^2) located near the Buzachi field. In 2005, the CNPC organized the most important foreign acquisition ever undertaken by a Chinese company, that of Petrokazakhstan (formerly Hurricane Hydrocarbons). The CNPC outbid its Indian competitor ONGC (Oil and Natural Gas Corporation) by offering to pay US$4.2 billion, regarded by some as an overvaluation. Kazakhstan thus became the second-largest foreign base of production, after the Sudan, for the CNPC. Petro-kazakhstan, based in Canada, possessed 12 percent of oil production in Kazakhstan, and managed twelve oil-bearing fields, including North Kumkol (entirely under its control) and South Kumkol (shared control with Lukoil).[35] Faced with this Chinese offensive, the Kazakh Parliament passed a law guaranteeing itself a right of pre-emption on energy issues, and thus preventing Petrokazakhstan from selling its shares without the agreement of the political authorities. Nursultan Nazarbayev finally agreed to this repurchase, but forced the CNPC to yield a third of its shares to KazMunayGas.

In the same year, CNOOC and KazMunayGas signed an agreement to explore jointly the Darkhan field in the Kazakh area of the Caspian Sea. Located east of the Kurmangazy site and 60 kilometers south of Bautino, its reserves are estimated at 480 million tons of oil.[36] The Kazakh government had long sought a partner for this venture, and only India's ONGC had displayed interest. While the Darkhan site cannot be compared to Kashagan, its acquisition finally makes it possible for Beijing to become a player in the vast, offshore Caspian reserves, after its failure to become part of the exploitation of Kashagan. In 2006, the Chinese state-run CITIC Group (formerly the China International Trust and Investment Corporation), based in Hong Kong, announced that it had just concluded the purchase of Nations Energy (Indonesia) for nearly US$2 billion. Nations Energy acquired the Karazhanbas Munay firm, which holds twenty-year exploitation rights for the Karazhanbas field, north of Aktau, whose proven reserves are more than 340 million barrels of oil.[37] Lastly, in 2009, CNPC acquired Mangistau Munay Gas, one of the largest of the country's oil enterprises, which exploits or explores thirty sites, in particular Kalamkas and Zhetybay.[38] Other Chinese companies such as Sinopec have also become more active in Kazakhstan: upon acquiring American First International Oil Company (FIOC), Sinopec became the owner of some small fields (like Fedorov, Mezhdurechensk, Sagiz, Begaidar, and Sazankurak) that are spread out over more than 17,000 km^2 in the west of the country; it often exploits them with Russian partners, and also manages the promising site of Aday with Rosneft.[39] In 2011, China announced it would target the large Urikhtay gas deposit situated in the Aktyubinsk region.

Chinese purchases in Kazakhstan were made within the space of a few years—with the exception of Aktobe Munay Gas, all were acquired after 2003—and have generated lots of tension, in particular with India's ONGC, which has always denounced the aggressive methods of the CNPC and its way of pressuring the Kazakh authorities.[40] The CNPC has also been forced to confront Lukoil, which shared a subsidiary with Petrokazakhstan, called Turgai Petroleum, and acquired Nelson Resources in 2006, a company that the CNPC also coveted. The legal saga between Lukoil and the CNPC, involving many complex twists and turns, has come to symbolize the emergence of Russo-Chinese competition for control of Central Asian hydrocarbons, and one that is destined to intensify in the years to come.

In 2010, China ran approximately a quarter of Kazakh production mainly through Aktobe Munay Gas, Turgai-Petroleum, Kumkol Resources, and Karazhanbas Munay. The strategy of Chinese companies is not totally focused on export to China: a large share of the production is bound for Europe through the Atyrau-Samara pipeline and the Caspian Pipeline Consortium. Some of the oil from Buzachi is also exported to the Iranian port of Neka, where it is then sold according to a barter agreement. However, Chinese installations have also the goal of implementing the pipeline link between the Caspian Sea and Xinjiang and thus ensuring that China has a minimal amount of supplies that are totally under its control.

Despite the initial failures and setbacks in the 1990s, the Sino-Kazakh pipeline project quickly took shape at the beginning of the 2000s, indirectly due to the difficulties China encountered in its negotiations with Russia. Moscow's hesitations around the construction of a pipeline connecting Angarsk in Yakutia (the Sakha Republic) to Daqing in the Heilongjiang province, Yukos' setbacks, and the discovery of the Kashagan deposit have accelerated Beijing's reversal of opinion in favor of the Caspian Sea over Siberia. The idea of an oil pipeline connecting the Caspian Sea to Xinjiang was confirmed in 2002.[41] The first section, in operation since 2003, connects the deposit of

Kenkiyak to Atyrau, and allows the oil extracted from the Chinese-controlled fields in Kenkiyak and Zhanazhol to join the Atyrau-Samara pipeline and the Caspian Pipeline Consortium for export to European markets. The second section connects the pumping station and the railway terminal of Atasu in the region of Karaganda to the Sino-Kazakh border post of Dostyk-Alashankou. The third one linking Kenkiyak to the Kumkol fields via the town of Aralsk has been completed, and the last part of the pipeline, situated between Kumkol and Atasu, has existed since Soviet times. In the years to come the first section will be reversed from west to east to enable the continuous transit of Caspian oil to China. Via the connection between Atasu and the already existing oil pipeline Omsk-Pavlodar-Shymkent, Russian oil could also use this route as a way of accessing Xinjiang.

This Sino-Kazakh pipeline has a total length of more than 3,000 kilometers, 2,818 in Kazakh territory and 270 in Chinese territory. During this first phase, the export capacity of the pipeline is approximately 10 million tons, and will increase to 20 million once the whole structure is operational. On the Chinese side, it is supplemented by an intra-Chinese pipeline, the Alashankou-Dushanzi Crude Oil Pipeline, which connects the border post to the Dushanzi refinery.[42] In 2008, the volumes transiting via the Atasu-Alanshankou pipeline were below its official capacity: 6.3 million tons, compared with a capacity of 10 million,[43] which caused some anxiety, but the gap will be filled with the expected rise in Kazakh production. In 2008, Chinese production in Kazakhstan reached 13 million tons: half of it was exported via the pipeline, while the other half was sent to Europe.[44] After completion of the pipeline, however, the CNPC hopes to direct most of the oil extracted from Zhanazhol, Kenkiyak, and Buzachi to China. In principle, the involvement of Russian companies in the transport of Siberian oil via the Sino-Kazakh pipeline is possible, as the connections exist, but it is likely that Beijing and Astana will want to maintain the bilateral nature of the pipeline so long as Kazakh volumes are sufficient. However, Lukoil could hope to see a share of its Kazakh-based production exported to China through it.

While this pipeline is the very embodiment of the success of the Sino-Kazakh oil cooperation, its capacity nonetheless remains limited and it by no means resolves the problems that both Beijing and Astana are faced with. On the Chinese side, the volumes of the pipeline will represent only 5 percent of the country's needs (20 out of 400 million tons). After costly optimization works, a volume of 40 million tons may be reached, but this will in any case remain low compared with China's exponential needs and will not undermine the domination of the Middle East. On the Kazakh side, the volumes transported by the pipeline will also stay modest: in 2008, they amounted to merely 10 percent of Kazakh exports (6.3 out of 62 million tons), although an increased figure was reported in 2010.[45] Even if China's share in the Kazakh oil sector increases quickly due to technical improvements, the exploration of still undiscovered sites, and the purchase of new fields, its proportional share of total Kazakh oil production will decrease as the exploitation of Tengiz, Kashagan, and Karachaganak increases the size of the pie. Indeed, Beijing cannot compete with the large Western companies that dominate the Caspian basin: the North Caspian Operating Company (NCOC) and Tengiz Chevroil together possess 67 percent of the country's total hydrocarbon reserves.

Chinese strategy toward Turkmen gas

The gas issue is more complex because its transportation is usually much more costly than it is for oil. It also requires a favorable regional context, as the agreement of several countries is necessary to allow the pipeline to cross their territories. In spite of a challenging regional situation, Sino-Central Asian gas projects have enjoyed rapid success, and, since the inauguration of the gas pipeline at the end of 2009, they have become the motor driving Sino-Turkmen rapprochement. Central Asian gas projects are part of a more global Chinese strategy involving the development of natural gas to replace coal for the production of electricity, in particular that earmarked for the Shanghai metropolis. With this aim in mind, in 2002 Petro China decided to build an intra-Chinese pipeline, the West-East Gas Pipeline, that runs from the Tarim Basin (Lunnan gas field) to the Yangtze River Delta area and then to Shanghai through Gansu, Ningxia, Shaanxi, Shanxi, Henan, Anhui, and Jiangsu over more than 4,200 kilometers.[46] With recent upgrades to 17 bcm, the West-East Gas Pipeline has sufficient capacity to accommodate a share of Central Asian gas.

Already in 1992, the Japanese firm Mitsubishi proposed building a Sino-Turkmen gas pipeline in the hope of linking Turkmenistan to the Chinese coast. The idea was mooted in 1994 during meetings between Turkmen President Saparmurat Niyazov and Chinese Prime Minister Li Peng.[47] The CNPC prepared a preliminary feasibility study in collaboration with Mitsubishi and Exxon-Mobil, which envisaged a gas pipeline of almost 6,000 kilometers able to transport up to 30 bcm each year from the Turkmen Dauletabat field to Shanshan in Xinjiang.[48] The excessive cost of this project—more than US$10 billion—and the need to negotiate with several transit states contributed to its eventual shelving. In the early 2000s, the rising price of oil and gas, the growth of exploitation of the Tarim Basin fields, and the construction of the Chinese West-East Gas Pipeline renewed interest in the project.

In April 2006, Turkmenistan and China signed their first energy agreement, according to which, by 2009, Ashgabat will deliver to Beijing 30 bcm per year for the next thirty years.[49] While some experts were questioning how Ashgabat might manage to deliver such quantities to a country with which it does not share a border—supplies have to transit through two other states—Chinese voluntarism rapidly came up with the solutions. Beijing actually succeeded in convincing the Turkmen, Uzbek, and Kazakh governments to build a common gas pipeline to transport 30 bcm annually, a capacity which will rise to 50 bcm in coming years. The CNPC was committed to investing more than US$2 billion in it, and, in 2008, offered to buy Turkmen gas at US$195 per 1,000 m^3, a price higher than that paid by Russia in the same period.[50] The Sino-Central Asian gas pipeline, inaugurated in December 2009, draws from the Turkmen reserves of Samandepe, on the right shore of the Amu Darya, runs 180 kilometers to Gedaim at the Turkmen-Uzbek border, and then crosses through Uzbekistan for 500 kilometers and Kazakhstan for more than 1,300 kilometers, before reaching the Chinese border at Khorgos. Each of the three countries is committed to delivering 10 bcm, although Ashgabat planned the delivery of the 30 bcm promised in the 2006 agreement by 2015.[51]

China became very popular with the Turkmen authorities.[52] In 2002, the CNPC signed a technical service contract for the Gumdak oil field, which has recoverable reserves totaling 44 million tons. In 2006, it demonstrated its goodwill toward the Turkmen regime by financing the restoration of the Seidi oil refinery. The following year, CNPC's Changqing Petroleum Exploration Bureau signed a new service contract for drilling twelve natural gas wells within three years for the Turkmen National Geology Company.[53] The CNPC hopes to be able to exploit a total of thirty wells situated on the Samandepe deposit, seven of which are new. In 2009, its subsidiary Petro China obtained a license for exploration and exploitation of the Bagtyiarlyk field on the right bank of the Amu Darya, whose reserves of 1.3 trillion m^3 are earmarked to feed into the Sino-Central Asian gas pipeline. This is the second time the Turkmen authorities have given exploitation rights to an onshore deposit, after the exceptional case of Burren at Nebit Dag, which dates back to the mid-1990s. This Amu Darya natural gas project is China's largest overseas natural gas project so far, but Chinese success does not stop there. In early

Chinese involvement in Turkmenistan, Uzbekistan, Tajikistan and Kyrgyzstan

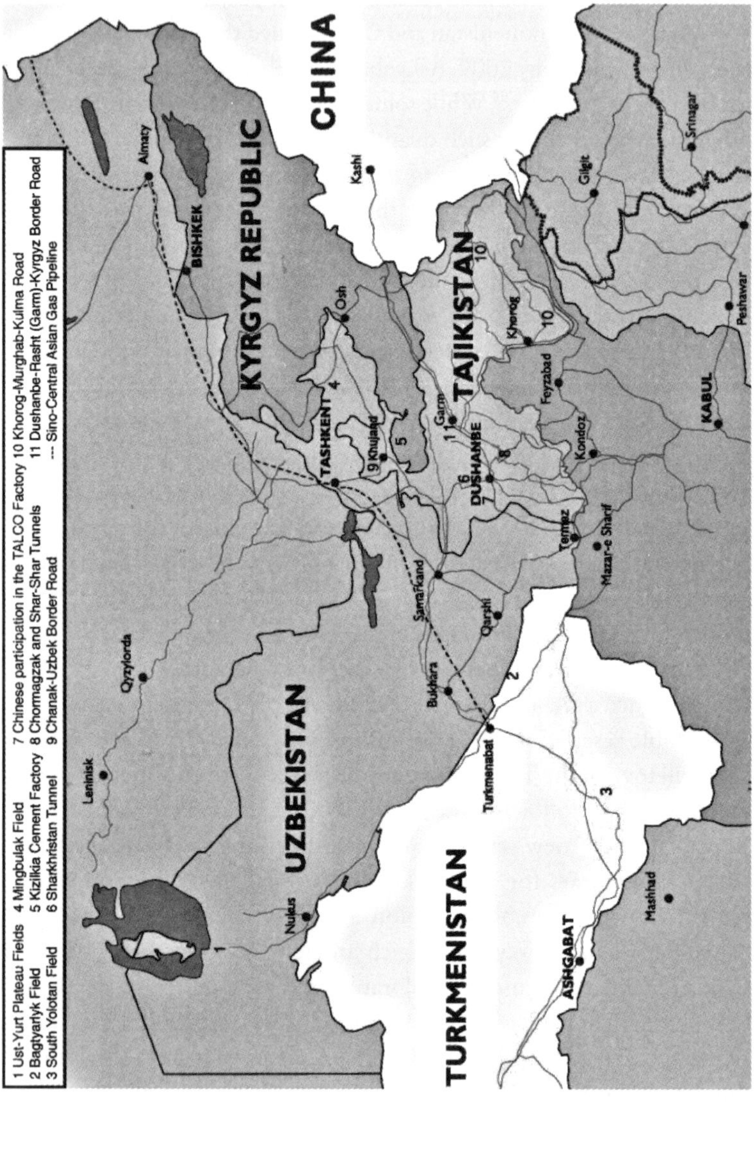

2010, Ashgabat announced that a consortium consisting of the CNPC, LG International (South Korea), Hyundai Engineering (South Korea), the Gulf Oil & Gas FZE (UAE), and Petrofac International had won the US$10 billion tender bid to develop South Yolotan. In this framework, the CNPC signed a US$3 billion contract, according to which it can produce up to 10 bcm per year and retain 3.13 bcm per year to fill the gas pipeline.[54] The Chinese Development Bank, for its part, provided Turkmenistan with a US$3 billion loan for developing South Yolotan, and the provision of another US$4 billion for the completion of the project's first stage.[55]

In March 2011, both countries announced a boost in their gas trade: Turkmenistan plans to supply not 30 bcm but 65 bcm to China by 2015,[56] which seems an unrealitistic number. In order to make up the supplies from Bagtyiarlyk, South Yolotan gas will also be delivered to China by the end of 2013. Having been designed for deliveries of 30 bcm, however, the currently operational gas pipeline does not have sufficient capacity to export of 65 bcm; its capacity may increase to 50 bcm after substantial enhancement works. Of these 50 bcm, Turkmenistan is only supposed to supply 30 bcm, as Tashkent and Astana are also delivering gas. To complement the first trunk, therefore, it will be necessary to build a second one able to transport 30 bcm. One of the most sensitive questions concerns tariffs. China is reported to have offered between US$100 and $150 per 1,000 m^3, a far lower tariff than that paid on the European market (between $250 and $400). China justifies these low tariffs by emphasizing the investments that it has offered for the exploitation of deposits. For its part, Turkmenistan has turned out to be reluctant to accept such low tariffs, even though it has urgent need of foreign currency.[57]

Driven by growing Sino-Turkmen cooperation, the gas projects with Kazakhstan and Uzbekistan have also been pushed forward. In the framework of this Sino-Central Asian gas pipeline, the CNPC and the Uzbek government reached an agreement involving contributions of as much as 10 bcm of Uzbek gas.[58] Kazakhstan also contributes an amount of 10 bcm toward filling the gas pipeline and in addition collects the transit rights for Turkmen and Uzbek gas. However, Sino-Kazakh cooperation is not limited to this project and there are larger plans for the construction of a gas pipeline linking the Beyneu-Akbulak deposits to Shymkent via Kzyl-Orda, a pipeline of 1,400 kilometers in length, part of which will deliver gas to the Sino-Central Asian pipeline, while the other half will be reserved for domestic consumption and end southern Kazakhstan's gas dependency on Uzbekistan.[59] Construction on this new pipeline should be completed in 2014, with an initial annual capacity of 10 bcm that is set to rise to 15 bcm per year.[60]

Kazakhstan and Turkmenistan largely dominate Sino-Central Asian hydrocarbons cooperation; however, some more modest partners, such as Uzbekistan, are starting to make inroads. As large Western companies are absent from the Uzbek hydrocarbons market, China can more easily establish itself there and hope that the underdeveloped Aral Sea and Ustyurt Plateau areas will live up to their promises. Energy relations between the PRC and Uzbekistan were consolidated only after the Chinese President Hu Jintao's visit to Tashkent in 2004, and Islam Karimov's visit to Beijing in May 2005, just after the Andijan events. The CNPC and Uzbekneftegaz signed an agreement instituting UzCNPC Petroleum, a joint venture responsible for the exploration and exploitation of oil-bearing fields in the Bukhara and Khiva areas.[61] In 2006, CNPC's subsidiary CNODC announced that it planned to exploit five gas and oil blocks located on the Ustyurt Plateau, in the Bukhara-Khiva region, and in the Ferghana Valley. If prospects appear profitable, a joint venture will be established and a new exploitation contract signed.[62] The Harbin Xiandai Group set up liquefied petroleum gas and water meter factories in Tashkent. In the same year, a Production Sharing Agreement was signed between the CNPC, Uzbekneftegaz, Lukoil, Petronas (Malaysia), and the National Company of South Korea, making provision for the exploitation of gas and oil fields located in the Aral Sea for the next thirty-five years. Finally, in 2009 CNPC and Uzbekneftegaz reached an agreement for the joint exploitation of the Mingbulak oil field in the Namangan region.[63]

Kyrgyzstan has also tried to rouse China's interest in its few oil and gas fields. CNPC and Sinopec subsidiary, China's Shengli Oil Company, confirmed their interests in renovating some outdated and eroding Kyrgyz oil wells, but these projects have remained on paper only. Lastly, in 2010, Tajikistan discovered 60 bcm of natural gas near Dushanbe, which is potentially enough to supply the country for the next fifty years.[64] China's interest was piqued by this discovery and it offered to help the Tajik government to exploit this heaven-sent deposit, which perhaps contains enough gas to give the country energy autonomy from its Uzbek neighbor.

* * *

China has advantages and disadvantages when it comes to the Central Asian hydrocarbons market: disadvantages because it has not been able to acquire shares in the main Kazakh oil deposits and thus to compete with the already well-established Western and Russian actors; advantages because it has very rapidly become a major player in the gas game in Turkmenistan, a country in which the CNPC is now the best established foreign oil and gas company. China has therefore succeeded, within the space of a few years, in establishing itself on numerous sites, and has demonstrated its tenacity with the construction of both oil and gas pipelines, which many observers had dismissed as being too costly and too complex to become rapidly operational.

Beijing seems interested in controlling the Turkmen market as much as possible. The growth of Chinese activity does not come without accompanying international community's anxiety for the autonomy of the Turkmen authorities: China enjoys preferential tariffs well below the gas market price, and Ashgabat risks becoming prisoner of Chinese supremacy in the coming decades once Beijing acquires a quasi-monopoly status. However, under current geopolitical conditions, it serves Turkmenistan to open its gas market to such a well-paying client and especially one that is so thirsty for energy. Kazakhstan finds itself in a more flexible situation, since it can play off several actors against one another, and does not risk seeing its oil dependency on China become too problematic since Russian and Western actors are long-term sustainable partners.

Among China's other advantages, it is worth mentionning that, in contrast to Western-oriented pipes, such as the trans-Caspian gas project designed to feed into Nabucco—which require the agreement of many partners, international majors, transit countries, and recipient countries—the Eastern-oriented ones involve chiefly bilateral relations between Central Asian governments and China, and are therefore easier to implement.[65] In addition, Chinese companies are not put off by the often excessive prices of the Central Asian market, since their commercial decisions are legitimized by much larger political and geopolitical rationales.

5

CHINA'S BRAND

INVESTMENTS IN INFRASTRUCTURES

China's economic presence does not only bear on hydrocarbons and trade, it also impacts on a multitude of other sectors, in particular those linked to infrastructures and communications. Infrastructure has often been neglected by the Central Asian states; since independence they have lacked the means to invest the large sums of money required, and so have ended up relying only on their Soviet legacy. Their infrastructures have aged, and since they are completely oriented toward the north they prevent a southward reorientation of flows. If advantage is to be taken of the new commercial rationales that opened up with the region's penetration in a global market, massive investments must be made in the domains of mineral extraction, transportation infrastructure, and communications, all of which are key sectors that may enable the Central Asian states to take advantage of their subsoil riches and/or their geographic location. It is precisely in these areas that Beijing has many trump cards up its sleeve. Its companies, whether public or private, have expertise to share, and offer much more attractive prices than other foreign firms. They are backed by the Chinese authorities and propose advantageous financial conditions for loans. In this way, China is trying to stake out an increasingly stronger position for itself within strategic sectors such as uranium, ferrous and nonferrous minerals, hydroelectricity, railways and roads, and communications. As the only state in the region able to demand more substantial investments from its partners in terms of technology transfers and human capital, Kazakhstan also aims to strengthen bilateral cooperation with China in the sector of high technology, even if this trend is still only in its beginnings. In 2011 for instance both countries concluded an agreement making provision for the creation of a large information technology center and a Sino-Kazakh university specialized in technological innovations.[1]

Sino-Kazakh nuclear cooperation and the export of Central Asian minerals

The Central Asian subsoil is rich in minerals.[2] With the exception of Turkmenistan, southern Kazakhstan, Uzbekistan, Kyrgyzstan, and Tajikistan all belong to the same rocky formations of the Tian-Shan range. Kazakhstan's central regions around Karaganda and the eastern regions in the Altay have also turned out to be well-endowed with minerals. Central Asia possesses significant reserves of them: not only does it have gold and uranium, but also silver, copper, zinc, and lead. Moreover, rare minerals such as titanium, beryllium, tantalum, cobalt, and cadmium have become increasingly sought after for the production of new technologies.

Kazakhstan's reserves of ferrous minerals are considerable, estimated to be about 16.6 billion tons, or 8 percent of global reserves. The country is second in the world in terms of manganese reserves, eighth in iron reserves, and has close to one third of the world's chrome deposits. Within the CIS, it has the largest reserves of chrome and lead, ahead of Russia, the second-biggest reserves of manganese, nickel, silver and zinc, and the third-largest of coal, gold and tin.[3] Among all minerals uranium plays a major role in the economic partnership between not only Kazakhstan and China, but also Japan and South Korea. To contend with its energy-devouring exponential growth, China is looking to develop its nuclear sector and plans nearly a five-fold expansion by 2020.[4] Priority is given by the Chinese authorities to partners with whom they have already established global economic cooperation, like Kazakhstan. After Australia, Kazakhstan is ranked second in the world in terms of reserves (with almost 20 percent of known world reserves, that is, between one and one and a half million tons), and became the world's leading producer in 2009 with about 18,000 tons—up 30 percent from 2009—and potentially around 30,000 tons by 2020.[5]

Beginning in 2001, negotiations got underway between the Kazakh national atomic energy agency Kazatomprom and the China National Nuclear Corporation (CNNC) on a joint venture to extract and export uranium from the deposits in South-Kazakhstan.[6] In 2004, the Ulba metallurgy plant, owned by Kazatomprom and based in Ust-Kamenogorsk, opened a branch in Shanghai so that it could sell its beryllium on the Chinese market.[7] The first contract for uranium extraction, valid until 2020, was signed between Kazatomprom and CNNC the same year. The 2005 strategic cooperation treaty between China and Kazakhstan advocates the strengthening of bilateral ties in the atomic energy sector and foregrounds "the unification of more segments of the industrial cycle for the production of enriched uranium."[8] In a further step in 2006, a new agreement was signed between Kazatomprom and the China Guangdong Nuclear Power Corporation (CGNPC) for the supply by Astana of nuclear fuel to Chinese power stations. According to the terms of the contract, Kazakhstan will send natural uranium to China, which will enrich it and then send it to Ulba, where it will be converted into fuel. Under the terms of this contract, Ulba will become the first foreign firm to obtain rights to supply nuclear fuel to the CNNC.[9] Kazatomprom is therefore the sole foreign supplier to the Chinese nuclear market, a strategic recognition of which the authorities in Astana are especially proud.[10]

In 2008, China confirmed its nuclear partnership with Kazakhstan. Several joint ventures under 51 percent Chinese control will be created to supply Beijing with natural uranium, and after 2013, to cooperate with enriching it. Kazatomprom also aims to participate directly in the construction of Chinese nuclear power plants so that it can gain experience in this sector and offer its services to countries other than China. Three uranium deposits, Irkol, Semizbay, and Zhalpak, will be exploited jointly.[11] In total, China planned to import 24,200 tons of Kazakh uranium between 2008 and 2012.[12] With a new contract signed at the beginning of 2011, Kazakhstan will deliver up to 55,000 tons of uranium to its neighbor, and plans to supply some 40 percent of China's uranium needs. The China-Kazakhstan uranium sales are now worth more than Kazakhstan's sales of oil to China.[13]

Along with hydrocarbons and uranium, gold constitutes one of Central Asia's main riches. The Tian-Shan Mountains, one of the largest and richest auriferous belts in the world, begin in Uzbekistan, cross through Tajikistan and Kyrgyzstan, and extend to China's northwest. Muruntau, one of the world's largest mines, situated in Uzbekistan, has estimated reserves of 170 million ounces of gold. While gold production is almost non-existent in Turkmenistan and rather modest in Tajikistan, it is significant in the three other states—Kazakhstan, Kyrgyzstan, and especially Uzbekistan. The cumulated extraction of these three producer republics is reported to be 120 tons of gold per year.[14] During the Soviet period, these resources were left practically unexploited, since Moscow gave priority to the mines in Siberia. For the newly independent states, the possession of gold constitutes a real opportunity, but for several reasons the industry's forecasted boom has not matched the pace of developments in the hydrocarbon sector. First, extraction requires considerable financial investments, which the Central Asian governments can only rarely put forward without foreign help. Second, multiple fluctuations in the gold rate in the 1990s have led the private actors to adopt a cautious attitude. And third, the gold market is at the core of several political and financial intrigues, often implicating highly placed figures.

Except for some joint ventures between the China National Gold Group Association and the Kazakh state company Kazakhaltyn to exploit gold deposits,[15] Beijing's main partners are Kyrgyzstan and Tajikistan. China has shown particular interest in Kyrgyz reserves. In 2005, as part of the "investments for natural resources" scheme, Beijing offered Bishkek to buy gold, tungsten, and tin in exchange for the construction of a section of the future railroad linking Uzbekistan and Kyrgyzstan to China, investments in the hydroelectric stations of Eastern Tian-Shan, and the construction of two metallurgic complexes, but the project did not get off the ground.[16] One year later, China came up with a new offer: to form a joint Sino-Kyrgyz venture that would be responsible for extracting Kyrgyz gold deposits, between 10 and 20 tons of which would be held at the Chinese Development Bank as guarantee. Many Kyrgyz politicians protested against the proposal, stating the security risk that this might entail: according to them, by divesting itself of its gold reserves too quickly and allowing other countries to have control over its strategic minerals, Kyrgyzstan would risk losing its political autonomy.[17] Beijing would like also to get involved in Kyrgyz tin mines, as well as in the silver deposits in Zhetymskoe, in the Naryn region; underexploited at present, they have the advantage of being situated on the path of the future Sino-Kyrgyz-Uzbek railroad, thus facilitating exports to China. Moreover, Beijing is interested in the deposits of tin, tungsten, molybdenum, and gold to be found along the Enylchek and Sarydzhaz Rivers in Eastern Tian-Shan, which is precisely where several Beijing-financed hydroelectric plants are due to be constructed.[18]

Tajikistan is in a similar situation to Kyrgyzstan: it cannot do without foreign investment for the exploitation of its metals reserves. To develop this extractive sector, regular meetings are organized with businessmen from China.[19] In 2007, the mineral domain represented 29 percent of Chinese overall investments in the country.[20] In 2008, China followed Russia's path by becoming involved in developing the Tursunzade aluminum smelter. The Tajik Aluminum Company (TALCO) and the Chinese National Heavy Machinery Corporation (CHMC) signed an agreement on the construction of two factories in the Yavan district that will supply TALCO with raw aluminum for further refining. Materials required to make aluminum (quartz and coal clay) will be mined from the Chashmasang deposit, not far from Dushanbe, which has enough reserves to be able to supply the smelter for the next fifty years. In addition, the Chinese partners are negotiating with TALCO over the construction of a factory for the production of coal and graphite.[21] Beijing's interest has been especially stirred by the Tajik deposits of fluorites in Agadzhan and Duncheldyk, tin and tungsten in Buguchi-Dzhilga, boron in Akarhar, monocytes (an alloy additive) in Baygumbez, and tantalum and niobium in Kuristik. However, compared to Chinese effectiveness in other sectors of investment, the extraction of minerals has been a mixed success for Beijing: the technological conditions of exploitation are challenging and the political environment is complex, to the extent that many projects have remained a dead letter or not attained the expected dimensions.

Participating in electricity development

In theory, the Central Asian region ought not to be suffering from large energy shortages: Kazakhstan, Turkmenistan and Uzbekistan are rich in gas, oil, and coal, while Tajikistan and Kyrgyzstan have a significant hydroelectric potential. The reality, however, is more complex since it necessitates, amongst other things, taking into account both the low level of interstate cooperation and the Soviet heritage. Energy exchanges between the states of the region fell by half between 1990 and 2000 and have never regained their Soviet levels.[22] Negotiations over the exchange of water for gas and oil regularly break down, through participants questioning the contractual terms. The stakes are not exclusively economic; geopolitical repercussions are also involved.[23] Until now, the states downstream of the large rivers, the Amu Darya and the Syr Darya, have been in a position of strength relative to the two "water towers," Kyrgyzstan and Tajikistan. By transforming water into a geopolitical weapon—Kyrgyzstan controls 70 percent of Uzbekistan's supply of water—the latter two countries hope to strengthen their position in the arm wrestle with Tashkent. A part of Central Asia's balance between these states is therefore dependent on the future of the water-electricity nexus.[24]

The Soviet legacy has shaped Central Asia's economic priorities around large energy-consuming industries and set up collective mechanisms of water and electricity management. Today, Central Asian governments can no longer maintain this joint management system and each in its own way tends to privilege its energy autonomy by reducing imports and exports and prioritizing domestic needs. The transition to the market economy also turned out to have paradoxical effects. Ageing installations and obsolete distribution networks required costly investments that the states could not finance without international aid.[25] However, their markets are relatively unattractive for investors: the corruption affecting their administrative apparatuses,[26] the governmental will to keep electricity prices low to avoid social discontent, and the difficulties involved in making bankrupt companies or those considered strategic pay their electricity bills thwart the desires of foreign actors to establish themselves. Lastly, the energy choices made by the Central Asian governments can sometimes appear contradictory: they often rely on national sovereignty arguments, without much relation to economic rationality. The multitude and diversity of problems, compounded by the further deterioration of interstate relations, as well as escalations in official discourses that systematically associate energy negotiations with state security, makes reaching nuanced decisions particularly difficult.

Nonetheless, the Central Asian electricity sector, still relatively underdeveloped, appears promising. With domestic demand for electricity expected to remain weak due to industrial crisis, coupled with high production potential, exports of electricity are destined to experience considerable growth. Beijing views Central Asia as an area capable of supplying it with cheap electricity. Contrary to its hydrocarbon policy, the aim of the Chinese here is not, at least not primarily, to have this hydroelectricity delivered to its large cities in the east (the electrical lines required would need to stretch over about 6,000 kilometers), but rather to make up for the energy shortfall in Xinjiang.[27] China would also like to be able to sell Central Asian hydroelectricity to countries of the southern corridor (Afghanistan, Pakistan, and India) because of the significant transit fees it would accrue. The establishment of Chinese companies in the region, like those it has set up in Russia and Mongolia, has thus been centered on two axes: first, the construction of new hydroelectric stations; and second, the installation of new electricity lines, in particular high-voltage ones.[28]

The China-Kazakhstan strategic partnership signed in 2005 provides for cooperation between the national electricity company of Kazakhstan, KEGOC, and China's GRID Corporation, and seeks the establishment of an "electricity bridge" between the two countries.[29] In this framework Astana and Beijing are discussing the construction of a huge electrical power station on the Irtysh River near Ekibastuz. The former site of a Gulag in the Pavlodar region, Ekibastuz already contains the two largest coal-fired power stations in

Kazakhstan. It is considered the country's largest open-cut coal mine and is one of the richest in the world, with reserves estimated at 13 billion tons.[30] With costs totally covered by Beijing, the production of the new station will be exclusively destined for China via a high-voltage line of 1,500 kilovolts able to export the electricity produced as far as Xinjiang, over 4,000 kilometers away.[31] The new power station will have an expected output of 3,600 megawatts, making it the most powerful in the CIS. Nevertheless it will present serious environmental problems, as it will need to consume huge amounts of coal, which can only worsen the situation in what is already one of Kazakhstan's most polluted towns. In addition, the high-voltage line to China has no provision for connection to neighboring Kazakh consumers, which implies that local residents will bear the ecological costs of the power station without receiving any of the benefits.[32]

The second project involves the Khorgos River at the Sino-Kazakh border. A new hydroelectric station called Dostyk ("friendship"), negotiated in 2005, will consist of a cascade of small stations with a combined capacity of 21 megawatts.[33] An 11-kilometer canal will also provide irrigation for more than 40,000 hectares of land on both sides of the border.[34] The third joint project concerns the hydroelectric station in Moinak situated on the Charyn River approximately 200 kilometers from the former capital, Almaty.[35] Completed in 2011, the station has a capacity of 300 megawatts, which means it will be partly able to make up for the electricity deficit in the south of the country.[36] The Moinak hydroelectric station represents the first Chinese "turnkey" construction project since Kazakhstan's independence.

Tajikistan is the second largest producer of hydroelectricity in the CIS after Russia, and accounts for more than half of the total hydroelectric resources of Central Asia. Its theoretical potential according to official figures is 40,000 megawatts, or around 4 percent of world hydroelectric potential.[37] With Dushanbe's support, China has decided to invest mainly on the Zaravshan River in the Penjikent region near Uzbekistan, while Russia dominates the southern projects. Thanks to a loan from the Chinese Development Bank, the state-run Sinohydro Corporation won the tender to construct the Yavan power station, which is designed to end the Penjikent region's energy dependence on its Uzbek neighbor.[38] Tashkent, however, has refused to have new stations built in Tajikistan for fear of having less water resources, and has succeeded in challenging Chinese voluntarism and putting a halt to the works for the time being.[39] China nonetheless continues to show its interest in the Tajik hydroelectric sector and has made known its desire to invest US$500 million in the construction of a new hydroelectric station at Nurabad, on the Khingob River.[40] China Theban Electric Apparatus Stock Company (CTEAS) is also building two strategic electric lines: the Lolazor-Obi Mazor in the Khatlon region; and the 350 kilometer 500 kilovolts high-voltage North-South line which, completed in 2010, is able to supply eight billion kilowatt/hour (kWh) to Afghanistan, Iran, and Pakistan.[41]

Whereas Kyrgyzstan is considered the third largest hydroelectric power in the CIS after Russia and Tajikistan, only 10 percent of its resources are currently being exploited.[42] A primary agreement was signed between Beijing and Bishkek as early as 1995 for the supply of electricity in exchange for oil, but the country's situation of permanent energy deficit has not enabled this cooperation to bear fruit.[43] In 2006, Beijing and Bishkek reached a new in-principle agreement for the export of 50 megawatts to Xinjiang, but they have been unable to agree on a price per kWh. The Kyrgyz authorities would like a consortium to be created, including Kazakhstan, Russia, and China, for the joint financing and exploitation of the huge Kambarata I and II hydroelectric stations to be built on the Naryn River. Negotiations are underway for Chinese financing of the construction of smaller stations on three cross-border rivers, the Sarydzhaz, the Enilchek, and the Akshiirak, which run from Kyrgyz glaciers in the Eastern Tian-Shan down to China.

As in the hydrocarbon sector, China has also arrived somewhat late on the Central Asian hydroelectricity market. The largest projects for hydroelectric stations were already launched during Soviet times and are today mainly in the hands of Russian companies, with Iran also involved in Tajikistan. However, multiple delays and conflicts of interest between the political authorities and foreign investors, as well as the Uzbek blockade, have grounded these large projects to a halt. Despite the repeated calls by Bishkek and Dushanbe, the Chinese authorities are mostly concentrating on small to medium-size projects, and are not participating in the two large projects of Kambarata in Kyrgyzstan and Rogun in Tajikistan. Though small and medium-size projects may not meet expectations for large-scale export, they nevertheless play a very important role in local economic development. China does not pretend, in any case, to be able to take exclusive possession of the Central Asian eletricity market. The financial weakness of Kyrgyzstan and Tajikistan requires the alliance of several foreign investors to guarantee the feasibility of these costly projects. It is therefore probable that cooperation with Russia and Iran, and with large international agencies, will increase without necessarily stirring up any competition between the actors themselves.

Focusing on transportation in a landlocked region

China is investing ever greater sums in the Central Asian transportation system, mainly road transportation, following a twofold strategy: it is seeking to improve the routes heading to its border posts in order to increase the flow of trade, and to open up its most isolated regions in order to facilitate internal communications. The financial allocations for these projects come either from the China Import-Export Bank, or from international financial institutions such as the Asian Development Bank, the Islamic Development Bank, and the OPEC Fund, and are directed mainly to the weakest states, Kyrgyzstan and Tajikistan. Chinese firms also offer their services in the cement sector and are involved in the construction of many large cement factories in Tajikistan and Kyrgyzstan, in particular that of Kyzyl-Kiia.[44] China has also proposed small-scale projects for the construction of mini mills and factories for the production of bricks.

It is in Tajikistan that the Chinese presence is most visible in terms of transportation. Thanks to China's US$900 million loan, China Railway Company built the Shar-Shar tunnel on the Dushanbe-Kulyab road, and the China Road Company another one at Shakhristan on the road leading to Khujand. In both cases, the junction between the capital and the large provincial towns is viewed by Beijing as a key element in the country's political stability. Chinese road construction has further sought to better link Tajikistan with neighboring Kyrgyzstan and Uzbekistan. The road linking Dushanbe to the Kyrgyz border, which passes through the Rogun site, and then traverses the Rasht Valley through Rasht (formerly Gharm) and Dzhirgital, has been widened and secured by Chinese companies.[45] The road linking Dushanbe to the Uzbek border via the Tursunzoda aluminium factory is also in the process of being renovated by Chinese companies, in order to provide better links with Termez situated on the Uzbek-Afghan border. A second road linking Khujand to Chanak at the Uzbek border en route to Tashkent is also in the process of reconstruction,[46] but it has been slowed down by the Uzbek rail blockade, since Uzbekistan supplies materials such as the bitumen used by China Roads.

On account of the rapid development of trade between Tajikistan and China, the road from Dushanbe to the border post of Kulma-Kalasu is also undergoing major renovation work. In 2004, China built the section of the road through the Kulma Pass on the Sarykolsk Ridge. Since 2007, it has renovated almost the entire route, starting out at a town that is famous for being the president's birthplace, Dangara—which the authorities have handsomely privileged—and then linking the Khatlon region to the Gorno-Badakhshan Autonomous Region (GBAO). The Dushanbe-Dangara section is currently undergoing renovation by Chinese companies. The Chormagzak tunnel, when complete, will reduce the travel distance between Dushanbe and Kulyab by close to 100 kilometers. The Chinese are also renovating key sections of the Pamir Highway between Khorgos and Murghab, and also between Murghab and Kulma-Kalasu.[47] Once the Chinese border is reached, the road opens onto the Karakoram Highway, which then heads toward Pakistan.

In Kyrgyzstan, Beijing has focused on the south of the country, mainly around the border post of Irkeshtam. It has partly financed and taken over the reconstruction of the Irkeshtam-Osh highway, built about 100 kilometers of the Madaniyat-Shamaldysay-Tashkumyr-Razan road to the Krupsay hydroelectric station, while the China Road & Bridge Corporation won a tender to construct a section of nearly 80 kilometers on the Osh-Dushanbe highway. The World Bank proposed the Sarytash-Murghab-Kashgar triangle, considered to be equally crucial on the economic and security levels, as a possible candidate for a pilot project on cross-border trade in Asia, with the support of the Chinese authorities.[48]

Despite being relatively well-equipped during the Soviet period, Central Asia has lost some of its railway potential. The progressive disappearance of the network has had detrimental effects on the development of freight travel, which is much less costly by rail than by road, and has also hindered the opening up of isolated regions. Indeed, without any rail links, the cost of the exploitation of mineral resources has skyrocketed: two-thirds of the cost price for a ton of coal extracted from the Kavak basin in Kyrgyzstan is attributable to transport costs alone.[49] Investments initiated after independence have been limited, and the Central Asian rail network continues to live on its Soviet legacy. According to the Kazakh Transport Ministry, the overall stock has aged considerably and depreciation affects between 50 and 80 percent of railway equipment.[50] On some lines, the speed of trains cannot exceed 30 km/h, so poor is the state of the tracks. The degradation of the infrastructure, considerable logistical problems, and poor renovation capabilities have resulted in severe cost increases in railway transport. In addition, the republics of Central Asia used to import their railway material from East Germany or Belarus, and today must either buy new equipment at higher international prices or acquire new production industries.

Russia, able to benefit from the long unity of Soviet railway grids, is trying to maintain its dominance over the equipment purchases of the Central Asian states, but the latter are increasingly looking toward China, which supplies them with cheaper wagons and locomotives. Since 2005, Turkmenistan has purchased dozens of diesel locomotives and about 200 passenger carriages from Capital-Lonqji Sci-Tech Corp. and CITIC.[51] Uzbekistan also seems interested in Chinese rail sector expertise and has ordered a dozen locomotives. Despite pressure from Moscow, Kazakhstan Temir Zholy, the national rail company, also ordered about 150 passenger carriages from the Chinese factory Tian-Shan,[52] as well as some electric locomotives, and opened negotiations with the China Railway New Express Transportation Equipment Corporation.[53] Beijing plans to participate in two railway projects in Tajikistan (Dushanbe-Kurgan Tyube and Rumi-Nizhnii Piandj), as well as in the electrification of the Kanibadam-Bekabad section of railway.[54]

Investing in the future: telecommunications

The telecommunications market is in rapid expansion throughout the entire post-Soviet space. Central Asia's main neighbors, China and Russia, have been classified by the British telecommunications regulator OFCOM as one of the chief driving forces of the world telecommunications market.[55] Another neighbor, Iran, has also manifested an undeniable infatuation for mobile telephony. For the Chinese, Iranians, and Central Asians alike, mobile telecommunications constitute not only a technological advance, but also a way to circumvent political coercion and to disseminate local information in real time. In Central Asia, the poor quality of the services on offer for landline telephony favors the rapid expansion of mobiles. Landline telephones are still dependent upon state companies, which lack the means to modernize their infrastructure and have not liberalized their prices. Uzbekistan is in the lead with more than 17 million subscribers in a country of 27 million inhabitants, while Kazakhstan is approaching market saturation with 14.9 million subscribers for a population of 16 million at the end of 2010. Kyrgyzstan and Tajikistan will also see their markets saturated within the space of a few years. Turkmenistan, for long far behind its neighbors, has now caught up with 2.5 million subscribers for a population of 5 million in 2010.[56]

China has not delayed in rushing to take advantage of the gap in the mobile telephone market. Since 1998, China Telecom, a participating member of the Transit Asia Europe (TAE) Fiber Cable System, connecting Shanghai to Frankfurt-am-Main, has been developing a telephone network for four Central Asian states (Turkmenistan only entered the project in 2004). Collective negotiations are also being undertaken chiefly within the SCO, which has decided to implement an Information Highway to enable better connections between the networks of member states so they can buy and sell telephone services from each other. In 2005, all the SCO national telecommunications operators, Rostelecom, Kazakhtelecom, Tojiktelecom, Kyrgyztelecom, Uzbektelecom, and China Telecom held their first meeting to coordinate their activities.[57] Chinese success in this sector can be explained partly by its technological know-how and competitive prices, but also by its capacity to control access to Internet. More and more Central Asian internet providers work with Chinese software capable of blocking dissident sites. Even if Russian companies dominate the Central Asian mobile market, Chinese firms are very well established in supplying technologies, mainly China Telecom, Shanghai Bell-Alcatel, ZTE (Shenzhen Zhongxing Telecom Equipment Corporation) and Huawei Technologies.

Thanks to its economic dynamism, the Kazakh market has turned out to be the most substantial. In 2001, Kazakhtelecom decided it should take advantage of the Transit Asia Europe Fiber Cable System to get internet connection via Chinese channels and not via European ones, which it considered too costly.[58] ZTE signed a contract with Kazakhtelecom for the development of wireless telephone networks and for the installation of a more effective system of message switching (commutation system), and invested in creating the CDMA-450 (Code Division Multiple Access) network in Kazakhstan.[59] In 2006, as part of the "Go beyond China" strategy, China Telecom opened an office in Almaty. The second largest market is the Uzbek one: even if the standard of living is well below that of Kazakhstan, the population is larger and the demand for mobile communications is considerable. In 2005, Shanghai Bell-Alcatel signed a contract with Uzbektelecom to modernize the Uzbek capital's telecommunications system. The Tashkent Information Technologies University also created a training center for 600 specialists from CIS countries, partly financed by China.[60] China Mobile Communications Corp. has expressed its desire to become a shareholder in Uzbekistan Telecom, while Uzbek company Perfectum Mobile signed a contract with Huawei Technologies to modernize the CDMA network.[61]

In Tajikistan, the establishment of ZTE attracted major attention. It first received an order from Tojiktelecom for a commutation station between Dushanbe and Kurgan-Tyube. Then it won the bid for codification of the Tajik national network, and became the sole owner of TK Mobile, the fifth-largest mobile communications company in Tajikistan. Since, ZTE has invested US$70 million in three large telecommunications projects in the country.[62] Huawei Technologies is also developing partnerships with local providers such as Babilon-Mobile, and the Russian Vympelkom, active in many CIS countries. In Kyrgyzstan, ZTE has shown interest in acquiring shares in Kyrgyztelecom, and Huawei Technologies has been supplying materials to all of the Kyrgyz mobile communications companies.[63]

The situation is very similar in Turkmenistan. Chinese companies are undertaking the modernization of telephone networks, the installation of stations with digital systems, and the development of internet access. ZTE won the tender for the codification of Turkmenistan's national network,[64] and Huawei Technologies has supplied Ashgabat with modern equipment and committed itself to establishing new telephone cable networks for the capital and the main cities. It has also agreed to modernize the commutation systems and to link Turkmenistan to the Transit Asia Europe Fiber Cable System.[65] In 2006, both countries signed a new cooperation agreement, which provides Ashgabat with a credit from the State Bank of Foreign Trade and Eximbank of China so that it can buy Chinese supplies for fixed telephony, mobile communications, and radio networks.[66]

* * *

China's economic presence in Central Asia is multifaceted. Beijing is seeking to establish itself in as many sectors as possible with an eye to occupying the vacuums left by the collapse of the Soviet Union. Whereas Western entrepreneurs often invest in the speculative sectors of the economy, by the acquisition of shares and bonds, Chinese companies direct their attention to the "heavy" sectors. These investments in infrastructure enable the Central Asian states to escape from the increased isolation from which they have suffered following the disappearance of Soviet-era infrastructure networks. Concerning the development of this landlocked region, China seems destined to play the same major role in the twenty-first century that Russia played in the nineteenth and twentieth centuries, though this time orientated toward the south and south-east, and not the north. Moreover, Central Asian societies benefit from cheap consumer products from China commensurate with their low living standards, but which are also capable of satisfying the growing consumer technology needs of the middle classes, in particular in Kazakhstan. The massive influx of Chinese products also gives the peoples of Central Asia the opportunity to reassume their traditional role as a transit culture exporting goods as far as Russia and Afghanistan, potentially further south and west.

This Chinese presence is of benefit to the Central Asian economies, but in an ambiguous way. Above all else Beijing privileges the extractive industry and exploiting subsoil resources. Small and middle-sized Chinese enterprises are rare, since the Central Asian market is very limited and the investment climate is regarded as negative, and is only developing in the trade sector. Heavy industry and the resale of Chinese products are both paradoxical elements of the Central Asian economies, and do not necessarily contribute to fostering the circulation of wealth and the production of knowledge. Moreover, these sectors enrich corrupted milieus such as the ruling circles and oligarchs linked to them, who control the profitable sectors of extraction, and the customs and police officers, who divert a share of the revenues generated by cross-border trade. In addition, the Chinese methods of economic settlement are decried by Central Asian actors: Chinese firms do not want to find equipment and materials locally and so come with their own, do not give work to local enterprises, mostly hire Chinese workers who live in isolation at their place of work and engage little with the host society, and often submit the few locals they do employ to appalling working conditions. There is nothing specific about this situation, which is replicated in the Chinese economic set-ups to be found in Afghanistan, Sub-Saharan Africa, and in Asia.

So does the Chinese presence bring sustainable societal development with it? Does it contribute to spreading know-how and techniques, to training locals, to interacting with the host country? Or is it rather an exploitation of partner countries' wealth in order to fuel the Chinese economic boom and domestic consumption? The response may be rather paradoxical, but whatever the negative or positive consequences, Beijing now represents the most credible economic alternative for the states of Central Asia to free themselves from an increasingly shaky Russian tutelage.

PART II

FROM INSIDE

DOMESTIC ORDER, SOCIAL CHANGES, AND NATIONAL NARRATIVES ON CHINA

The "Chinese question" in Central Asia is a multidimensional issue: it is not limited to changing the international environment of the new states, or structuring their economic development, but is also part of domestic evolutions. This domestic dimension, largely unknown, is nevertheless fundamental if we seek to articulate what is left unsaid, unconsidered, and unseen in international relations and how representations shape the twenty-first century even more than the decades of the Cold War. The question is all the more relevant for Central Asia as the region has been through drastic changes since the collapse of the Soviet Union: the countries are in a phase of nation-building that implies significant processes of myth-making; the self-representation of their place in the world is still shifting; and the social fabric is being fully recomposed.

In such a context, China cannot be regarded as solely an external actor that is absent from the domestic evolutions of the Central Asian states. On the contrary, it partially structures the domestic orders, social changes, and national narratives. Beijing has made it possible to act as a catalyst for indirect political debates on the choices made by governments; it fosters a reorganization of the social fabric by giving rise to new professional niches in which are engulfed all those who present themselves as "go-betweens" between China and Central Asia; it is an object of academic knowledge, and of expertise, and has entered into the popular imagination. Analyzing China as part of the domestic environment proves to be a revealing prism through which to look at Central Asian societies' evolutions, concerns, and representations.

However, ascertaining a precise picture entails overcoming several challenges related to the authoritarian character of the majority of Central Asian regimes. First, the limited nature of political life in the region makes it difficult to identify any opposition circles with divergent opinions from those espoused by the ruling elites. No political dissent is permitted in either Turkmenistan or Uzbekistan, while in Tajikistan it is reserved for the Islamic Rebirth Party, which has no elaborated opinion on foreign policy. In Kazakhstan too, the opposition concentrates on questions of domestic political and social affairs rather than international relations as such. In addition, the only country in which the opposition has succeeded in attaining power, Kyrgyzstan in 2005 and 2010, shows that changes in political leadership does not necessarily have an impact on foreign policy choices—so limited is the room for maneuver. In addition, as the survey institutes in these countries are rather underdeveloped, it would be futile to hope for detailed works on public opinion in Central Asia of the sort to be found in Russia, Ukraine, or the South Caucasus. In Kazakhstan, Kyrgyzstan, and Tajikistan, survey institutes and sociological study centers exist, but they remain rather limited, while in Uzbekistan and Turkmenistan it is impossible to conduct such surveys. The available information is therefore thin, varies according to country, and necessitates focusing on the written publications representing the opinion of the elites. A more sociological and anthropological approach, making it possible to better define "popular" opinions is nonetheless possible and illustrated here through cultural and economic mediators.

6

DISCUSSING CHINA

SINOPHILIA AND SINOPHOBIA IN KAZAKHSTAN AND KYRGYZSTAN

Since the beginning of the 1990s, the declarations made by the Central Asian leaderships have emphasized the need to develop good neighborly relations with Beijing. As early as 1995, Kazakh President Nursultan Nazarbayev argued that relations with China were a crucial focus of his country's foreign policy.[1] In the 2000s, the official friendship came to broaden so much in scope that all Central Asian heads of state have made pointed statements about the major role that they reserve for China. In May 2005, Uzbek President Islam Karimov underscored his appreciation of the Chinese authorities by visiting Beijing immediately after the repression in Andijan, and ever since the two countries seem to be enjoying a honeymoon period. In 2006, Turkmen President Saparmurat Niyazov also visited Beijing with great fanfare in what was one of his rare trips abroad. In 2007, President Nazarbayev announced in his annual message to the nation that he considered the partnership with China second in importance only to that with Russia.[2] The same year, Kyrgyzstan's Foreign Policy Blueprint stated that China was a close second to Russia in terms of foreign policy priority.[3] And, for his part, Tajik President Emomali Rakhmon regularly boasts of the century-old friendship between the Chinese and Tajik peoples.[4]

Notwithstanding these official discourses, the two most liberal countries in the region, Kyrgyzstan and Kazakhstan, have been rocked by debates about China's influence, and government opponents regularly try to instrumentalize the question of China to discredit the established powers. While in Turkmenistan and Uzbekistan there can be no question of having a genuinely pluralistic debate on China or any other foreign or domestic policy issues, political life in the other three states does allow for a greater expression of differences of opinion, giving the media limited license to discuss topics other than those directly involving the presidential family. The controversies about relations to China have ranged from issues of national integrity to economic questions. Both Sinophile and Sinophobe groups rapidly formed, and the economic issues soon became the principal driving force behind them. Whereas groups have appeared whose commercial interests coincide with China's growing presence in the region, other milieus are also starting to organize themselves to resist Beijing and the competitive threat it presents. Being a new phenomenon, this structuring of pro and anti-forces is only beginning to take shape, but it is already possible to make out the most problematic aspects of this issue which will shake the political sphere over the coming years.

Pro-Chinese groups of influence in Central Asia

With the exception of Kyrgyzstan, Central Asian regimes can be classified as authoritarian, with more or less graduation between, Turkmenistan and Uzbekistan on one side, and Tajikistan and Kazakhstan on the other.[5] In these four states, loyalty to the president is a precondition for participation in public life, meaning that severe restrictions are placed on the public expression of opinions not sanctioned by the state. In Kyrgyzstan, the diversity of opinion is larger, but it is also accompanied by a state in the process of failing, by the massive criminalization of political life, and by regular "revolutions." Politics in Central Asia is not marked by ideological struggle: other governing lines of division are more structuring, for instance, struggles for control over resources and over the dividing up of property. Conflicts are thus emerging between patronage groups seeking, for the most part, to defend their own corporatist and regional, or occasionally clan, interests. These economic groups have no small influence over domestic policy choices. They also play key roles in the development of foreign policy, since they tend to prioritize those states whose economic interests correspond to their own private strategies.

The question of China's increasing influence in Central Asia is a sensitive one and no one has an unequivocal response to it. In the region, the phenomenon of pressure groups is a taboo subject as it bears within it the threat of discrediting the elites, who may be suspected of defending their own interests rather than those of their country. The Kazakh and Kyrgyz media, in addition to some local analysts and political opponents, regularly mention the existence of a "Chinese lobby," and thereby attempt to denounce the economic woes and policy errors of the government. Rarely, however, are they in a position to be able to name the persons or groups that they consider to be Beijing's lobbyists. A critical analysis of this issue implies that we define the notion of a pressure group in the region; indicate public figures or circles that present pro-Chinese positions; and demonstrate the influence they may have in contrast to the groups that are indifferent, or indeed opposed, to China. These three levels of argumentation are difficult to pull together in the Central Asian context, but the mechanisms and articulations of Chinese influence networks are nonetheless visible.

First of all, the notion of a "lobby" defined as an established pressure group that defends choices based on ideological convictions is rather incongruous with the functioning of Central Asian political life. Although politicians hold discourses that are sometimes classifiable in terms of doctrinal elements (pro-Western stances, more nationalist convictions, relation to Islam, etc.), such a classification would be misleading insofar as political opinions do not determine party affiliation or career path. Although some Central Asian political figures are reputed to be pro-Western or pro-Russian, or to promote a nationalist or pan-Turkic sensibility, it is particularly difficult to identify a pro-Chinese lobby. Moreover, while favoritism for either the "West" or Russia, or the Muslim world, is perceived to be partly an ideological choice, China is viewed in an exclusively pragmatic fashion: in Central Asia, one is pro-Chinese out of economic interest, or because one thinks that there is no other rational choice for the future of the country. Accordingly, such a stance is not borne of ideological conviction. Neither does it consider the Chinese regime a role model or indicate a willingness to embrace Chinese civilization.

When the Central Asian states acquired independence in 1991, the Chinese authorities immediately established close relations with the countries' presidents. This enabled Beijing to convey its interests directly to the holders of political legitimacy without having to finance institutional go-betweens or individual mediators. To date, all Central Asian heads of state have spoken enthusiastically about their excellent relations with Beijing. They have encouraged Chinese companies to settle in the country and declined to comment in public about any contentious issues. Nevertheless, although they seem to speak with one voice on the question of China, we should not be deceived.

Beijing's capacity to influence them does not mean that the heads of state and their close aides are Sinophile by conviction; it is rather for lack of any alternative. Moreover, private interests essentially orient some sections of the elite toward China. The members of presidential families, most of them being directly involved in the most profitable sectors of the national economy, often have private interests linked to China.

Outside of the presidential families, some political actors are more oriented toward China than others, mainly due to their professional training or economic specialization, although this by no means implies that they form an established lobby. Such is the case, for example, of Kasymzhomart Tokayev, a Sinologist by training, Foreign Affairs Minister of Kazakhstan from 1994 to 1999 and Prime Minister from 1999 to 2002, or of Karim Masimov, Kazakhstan's Prime Minister since 2007. Of Uyghur origin, Masimov studied in Beijing and is fluent in Chinese. He is the former representative of the Kazakhstan Ministry of Foreign Affairs in Urumqi, a former director of a Kazakh business house in Hong Kong, and is considered by some experts to be *the* representative of the Chinese lobby. A similar situation can be found in Kyrgyzstan with Daniar Usenov, deputy Prime Minister for Economic Affairs in 2006–2007, former Mayor of Bishkek, and thereafter Vice Prime Minister from 2009 to 2010, famous for having played an important role in the negotiations with Beijing concerning the Uzbekistan-Kyrgyzstan-China rail link. However, it is not specific prime ministers per se that are responsible for initiating Central Asia's pro-Chinese policies: the issue of China arises at the level of the state itself and has nothing to do with the personality of leaders. Indeed, never has any of its prime ministers declared himself to be anti-Chinese, nor has any of them sought to modify his country's pro-Chinese policies.

As for the Central Asian oligarchs with interests centered on Beijing, they turn out to be the supporters of the authorities' pro-Chinese policies. In Kazakhstan, two oligarchic groups, Alexander Mashkevich's Eurasian National Resources Corporation—which controls the London-based Alferon Management and holds several mines in Africa, as well as Kazchrome, Aluminum of Kazakhstan, and some of the main industrial and mining complexes in the country—and Vladimir Kim's company Kazakhmys, Kazakhstan's largest copper producer, desire strengthening of ties with Beijing; China has rapidly become a quasi-monopolistic client of Kazakh metallurgy. In Kyrgyzstan, the Salymbekov family—which possesses the Dordoy market in Bishkek and controls the trade flows from China that pass through Naryn, the region whence the family hails—also plays a major role in fostering good relations with Beijing. In the south of the country, the late criminal boss Bayaman Ereinbayev, whose business was later ambushed by other groups, monitored the export of raw materials to China. In Uzbekistan and Turkmenistan, many heads of large national companies, in particular in the energy, precious minerals and railroad sectors, also have personal interests in maintaining good Sino-Uzbek and Sino-Turkmen relations.

It is true that China knows how to buy, in the proper sense of the word, its partners. At the end of the 1990s, several corruption scandals came to light in the press concerning the establishment of the China National Petroleum Corporation in Kazakhstan.[6] In 2001, the director of the Kazakh Customs Committee, Maratkali Nukenov, spoke openly about the supposed existence of a Chinese lobby in the government that was going to provide Chinese companies with an export duties exemption on metallurgical products from the former military-industrial complex.[7] Some newspapers regularly express their doubts about the China-Kazakhstan Cooperation Committee—established in 2004 and headed by the Chinese and Kazakh Prime Ministers—claiming that it can be easily "bought." This committee comprises around a dozen specialist sub-committees in areas such as finance, biotechnology, petroleum and gas, and the use of nuclear energy for civilian purposes, all strategic sectors in which Chinese companies would not hesitate to invest black money so as to secure markets. In 2007, the Aktyubinsk Court of Justice found against Aktobe Munay Gas for the possession of classified state documents relating to oil reserves in the Caspian Sea.[8]

The crossing of borders naturally comprises a key component of the shadow economy, in which many organized groups prosper with international networks and associates in political circles, and for whom neighboring China is a financial godsend. At the Kazakh customs post in Dostyk, smuggling was overseen by the so-called Karimov brothers, known as the Rybachinsk group, while the Krykbayev brothers—one of whom had been a deputy of the presidential party Nur-Otan—controlled the transit of Chinese goods over the Kyrgyz-Kazakh border. In Uzbekistan two famous criminals, Gafur Rakhimov and Salim Abduvaliyev, managed illegal trade to China. In 2011 Kazakh authorities arrested the head of customs at Khorgos, and a deputy head of the Committee for State Security (KNB), thereby dismantling an organized criminal group comprising more than a hundred people, which had for a long time dominated the smuggling of goods, especially cars, from China.[9] In Kyrgyzstan, the shadow economy is divided between groups in the north and the south of the country, with links either to drug trafficking, or to the large bazaars of Osh and Karasuu.

Chinese businessmen make regular complaints about the high degree of corruption of the customs services and administrations in Central Asia, which sometimes forces them to halt their commercial activities.[10] Many articles published in the Kazakh press in 2006–2007 denounced the situation at the customs border of Khorgos where, according to the KNB, the shadow turnover amounts to about US$3–4 million per month.[11] To get Chinese commodities into Central Asia, businessmen, both local and Chinese, have to negotiate multiple bribes, either to avoid paying custom taxes, or so that trucks contents are not checked, and often use intermediaries that will take over the delivery of goods via illegal schemes. The Chinese trucks that travel to Kazakhstan often tend to make a detour via Kyrgyzstan, where the bribes are less expensive, in order to then cross the Kyrgyz-Kazakh border, less monitored at least until the Customs Union came into effect in 2010. Attempts by the Kazakh government to stop the practices of corruption low down in the hierarchy have led to an increase in prices, since bribery then has to be managed at a higher level in order to guarantee its efficacy.[12]

A structuring component of the pro-Chinese interests in Central Asia is therefore the fact that nearly the entire trading system is based on corruption and criminal schemes. The so-called "red" (*krasnyi*) trade involves high ranking political figures, while the "black" one (*chernyi*) is conducted underground, albeit also relying on influential senior officials. These pro-Chinese shadow groups and cases of corruption are by no means unique. All the foreign companies established in Central Asia work within this same conjunction between state interests and the personal networks of leaders. This assessment therefore only confirms that corruption is a widespread practice in Central Asian societies, one in which foreign companies participate voluntarily or otherwise, and says nothing specific about China and its networks. Moreover, corrupt practices cannot be simply likened to the formation of a lobby consistently promoting pro-Chinese policies across many years, as they are temporally circumscribed and product dependent. The black money spent by Beijing in Central Asia may help to formalize a contract or to facilitate a specific project, but it does not provide a level of influence that could sway high-ranking political decisions. Therefore, there are no lobbies financed by China that have developed independently of the ruling elites, and none that could duplicate high-level decisions. This phenomenon is strengthened by the current collusion in Central Asia between decision-making circles, high-level state employees, and private- and public-sector oligarchs.

It is therefore not possible to identify "Chinese lobbies" in Central Asian political life like those existing, for example, in the United States. Beijing has no need to finance institutional mediators capable of conveying its viewpoint to decision-making circles, and any overt formalization of a pro-Chinese lobby could have the counter effect of inducing the organization of an anti-Chinese lobby. It is nevertheless likely that such a situation is provisional, for several reasons. First, historically Beijing has always fostered Sinophile circles in neighboring countries, and so it seems likely that what happened in South Asia, where China has managed to co-opt sections of the intellectual and political elite, will also occur in post-Soviet space. Second, Sinophile circles are currently being formed in Russia, where ideological commitments tend to be more openly proclaimed than in Central Asia.[13] Last, economic issues relating to the dividing up of the region's wealth and the conflicts of interest between the great powers may lead to the formation of pro-Chinese lobbies to counteract the already extant pro-Russian and pro-Western lobbies.

The Kazakh "Chinese Question": labor conditions, energy sector, and the land issue

Although the Sinophile lobbies are not yet very structured in Kazakhstan, China's presence is not a matter of indifference to wider political and social circles. There are indeed numerous grounds for tension, which include the dynamism of the Uyghur diaspora, border disputes, the difficulty of resolving issues connected to cross-border rivers, growing tensions over Chinese activity in the energy sector, the setting up of Chinese firms, and fears about unchecked migration flows.

In the early 1990s, with tensions running high in Xinjiang, Beijing demanded that the Central Asian states clamp down on the most pro-independence Uyghur diasporic associations. These pressures seem to have been applied at the highest level, that is, directly on the presidents. The Chinese secret services are alleged to have entered Kazakh territory with the forced consent of the authorities in order to track down Uyghur dissidents and, if possible, to have them deported to China.[14] Almaty's decision of abandoning the Uyghur diaspora to Beijing's interests was legitimated in the name of national independence: the authorities argued that if they had refused to yield to Chinese pressure, then Beijing would have simply sent its secret services in to deal with the situation on their own terms, and this would have weakened Kazakh state control over its own territory and population.[15] With the exception of those concerned, the crisis between China and Central Asia over the Uyghur question was hardly remarked upon: there were almost no local reports about it, and the authorities had no problems in co-opting local politicians and public opinion, neither of which desired to see a potentially threatening Uyghur minority being granted special rights.

There was not the same unanimity over the border settlements, even if in 1999 Nursultan Nazarbayev did eventually manage to get the parliament (Mazhilis) to ratify the final agreement by a large majority. To convince public opinion, the Kazakh authorities launched an intense propaganda campaign to justify the transfer of territories to Beijing. They argued that the tracts of land being ceded were worthless, were uncultivable, contained no deposits of precious minerals, and were of no strategic value. In spite of this campaign, a share of public opinion, supported by political opponents at the time, interpreted the border agreement as a betrayal, believing that the authorities were simply ready to sell off the country's territorial integrity only a few years after attaining independence. The opposition was united in rejecting the arguments put forward by the authorities to justify the agreement. Murat Auezov, in particular, skillfully used his familial and personal prestige to draw public attention to the "Chinese question."

Murat Auezov, son of the famous writer Mukhtar Auezov[16] (1897–1961), is an essayist known for his works on the cultures of the Steppes. He is also a Sinologist by training and worked for many years at the Institute of Oriental Studies before taking up a position in the diplomatic service. In 1992, he was sent to Beijing to take up office as the first Ambassador of independent Kazakhstan to China. Returning to Almaty in 1995, he became involved in politics, creating a democratic platform called Azamat, which was transformed into a political party for the 1999 legislative elections. He also took up the directorship of the Soros-Kazakhstan Foundation from 1999 to 2002. Auezov, who was a key leader of the opposition against Nazarbayev, has been a constant critic of the authorities' handling of the "Chinese question," from the first Sino-Kazakh treaty in 1994 to the 1999 agreements over outstanding land disputes. He personally participated in some of the commissions presiding over issues of border demarcation and this experience, he claims, enabled him to witness Chinese pressures first-hand.[17] Auezov virulently criticized the "disinformation campaign led by the organs of power to deceive public opinion" and claimed that official discourses "bordered on state crime."[18] This intensified his personal conflict with President Nazarbayev and obliged him to quit politics in the early 2000s.

In addition to the support of his own party, Azamat, Murat Auezov was also backed by another great literary figure, namely Olzhas Suleimenov

(1936–). Suleimenov was the former president of the ecological and anti-nuclear Nevada-Semipalatinsk movement and the then leader of the People's Congress of Kazakhstan. In 1993, he argued that such a small amount of land would not content the Chinese. This point, he stated, was betrayed by Chinese textbooks, which he reproached for persistently depicting large tracts of Kazakh land within the borders of the Chinese Empire.[19] Auezov also received the full support of the opposition parties, including the ecological movement Tabigat, the Kazakh nationalist circles linked to Azat, the Russian opposition such as the Lad party,[20] the Communist Party of Kazakhstan, and the Pokolenie Retiree Movement.[21] For his part, the Prime Minister at the time, Akezhan Kazhegeldin, declared, once in exile in London, "the greatest political error of Nazarbayev was the territorial agreement with China. These agreements directly threaten our security."[22]

No sooner was the border question settled than Kazakh public debate again focused on China, but this time in relation to the question of cross-border rivers. Here again, Murat Auezov tried to galvanize public opinion, accusing the authorities of missing the chance to ally Kazakhstan with Kyrgyzstan and Russia in order to stand up to Beijing and force it to accept a post-Soviet point of view.[23] As he saw it, China was merely seeking to gain time. Beijing knew that sooner or later it would be compelled to sign an agreement on the use of cross-border rivers, but was delaying this so that it could modify the status quo as much as possible in its favor, by canalizing the Ili and the Irtysh upstream; with this *fait accompli*, Astana would not be able to refer to the initial situation.[24] In Auezov's eyes, this failure is that of Central Asian cooperation in general: China had succeeded in gaining territories from Bishkek that contained both glaciers and the sources of several rivers flowing into the Tarim Basin without having to cede anything to Kazakhstan in return. On this issue, Auezov, once again, enjoyed the support of the entire political opposition, in particular that of Democratic Choice of Kazakhstan, which at the time was backed by a part of the political and business elite.

The question of cross-border rivers no longer dominates either the political scene or the Kazakh media. However, it is bound to take center stage again in the years to come if no equitable solution is found. In the meantime, the "Chinese question" has become more of an economic one. At the 2004 legislative elections a new political bloc, the Agricultural and Industrial Workers' Union (AIST), defended the interests of large Kazakh industrial groups from the metallurgy and agriculture sectors, whereas its allied party Enbek, close to the unions, worked to promote the rights of workers and state employees.[25] These two political factions rivaled the official party Otan, as well as the Asar party headed by the President's eldest daughter, Dariga Nazarbayeva. Both positioned themselves in an electoral niche that promoted social and corporatist demands. They were therefore particularly sensitive to Beijing's advances in the industrial sector and to the social issues raised by the practices of Chinese companies, which have a reputation for not respecting Kazakh workers' rights. Their influence reached such levels that in December 2004 the Chinese Ambassador to Kazakhstan, Zhou Xiaopei, made a point of meeting with deputy members of both factions.[26]

Indeed, Chinese companies based in Kazakhstan have had to confront growing discontent. As the CNPC brings all its extraction equipment from China, local entrepreneurs receive no benefits from this presence in terms of increased sales. In Aktobe, Atyrau, and Kzyl-Orda, Chinese companies are criticized for primarily employing workers from China, and consequently for doing little to tackle the high levels of unemployment in these regions. While there is a requirement to employ a minimum number of locals, Kazakhs who work in these enterprises are said to receive lower salaries than the Chinese and to be relegated to the most difficult jobs.[27] In addition, Astana is reported to have permitted these enterprises to operate according to Chinese rather than Kazakh labor law, thus inhibiting union activities by Kazakh employees, and outraging public opinion by requiring Kazakh employees to salute during the Chinese national anthem.[28] In only a few years, Kazakh courts have issued penalties to Chinese companies for more than 300 contraventions of the labor code or environmental standards.[29] In 2007, many hundreds of workers from a branch of the CNPC, the China Petroleum Engineering and Construction Corporation (CPEEC), succeeded in organizing big-scale protests.[30] The regional administration, concerned by the distribution of leaflets and the articles published in local newspapers that denounced the "Chinese as exploiters of the Kazakh people,"[31] launched an official inquiry, while the CNPC announced it was willing to enhance salaries and working conditions.

The growing Chinese presence is also the barbinger of other problems. The possibility that some regions could become economic enclaves entirely dependent on Chinese businesses is a concern: 90 percent of the Kzyl-Orda region's budget, for example, is reported to be funded by taxes levied from the petroleum sector, which is mainly dominated by Beijing.[32] The question of competition is obviously dominant. The President of the Association of Companies of Light Industry of Kazakhstan has expressed concern about the future of the textile and weaving industry, which will, in all likelihood, be quickly wiped out by the arrival of Chinese products.[33] The Kazakh Chamber of Commerce and Industry has recognized the inability to compete with Chinese products, and considers that the only markets left open are those of Xinjiang, and of a few developing countries.[34] Even if it is rather unstructured in institutional terms, it is therefore possible to observe the emergence of anti-Chinese groups supported by some working middle-class people, concerned about Chinese competition and the deterioration of the labor market.

Beijing's offensive in the energy sector has also elicited a growing number of reactions, even within official circles. In fall 2006, several members of parliament, including members of the presidential party Otan, censured "China's aggressive expansion in the oil sector" as well as its new acquisitions.[35] After the CITIC Group purchased Karazhanbas Munay, the deputy Valeri Kotovich asserted that the country was about to lose its energy independence, declaring that China already controlled 28 percent of Kazakh oil production and that, if it were to purchase Mangistau Munay Gas, it could acquire as much as 40 percent of the market share. The polemic that arose was such that the Energy Minister Bakhytkozha Izmukhambetov himself was obliged to intervene by saying he would do everything in his power to block the purchase plans, which did not happen. The lack of transparency in oil transactions constitutes one of the great topics of debate in the Kazakh parliament and features regularly in the media. Every transaction with China provokes more reactions than those with Western companies, even though the majority today believes that the Kazakh state ought to remain in control of its natural resources.

Throughout the 1990s Kazakhstan was a country of emigration, but during the mid-2000s it turned into one of the main migration crossroads in the post-Soviet space, with the second largest intake of migrants from Central Asia after Russia.[36] Since 2004, the country's migration balance has been positive, despite the many Kazakhs who have emigrated to Russia. According to official reports, the country hosts between half a million and one million illegal workers. However, taking seasonal flows and the shuttle trade into account, other experts advance a more plausible figure of about two million migrants.[37] The migration issue is very present in the Kazakh press, which also tends to emphasize the increasing dangers of the "Yellow Peril," yet Chinese migration is statistically far less and sociologically very different from the one coming from Central Asia. The migrant issue has been raised in parliament while Valeri Kotovich, once again, attacked the official migration policy, expressing his concern that too many migrants, not only Central Asian but also Chinese, were being let in.[38] The arguments put forward by some groups, according to which migrants steal work from Kazakhs, are likely to prove difficult to justify inasmuch as these migrants occupy economic niches that citizens refuse to enter because of the meager salaries. But precisely insofar as the "Yellow Peril" narrative has no rational basis, it is likely to remain a politically potent topic. Murat Auezov, for instance, continues to head the debate on this question. Although he abandoned politics under pressure from the authorities and returned to do research, he has retained a prominent media presence, especially on the topic of Chinese migration.[39]

These political debates have been intensified by fears that parcels of agricultural land will be sold to China. In the spring of 2004, the local authorities of the autonomous Kazakh region of Ili in Xinjiang obtained permission to rent 7,000 hectares of agricultural lands—which had been left fallow since the 1990s—from the Kazakh governor of the border district of Lake Alakol. The lands were rented to about 3,000 Chinese colonists for a period of ten years to grown soybeans and wheat.[40] This transaction provoked scathing attacks in the media and in public opinion against the authorities. For many years afterwards, no such deals were made again, precisely because Sinophobe social pressures quelled the ambitions of local politicians. However, at the end of 2009, Nursultan Nazarbayev announced that China had expressed a desire to lease a million hectares of Kazakh land upon which Chinese growers would cultivate soybeans and rapeseed. This statement provoked a demonstration of 2,000 people, a relatively large number for a non-authorized meeting, comprising prohibited parties, mainly the United Social Democratic Party, the Azat Party, as well as Kazakh nationalists and the Russian opposition.[41] On this occasion Murat Auezov again issued a fresh denunciation of the risk of Chinese colonization.[42] As land remains a highly emotive issue everywhere in Central Asia, the likelihood of settlements of Chinese farmers in the years to come is liable to amplify the growing Sinophobia.

The so-called "Chinese question" is therefore bound to reappear in Kazakh public debate at regular intervals. Its traditional protagonists comprise oppositional groups of diverse political sensibility: pro-Westerners who criticize China's influence on the authorities' authoritarian orientation; Kazakh nationalist circles, for whom China is a major preoccupation;[43] and associations of the Russian diaspora, who are anxious about the strengthening of ties between Astana and Beijing and raise the specter of Kazakhstan as a future Russian Far East in Chinese hands.[44] However, in recent years, the question of China started to shake up more than just the political opposition, and has also become a recurrent preoccupation of some groups within the establishment.

The latter are representative of the specific industrial and commercial interests that have become threatened—or feel themselves to be—by the rise of China's economic influence in the country. Over the long term it is this "economic-based" Sinophobia, and not the more ideologically based opposition, that the authorities will have the most trouble in managing, precisely because it is developing in social groups central to Nazarbayev's support base.

The Kyrgyz "Chinese Question": border demarcation and bazaar competition

More than in Kazakhstan, the process of settling border issues with China has profoundly structured political life in Kyrgyzstan. This issue provoked the largest popular demonstrations seen in the country since independence until the "revolutions" of 2005 and 2010. The first border agreement, according to which approximately 30,000 hectares were ceded to China, was ratified by the parliament (Zhogorku Kenesh), but the second, signed in 1999, provoked the wrath of the opposition, which decided to draw on nationalist feeling to try to topple the incumbent government. Far from being subordinate to the President, Askar Akayev, the Kyrgyz parliament claimed that Beijing had not contested the territories ceded and would have recognized Kyrgyzstan's borders upon the establishment of diplomatic relations in 1992.[45] In the fall of 2001, MPs refused to ratify the treaty, arguing that the final text of the agreement had not been made known to them, that no maps with precise geographical boundaries had been attached, and that it contained no assessment of the value of the lands.[46] A parliamentary commission visited the Uzengi-Kuush area to report on the ceded territory and confirmed that the new border was being materially demarcated even prior to ratification. Presented with a *fait accompli*, the MPs revolted. General Ismail Isakov, who became Defense Minister after the "Tulip Revolution," a key figure among the opposition party leaders, called for the President's resignation on grounds that only the parliament, and not the president, is empowered to alter state borders.[47]

The opposition launched a petition calling for a popular referendum over the matter, but it was unable to collect the 300,000 signatures required, largely because the authorities maintained a tight control over the use of "administrative resources."[48] The deputy Azimbek Beknazarov, an important political figure in his natal region of Jalalabad, was also a vociferous critic of Akayev's handling of the "Chinese question." At the time, Beknazarov was president of the Parliamentary Committee for Judiciary Affairs and Constitutional

Reform and regularly threatened the President with impeachment.[49] In early 2002, legal charges were brought against Beknazarov by the authorities, which were moving to quash protest, but this gave rise to pro-Beknazarov demonstrations in his home village of Aksy. Demonstrators and hunger-strikers turned out to demand his freedom, that of another political opponent Felix Kulov, leader of the Ar-Namysh party, and also the President's resignation. The protestors were violently repressed: a March 17, 2002 confrontation with the police in the small town of Kerben left five dead and close to a hundred wounded among the demonstrators, with a sixth person dying as a result of his hunger strike. Confronted with this scandal, the Prime Minister Kurmanbek Bakiyev was obliged to hand in his resignation, but the police officers responsible for the violence were never arrested.[50]

Akayev misunderstood the symbolic significance of the crisis provoked by the loss of territorial integrity and had no way of countering the fomenting feelings of betrayal. In addition, this conflict broke out at a time when tensions with Uzbekistan were aggravating the situation, since Bishkek was also in the middle of negotiations with Tashkent over the two countries borders. In 2001, under pressure from the parliament, Prime Minister Kurmanbek Bakiyev was struck by a scandal that forced him to revoke a secret memorandum of territorial exchange that he had signed only shortly beforehand with Uzbekistan. Fears that the Uzbek neighbor would demand much territory as Beijing seem to have led the parliament to taking a more hard-line approach. Moreover, rumors—which have since proved unfounded—about a rent deal giving agricultural lands to Chinese farmers in the Issyk-Kul region to form enclaves under Chinese rule, fuelled the population's phobias.[51] Popular resentment against Akayev over the "Chinese issue" thus crystallized, and the political opposition, in particular Azimbek Beknazarov, were successfully able to exploit the Kyrgyz patronage system against the President.[52]

In May 2002, Askar Akayev took a sterner approach and in behalf of the national interest asked the parliament to ratify the agreement, arguing that China had forgone 70 percent of the contested territories and that no more could be expected.[53] Despite renewed demonstrations involving many thousands of people in Aksy, the agreement was ratified in parliament by a large majority.[54] Officially closed, the debate is occasionally reignited in the media and political spheres. In 2005, after the peaceful overthrow of the President, some demanded that the border agreements be revoked on grounds that Akayev's acts were unconstitutional, but the idea was quickly forgotten.[55] The successive governments of the second President, Kurmanbek Bakiyev, have seen no interest in provoking a diplomatic crisis with China. So, despite the anti-Chinese remarks that many politicians uttered while in opposition to Akayev, no change in Bishkek's China policy emerged after the "Tulip Revolution." Bakiyev himself has even enthused over the cordial relations that the two countries have enjoyed for more than fifteen years,[56] and his successors, Roza Otunbayeva and Almazbek Atambayev, have continued to pursue a friendly policy toward Beijing.

With the border question at last resolved—although traces of it exist in the collective memory and its long-term impact on Sinophobe feelings remains obvious—the debate then shifted to the issue of migration. In contrast to Kazakhstan, where demographic fears are mainly linked to the potential transfer of agricultural lands, in Kyrgyzstan the presence of Chinese migrants working at bazaars has raised much concern. The country is in quite a quandary: about half a million of its citizens have left to work abroad, while at the same time more and more Chinese migrants are establishing themselves in the small-business sector. This has caused acute social and interethnic problems, since, with the exception of gold and a few precious metals, Kyrgyzstan has no raw material resources and relies on a trade-based economy. Bazaars thus constitute the backbone of the Kyrgyz economy and comprise particularly politically reactive milieus.

Kyrgyzstan has two main bazaars: Dordoy in Bishkek, from which goods are re-exported to Kazakhstan, and the Karasuu bazaar on the Kyrgyz side of the Ferghana valley, near Osh, which is the largest in Central Asia and functions as a transit area for goods from the Irkeshtam border post, three-quarters of which end up in Uzbekistan. The owners of these bazaars have all entered politics in order to obtain parliamentary immunity. The Dordoy bazaar owner, Askar Salymbekov, is also the former mayor of Bishkek and the former governor of Naryn. His brother and nephew have won parliamentary seats, while his sons organize the sale of land parcels and market boutiques through the Dordoy Corporation. The construction of this family business was largely guaranteed through the family's success in securing control of the Naryn road, which links the capital to the Torugart border with China. In the country's south, the chief owners of Karasuu, Bayaman Erkinbayev (who was murdered in 2005) and Alisher Sabirov, both managed to get elected to parliament, and members of their families to the municipal council. This milieu is highly criminalized: since 2005 more than ten Kyrgyz businessmen working in the bazaar sector who have also had administrative posts have been murdered, which stands as confirmation of the high degree of collusion between the mafia economy and political circles in Kyrgyzstan.[57]

Internal conflicts between the bazaar's main owners regularly threaten the stability at the local and regional levels. Several deliberately lit fires struck the Uyghur and Chinese sections of the Dordoy, Madina and Karasuu bazaars in 2002, 2004, and 2008, as well as during the "Tulip Revolution" in 2005 and the interethnic riots in Osh in 2010. It is difficult to assess whether these fires concerned only groups of the shadow economy settling their accounts, or whether the ethnic intention is really pertinent and Chinese containers were targeted as such. The authorities are therefore particularly sensitive to demands made by small groups of sellers. In early 2007, the Kyrgyz government announced that it would introduce bills similar to Russia's recent adoption of legislation to clamp down on foreign citizens working in wholesale and retail, first by limiting them through quota restrictions, and then by banning them altogether.[58] While the Russian legislation principally aims at Caucasians and Central Asians, and was drafted by the Kremlin in response to a rise in xenophobia, in Kyrgyzstan this situation was used as a chance to curtail the commercial activities of the Chinese. An official directive titled "On the establishment of an authorized quota of foreign citizens and stateless people maintaining commercial activities in wholesaling and retailing in the Kyrgyz republic" was due to come into effect in April 2007: only 4,500 foreigners were to be allowed to work at Kyrgyz markets. However, with an SCO summit to be held in Bishkek just a few months later, the government grew concerned about the negative impact this decision might have on relations with Beijing ; implementation of the decision was initially delayed until 2008, and has since been indefinitely postponed.[59]

The director of the State Committee for Labor and Migration, Aigul Ryskulova, who was the bill's main instigator, tried to alleviate the concerns of Chinese entrepreneurs. She explained that this law did not target either investors or company heads, but rather those who undertook individual entrepreneurial activities.[60] The official reason for the decision was a response to a threefold challenge: to reduce the competition from Chinese traders; to decrease pressures at markets where conflict between groups had intensified since the "Tulip Revolution"; and to facilitate the return of Kyrgyz workers from Russia. According to the above-named Committee, Kyrgyzstan's membership of the WTO means it cannot impose customs duties on Chinese products, and so must employ other measures such as imposing quotas on foreign traders and increasing the cost of rental licenses for sites at bazaars, which until then had been relatively low (around US$15 per month). Aigul Ryskulova nevertheless conceded that pressures from the two chief organizations of Kyrgyz small entrepreneurs lay behind the drafting of the law.

The first, the Dordoy Association, unites 1,500 sellers from the Dordoy bazaar located on the outskirts of Bishkek. It lodged formal complaints about dumping by Chinese traders, claiming that they bought cheaper Chinese products than their Kyrgyz counterparts and were even given fiscal relief for exports by their government. The allegedly inferior quality of Chinese products is also an argument often employed by unions. The Dordoy Association, for example, has complained that Chinese fabrics, which are not certified, give fashion designers illnesses.[61] The second largest association, Ishker, is a union of 10,000 entrepreneurs and sellers from the Karasuu bazaar, which formed in early 2006. Committed to reducing investment costs and improving sanitary and security conditions, Ishker regularly decries so-called Chinese competition as well.[62] These two powerful economic lobbies have thus tried to convince the government that certain labor sectors should be officially reserved for nationals. Ishker even orchestrated big demonstrations of thousands of people against Chinese traders.[63]

Nevertheless, the government's decision to introduce quotas for Chinese traders did not receive unanimous support from Kyrgyz economic and political circles. In point of fact, the former governor of the city of Osh, Zhantoro Satybaldiyev, supported by the Secretary of State Adakhan Madumarov, has argued that the introduction of quotas will by no means induce those migrants settled in Russia and Kazakhstan to return, but instead will lead to a great loss of money for the region, since more than two-thirds of Chinese products are actually re-exported.[64] Tursuntay Salimov, director of the Madina bazaar, specializing in textiles, sanitary and construction materials, 90 percent of which come from China, was also opposed to this idea. He argued that Chinese traders bring money into Kyrgyzstan by paying for licenses for their boutiques and rents for their apartments. He has called attention to the fact that many Kyrgyz traders actually make profits by reselling cheaply bought Chinese products at higher prices in Russia and Kazakhstan.[65]

In addition, several businessmen have stated that, since competition between Kazakhstan and Kyrgyzstan for the transit of Chinese products is growing, Astana will acquire the Chinese wholesale bazaars that were obliged to leave Kyrgyzstan.[66] Others also mention the possibility of reprisals against Kyrgyz traders established in China. The press has remained rather reserved, interpreting this decision as a judgment in favor of Kyrgyz commercial lobbies to the detriment of ordinary citizens. It has argued that the weak consumer capacity of the latter will be unable to respond to the price increases resulting from the partial disappearance of Chinese traders. After this crisis, the Kyrgyz government has left the question hanging and has not introduced the quotas announced. But the tensions at the bazaars have nonetheless not been defused. New conflictual niches have emerged. Kyrgyzstan now regularly experiences protests of truck drivers who are not allowed to enter Chinese territory, in contrast to Chinese drivers who are allowed access to all Kyrgyz roads. It is argued that this deprives the locals of work opportunities. In spring 2010, these large-scale strikes blocked the truck flows between Irkeshtam and Osh for several days.[67]

* * *

If one had to define a "Chinese lobby," then the heads of state themselves would be the most obvious candidates, insofar as they appear to have taken on the role of heralds of Sino-Central Asian friendship. They are backed by their relatives and personal networks involved in "red" business, and by numerous powerful economic circles with interests in seeing further development in official and underground trade relations with China. While the ruling circles actively promote friendly relations with Beijing, government opponents try to undermine them by denouncing their favoring of China. However, even if they succeeded in taking the reins of power, they too would find themselves constrained in promulgating the same Sinophile discourse as their predecessors. In view of the large economic, political, and demographic differential, no Central Asian regime can afford to present itself as Sinophobe. As for the orientation of the armies and secret services, which is beset with uncertainty, it seems that China is held in relative suspicion, both because of its disquieting capacity for penetration, and because old traditions of cohabitation with Russia are still dominant. It is probable that in economic circles more distinctly pro- and anti-Chinese lobbies will form in the coming years. Some social groups, such as employees, labor unions, independent small businessmen, and directors of medium-size companies, tend to concentrate on criticizing competition from the Chinese, while big national groups, both public and private, generally stand to gain from pursuing closer relations.

In Kazakhstan and Kyrgyzstan, political life has come to be stamped by crises and public debates involving their relations with their great neighbor. With the "Chinese Question," public opinion has found a means to express its concerns over issues including whether the authorities are justified in exercising regalian rights, such as the cession of sections of territory, without calling for a national referendum; whether leaders who sell economic wealth to foreign actors ought to be suspected of seeking personal gain; and what migration and labor policies the region needs to implement in order to address its own demographic weaknesses vis-à-vis its overpopulated Chinese neighbor. Nevertheless, this situation remains specific to these two republics alone, for neither Uzbekistan nor Turkmenistan are arenas for such pluralistic debates. In Tajikistan, China is slowly becoming a major topic of discussion, but the media and politicians are still more focused on domestic problems, questions of migration, and drug-trafficking from Afghanistan. It is nevertheless likely that the "Chinese question" will become an important one for the authorities in Dushanbe, and in a way that is rather similar to what has happened in Kyrgyzstan over the last decade.

Changes in the nature of the "Chinese question" move apace with shifting political and economic stakes. In Kazakhstan, the question was chiefly raised in conjunction with the highly symbolic issue of territorial integrity and the Uyghur problem, before economic considerations then came to the fore, in particular related to energy. The as-yet unresolved question of cross-border rivers is likely to recur regularly, especially as it will have many long-term repercussions; and doubtless the migration question linked to the rental of agricultural lands will also become more important in coming years. Debates in Kyrgyzstan have also shifted from border delimitations, which played a fundamental role in delegitimizing Askar Akayev, to migration and bazaar-related economic issues. Four major aspects of the "Chinese question" are thereby likely to remain in play in Central Asia: first, the transparency of transactions in the energy and mineral sectors, which form some of the largest contributors to all state budgets; second, the establishment of non-energy sector Chinese companies, which raise issues of competition for work and due respect for labor regulations; third, the issues of land ownership, which has long been a particularly sensitive topic for Central Asians;[68] and last, the control of commodity flows coming from China, in particular to the bazaars, which are the driving forces of the Central Asian economies, especially of Kyrgyzstan's.

In the framework of this "Chinese question," public opinion in Central Asia has found a way to formulate its legitimate anxieties over the threats to national territorial integrity that emerged shortly after independence. It has also come, if discreetly, to raise its opposition to the selling of national subsoil resources at bargain basement prices by elites suspected of promoting their personal interests. The "Chinese question" also provides a way to express social anxieties related to the market economy, such as the development of the labor market, the deterioration of working conditions, and the difficulties faced by those classes of small entrepreneurs who have made their fortunes in very unregulated commercial sectors. Fears of the potential massive migratory flows from China are also part of this context. China's rise to power has therefore acted as a catalyst, exposing the dysfunctional aspects of the local economies, and compounding the phobias connected to the last two decades of major social upheavals.

7

THE NEW MEDIATORS

DIASPORAS, TRADERS, MIGRANTS, AND YOUTH

The impact of the growing Chinese presence in Central Asia is not limited to the emergence of pro- or anti-Chinese influence groups, or to the formulating of a "Chinese question" in Kazakh and Kyrgyz public space. Social transformations of greater magnitude can also be explained by Chinese proximity. Even though labor migration flows bound for Russia are the most visible, similar movements are in the process of taking shape in the direction of China. Of less magnitude in statistical terms, they are more multiform, symbols of the diversified interaction that is being created between the Central Asian societies and their large neighbor. The local social fabric is being modified in depth by the economic opportunities made available by Beijing, and emerging niches are taking shape, through which groups of very different natures try to play the role of economic mediator and "cultural smuggler": cross-border minorities who are rediscovering their historical role as "go-betweens;" shuttle traders who disseminate the image of China as a land of plenty; Chinese migrants and expatriates who happen to embody a new place in the Central Asian imaginary; and young generations attracted by Chinese success who are in search of new professional opportunities.

Cross-border minorities: reviving an historical "go-between" role

Although in 1991 the feeling in Central Asia was that China was largely an unknown world, there have always been population exchanges between the two zones. From the 1870s until the 1960s, hundreds of thousands of people crossed over the border from Xinjiang to settle in the Russian-Soviet space, a phenomenon that continued throughout the 1990s and 2000s with the repatriation programs for co-ethnics abroad.[1] Today, old and new cross-border minorities play, each at specific levels, the role of cultural and economic mediators. Even if their trade-related niche remains modest by comparison to the overall Sino-Central Asian commercial flow, it constitutes an important element in their social strategies. Trans-nationalization is not new or specific for either of the two areas: the national minorities in China have been part of processes of globalization,[2] as have the Koreans, the Greeks, the Germans and the Russians in Central Asia, all of whom started up trading links with their countries of origin during the transition to the market economy.

The Uyghurs: commercial opportunities hampered by political suspicions

Though there were limited exchanges between the Soviet and Chinese Uyghurs in the 1980s, the opening of the borders at the end of *perestroika* enabled many of them to visit family members and to combine this with some modest shuttle trade. In China, Soviet products were considered of higher quality than the national ones, while the Central Asians expressed an interest in Chinese household appliances and plastics that could not be found in the Soviet Union. Despite strong suspicions on the part of the central authorities, Beijing then had every interest in playing up the Uyghur card, since it wanted to make its border economy more dynamic. Moreover, Deng Xiaoping's reforms encouraged the ethnic minorities, not to mention the Han Chinese, to set up small private companies for the transit of commodities, and to enter into retailing or the restaurant business.

From the start of the 1990s, the main flea market (*barakholka*) of the then Kazakh capital, Almaty, located at the city limits on what was previously an abandoned site, was transformed into a place for the resale of Chinese goods transported from Xinjiang. It was quickly taken over by Dungan and Uyghur traders, since it was located near a former *kolkhoz*, Zaria Vostoka (The Dawn of the Orient), which had a Dungan majority at the time of its foundation in the 1930s, but then came to be numerically dominated by Uyghurs arriving from China in the 1960s. These latter, who maintained close links with relatives in Xinjiang, set up in the cross-border trade by investing in the *barakholka*, or by developing related businesses, such as restaurants, the hiring out of warehouses, or the supply of lodging for traveling traders.[3] Smaller markets selling Chinese goods were also set up on both sides of the border in Zharkent and Yining, allowing traders to commute between them without having to cross the entire Ili valley from Almaty to Urumqi. Similarly in Kyrgyzstan, cross-border trade at the Torugart Pass boomed in the Naryn region and then developed around the bazaar of the capital, Dordoy.

The cross-border shuttle services quickly came into competition with the new Almaty-Urumqi railroad, which enabled trade to take place across greater distances. As a result, trade practices became more diversified: the Central Asian Uyghurs started to spend less time in Xinjiang, where they went only to purchase goods, while the Chinese Uyghurs who went to Central Asia stayed longer to establish their own stands at the *barakholka* or at one of the other bazaars of the region. To reduce transport costs, Uyghur traders tried to have larger quantities of goods freighted. They organized whole containers to enable the storage of significant quantities of goods, which then became sites of sale in their own right—something that is still observable today. Cross-border movements were also reduced by structuring networks that made it possible for a trader to establish links with a permanent contact in Xinjiang for the purpose of buying the required goods and freighting them, and by establishing a method of payment that involved the mutual repayment of diverse types of debt and avoided the transfer of massive sums of money.[4]

In the second half of the 1990s, many obstacles stood in the way of Uyghur trade. First of all, the cross-border character of the trade diminished as it increased in magnitude at regional and then state levels with the development of official Sino-Central Asian commercial relations. Kazakh businessmen quickly became aware of the economic stakes and put pressure on the authorities to alter the rules of the game in their favor. Hence, beginning in 1995, the Kazakh government passed a series of laws aimed at making cross-border trading more difficult for small traders and preventing the importation of specific products to safeguard local production (Chinese beer, for example).[5] Preparing for the emergence of new competition, Uyghur traders on both sides of the border strove to define their objectives with more precision. Some tried to specialize in specific niches, such as imitations of brand name products, but they were rapidly outstripped by the arrival of companies owned by Han Chinese, who received their supplies directly from large production centers in the Chinese south-east. Others have tried to open larger enterprises in collaboration with the Chinese and Central Asian authorities, but the general suspicion that Uyghurs encounter has cut down on their success, as has the fact that the Dungans, the Han Chinese, and the titular nationalities of Central Asia have all targeted the same market.

Fostered by international trade, the trans-nationalization of the Uyghur communities and the development of links with the diaspora were quickly seen to be a dangerous phenomenon by Beijing and the Central Asian capitals. China has thus dissuaded many Uyghurs suspected of harboring separatist sympathies from engaging in cross-border trade. In the 2000s, good relations between China and Central Asia, not to mention the presence of other trans-national communities in the same commercial niche, meant that the Uyghurs became marginalized. They found it increasingly difficult to find a Central Asian or Han partner willing to associate with them. They have therefore been reduced to engaging in very small-scale, low-profit trading or else working as assistants or translators either for Central Asian businessmen who trade with Xinjiang or for Han businessmen settled in Central Asia, although competition from the Dungans has also put them at a further disadvantage.

In addition, the Uyghurs are often forced to take sides during tensions between Central Asian and Han traders, and feel discriminated from both sides. They are also subject to particular pressure from the local mafias, since the police services are not inclined to rush to their aid. In Uzbekistan in 2002, the authorities closed the Hippodrome, a large Chinese market in the capital, and began a campaign of persecution against Uyghur businessmen settled in the country. Some Uyghurs have thus tried to switch into more specialized domains, such as traditional Muslim catering, a domain from which the Han Chinese are excluded.

Another category of Uyghur businessmen has preferred to play the game of officialdom by integrating into much more state-regulated commercial networks. It is therefore possible to be an important businessman and to be Uyghur, provided one knows how to use personal contacts at the state level—on both sides of the border—and how to collaborate with the majority nationalities.

A small number of Uyghur businessmen continue to be motivated by reasons that are more political than commercial, and therefore do not envisage ceasing their business activities, not even when they become less profitable. Such trade activities make it possible to become a notable in one's region or town, to set oneself up as a sponsor for the construction of mosques and schools, or as a financer of Uyghur-related cultural activities, all of which provide the community with more visibility.[6]

In two decades, the Uyghurs have partially lost the unique niche that they had occupied in Central Asia. This can be attributed to three main factors: first, Sino-Central Asian trade has been brought under state control, with the greatest share going to the titular nationalities—Han Chinese and Central Asians—and not to the minorities; second, even among the cross-border minorities themselves, the Uyghurs have been marginalized by the political suspicions that weigh on them and impede their ability to make use of the transnational networks customary among diasporic peoples; and third, in Xinjiang the Uyghurs have been to some extent outstripped by the Han Chinese, who themselves are now reaping the benefits of bordering Central Asia. The extreme political acuity of the Uyghur question, which Beijing considers more dangerous than the Tibet question, has therefore dispossessed the Uyghurs of their historical role, while the other cross-border minorities are in the process of taking up all the advantages that the trade dynamism between China and Central Asia has to offer.

The Dungans: a double bet on ethnic business and state-level activism

Approximately 100,000 Dungans live in Central Asia, predominantly in Kyrgyzstan and Kazakhstan. After the 1861–1877 uprising against Qing domination, several tens of thousands of Muslim Chinese, or Hui, from the provinces of Shaanxi, Gansu and Xinjiang went into exile on the territory of the Russian empire. Called Dungans in Russian, they were recognized as a national minority by Soviet power in the 1920s. In the PRC, they also obtained the status of minority (*minzu*), making up one of the 56 ethnic groups recognized by the Communist regime. Today, China counts a diversified population of about ten million Hui, who live in various situations and in complex relations with the Han majority. Considered as a national minority due to their religious specificity, they endure social, cultural and religious marginalization, which occasionally leads to open conflicts; they are also subject to processes of acculturation, but are much better integrated into Chinese society than the Uyghurs.[7] In Central Asia, like all the peoples of the Soviet Union, the Dungans endured social transformations that modified their cultural and identity references.[8]

Traditionally, the Dungans have been known for their agricultural skills, which enabled them to assure the success of their *kolkhozes* and *sovkhozes* in the Soviet era, in contrast to the Kazakh and Kyrgyz, who were involved in transhumance and herding cultures. The Dungans are specialized in two domains, rice growing and market garden produce, and have gradually set up in a new commercial niche, that of fresh produce sold on Central Asian markets. Since the privatizations of the 1990s, many Dungans have invested in the restaurant business, as their so-called "Muslim" cuisine is well-reputed in Central Asia and they enjoy special relations with agricultural enterprises supplying them with fresh produce. Still today, half of the Dungans of Kazakhstan and Kyrgyzstan continue to work in agriculture, while approximately 20 percent are reported to have been working in the state administration since Soviet times. In Uzbekistan and Tajikistan the Dungans tend to be limited to agricultural activities. However, in Kazakhstan and Kyrgyzstan a new economic niche has appeared—trade with China.

Approximately 30 percent of Dungans in Kazakhstan and Kyrgyzstan, employed in diverse professions, are involved in trade with China.[9] Some of them, especially those from the border towns, have set themselves up in the shuttle trade. The geographical proximity to China exempts them from having to obtain a visa, so they are able to visit the Chinese shopping centers situated on the other side of the border, where they can buy products and then resell them back home. This trade, which is dominated by rural people trying to escape from the agricultural crisis, is very modest in scale and often organized in a familial framework. Others have gone into the tourist agency sector: using their linguistic skills and their contacts in Xinjiang, they organize "shop-tours" for their compatriots in China and look after the administrative formalities as well as the arrangements for their shopping. Some specialize in medical tourism in China, an area that is enjoying growing success in Central Asia.[10] A third group has found employment with Chinese businesspeople set up in Kazakhstan and Kyrgyzstan, since their Chinese-language ability, even if dialectal, enable them to serve as assistants, intermediaries, or as translators, all the more so as they are often both Russian-speaking *and* Kazakh- or Kyrgyz-speaking. The Dungans in these last two categories come mostly from urban populations and are chiefly represented by the younger generations.[11]

Lastly, a fourth group has branched out into commerce by opening stands at bazaars specialized in certains goods. The shoes sector in Almaty, for example, is considered to be a Dungan specialization. Some Dungan traders attempt to obtain agreements signed directly with Chinese clothing and shoe factories based in Shenzhen and Guangzhou. Others specialize in construction materials from the Urumqi area.[12] Others still have set up in the transportation (road but not rail) of commodities as far away as Russia, taking advantage of their transnational networks, which sometimes extend to Western Europe.[13]

In China, the Dungans trade either with the Hui or with the Han Chinese, but very little with the Uyghurs. Historically, the relations between Uyghurs and the Hui have been conflictual. The two peoples do not in the least foster Muslim solidarity; the Hui and the Dungans are actually keener about working with the Han Chinese. In addition, although the Dungans from Kyrgyzstan mostly come originally from Gansu and those of Kazakhstan mostly from Shaanxi, links with their places of origin have all but evaporated as a result of the history of twentieth-century Sino-Soviet relations. It is therefore very rare that the Central Asian Dungans are able to re-establish familial links in China and use them as a driver of trade. In confirmation of this absence of family networks, the Dungans trade almost systematically with Xinjiang, in particular via the Urumqi industrial park and the free-trade zones at the borders, or in the Pearl River Delta, but they do not venture as far as Gansu and Shaanxi.[14]

Since the late 1990s, the Dungan Association of Kazakhstan, led by the businessman Husei Daurov, has organized cultural exchanges between Kazakhstan and the Shaanxi and Gansu provinces for Dungan students. In 2003, anxious to avoid communitarianism criticisms, it launched a massive program to send Kazakh students to China without regard to nationality, and it currently oversees about 600 Kazakh students in Xi'an. The Association has also succeeded in transforming cultural exchanges into commercial partnerships, and moving from the non-governmental sector to the governmental one. It has played the hand of ethnic solidarity, recreating from scratch the links between the Kazakh Dungan diaspora and China. But it has also managed to avoid getting stuck in too restrictive a Dungan/Hui framework, by convincing the provincial administrations of Gansu and Shaanxi, and also the Kazakh authorities in Astana, to utilize it as a cog in state-level commercial relations.

The association serves as an intermediary for Kazakh businessmen looking to do business in China and has opened offices in Xi'an, Shenzhen, Beijing, Shanghai, Lanzhou, Urumqi, and Yinchuan, and has been involved in the signing of important bilateral contracts, for instance in the railway sector. Daurov's own company is involved in transfers of agricultural technology from China, which is being tried out mainly on Dungan farms in the Korday district, near Dzhambul. The association has also signed agreements with Chinese companies to build modest hotel infrastructure in two areas of compact Dungan settlement. This tourism is expected to provide additional income to rural Dungans based on the folklorization of culture. The hotels are built in a Qing-era Chinese style and offer "traditional" activities such as festivals in Dungan costume. The Dungans could then come to be a symbolic gateway for Chinese culture in Kazakhstan, by encouraging a sort of re-ethnicization of their identity.

China's Central Asian minorities: the rise of the Kazakhs

China also includes Central Asian minorities, recognized as ethnic groups in the Chinese system of national classification. There are around 16,000 Chinese Uzbeks, about 44,000 Tajiks, who are based mainly in the Tajik autonomous district of Tashkorgan, and about 181,000 Kyrgyz, settled mainly in the autonomous district of Kyzylsu. China's Kazakhs, two-thirds of whom live in more densely populated communities in the Ili Kazakh autonomous prefecture, are the most numerous with a population of about 1.5 million.[15] These Central Asian minorities benefit only little from the economic and cultural niche that has opened up with the proximity of the Central Asian states, and are barely involved in cross-border commerce. Not only do they mostly live in remote areas, but their mobility is confined to their region, and the Chinese authorities are very reluctant to issue them with passports, which is a precondition for crossing borders and obtaining a commercial export license. In addition, they live mostly from agriculture and stockbreeding, do little business in urban environments, and above all, lack the means to accumulate a starting capital that would enable them to set up in business.[16]

In its relation to Central Asia, Xinjiang can be divided into two regions. The first, Kashgaria in the south, has relatively little contact with post-Soviet Central Asia, despite being situated on the Karakoram Highway that leads to Pakistan; the Kashgar bazaar, furthermore, has been marginalized by Chinese strategies.[17] The second region, Dzungaria in the north, is by contrast developing increasing links with Central Asia, notably the Ili Valley and the city of Urumqi. In these northern border areas, an increasing number of China's Kazakhs are seeking to open small stands along the roads traveled by buses from Kazakhstan in order to sell basic consumption goods as well as traditional Kazakh foodstuffs (milk products, etc.). Others have become intermediaries in the cross-border metal trade, buying metal scraps transported by Kazakhs and then selling them to larger intermediaries who take them to Chinese factories.[18] Some try to get employment as translators in the shopping centers and industrial parks that are multiplying along the edge of the Sino-Kazakh border. However, being proficient in Kazakh does not suffice to get a start in this type of job since many Kazakhs from Kazakhstan, not to mention the non-Kazakh citizens of Kazakhstan, only speak Russian. This is why, like the Uyghurs, more and more of China's Kazakhs are learning Russian.

Some members of the Kazakh and Kyrgyz minorities of China have also benefited from the opening of the borders to emigrate to the two neighboring republics. While China's Kyrgyz have settled in Bishkek or Naryn, using their linguistic abilities in Uyghur and Chinese to get work as translators at bazaars or to develop a shuttle trade, the phenomenon essentially concerns China's Kazakhs. Between 1991 and 2007, more than 600,000 ethnic Kazakhs—called Oralmans—settled in Kazakhstan, 60 percent from Uzbekistan, 14 percent from Mongolia, and only 7.7 percent from China: a total of about 42,000 persons. All have experienced difficulties in integrating into Kazakhstan, but some Oralmans from China have been able to make use of the trade between the two countries to find work. With their Chinese language skills and their family links with China, some of them have specialized in petty trade. Many work at the bazaars, either for themselves or for Chinese businessmen, in particular at the *barakholka* in Almaty, which is a regular cause for protest from Kazakh traders.[19] Some also specialize in providing legal advice on export matters: their familiarity with Chinese formalities makes it possible for them to sell their services to Kazakh businessmen, who are generally not up to date with the Chinese administrative system.[20] Those at the bottom of the social ladder, who have often received an intermediate-level technical education in China, are unable to find any work in their area of specialization and are therefore limited to petty street trade: this is the case, for example, in the village of Baibesik in a suburb of Almaty, where numerous Oralman families are settled,[21] while others open call centers to enable the population to make calls to China at reduced prices.[22]

While the Oralmans from Uzbekistan or Mongolia often come from the rural population, a non-negligible segment of China Kazakh emigrants belonged to the intelligentsia. These latter have completed higher education degrees in Urumqi but have been unable to find appropriate positions, as Beijing has refused to indigenize Xinjiang administrative organs. For these university graduates, emigration to Kazakhstan guarantees social promotion. Indeed, the kazakhization of the state administration being implemented by Astana requires employing individuals with a mastery of the Kazakh language. Given the insufficient number of Kazakh-speaking elites in Kazakhstan, China's Kazakhs have therefore helped fill the linguistic quotas of state employees. China's Kazakh intelligentsia is also specialized in a specific niche, that of teaching Chinese. This linguistic advantage also has its downside, however, with the Oralmans regularly complaining that they have been refused positions of high responsibility due to their lack of Russian language skills.[23]

Central Asian shuttle traders and Chinese migrants

Cross-border minorities are not the only actors to serve as intermediaries in Sino-Central Asian relations. The opening of the borders has made possible the development of more long-term and two-way migratory flows, mainly from China toward Central Asia. These population flows play a major role in the perception of the "other." For the Central Asians who regularly travel to China, trade provides a specific access to Chinese culture, and spreads an image of the country as filled with unique commercial opportunities, in which cutting-edge technology mixes with everyday plastic objects, thus reinforcing old Central Asian stereotypes of the Middle Kingdom as a land of plenty.[24] For those who remain in their own country, the discovery of Chinese "otherness" materializes in the awareness of migratory flows, which provoke mixed reactions on the part of the local populations. For the moment, the Chinese migrants do not occupy roles as cultural go-betweens: they are very few in number and many of them live without much interaction with the host societies. Nevertheless, this situation is likely to evolve rapidly in the near future.

Central Asian petty traders and "shop tourists"

The flows from Central Asia heading toward China mainly comprise small traders or "shop tourists," who have no intention of settling in China in the long term. The salaries there are considered too low, the legal conditions for foreigners too complicated, and the cultural context somewhat unpropitious for integration. Some Central Asian citizens are employed in Xinjiang in some agricultural, mining, and processing industries, and have been trying to take advantage of the "Far West development programs," which makes it possible for foreign nationals to enjoy tax exemptions,[25] but they are largely in a minority. The main population movements are therefore temporary. Ever since the *perestroika* years, Central Asian petty traders, mainly Kazakh and Kyrgyz, have traveled to China, above all to neighboring Xinjiang, to compensate partially for the collapse of goods flows from Moscow. Upon independence, they benefited from the decline of the local industries to export scrap metal, non-ferrous products containing rare metals, and plastic waste to China, and returned with consumer products. This shuttle trade points to a major upheaval in the social fabric, as it has enabled the professional redeployment of a whole class of engineers and industry workers, who lost their employment when the Soviet industries collapsed.

In the summer of 1991, the first China-Kazakhstan agreement was signed in Khuldja, encouraging the development of shop tourism: in the following year, approximately 700,000 Kazakh citizens crossed the border to buy common consumer items in China with the intention of reselling them back at home.[26] Blame was pinned on the shuttle trade for importing poor quality Chinese goods, which were bought at the lowest possible prices by Central Asian traders. The Beijing authorities then expressed concern about the deteriorating image of Chinese products in the region. In 1993, after a recommendation by the Committee of Chinese entrepreneurs, the authorities issued an order making it a criminal offence to produce and distribute poor quality goods, while the Kazakh authorities agreed to exercise greater control over the activities of Kazakh and Chinese traders. In 1995, during Nursultan Nazarbayev's visit to Beijing, the two parties signed a document on quality control for imported and exported goods.[27] In any case, the establishment of more substantial trade relations has since weakened the profitability of this shuttle trade. However, in 2002, it reportedly still provided employment for nearly half a million Kazakh citizens, who are estimated to have spent more than US$1 billion in Xinjiang between 1989 and 2003.[28] In 2006, Kazakh shop tourism to China was reportedly responsible for the purchase of US$4 billion worth of goods.[29]

In Kyrgyzstan also, shuttle trade increased quickly with the end of *perestroika*. Possessing more modest financial means than their Kazakh neighbors, Kyrgyz petty traders quickly found themselves in competition with the Uyghurs or Han Chinese wanting to occupy the same sector. Profit rationales thus developed, involving the organization of traders into small groups of ten or so, joint rental of buses or trucks to freight the commodities, collective ordering of products, etc.[30] Kyrgyz women played a relatively important role in this shuttle trade, as they were allegedly able to pass more easily through customs. However, since the second half of the 1990s it has become more difficult for Kyrgyz traders to compete with the more organized Chinese businessmen. In Uzbekistan, Tajikistan and Turkmenistan, shuttle trade to China only developed its full scope in the 2000s: Turkmen and Uzbek petty traders had previously tended to travel in much larger numbers to Turkey, Iran, and the United Arab Emirates (Dubai in particular), whereas Xinjiang remained a less fashionable destination. Today the situation has changed: opportunities have increased with the growing numbers of flights from Ashgabat, Tashkent, and Dushanbe to Urumqi, Beijing, Shanghai, and Guangzhou, as well as shop tours by bus that leave from the Ferghana Valley or Tajikistan to Kashgar and Urumqi.[31]

Despite Chinese competition, increasingly structured and organized Central Asian shop tourism has grown in magnitude. This involves specialized tourist agencies with Russian-Chinese translation services and hotels reserved for post-Soviet citizens, which supervise those who travel to China for a few days in order to gather supplies.[32] Some people, often called the *kubovshchiki*, have specialized in dealing with cargo transit, transportation companies, and customs formalities. To create a small business, organize the marriage of one's children, or furnish a large family house, the wealthiest go directly to the major production centers on China's maritime façade, such as Zhejiang or Guangzhou provinces, to get their supplies, the less well off go to Xinjiang.[33]

Chinese migrants: beyond the clichés, a large diversity of situations

The migration flows arriving in Central Asia from China comprise another structural component of cross-border population traffic. The situations in each country are, however, extremely different. Beginning in the early 1990s, emigration from China had most impact on Kyrgyzstan and Kazakhstan. In 1988 the Soviet Union and the PRC signed an accord enabling citizens living in border areas to travel without visas. Consequently, a small number of Chinese businessmen of Kazakh, Kyrgyz, Dungan, or Uyghur nationality began to cross the border. But cross-border travel without a visa was revoked by Kazakhstan in 1994, when the government, which was concerned about its inability to regulate migration flows, decided to curtail the presence of the Chinese. In Kyrgyzstan the system of travel without visa was only abolished in 2003; until then Chinese citizens were able to move freely across the Kyrgyz border, and from there to proceed to Kazakhstan or Russia thanks to the intra-CIS free circulation agreement.[34] In Tajikistan, simplified procedures for border crossing were put in place only in the mid-2000s, in a bid to dynamize the cross-border exchanges at Kulma-Kalasu pass. The two other states, Uzbekistan and Turkmenistan, have particularly restrictive entry policies and have not yet experienced any significant Chinese migration.

Migration flows are difficult to measure in any reliable way: first, the Central Asian governments are reluctant to collect or provide any statistics; second, they assimilate two notions which correspond to rather divergent social realities, that is, expatriates and migrants; and third, a large part of this migration, especially in Kyrgyzstan, is illegal. However, the notion of illegality is complex. The Chinese migrants come to Central Asia either on tourist visas or on 30-day work invitations, which they obtain from Central Asian or Chinese companies that specialize in this type of service. Once there, they extend their stays for 90 days with the relevant authorities. Some then choose to stay on and work illegally, others to leave for Russia, while others return to China to start the administrative procedures again so they can return.[35] These migrants therefore do not enter the country illegally, but they stay longer than their papers allow, and thus become so-called illegals. In such a context, the migration figures are very imprecise and large in scale. Russian experts often declare that Kazakhstan has between 150,000 permanently settled Chinese and 300,000 migrants who regularly cross the Chinese border, but these numbers appear to be inflated.[36] In Kazakhstan, the customs services of the Interior Ministry registered 30,000 Chinese citizens crossing the border in 2006,[37] while for the same year, the customs service of the Committee of National Defense estimates that the flow was around 170,000 people per year.[38] In Kyrgyzstan, the chairman of the Border Service declared that there were about 60,000 Chinese persons living in Kyrgyzstan at the beginning of 2008.[39] In Tajikistan, according to the Interior Ministry Migration Service there were a little more than 10,000 Chinese laborers in 2008.[40] No figures are available for Uzbekistan or Turkmenistan.

These migrants can be classified into several ethnic and professional categories. In Kazakhstan, the majority of the official migrants from China are Oralmans, that is to say Chinese Kazakhs who have taken advantage of the repatriation program offered by Astana. The Chinese citizens who make requests for Kazakh citizenship or for permanent residency are almost exclusively Oralman.[41] In Kyrgyzstan too, Kairylmans comprise a significant percentage of the official Chinese migration, but to a lesser degree given the relative unattractiveness of the country's economic situation. Although there exist no figures that take into account the ethnic origin of the migrants, it seems that, even outside of the official repatriation programs, about half the migrants hailing from China have a Central Asian or Uyghur background, and the other half comprise Han Chinese.[42] The regional and ethnic origin of the Chinese private entrepreneurs has rather drastically altered since the beginning of the 1990s: traders from Xinjiang are becoming fewer and fewer, and about twice as many Han Chinese have come from the maritime provinces since the beginning of the 2000s. The majority of them originate from Zhejiang province, especially from the city of Wenzhou, considered to be one of the biggest centers of Chinese entrepreneurs. More than 80,000 traders from Wenzhou have established themselves in Xinjiang, principally at Kashgar, and half of these engage in trade with Central Asia.[43]

In the case of Kazakhstan, about only 5,000 Chinese citizens (non-Oralmans) are officially registered as working in the country. They can be divided into three groups. First are the employees of the large Chinese companies established there, in particular in the energy sector: mostly high-level salaried graduate engineers, who live in Kazakhstan as expatriates with their families, in apartments, for the duration of their contract. Second, there are workers in the construction sector, in both real estate and energy projects, who mostly comprise poorly paid employees, few of whom have graduated, and who come as singles and mainly live in encampments close to the building sites, and do not integrate into the host society.[44] Kazakhstan is reported to be the CIS country that registers the most Chinese in this sector, especially because many Russian construction companies employ them. The third group comprises retailers and private businessmen, whose business can be either large- or small-scale: the most modest arrive as individuals to sell their goods to Kazakh retailers, but they are rather rare in the country, since its legislation is not conducive to their presence (they must go through a joint-venture system requiring each to have a Kazakh partner), while the wealthier have developed local intermediary networks and are therefore relatively well integrated.[45]

The Almaty and the northeast (Ust-Kamenogorsk) regions, both bordering China, receive the most number of Chinese, where they work in the trade sector (small or large import-export businesses) and in the small brick or food processing industries. Dominant in Almaty and Astana are either expatriates of large companies and people connected to the embassies, or those who work in the booming construction sector. In Atyrau, Kzyl-Orda, and the Mangystau Peninsula, Chinese migrants are mostly employed in energy companies, from the highest to the lowest echelons. In terms of the labor market, Han migrants and expatriates occupy specific professional niches.[46] The engineers and technicians invited to work by Chinese companies or joint ventures have skills that the Central Asians often do not have. However, the criticisms directed at Chinese companies are growing: by bringing their own engineers with them, they are accused of thwarting the training of a new professional category of Kazakh engineers, and the official quotas that oblige them to employ at least 50 percent of local workers are not respected. As for the Chinese migrants who work in very poorly paid positions—in particular in construction—they have to compete with the Uzbek, Kyrgyz, and Tajik migrants who have established themselves in part in the same sectors.[47]

In Kyrgyzstan, relatively few Han Chinese work in large companies, which are practically non-existent in the country; instead they have invested massively in the trade sector. The very first stores to sell Chinese goods, such as "Artush" and "Kashgar," opened in Naryn on the eve of the Soviet Union's collapse. At the time, these stores sold products that were in shortage like sugar and rice, and large profits were also made from the sale of Chinese alcoholic drinks like vodka and beer. They then established a sizeable presence in the bazaars of Dordoy and Osh, and later at Karasuu, where they often have their own special Chinese sections, such as Dordoy-Dzhunkhay. They are also established in Madina, a market specializing in textile products manufactured in China.[48]

The Chinese traders in Kyrgyzstan—estimated to be about 30,000—can be divided into two broad categories. The small operators often make the trips between China and Kyrgyzstan themselves and do not seek to obtain long-stay entry permits. They rent one or two containers in which they stock and resell their goods, and employ one or two local workers, whether Dungans or Kyrgyz students wanting to practice their Chinese. Their poor knowledge of Russian and Kyrgyz, as well as their ignorance of the local culture, does not facilitate contact with clients. As a result, specialized commercial rationales have taken shape: those containers offering electronic equipment are often run by Chinese sellers, since they are considered to be competent by the Kyrgyz, while those that sell clothing or sewing textiles are manned by Kyrgyz sellers, since they presume an implicit knowledge of the local "Muslim" tastes, while the Chinese owner remains in the background.[49] The wealthiest Chinese businessmen, referred to as *loben* or *bashlik*, work only in wholesale, not retail; they are not present at the bazaars. They may employ up to several tens of locals for reselling and performing transactions. They have also hired intermediaries whose role it is to make contact with the police and the administrative services, and have access to Kyrgyz political networks, which protect them (*krysha*). In addition to their sites on the markets, some Chinese entrepreneurs have opened small factories, often on the ruins of old Soviet industries, and produce a diverse array of products, which range from toilet paper to flour and bricks. Most of these are located in the Chui Valley, which is the most industrialized region in the country.[50] Shopping centers such as Taatan in Bishkek and in Osh have also blossomed over recent years, offering expensive products, in particular electronic goods, and brand clothing labels.

Faced with the tensions provoked by their presence, the demonstrations organized by the Kyrgyz unions, and the arson attacks, the Chinese traders of Karasuu have formed an association, Shat i Co., which defends their rights, whereas an association of Chinese traders has also been created in Bishkek for the whole of Kyrgyzstan.[51] It has suggested the setting up of wholesale markets in the poorest regions of the country to make it clear that the only way the country will develop is by trading with China.[52] Even if the traders comprise the majority of Chinese migrants in Kyrgyzstan, other categories of workers are also settled there. The small Chinese factories—essentially brick, flour producing, and iron-smelting factories—employ mostly Chinese personnel, who have the reputation of being more reliable, harder working, and less demanding in terms of salaries than the local population. Public opinion is often critical of these migrants who are blamed for "stealing" work and living in a closed world, even if Kyrgyz themselves refuse to work under such difficult conditions and under Chinese authority. Workers on the road construction sites are also almost exclusively Chinese, and contacts with locals are extremely uncommon. Lastly, some Chinese work seasonally on vegetable or cereals farms, but this agricultural sector is politically sensitive and the Chinese colonists are not welcome there.

In Tajikistan, bazaar trade has only begun to develop, a decade later than that in Kyrgyzstan. Chinese traders are therefore less numerous than in the neighboring republic, but they are beginning to set up new wholesale markets in Dushanbe, Khujand, Kayrakkum, and Istaravshan in the Sogd region, where the local markets are directly supplied from Karasuu. Most Chinese migrants in Tajikistan are workers, and engineers employed by large Chinese companies such as the Sinohydro Corporation, China Road, and China Railway. Others are employed in brick factories, such as that in Hissar, a foundry factory in Dushanbe, and concrete-producing companies or chemical factories at Yavan and Kurgan-Tyube.[53] In most cases, these workers live in closed camps, with poor sanitary conditions, and are fed on site by Chinese cooks. They have very little interaction with the local population, especially because they do not speak any Russian or any of the national languages. China's managerial culture of vertical integration, and residences located in separate enclaves, therefore disadvantages Chinese migrants in terms of integrating into the host society. Only the engineers live in towns in better material conditions. Officially, the proportion of local—Tajik—personnel employed by Chinese companies is set at 30 percent, but, as in the other republics, this figure is rarely adhered to.[54]

The few existing sociological studies provide a diversified picture of these Chinese migrants in Central Asia. Engineers and wage earners employed by the big energy companies were urban dwellers prior to their departure with average or above-average professional qualifications.[55] Those who work on the construction sites belong to more impoverished populations of Central China, but some have degrees and have not found work matching their levels of qualification in their home country. Those working in the small private Chinese factories are in the most difficult situations, and are often suspected of being "illegals" within the Chinese system, that is, undeclared third or fourth children.[56] As very few Chinese migrants wish to establish themselves permanently in Central Asia, they do not make applications for permanent work visas or nationalization procedures. The length of their stays abroad generally range from a few months to a few years, their sole aim being to accumulate enough capital so that they can start up a private business in China, Russia or Western Europe.[57] Intermarriages with Central Asians are very uncommon, a sign of the low-level of integration into the host country, even if the phenomenon is growing in Kyrgyzstan. However, there has been a notably quick development of infrastructure to manage this diaspora, including tourist agencies to organize administrative formalities, special banks to cater for Chinese citizens, restaurants, medical centers, hotels, dry-cleaners, as well as hotels or residences.[58] This suggests therefore that the number of migrants who decide to remain in Central Asia for a long period will increase, and consequently, the level of interaction with the host societies is likely to grow rapidly.

The generation gap? Central Asian youth and the fashion for China

Whereas knowledge about China and the Chinese language was practically non-existent at the time of the Central Asian states' independence, the situation changed quickly in the second half of the 2000s. Today Chinese would appear to be the second-most taught foreign language, after English, at universities in Kazakhstan and Kyrgyzstan, although figures are lacking to definitively confirm this trend.[59] It is also being taught more widely in Uzbekistan and Tajikistan, but at a less sustained pace.

In the first decade or more of contact with independent Central Asia, China had not sought to implement any cultural or linguistic policy. Indeed Chinese embassies have played practically no role in the promotion of "Chineseness" (*zhonghuaxing*). The first Confucius Institute, which promotes Chinese in a similar manner as the Goethe Institut does for German, opened in Almaty only in 2004, whereafter the establishment of the Institute expended between 2006 and 2008.[60] Today, all the Central Asian capitals with the exception of Ashgabat have at least one Confucius Institute, and in Almaty, Astana, and Bishkek there are even two or three. They are often integrated within the local universities, where they function as Chinese departments, and have been funded by the Chinese government in partnership with some Chinese universities. In addition, all the main public and private universities, in particular in Kazakhstan and Kyrgyzstan, have founded chairs in Chinese in order to meet student demands. Institutional structures of learning Chinese are therefore growing, though the practical realities of teaching Chinese are somewhat more complex.

In the Confucius Institutes, the overwhelming majority of teachers are Han Chinese, who are usually not very proficient in Russian and even less so in the local languages. They often have to teach by way of English, although the textbooks are edited in Russian. Trained in teaching Chinese as a foreign language, they seek to leave for the West; as the demand for Central Asia is low, it is often the least competent who end up there.[61] In the universities, the standards of the local teachers are also very poor, as the most competent Central Asian Chinese-speakers have left what is an unprofitable sector to become translators or interpreters in private companies that trade with China. This lack of teachers has thus been filled by the return of "ethnic repatriates"—the Oralmans to Kazakhstan, and the Kairylmans to Kyrgyzstan—but this situation presents a certain number of problems: first of all, the Chinese proficiency of these non-Han Chinese is often average at best, or even rather mediocre or dialectal, and does not conform to the standards of *putonghua*; second, these teachers have not received any training in teaching Chinese as a foreign language since they often become teachers only after emigrating; third, they very rarely speak Russian, which means that Chinese courses are often only accessible to Kazakh- or Kyrgyz-speaking students and not to Russian-speaking ones, who form the large majority, or else they are obliged to combine both languages, which thus diminishes the pedagogical efficacy.[62]

Chinese activism in cultural matters is only just beginning to take shape. Since the second half of the 2000s a few exhibitions that promote Chinese history and culture have been organized, mostly with the financial support of the large Chinese companies. Since 2006, the CCTV Chinese television station dedicated to foreign broadcasting has been retransmitted to Kazakhstan and Kyrgyzstan, mainly in Russian but with some programs in Kazakh and Kyrgyz.[63] In the same year the writer and former politician Murat Auezov, despite being known for his Sinophobe stances, opened a Chinese cultural center in the National Library of Almaty, and launched a journal called *Korshi* (The Neighbor). Financed by Chinese companies established in Central Asia and by the Xinjiang Association for Cultural Exchanges with Foreign Countries, *Korshi* presents Chinese history, culture and heritage from a touristic viewpoint, but also provides commercial information for Kazakh businessmen (holding of trade fairs in Xinjiang, etc.).[64] Unfortunately, as it is published in

Kazakh, this greatly limits the readership of the journal in the country. In Kyrgyzstan, aided by the same Xinjiang Association for cultural exchanges with foreign countries, a monthly journal called *Kontimost* was launched which has the same scope. However, as compared with the cultural presence of India, well-established since the 1960s and 1970s and now undergoing a revival via music as well as cinema, China's cultural presence remains minimal.

The fashion for learning Chinese can also be observed at Russian universities; it is also increasingly being taught in secondary schools in the Russian Far East. In parallel, though the study of Russian has declined at all the major Chinese universities, in conformity with a worldwide trend, the learning of Russian has become fashionable in the Chinese provinces bordering Central Asia and Russia, in particular in the Yining region, a historically Russified region since the nineteenth century. The boom in border trade, the growing number of exchanges, the opportunities for tourism, and the demand to open small tourist agencies specializing in "shop-tours" for Central Asians as well as for Russians from the Altay region explains this craze. Numerous small private schools have opened, in which the teachers of Russian are either former Soviet citizens or Chinese compatriots who have lived in the former USSR.[65] Russian thus offers attractive professional prospects, just as Chinese does in Central Asia or in Russia. In the same way as the province of Heilongjiang, where Harbin has recaptured its historical role as a contact zone with Russia, Xinjiang is therefore trying to take advantage of its regained proximity with Central Asia. Throughout Dzungaria, having skills in Russian language opens professional opportunities similar to those of having skills in Chinese on the other side of the border. However, the complexity of Xinjiang's political status makes the appropriating of that niche more complex than in Heilongjiang.

In Central Asia, the interest in learning Chinese entered a new phase with a growing number of students departing to do their studies in China. The Kazakhs comprise the majority with about 3,000 students, including 1,500 in Beijing, 500 in Shanghai, about 600 in Xi'an, and the rest spread throughout Lanzhou, Urumqi, and other provincial towns. There are reported to be about 700 Kyrgyz students and 600 Tajiks in China, while some several hundred Uzbeks and relatively few Turkmens are also present.[66] The administrative possibilities for studying abroad greatly increased in the 2000s. Interstate exchanges have been set up between Beijing and the five states, albeit only offering a limited number of stipends per year. The SCO also has a limited exchange program. In Kazakhstan since the end of the 1990s, the CNPC has offered to finance energy-related study programs: Aktobe Munay Gas has thus created a foundation for educational purposes which each year sends a hundred Kazakh students for training in oil-related professions to the China University of Petroleum and the Xi'an University of Oil and Gas, as well as to Russia.[67] Such company-sourced financing remains limited in the other republics, but it is likely to develop, in particular in Uzbekistan and Turkmenistan, where Chinese energy projects attract significant amounts of financing.

In 1993 the Kazakh authorities created a specific scholarship program called Bolashak, which sends thousands of students abroad, to Russia, the United States, Western Europe, Japan, and South Korea. China became part of the program in 2005, and since 2008 has been the third most popular destination after Russia and Western countries. Despite cases of corruption, the Bolashak students are often among the best, and the program's strict conditions oblige them to return to work in Kazakhstan in order to prevent a brain drain. Those who successfully complete their degrees are guaranteed a fast track to the upper echelons of the public service.[68] However, the scholarship program was undermined in 2010 with the creation of the new Nazarbayev University, which has been designed to make the "best of world higher education" come to Astana without the need to finance the sending of students abroad, and this has contributed to the drying-up of funds available for Bolashak.[69]

Exchanges signed between the Chinese and Central Asian universities also mean that the Central Asian students can take advantage of preferential fees for enrolment in China: for instance, agreements have been signed between Aktobe and Urumqi, between Shymkent and Xi'an, between the Slavic-Kyrgyz University in Bishkek and that of Lanzhou, between the Agrarian University of Almaty and that of Urumqi, etc.[70] Lastly, the local provincial governments of Gansu and Shaanxi have created stipend programs for Central Asian students, mainly thanks to the Dungan lobbying. Some prestigious Chinese Universities such as Beida in Beijing have even set up co-optation strategies with Kazakhstan: a headhunter intermediary is tasked with selecting "children from good families," that is, those with whom the Chinese government hopes to establish privileged links.[71] Chinese logics for creation of a Central Asian clientele are therefore starting to take shape.

The strategies of Central Asian students are twofold: some want only to learn Chinese and aim at the languages universities or normal schools that are established in the major university towns in China. Others aim at complete degree courses and in this case tend to begin by one or two years of intensive Chinese lessons before starting a Bachelor of Arts course. Central Asian students rarely take an interest in studying humanities and social sciences since the cultural traditions of China are too different and passing the exams requires having an excellent mastery of written Chinese, which they seldom have. The most usual degree courses taken, therefore, are economics, international commerce, international law, management, and finance. In addition, some components of these degrees can be delivered in English, which continues to be more accessible than Chinese for Central Asian students. The most ambitious students aspire to enter into the prestigious universities of Fudan in Shanghai, and Beida or Tsinghua in Beijing. The Bolashak students are, as a priority, sent to study information technologies and technological specializations. Many also aim to get into the Oil and Gas Universities, as well as that of Transports and Communications, and even into the Textile University (Dong Hua) in Shanghai, since this is a guarantee of getting quick and well-paid employment.[72]

It is possible to draw up a social map of Central Asian student enrollment in China.[73] The children of the elite go to Shanghai or Beijing via the Bolashak program or interstate exchange programs; family networks enable them privileged access to public financing. Enrollment in the best Chinese universities costs around US$5,000 and daily living expenses are high. The degree courses chosen are among the most prestigious (international law, international trade) and some students also complete a Master of Arts or even a PhD in China. In this category, the Kazakhs dominate since they are both the most numerous and the richest—they include the children of politicians, diplomats who have been posted to Asia, of directors of companies with links to China (energy, air and railway transport), and representatives of Chinese energy companies in Central Asia. These children of the elite do not plan to remain in China: their family networks, combined with their knowledge of Chinese, guarantee them access to the best positions in their home country, either decision-making jobs in the administration, or high-up positions in the major companies with links to China.

The students of the middle classes succeed in getting preferential rates to study through university exchanges, or are financed by their families. They cannot afford to study in Beijing or Shanghai and choose Urumqi, Lanzhou or Xi'an, where the cost of studies is about US$2,000 and the everyday living costs more moderate than in the big cities. The degree courses chosen aim to be functional and pragmatic. Students chiefly opt for management and commerce, and most of them limit themselves to doing a Bachelor of Arts. Upon their return, their foreign degree and knowledge of Chinese enables them to make their way rapidly up the social ladder: whether to a modest level within the administration, or to employment as a translator or intermediary in companies that trade with China.

The children of petty traders go at their own expense. Usually the whole family joins together to pay and with quick profits in mind. The immense majority among them do not go further than Xinjiang: the cost of studying there is moderate, the living standards lower, and the transportation fees are reduced since one can get there by train or bus. The living and study budgets do not exceed US$2,500 per year. In this category, it is probable that the Kazakhs are no more numerous than the Kyrgyz or Uzbeks. The luckiest obtain a place at the Urumqi University, while the others go to small provincial towns such as Yining. Although some choose economics and commerce courses, the aim of the majority is not to learn a profession, but rather to speak Chinese and establish new networks. Their parents are often involved in the shuttle trade with Xinjiang, or have clothing or shoe stands at the Karasuu bazaar. During their studies, these students work as translators or traders, helping with the family business. Once they return home, they streamline the trade with China so that the fewest possible intermediaries are involved.

The experiences of expatriation to China are thus different depending on the social origin of the Central Asian students. The children of the elite come to know a modern China, one that is turned toward the West, consumer-oriented, technological, and globalized. Their lifestyle in Beijing or Shanghai differs little from the one that they could have in Moscow, London, or New York. They live in a more internationalized environment: they have an obvious proximity to the other students from the CIS, in particular those from Russia, and have privileged Chinese friends with a more global outlook. Many of these students embrace a party-like lifestyle, and have earned a bad reputation in the major Chinese universities for trying to pay bribes to get better marks and/or to obtain degrees. The Kazakhs—as well as the Mongols—also have a bad reputation for their behavior: alcohol-fuelled evenings regularly end up in fights, in particular with the South Koreans, who comprise the largest number of foreign students in China. The situation has indeed become so problematic that the Bolashak program has dispatched a permanent emissary attached to the Kazakhstan Consulate in Shanghai to "supervise" the students in order to prevent their excesses or problems with the Chinese police.

The children of petty traders have access to another China, one that is more remote and less internationalized, and that represents the "China of minorities." The Xinjiang that they discover, though very different from their country of origin, remains a Turkic and Muslim space. Interviews conducted locally confirm that these students come from predominantly non-privileged backgrounds and that they have poor Russian-language abilities, and are therefore satisfied to remain in a Turkic-speaking world. This however means that their linguistic integration into the Chinese world is limited; they tend to speak "Turkic" among themselves and in their contact with the Uyghurs, and Chinese only at university. Often more religious than the children of the elite, they are also pleased to arrive in a land that is not too unfamiliar. However, the Central Asians still generally practice religion much less than the populations of Xinjiang: as cultural elements of their Islamic identity, they mention, for example, the pleasure of "eating Muslim food" in Xinjiang. Nonetheless the re-Islamization of Central Asian students in Xinjiang is noticeable: their contact with another way of practicing Islam tends to reinforce their Islamic identity, a phenomenon that is also to be seen among the Dungans and Kazakhs present in Xi'an—the "capital" of Chinese Islam—who tend to frequent the mosque more often than they do in their home countries.[74]

Irrespective of their social belonging, these Central Asian students perceive China as a professional option that will remain unaffected by geopolitical machinations. Whether the Central Asian countries incline more toward the West or Russia, they will remain unchanged in their proximity to the Middle Kingdom. This "Chinese given" is analyzed in pragmatic terms: while Russia and the West are allegedly out to manipulate Central Asia in accordance with their own immediate interests, China is credited not with an absence of national interests, but with the additional ability to foster Central Asia's own long-term interests. A career based upon knowledge of the Chinese language is therefore seen to be a professional asset irrespective of political vacillations. Fluency in Chinese also guarantees being fast-tracked up the social ladder in both the public administration—especially in the Ministry of Foreign Affairs—and the private sector, mainly that relating to trade, transit, freight, legal supervision, translation, etc.

The pro-Chinese orientation of the new generations, who view their large neighbor pragmatically as an opportunity to be taken, will therefore probably have an impact on the balance of relations over the next decades, when knowledge about China will have become synonymous with a successful professional career and higher incomes. One of the driving forces of this shift in relations is the process of replacing the former Soviet elites, particularly through the education of the young generations from the middle and upper classes abroad. The current fashion of studying Chinese will thus give rise to a milieu where China is no longer perceived as an inaccessible, incomprehensible, and alien country, but on the contrary the very example of successful modernity. Nothing suggests, however, that the Chinese government's cooptation strategies will be successful, in the sense that these young generations will necessarily take a stance in favor of a China-oriented "choice of civilization." Regardless of whether these young generations then form Sinophile or Sinophobe lobbies, they will embody Central Asia's newfound proximity with China and view Beijing as a model of development capable of rivaling that of Moscow as much as that of Western Europe. Further studies will need to be carried out to ascertain whether or not this new generation, which will be at once indifferent to old Soviet clichés and familiar with contemporary China, has the effect of modifying social apprehensions, in particular on demographic and identity issues.

* * *

Despite the social anxieties provoked by Beijing's growing influence in Central Asia, China's proximity has also proved a guarantee of development and insertion into world markets. As Kyrgyzstan has shown, the re-exporting of Chinese products throughout the rest of Central Asia, to Russia and potentially the Middle East, makes it possible to set up new dynamics that transform the social fabric. A whole range of new professions are being structured, all linked to the service economy: transportation, freight, logistics, translation, legal and commercial services, foreign sales networks, etc. Transnational minorities and petty traders from both sides of the border have also taken over this niche. The Uyghurs, who were the first to develop it at the beginning of the 1990s, were quickly dispossessed, while the other, less politically dangerous minorities, like the Hui/Dungans and China's Kazakhs, only really began to enter it in the 2000s. Other small interconnected networks also appear to be emerging, for example between the Dungans and Koreans, in the direction of both China and South Korea.[75] Even if Central Asian and Chinese shuttle traders do not modify the overall impact of relations between the two worlds, their role as mediators nevertheless remains central in crystallizing a form of popular knowledge on the Chinese "other," and in the dissemination of a narrative that is at once Sinophobe and Sinophile. Similarly, Chinese migrants, who are destined to become increasingly numerous and better integrated into the host societies, will also play a growing role in cultural interactions between Central Asia and China.

Since the second half of the 2000s, this Sino-Central Asian niche has been entered in an ever greater way by the young generation, which finds in it ways to meet its own aspirations: it foregrounds mastery of market-economy principles, emphasizes knowledge that is at once individual (foreign languages) and institutional (university diplomas), and enables an opening up to foreign countries and the earning of much higher incomes than those provided by traditional tertiary, state-dependent professions (teaching, medicine, etc.). In addition, it accentuates economic mechanisms that are at once formal and informal, giving individuals a certain autonomy faced with the stranglehold exerted by state structures over "business." This niche of services is bound to develop throughout the entire region and could act to curb, at least partially, the brain drain due to migration flows. It is therefore likely that the Central Asian social fabric is only beginning its process of transforming under Chinese influence.

8

CHINA AS AN OBJECT OF ACADEMIC KNOWLEDGE

STRUCTURING NATIONAL SINOLOGY

Part of the process of constructing national identities involves acquiring knowledge about the "other": the representations a society makes of its neighbors are never anodyne and form part of complex identity and societal strategies, the stakes of which exceed the desire for any simple knowledge of the other's differences. China is not just a political but also a scientific object; indeed both aspects are intrinsically linked, as the authorities are supposed to ground their decisions in a correct understanding of national interest formulated by specialized expertise groups, which legitimate their work by disseminating information. Although decision-making as practiced in Central Asia is often determined by personal rather than national interests, the interaction between science and power cannot be ignored. Academic circles and think tanks specializing in China are therefore a key component in shaping Sino-Central Asian relations insofar as they are assigned the task of making sense of the relationship, and, to this end, of formulating the state's political and economic interests with respect to China. But they are also called upon to provide rational interpretations of complex phenomena such as migration, political pressures, and cultural influence, which are bound to impact upon Central Asian concerns of China in one way or another. Central Asian circles specializing in China may be divided into three broad categories: first, academia, in which the discipline of Sinology only emerged with independence, despite having been part of Russian-Soviet academia; second, the state-financed institutes for strategic studies, whose degree of autonomy in large part depends on the level of freedom of expression in their country; and third, the private consulting groups that emerged during the 1990s partly in response to foreign policy needs, but also because individuals wanted to take advantage of the new economic conditions so as to sell their intellectual skills outside state organs.

The difficulties of launching Sinology in academia

For its expertise, the Soviet regime relied very heavily on university professors and scholars at the Academy of Sciences, in particular in the domains of both international relations (the Institute of World Economy and International Relations, the Institute of North-American Studies, etc.) and nationalities policy (the Institute of Ethnology). Soviet Sinology was based on an old Orientalist tradition that had taken shape in Tsarist times and was generally inspired by the Western model of Sinology. A national Sinology, based on research conducted first-hand by Russian scholars in China, emerged in the second half of the nineteenth century.[1] During Soviet times, Sinology was deeply politicized and the Communist Party was intimately involved in the shaping of scientific discourse. Sinology was also subject to the twists and turns of Sino-Soviet relations. It was represented by two main institutions: the Institute of Oriental Studies, which adhered to a classical definition of Orientalism (language, culture, literature, and ancient history), and the Far East Institute, which dealt with contemporary topics.

In Central Asia, the difficulties that academia has experienced since the disappearance of the USSR have been accentuated by the enduring impact of the former Soviet division of knowledge, within which Moscow and Leningrad alone were permitted to formulate discourses about the external world. Indeed, studies of areas outside the Soviet world were conventionally understood to be a domain reserved for Russians. The federated Soviet republics, the autonomous republics of Russia (then the Soviet Federative Socialist Republic of Russia), and Russian provinces were all limited to studying their own national or regional culture. They were not supposed to access the outside world other than through the prisms constructed by Moscow or Leningrad.[2] This logic was even more marked in the case of Sinology, such that relations with Communist China, whether amicable or conflictual, were always highly political. In Russia, the only city that was able to create a school of Sinology with some degree of autonomy from Moscow and Leningrad was Vladivostok, and to a more limited extent, Irkutsk and Barnaul.

In Central Asia, the departments of Oriental Studies were modeled on the Institute of Oriental Studies in Moscow, and therefore focused on historical, linguistic, and cultural questions. But nowhere in the region did there exist a center on a par with the Far East Institute that specialized in contemporary issues. In addition, these departments of Oriental Studies did not furnish any knowledge on areas outside the Soviet Union, but reproduced the Russian prism in which their very own culture was classified as "Oriental." Oriental Studies, then, were principally understood to involve the ancient history of Central Asia, including the study of manuscripts, and the history of Islam, but not Asia outside of the Soviet Union. However, the regionalization of Soviet sciences meant that these departments were allotted a specialization in studies on the Uyghur and Dungan minorities. The Kyrgyz Soviet Republic established a department of Dungan Studies (*dunganovedenie*) at the end of the 1930s, a time when Russian folklorists, exiled in the region as a result of Stalin's repression, began to take an interest in the local cultures. From the 1940s on, the Academy of Sciences of the Kazakh Soviet Republic set up a department of Uyghur Studies (*uigurovedenie*) within its Linguistics Institute.[3] Although their researchers were confined to the disciplines of philology, history, folklore, and ethnology, a minority among them were allowed to learn Chinese so they could carry out their research.[4] A modest milieu of Central Asian Sinologists thus formed in the 1960s and 1970s among the specialists of these two minorities and the historians of the relations between ancient China and the steppe cultures. Due to the system of regional studies promoted by Soviet ideology, they were able to take an interest in their Chinese neighbor without incurring the wrath of Moscow or Leningrad.

This first Soviet-born attempt at establishing Sinology in Central Asia nonetheless remained limited. It was distinguished by only a handful of personalities, whose personal and professional trajectories illustrate well the chaotic nature of Sino-Soviet relations. Ablat Khodzhayev, for example, is a founding father of Sinology in Central Asia. Of Uyghur origin, he spent some of his childhood years (1955–1959) in China with his father, one among the very few non-Russian Soviet citizens permitted to take part in the specialist groups sent by the Communist Party of the Soviet Union in order to help build Chinese communism.[5] In fact, between Mao's seizure of power in 1949 and the Sino-Soviet split in the early 1960s, Communist China enjoyed significant amounts of Soviet aid, particularly in the form of technicians, engineers, and political and military advisors. But with the rupture in Sino-Soviet relations, no Central Asian scholars with an interest in China were any longer permitted to go to the People's Republic until the beginning of *perestroika*. The Faculty of Oriental Studies at Tashkent University, which had the only Sinology chair in all Central Asia (created in 1958 on the basis of the former Uyghur language chair), provided an opportunity for students with an interest in China to graduate in Sinology. However, the chair was abolished during the most difficult periods of Sino-Soviet relations, from 1964 to 1977, during which time students were obliged to read for their Sinology Masters degrees and doctorates either at Leningrad University's Far East Institute or at the Institute of Oriental Studies in Moscow.

As an illustration of the highly political character of Soviet Sinology, it was only at the end of the 1970s, when relations with Beijing began to normalize, that Moscow decided to reopen the Sinology chair in Tashkent. The chair was initially renamed the "History of Cultural Relations between Central Asia and China," and then the "Department of Central Asia and the Far East," and assigned to Ablat Khodzhayev. The latter was a disciple of the famous Russian Sinologist Sergey Tikhvinsky, a member of the Study Commission of Diplomatic Documents of the Foreign Affairs Ministry, as well as the director of its Historical Diplomatic Section.[6] In this function he was entrusted with the mission of gathering archival evidence to justify the Soviet borders with China. When Ablat Khodzhayev took up his post he was given the task of drafting reports to provide justification for the Central Asian borders, using Chinese sources from the eighteenth and nineteenth centuries to argue that areas contested by China lay outside the Qing Empire's borders.[7] Historical research on China undertaken in Central Asia has thus always had strong ideological underpinnings responding to urgent political demands.

Ablat Khodzhayev was practically one of the only academics to act as a bridge between the principal Russian Sinologists of the 1960s and 1970s and post-Soviet Sinology. With the exception of the chair in Tashkent, there were some good trained specialists in Kazakhstan (Murat Auezov, Klara Khafizova and Konstantin Syroezhkin, all linked to Oriental Studies) but with no other appointed chairs, they have found it difficult to institutionalize the transmission of knowledge. In Turkmenistan and Tajikistan, researchers interested in foreign countries were accustomed to studying neighboring countries that had some cultural similarities, such as Iran and Afghanistan, rather than China. The Sino-Tajik border being inaccessible, the Tajik Soviet Republic was never considered by Moscow as being close to China, in contrast to the Kazakh and Kyrgyz Soviet Republics, and therefore never had any Sinologists or any departments of Uyghur or Dungan Studies.

The brutal collapse of state budgets in the 1990s aggravated this already precarious situation. In Tajikistan, the 1992–1997 civil war caused many researchers to flee, in particular those of Russian origin, thereby breaking the chain of intellectual transmission. Today, the Institute of Oriental Studies in Dushanbe includes a fairly well developed unit focusing on Iranian and Afghan studies, which is sure to further expand, but as yet it has no researcher working on China. In Ashgabat, the closing of the Academy of Sciences in 1997 by President Saparmurat Niyazov meant that the knowledge accumulated during Soviet times was dramatically lost.[8] The Institute reopened in 2007, but it does not yet constitute an established academic milieu. If and when this does eventually occur, it is likely that it will initially be limited to the study of Turkmenistan and its neighbors. A section of Uyghur and Dungan Studies did survive in Kazakhstan and Kyrgyzstan, but it has been fraught with difficulties. The lack of state funding for the Kyrgyz Academy of Sciences has forced some of the last remaining specialists to leave the institution, leading to a loss of knowledge that has been further accentuated by the retirement of older generations. The Dungan Studies section today includes only a few researchers, all of whom specialize in historical, ethnological, and linguistic questions, but few of whom speak Chinese. In addition to a few scattered publications, the Dungan Studies Department, reeling from a lack of both financial and human resources, has its main *raison d'être* in the writing of textbooks of Dungan language and literature for Dungan-speaking schools in the country upon the request of the Ministry of National Education. Almost no sponsorship from Dungan businessmen has been forthcoming to make up for the state's withdrawal.[9]

In Kazakhstan, the difficulties confronting specialists in Uyghur studies are more political than economic in nature. In 1986, before Mikhail Gorbachev visited Beijing to make the reconciliation with China official, the political authorities deemed it necessary to develop Uyghur studies, and so had the section transformed into an autonomous institute directly linked to the Kazakh Academy of Sciences. In the first years of independence, this Institute was highly coveted by Uyghur activists, who sought to politicize the institution and transform it into a flagship of militancy. In 1996, however, Beijing pressured the Kazakh authorities into merging the Institute of Uyghur Studies with the small Center for Oriental Studies, the result of which was the Institute of Oriental Studies, which carefully avoids embroiling itself in any political issues connected to the Uyghur question. Today, the Institute's Uyghur section includes a dozen researchers, all of whom work on apolitical historical, ethnological, and linguistic topics. With the exception of Ablet Kamalov, who is a specialist in Chinese medieval sources on Xinjiang, none of them are Sinologists.[10]

Like their colleagues in Dungan studies, the Uyghur studies specialists, at the request of the National Education Ministry, have been assigned the task of writing language and literature textbooks for Uyghur-speaking schools. However, these specialists have managed to diversify their funding sources, some of which are private. The section thus entertains low-profile relations with some Uyghur businessmen, who agree to act as sponsors for publications, conferences, and fieldwork research. Uyghur and Dungan Studies comprise specific domains of research that are still influenced by methods of intellectual work dating from Soviet times (including, for example, the idea that a *native* is more competent to study his or her own culture than a non-native, which explains why the majority of scholars in Uyghur/Dungan studies are of Uyghur/Dungan origin) and are having difficulties adapting to contemporary upheavals. Rarely are the scholars in these departments actually Sinologists, and, even when they are, they focus on the Dungan and Uyghur populations established in their own countries or in Xinjiang rather than on China proper.

The study of China in the Academies of Sciences in Central Asia is therefore confined to two states, Uzbekistan and Kazakhstan. There is a longstanding rivalry between them, in the domain of Sinology as in numerous other spheres of intellectual life. But the status quo changed as of the early 2000s: while Tashkent still rides on its legacy as the cultural capital of Soviet Central Asia and has been unable to take advantage of the new political situation to increase its knowledge on China, Almaty, regarded as a provincial town during Soviet times, tried to institute mechanisms for the renewal of its intellectual elite. Although the Tashkent Institute of Oriental Studies is particularly competent on questions of Islamology and Middle Eastern studies, the Chinese section is moribund, has had to call Ablat Khodzhayev out of retirement to take up its leadership, and faces difficulties attracting new disciples, save for a few researchers working on linguistics and ancient history. The meager salaries on offer (less than US$100 per month for a higher doctorate degree—a *doktor nauk*—at the end of the 2000s), the difficulties of doing fieldwork in China, the political pressures, and the lack of publication prospects drive young researchers away to work in the private sector.[11]

For lack of rivals, the Institute of Oriental Studies at the Academy of Sciences in Kazakhstan is today the driving force of academic Sinology in the whole of Central Asia. Apart from the Uyghur studies section, it includes an International Relations section, which works mainly on the Kazakh diaspora abroad, especially in China.[12] The Far East section is the only one that studies contemporary developments in China, Japan, and the two Koreas, but as it has only half a dozen researchers to cover these four countries, it is unable to carry out any in-depth research on China. Its main Chinese focus, Xinjiang, is looked at from the point of view of its being a neighbor of Central Asia, and chiefly from that of trade relations with Kazakhstan.[13] Thus, of a total of more than sixty scholars working at the Institute of Oriental Studies, only half a dozen deal principally with China, and even they work on Kazakhstan-China relations, and do not study China per se. Moreover, the few existing Chinese-speaking scholars are mostly Kazakhs from China who have settled in Kazakhstan, and arrived with Chinese intellectual traditions very different from Soviet Sinology.[14] Despite this glaring shortage of cadres, the Institute's management is trying to expand its Sinology section, in particular in the domains of historical interactions between the Steppes and the Middle Kingdom, and that of contemporary questions. As a result, it is making an attempt to set up mechanisms to train and recruit Sinologists, but has not yet been able to counteract competition from the private sector and the strategic institutes, which offer far more attractive terms.[15]

Outside the Academy of Sciences, Sinology is being developed within the universities, but here again the results have been modest. After enduring huge difficulties throughout the 1990s, Central Asian universities have started to see slow improvements in their financial situations: they can now provide professors with salaries higher than those of researchers in the Academy of Sciences; they can obtain external funding; and they can also charge more expensive tuition fees to boost revenues. However, except for the teaching of Chinese, which cannot be considered as part of Sinology proper *qua* knowledge on China, there are very few universities that can claim to have a Sinology department. Kyrgyzstan, for example, does not have one, since none of its numerous Chinese language teaching sections included, at least in 2010, any scholars who published research on China. In Tajikistan, only the Center for Geopolitical Studies, which is part of the Slavic Russian-Tajik University created in 1996, produces any knowledge on China. It is headed by a scholar of Uyghur origin and a specialist in international relations with a particular interest in China;[16] and seconded by a historian, vice-director of the History Institute of the Academy of Sciences, who works on geopolitical questions that induce him to focus partially on China thanks to his Eurasianist convictions.[17]

In Uzbekistan, the Institute of Oriental Studies at the National University includes some scholars who specialize in questions of the ancient history and linguistics of China, but it does not really generate expertise on contemporary questions, even if links with Beijing are developing.[18] In Kazakhstan, some units in Sinology exist in the universities. The most prominent among them is that at the National University Al-Farabi (KAZNU), where the first China chair was established by Klara Khafizova in 1989. But, here again, little research is undertaken, save in ancient history and linguistics, and publications mostly consist of language textbooks. Klara Khafizova, who teaches at the Kainar private university and undertakes research on the history of Qing China, worked for some years on more contemporary topics at the Institute for Strategic Studies. It is also worth mentioning the Center of Practical Sinology of the Kazakh Academy of Work and Social Relations. For its part, the Lev Gumilev Eurasian University in Astana, which is often presented as one of the most political higher education institutions in the country, has a small Chinese section, but it only gives language courses, and produces no expert knowledge.[19] Hence, even in the most dynamic university system in Central Asia, namely Kazakhstan's, there is almost no expert knowledge on contemporary China produced in the universities.

The position of the academic sector in Central Asia is thus paradoxical. Historically, academia has been the main site for knowledge formation on China. Since independence, however, Central Asian academia has not yet been able to overcome the Soviet division of labor, which limited Central Asian scholars to being specialists in their own culture, their national minorities and their diasporas, but disqualified them from working on international relations. The Academies of Sciences have paid a heavy price for their specialization in disciplines such as linguistics, folklore, and ancient history, since they are unable to present themselves to the authorities as centers of expert knowledge on contemporary issues. Moreover, they only have very limited access to decision-making circles; when such links do exist, they are not based on institutional mechanisms, but rather on a particular individual's network. In addition, the Academies of Sciences continue to be at the mercy of small government budgets, which impedes generational renewal and makes it impossible to compete with the new institutions, since the latter can exploit alternative sources of funding. However, this lack of interest in academic Sinology presents a long-term danger: no applied research can develop if no knowledge is generated independently of political and economic contingencies.

Public research: the Institutes for Strategic Studies

In 1991, the new states of Central Asia found themselves catapulted into the international arena with no experience in foreign policy and no established diplomatic corps. Neither did they have any tradition of expertise on international topics, since international relations had always been a domain reserved to Moscow and the Russians. During the first years of independence, no foreign policy knowledge on China was available, and so university academics were solicited to enter the diplomatic service: this was the case, for example, with Murat Auezov, Kazakhstan's first Ambassador to China (1992–1995), as well as Muratbek Imanaliyev, Kyrgyzstan's Ambassador to China (1993–1996), and Ablat Khodzhayev, the political advisor at the Uzbek Embassy in China (1996–1999).[20] Creating a field of expertise from scratch has proved especially difficult: currently the Central Asian states are still either undergoing a long social and economic crisis, which means being deprived of resources, or living under an authoritarian political regime, which means that the intellectual circles are denied the autonomy necessary to generate expert knowledge. In addition, in the 1990s a large number of academics left these countries, whether for Russia or the West, or abandoned research to set themselves up in the private sector.

Apart from the schools of the Communist Party, which the new states transformed into superior cadre-training schools, the first official think tanks to appear were the Institutes for Strategic Studies. These institutes were created in the years following independence and have direct links to the presidency. In addition, all ministries, in particular the Ministries of Foreign Affairs and of Defense, have their own internal centers of analysis, which produce classified reports on demand. This is also true for the Presidential Administrations, each of which has its own Center for Foreign Relations, which itself produces papers, but are kept confidential. In Kazakhstan, the principal foreign policy think tank remains the Kazakhstan Institute for Strategic Studies (KISI). However, in the early 2000s, the authorities understood that if the country was to retain its status as a regional power, they had to promote the field of expert knowledge. Nursultan Nazarbayev's private foundation (called the "Foundation of the First President of Kazakhstan") thus undertook to create several other think tanks such as the Institute for World Economics and Politics (IWEP).

Official Kazakh expertise on contemporary China remains in the hands of these institutions. The Institute for Strategic Studies has some China-oriented researchers working on international relations or on regional organizations including the SCO, and one of the great names in Central Asian Sinology, Konstantin Syroezhkin, for a long time employed in the Uyghur section of the Institute of Oriental Studies.[21] The International Institute for Modern Politics, created in 2003, was granted the title of an "SCO expert center," organizing annual conferences with the expert centers of other member states and carrying out press surveys to monitor perceptions of China in Kazakhstan,[22] but it did not survive the economic crisis in 2008. The Institute for World Economics and Politics had the most serious ambitions to be the future center for Kazakh Sinology: it opened a Center for Chinese Studies with the goal to "construct more adequate and profitable relations with China for Kazakh society (...) with the aim of defending Kazakhstan's national interests,"[23] but its main researchers left it in 2008 and are now employed by other institutions. Despite being closely aligned to the presidency, the two main institutes, the KISI and the IWEP, do enjoy some freedom of speech; they are able to express veiled criticisms concerning the authorities' handling of the relationship with China and researchers speaking off the record will occasionally issue severe criticism of Beijing's role in Central Asia.

In Kyrgyzstan, in the 1990s and the beginning of the 2000s the International Institute of Strategic Studies (MISI) was a smart outfit run by several renowned researchers such as Muratbek Imanaliyev, Akylbek Saliyev, and Valentin Bogatyrev. In the mid-2000s, however, the MISI has become increasingly disorganized. This disorganization has resulted from the conflicts of interest that plagued Askar Akayev's presidency, as well as the reorganizations that followed in the wake of the March 2005 "Tulip Revolution."[24] With Valentin Bogatyrev's resignation in 2006, the institution was reduced to an empty shell, and its key researchers on China left to take up positions in private institutions. In Tajikistan, the Center for Strategic Studies under the Tajik presidency is heir to the former Institute of Economic Research of the Economy Ministry of the Tajik Soviet Republic. Still today, the Center lays much emphasis on the economic questions crucial to Tajikistan's future.[25] Although it has several researchers working on Dushanbe's relationships with neighboring countries, including China, and although it enjoys a status as a Tajikistan's "SCO expert center," only one of its researchers is a Sinologist by training. However, the Center does currently have a few young doctoral candidates writing PhD theses on China who will soon be able to make up for the lack of expertise in this area.[26]

Similar to the academic domain, the situation of expert knowledge in Uzbekistan falls short of the country's traditional intellectual standards. The

Institute of Strategic and Transregional Studies, which is close to the presidency, has largely lost its dynamism as a result of the restrictions placed on public freedom. Today it is confined to organizing conferences and seminars, which do no more than showcase government opinion.[27] The field of expert knowledge in international relations is shared with two other institutions, which only reflect official narrative: the Center for Political Studies (run by the president's eldest daughter, Gulnara Karimova), which is one of the best-known Uzbek think tanks in China and seems to maintain close relations with Chinese scholars,[28] and the Foundation for Regional Politics, both created in 2005.[29] Although these three centers regularly organize international conferences devoted to the SCO, they have very few Sinologists. The University of World Diplomacy and Economics, one of the country's most prestigious university institutions, for a while employed one of the main specialists on the SCO, but his pro-Western opinions obliged him to return to the National University.[30] In Turkmenistan, the extreme authoritarianism of Saparmurat Niyazov's regime prevented the constitution even of a restricted milieu of specialists, but in 2008, an Institute of Studies in International Relations connected to the Ministry of Foreign Affairs was created. This seems to suggest that provision is being made for a structure of expertise to provide the authorities with expert reports.[31]

Official expertise constitutes one of the most dynamic sectors of the world of the Central Asian think tanks. In the early 1990s, Central Asian governments were quick to understand that they needed a structured narrative presenting their stance on international issues, not to mention circles capable of providing analyses for use in decision-making and justifying policy choices. As all their funding comes from the state, these institutions have as much room for maneuver as their country's overall political situation allows. Hence, in Uzbekistan, where the regime has become more and more authoritarian, the centers for strategic studies have been unable to develop any autonomy. In Kyrgyzstan, meanwhile, the dismantling of the MISI highlights not only the absence of state funding for research, but also the structural weakness of the presidential apparatus and its inability to develop any long-term political conception for the country's future. In this regard, Kazakhstan has an unambiguous superiority over its neighbors: Astana has made very clear the importance that it assigns to the question of expertise, and is willing to set aside substantial amounts of funding for it.

The small sector of private expertise

Privately-funded think tanks comprise a very heterogeneous group with much greater diversity than in governmental centers of expertise or in academia. Nonetheless their spectrum in Central Asia is quite reduced, since it depends on the economic, not to mention the political, situation of each state. Accordingly, they are circumscribed either by the intrinsic weakness of the domestic economy (in the cases of Kyrgyzstan and Tajikistan) or by the state's quasi-total stranglehold over the political sphere (Uzbekistan and Turkmenistan). Only in Kazakhstan do things come close to providing relatively good conditions for the flourishing of private expertise, both in terms of the room—albeit reduced—for political expression, and the substantial financial means placed at their disposal, which has seen some entrepreneurs able to free up sufficient funds to commission expert reports.

Think tanks connected to political parties are non-existent, and private foundations that base their autonomy on the diversity of their sources of funding are very rare. In the 1990s the main source of funding for these think tanks and NGOs came from large international institutions: the World Bank, the Asian Development Bank, the European Bank for Reconstruction and Development, specialized United Nations agencies such as the United Nations Development Programme (UNDP), the US Agency for International Development (USAID), the Organisation for Economic Co-operation and Development (OECD), the Organization for Security and Co-operation in Europe (OSCE), the European Commission, the former TACIS program, and private funds from the West, mostly from the United States (the MacArthur Foundation, the Open Society Institute, the Eurasia Foundation, and various think tanks) and Germany (the Konrad Adenauer Stiftung and the Friedrich Ebert Stiftung). With the growing distrust of the ruling elites toward foreign and especially Western financing, NGOs had to apply to state-run funds, which enabled the authorities to increase their control over these politically sensitive associations.

In Kazakhstan, the first independent think tank to emerge was the Public Policy Research Center, which has published several analyses on sales of Kazakh oil company assets to China, and has often taken a critical view of such such transactions. The Risk Assessment Group specializes on the political and economic elites, pressure groups and lobbies, and provides reports on the financial and political risks facing Central Asia and the Caspian region.[32] It is therefore in a good position to gauge China's rise in power in Kazakhstan and the question of the emergence of Chinese pressure groups. Last, the Central Asia Institute for Economic Strategies, in partnership with the Moscow Institute of Economic Strategies, is showing a growing interest in China's commercial activities throughout Central Asia and the impact of these activities on the region's national economies.[33]

In Kyrgyzstan, one main foundation has emerged outside the academic and state sector thanks to private funding, the Institute for Public Policy (IPP). Regarded as the MISI's successor, it acts to pool the country's expert knowledge on international matters. Due to the large personal networks of its former director, Muratbek Imanaliyev, who was the Minister of Foreign Affairs in 1991–1992 and again in 1997–2002, it has good access to decision-making circles and often carries out research on China.[34] The small Alexander Kniyazev Foundation, which receives most of its financing from Russian sources, also specializes in questions of regional security, in particular concerning Afghanistan, and on various occasions has published its opinion on China's rising influence in the region.[35] While private foundations are rare in Kyrgyzstan, there have been many small private research centers set up as part of the university system. For the most part, they specialize in domestic questions, due largely to Kyrgyzstan's lack of international influence and to the considerable presence of NGOs and Western foundations, which do research on domestic issues.[36] In Bishkek, only one university center concentrates on international questions, the Institute for Strategic Analysis and Forecasting (ISAP), created in 2005 as part of the Slavic-Kyrgyz University.[37] The ISAP organizes several types of projects, including the information portal East Time, which disseminates analyses on Central Asia, Afghanistan, the Middle East, and Asia.[38] It aids with decision-making on domestic and foreign policy issues and conducts research on Islamism in Central Asia, as well as on the Kyrgyz population's perception of foreign activities and NGOs in the country.[39]

The last category of centers of private expertise is the broad grouping formed by the NGOs that emerged in Central Asia from the early 1990s on. Western researchers often take these centers as objects of study expressing "civil society" as such, but not all can be considered to belong to the expertise world. Only sociological and survey centers specializing in studying public opinion, which are run by teams of sociologists who have quit academia, can be added to this analysis of China as a subject of study. Several sociological centers occasionally deal with international topics when conducting studies on public opinion. These include the Sange Research Center[40] and the Institute for Comparative Social Research Studies[41] in Kazakhstan, Valentin Bogatyrev's Perspektiva Analytic Consortium in Bishkek,[42] the Analytical Center Sharq,[43] the Panorama Association, the Zerkalo Center for Sociological Research in Dushanbe,[44] and so on. Beijing's rise to power in the region is starting to appear within their purview, since Central Asian societies are increasingly affected by certain socio-economic phenomena linked to China (importing of Chinese products into bazaars, road-building to open up isolated regions, migration flows etc). In addition to the already long-studied activities of Russia and the West in the region, these sociological centers are bound to become more distinctly interested in the "Chinese question."

These private centers are halfway between academia, since their researchers often have a university background, and the official think tanks, since they work on current issues and are interested in the multiple transformations that have occurred in Central Asian societies since independence. Even if their political opinions are not publicly expressed, their members are committed to more global ideological aims: in terms of their activities, these private centers are often pro-Western, regret that the populations are not more engaged in political debates, and desire more interaction with the international community. However, with rare exceptions, they have a far smaller influence over the authorities than do the official institutes for strategic studies, as their staffs mainly come from academic or journalistic circles, not from political and/or diplomatic circles.

This brief analysis of Central Asian expertise on China shows the difficulties that these countries are experiencing in overcoming the Soviet heritage of the division of academic labor—a division which meant these new states were catapulted onto the international arena devoid of the intellectual resources required to engage in international affairs. Although diplomatic milieus, notably in Kazakhstan, are beginning to develop in professionalism, the field of expertise has—inasmuch as it requires greater independence of mind and distance from politics—encountered problems in establishing an institutional structure with regular funding, and in recruiting well-educated and motivated younger generations. With the exception of Kyrgyzstan, the domination of state institutions over the private sector is part not only of the Soviet legacy, but also of a political system that prioritizes mechanisms of state control over the formation of expertise. The loss of knowledge acquired during the Soviet period, in particular in Uzbekistan, as a result of the fact that a new generation of intellectual elites has not emerged, appears to be a problem that will afflict the future of the whole region, the effect of which is a weakening of public policy and of the population's capacity to interpret the information disseminated by the authorities about current challenges.

* * *

After two decades of independence, Central Asian intellectual circles have displayed minimal interest in China, since their geopolitical orientations have already been structured by Russia, the West, and Turkey. However, expertise on China is starting to develop concomitant with a growing awareness of authorities, academia, and experts alike, that continued ignorance will be detrimental. In the years to come, these circles will therefore become more distinctly divided in accordance with their opinion about China. For the moment, the Soviet legacy still largely structures the complex relations between Central Asia and China: the dearth of institutionalized knowledge on China is a major reason for the simultaneous presence of very pragmatic directives and old phobias. In Central Asia, Beijing continues to be seen through a predominantly Russian prism: politicians take good Sino-Russian relations as their main point of reference; the Kazakh and Kyrgyz media outlets reproduce the clichés on China that circulate in Russia; and local researchers tend to base their analyses on the publications of Russian Sinologists. This Russian prism derives from the long, shared history of the two regions: the "de-Russification" of Central Asian knowledge will first of all require generational change, and the training of new elites with their own vision and knowledge of China.

9

SECURITY AND ECONOMIC CONCERNS AS THE MATRIX OF CENTRAL ASIAN EXPERTISE

While the official declarations proclaiming the need to maintain friendly relations with Beijing have been unanimous, this has not been the case among Central Asian experts and academic specialists, who present more variegated and critical viewpoints. Almost all of them express concern about the silence cultivated by the authorities in relation to China, and do not hesitate to condemn their lack of willingness to provide more detailed information about Chinese activities in Central Asia. They are concerned about the atmosphere of suspicion—generated precisely through the dearth of information—that surrounds the topic of China in public opinion, and argue that if the issue does not receive adequate expression, it will only contribute to increasing social tensions. The discourse that has been developed by Central Asian expertise on China's role in the region is therefore a complex one.

While some key figures are on record as expressing their unilateral critiques of Chinese activities, others do not conceal their appreciation, and even admiration, for China's dynamism. However, the majority of experts tend to identify both pros and cons regarding China's engagement. This balanced argumentation can in part be explained by the variety of issues involved. In relation to geopolitics, China is mostly viewed as a positive factor, whereas in questions of identity and culture, it elicits negative reactions. Moreover, perceptions of China differ according to country: Kazakhstan seems in general more Sinophobe, while Kyrgyzstan's and Tajikistan's attitudes are more Sinophile. What is striking, however, is just how little overall sympathy China elicits: there is a prevailing feeling of mistrust about Beijing's possible "hidden" objectives. Local experts suspect, despite the current positive effects China is having on Central Asian nations, that its presence will cause huge problems in the long term. They also tend to believe that after centuries of near invisibility, China's rapid rise over recent years has once again made it a cumbersome neighbor, one which Central Asian states will have to reckon with regardless of future regime changes and geopolitical developments vis-à-vis Russia and the West.

China: a credible partner in matters of security?

All Central Asian experts profess their astonishment at the rapidity with which China has managed to impose itself on the Central Asian scene. Nevertheless, their viewpoints concerning the region's place in China's foreign policy are varied. While recognizing that the Caspian Basin is not a priority compared to Taiwan or Japan, some contend that the Chinese authorities see Central Asia as having real strategic interest.[1] Others more modestly maintain that China's objective is less to impose itself on the Central Asian domestic scene than it is to demand loyalty with respect to sensitive questions such as Taiwan, Tibet, and Uyghur separatism.[2] But irrespective of their particular opinions on the foreign policy of their neighbor, all insist on the long-term nature of Chinese geopolitical thinking. They remark upon the specificities of Chinese diplomacy, claiming that it is defined by restraint and patience rather than confrontation and use of force, and that it thus stands in sharp contrast to the more brutal Russian policies.[3]

All experts—particularly those in the weakest countries, namely Kyrgyzstan and Tajikistan—remain positive about China's stabilizing role in regard to security matters, and often support unreservedly its strategic commitments in the region: the more actors present, the better for the region.[4] Some argue how much more effective the Chinese border guards are compared to the Central Asian customs officers, who have been corrupted by the drug trade.[5] They also welcome China's genuine efforts to combat Islamism since this leads it to invest in Afghanistan, which can only be of benefit to Central Asia as a whole.[6] While the majority of Uzbek experts, whose capacity for public expression is limited, have adopted the official pro-Beijing discourse on the "three evils," Kazakhs, on the other hand, remain rather more skeptical. Konstantin Syroezhkin remarks for instance that Chinese policy in Central Asia is not without ambiguity: even if Beijing strives to maintain stability, it also discreetly fosters disagreement among Central Asian states. Its aim, he claims, is to prevent the Central Asian states from establishing a common front that might jeopardize the advancement of its interests.[7] He thus tends to think that China's multilateral aims in the SCO are deceptive, arguing that all the fundamental questions have been settled through bilateral agreements. Other, more moderate, experts consider that China has always put more emphasis on bilateral relations, but was led to develop a more ambitious policy of multilateralism after the Soviet Union's collapse, and even more pointedly after the success of Asian multilateral organizations such as the Association of Southeast Asian Nations (ASEAN).[8]

Opinion remains more divided, however, as regards China's ability to improve regional security. In a survey conducted in 2006 by Adil Kaukenov, among thirty Kazakh experts, only 20 percent thought that Beijing was going to be a major player in Central Asian security; and 44 percent declared that over the short term it would not even have the least interventionist capacity.[9] None of the experts surveyed believed that Chinese policy was fully compatible with Kazakhstan's interests. A large majority of them (three quarters) even reckoned that China's increasing geopolitical influence would have contradictory effects and basically run counter to the interests of the Central Asian republics.[10]

The issue of China's potential military presence in Central Asia is a particularly sensitive one. The idea is widely decried in the media, above all in Kazakhstan, and in populist books, many of which promulgate alarmist perspectives on the Chinese military's supposed hidden presence in the region.[11] Several experts also have expressed direct concern about Chinese military power. They see Chinese military reforms and Beijing's massive investments in military technology as being of major concern, a development that Central Asian governments should closely follow.[12] The build-up of military forces in the Lanzhou region, for example, is said to be more than three times as large as the combined forces of the Kazakh army.[13] Furthermore, the issue of nuclear weapons in Xinjiang is not yet resolved, with the Chinese still performing tests on short- and mid-range weapons at the Lob Nor test site.[14]

Kaukenov's survey also revealed that 50 percent of experts placed Russia as their country's number one partner, ahead of the US and China, while none placed China first.[15] Indeed the majority of Central Asian specialists we have interviewed claimed that the only partner who would really be willing to accept the political and financial burden of a military intervention in case of serious destabilization is Russia. They consider it most improbable that the Chinese armed forces might try to use the auspices of the Regional Anti-

Terrorist Structure—which they view as an empty shell with virtually no efficacy—to intervene in Central Asia.[16] No one goes so far as to call for the creation of a Chinese military base on national territory. Even those who see China as a necessary counterweight to Russia claim that the arrival of Chinese troops on Central Asian territory would be opposed by the local governments and would provoke violent reactions among the population.[17] Only a handful of Kyrgyz experts, such as the former pro-rector of the Diplomatic Academy of Kyrgyzstan, Murat Suyunbayev, actually envisage the arrival of Chinese troops in case of serious conflict with Islamist groups. He also argues that Kyrgyzstan should be turned into a polygon of anti-terrorist combat in which not only Russia and China but also the West might participate.[18] Direct intervention by the Chinese authorities following political destabilization in any one of the Central Asian states is considered to be a serious risk for Kazakhstan's geopolitical security.[19] Although there is no official information available on this issue, a large number of experts privately voice the opinion that too much intelligence exchange between the Chinese and Central Asian secret services might well backfire on national interests. They also state their belief that the Chinese secret services are already too well established in Central Asia.[20]

The SCO—a balancing act for or against Central Asia's interests?

The Shanghai Cooperation Organization is by far the most studied topic by Central Asian experts. The overall opinion of it is very positive: it is the main regional organization to which four of the five Central Asian states belong, it is not limited to the post-Soviet space, and also garners considerable international media attention. Despite the profusion of publications relating to the SCO, Central Asian experts contend that the major issue concerning the relationship to China is not multilateral but bilateral. Questions about the organization's future revolve around three major axes: Does the SCO function solely as an instrument to promote Chinese interests or is it designed to help address Central Asian problems? Will the balancing act between Moscow and Beijing continue? And if so, will it enable Central Asia to increase its autonomy or does it thereby risk becoming a dominion of the Russians and Chinese? Is the anti-Western orientation of the organization an asset to stability or is it liable to cause destabilization in the region?

Central Asian experts dismiss simplistic Western critiques that cast the SCO as the precursor of a future supranational political or military-political organization on the model of the defunct Warsaw Pact. They remind us that neither Russia nor China desires to give up national sovereignty. On the other hand, whatever direction the organization takes in the coming years, a large majority of experts state that Central Asia will have little influence over it. Only a little more than 10 percent of the Kazakh experts interviewed by Adil Kaukenov in 2006 considered that Central Asia would be able to determine the development of the organization in the coming decades. Conversely, more than 60 percent stated that the SCO's future would be decided by direct negotiations between Moscow and Beijing, irrespective of the Central Asian viewpoint.[21] On this issue researchers in Tajikistan and Kyrgyzstan again seemed more enthusiastic than their counterparts in Kazakhstan and Uzbekistan, stating that their countries had everything to gain from the development of an SCO fostered by the Russian and Chinese giants.[22]

In Kazakhstan, the SCO arouses even less enthusiasm. The majority of researchers doubted the effectiveness of the organization, especially as an instrument for tackling the important questions that Central Asia faces.[23] The absence of any binding foreign policy agreement between member states, as well as potential conflicts of interest, are regularly cited as reasons that speak against the organization.[24] An expert from the Al-Farabi National University, Gulden Zholamanova, has argued that the SCO's declarations of intention are all well and good, but that only the specialized commissions designed to strengthen cooperation in specific areas are of any real efficacy.[25] Konstantin Syroezhkin similarly contends that the SCO's capacity for action is essentially limited to declarations of intention, arguing that the more the organization develops, the more it is confronted with multiple problems such as the question of enlargement, unequal development between member countries, and the competition, or indeed antagonism, between Russia and China.[26] These multiple inconsistencies are further evident in the fact that the SCO has been unable to establish any sort of unified approach to the priorities of its member states.[27]

Nearly all experts accuse the SCO of talking too much and doing too little, a reproach that is usually directed at Western countries and Russia, but never to China as a bilateral partner. Its refusal to become a discussion platform for water management negotiations is of big concern to Astana, Dushanbe, Bishkek and even Tashkent, as all governments have raised this issue as being a potential element of regional conflict. The water question is often presented as the reason for the organization's future failure.[28] This refusal is explained both by Beijing's fear of having to take sides, but also by its not wanting to turn the spotlight on the tricky issue of Sino-Kazakh cross-border rivers.[29]

Beijing is also often held to be solely responsible for the SCO's refusal to look into questions of human security in Central Asia, especially those relating to migration. The Central Asian experts are therefore critical about the real willingness of member states to put "explosive subjects" on the discussion table: by fostering consensus, the SCO is liable to lose its ability to influence future developments.[30]

The great majority of Central Asian experts agree in recognizing that since 2007–2008 the SCO has been going through a form of "growth crisis." Some consider that this stagnation was born from an interpretive error: having attained its goals, the SCO was always unlikely to elaborate other, more complex mechanisms. According to Konstantin Syroezhkin, for example, the SCO's only functions were to settle the question of border disputes and neutralize the Uyghur diaspora; to build relations of trust between member states and regulate Sino-Russian dialogue; and to supervise China's rise in economic power, all objectives that were attained successfully.[31] All the other domains fall under bilateral relations with Beijing, or amount to geopolitical speculations about the SCO security missions, which are deemed to have no more than a declarative, rhetorical value. For others, the SCO is a mechanism with a merely defensive, anti-NATO function; it is therefore no surprise that it has become stagnant now that the North Atlantic Alliance is no longer perceived to "threaten" through further eastward expansion, and because American interests in Central Asia have waned in significance.[32]

However, it is on the level of security that the SCO's competencies are most discussed, and the events in Tajikistan and Kyrgyzstan in 2009 and 2010 have, of course, reinforced this discussion. The gap between the organization's official discourse on the fight against non-traditional threats and the—quasi-non-existent—mechanisms in place to enable collective, or at least concerted, action is the main reason of Central Asian experts' disillusionment. While a few people consider that the SCO has the potential to replace the international coalition in Afghanistan, such as Alexander Kniyazev in Bishkek[33] and Viktor Dubovitsky in Dushanbe,[34] the others criticize its lack of common will in spite of its increasingly active rhetoric on the "Afghan question."[35] They all cast doubt on the will of the Russian and Chinese armed forces to work together even in a defensive form, for example by forming brigades to monitor the Central Asian borders against drug-trafficking. According to them, it would be naïve to expect anything whatsoever from the SCO on the Afghan question: each member state is developing bilateral economic relations with Kabul but nobody wants to get involved more directly, or in a collective way.[36]

China's position within the SCO also raises numerous questions, and opinions on this issue diverge accordingly. The majority of experts agree that the organization's statutes make it impossible to stop Chinese expansion in the region but that at least they provide Moscow with possibilities to curb it;[37] others have less nuanced views. For them the SCO is an instrument that directly serves Chinese interests and works to justify Beijing's activities in the region in the eyes of the international community.[38] A professor at the Slavic-Kyrgyz University in Bishkek, Nur Omarov, talks of the "Chinese SCO."[39] Farkhat Tolipov, at the National University of Uzbekistan, suspects the SCO of wanting to become an "Eastern NATO" and compares it to the Holy Alliance of 1815, the objective of which was to maintain the political status quo and therefore to work in favor of the major powers.[40] A researcher from the KISI, Venera Galiamova, has pointed out that SCO treaties will have to be renegotiated in 2020, when China will be able to put even more pressure on its partners.[41] A highly placed Uzbek official who participated in Uzbekistan's SCO membership process in 2001 stated off the record that the fifth founding point of the organization—which stipulates that member states cannot act against one another—ought to be revoked: he is concerned about the possibility of Chinese intervention if any state's policy options begin to run counter to Beijing's interests.[42] According to Konstantin Syroezhkin, the SCO has made it possible for China to institutionalize its legitimacy in the region without being accused of expansionism.[43]

Although all the Central Asian experts support Moscow's presence in the SCO and refuse to envisage any head-on clashes with Beijing in case of Russia's absence, their opinions diverge when it comes to the positive or negative value they accord to the Russian-Chinese partnership. Some of them contend that it represents a balance of forces that plays in favor of Central Asia; others denounce it as a simple mechanism of bilateral domination. An expert at KISI, Murat Laumulin, expresses the concern that Moscow actually discusses the region's future more with Beijing than with the Central Asian governments themselves. Not only is such a tendency disadvantageous to Central Asia's autonomy but, were the Russian-Chinese partnership to collapse, it would expose the region to a major risk of destabilization.[44] In this balancing act, many experts point out the difficulties that stand in the way of the SCO forging a role to rival that of the CSTO, which is conceived to be far better structured and much more effective.

Other experts judge the Russian-Chinese partnership in Central Asia more positively. Maria Disenova and Aitolkin Kurmanova of the Institute of Economic Strategies in Almaty, for instance, have remarked that Kazakhstan has always had to maneuver between its two larger neighbors and that history shows this game to be optimal for the country.[45] Esen Usubaliyev at the Institute for Strategic Analysis and Forecasting in Bishkek maintains that China will enable Central Asia to set limits on Russian policy, since Beijing has been readier to accept the US military presence in Kyrgyzstan than Moscow.[46] Hence many experts believe this Sino-Russian arrangement to be optimal, at least for the time being, and note that Beijing at any rate favors maintaining Russian domination in the region.[47] Farkhad Khamrayev, who works at the Uzbek Ministry of Foreign Affairs, has stated that Beijing is discreetly supporting Russia's anti-American position in order to kill two birds with one stone: getting the United States to withdraw from Central Asia, and prompting Washington to blame Moscow for this instead of Beijing.[48]

Nevertheless, despite the apparent cooperation between China and Russia, many researchers question the future of this collaboration and think that the long-term interests of the two countries are contradictory.[49] According to Ablat Khodzhayev, the potential for competition over the control of Central Asian resources is bound to increase,[50] an opinion that is shared by Ainura Dzhorobekova at the National University of Kyrgyzstan, and Murat Asanbayev in Almaty.[51] For his part, Konstantin Syroezhkin surmises that Russia will one day have to choose between the West and Beijing.[52] Other researchers, such as Adil Kaukenov, hope that Moscow will prevent Beijing from entering into a domain which hitherto has been firmly in the Russian orbit. The vast majority of experts hold this opinion, believing that Russia will do everything in its powers to curb Chinese expansion.[53] They dismiss the idea that a real partnership could develop between the SCO and the CSTO, since they do not believe that it is in Moscow's interest to merge an efficient organization—one that it has complete control over—with the SCO.[54]

From a Central Asian viewpoint, the last major issue concerning the SCO relates to Central Asia's attitude about the place that the West, and especially the United States, occupies in the region. The SCO's anti-Western overtones tend to be evaluated positively or negatively depending on the specific political convictions of each expert. The most pro-Russian complain about Western interference, whereas those with more Western-oriented sensibilities worry about the disappearance of American power in the region. For example, the vice-director of the Center for Geopolitical Studies in Dushanbe, Viktor Dubovitsky, and Leonid Skakovsky, a researcher at the Center of Geopolitical Research at the Russian-Kazakh University in Astana, positively welcome the Russian-Chinese alliance in its desire to counter the United States.[55] The director of the Center for Social Research in Bishkek, Nurbek Omuraliyev, has stated his concern about China's desire to enlist Muslim countries in what he views as potentially dangerous anti-US politics.[56] Numerous Central Asian experts express their apprehension about the deteriorating relationship with NATO and would like to see the European Union and/or NATO obtain observer status in the SCO so as to be reassured about the latter's intentions.[57] According to Konstantin Syroezhkin, despite the rise of anti-US sentiment among the Central Asian elites in recent years, all experts tend to perceive Western presence in the region as a guarantee of stability and that it would be dangerous if the Russo-Chinese partnership were to have an exclusive grip over Central Asia.[58]

China in Central Asia: economic opportunity or resource vassal?

Central Asian experts are all acutely conscious of the region's landlocked character, a factor that drastically augments the cost of transporting commodities for export and import. In both Kyrgyzstan and Tajikistan, experts express enthusiasm for the prospects that China presents for opening up the region, which was a mere dead-end point in the Soviet circuit of distribution.[59] Proximity to Chinese neighborhood is therefore seen as not only having opened up new routes to the southern seas, either via Chinese territory or the Karakoram Highway heading toward Pakistan, but also for having transformed the region into a transport corridor from ASEAN countries toward Iran and Afghanistan,[60] and for having provided a unique opportunity for greater long-term development thanks to the re-export of Chinese products.[61] Kyrgyz and Tajik experts also view positively the practical effectiveness with which China participates in tunnel and road construction, highly publicized projects that are greatly appreciated by the local populations.[62] According to them, such projects have enabled an "invasion" of Chinese products, which is good insofar as it lowers prices and raises the transit value of some of the more isolated and mountainous regions situated on the trade routes from China.[63]

For Kazakhstan, the promising energy partnership is also an argument for consideration. According to some experts, the numerous export opportunities offered by China are beneficial to the country insofar as Beijing makes it possible to counter the large international majors that are already well-established, particularly as Chinese firms offer contracts that are more advantageous for KazMunayGas than Western firms. However, the energy issue also raises concerns for others, who think that increased dependency on China jeopardizes national sovereignty.[64] They argue that the Kazakh authorities have transferred too many energy resources into Chinese hands, and denounce the dangerous opacity that surrounds the awarding of tenders for deposits' exploration and exploitation.[65] The Sino-Kazakh pipeline, in addition to its ecological risk, is suspected of being unprofitable to date.[66] Moreover, the Kazakh government has not shown any transparency on fundamental questions such as whether China or Kazakhstan will ensure the pipeline's maintenance and security arrangements. Many are therefore worried that Chinese firms will be given responsibility for security instead of the Kazakh forces.

While Chinese and Central Asian official discourse lays emphasis on the complementary nature of their respective economies, which is held up as a win-win trade situation, several Central Asian experts, including economists and specialists in Chinese political economy, question such a one-sided view.[67] Their key accusation is that China restricts the Central Asian economies to the role of producers and exporters of primary resources. On this matter, also, the level of criticism of Chinese economic policy varies depending upon the country. Neither Kyrgyzstan nor Tajikistan has an efficient industrial or agricultural sector and they already import most of their goods from Russia, Kazakhstan, Iran, and Turkey. China's arrival is therefore not viewed as jeopardizing but as dynamizing because its prices are competitive. Local experts even complain that there is a lack of small- and medium-size Chinese companies, which could play a key role in domestic industrial development via the joint-ventures system.[68] However, others express their fears about the disappearance of the last national companies.[69] For instance, the Tajik economist Khodzhimukhammad Umarov criticizes Beijing's policy, arguing that investments in the upgrading of local factories (cement, food processing, or agriculture machinery factories) will suffer as Beijing merely seeks to export its own finished products. He calls upon the Chinese authorities to change the structure of trade relations by promoting investments that could help the country develop indigenous production.[70]

The issue of over-specialization is often raised by experts in Uzbekistan, and more so in Kazakhstan. In Tashkent, the subject remains off-limits and very few specialists are able to question the official discourse on the current honeymoon in Sino-Uzbek relations. Nevertheless, Ablat Khodzhayev used his high-level position to obtain political approval to publish a critical work entitled *The Chinese Factor in Central Asia*, printed in a limited edition of a hundred copies in 2004, and five hundred in a second edition in 2007. As he explains,

"Chinese investments are not aimed at the development of local production but at the creation of conditions to boost the export of Chinese products and the import of primary resources."[71] He continues by stating, "China is not ready to offer large-scale economic aid to the states of Central Asia for the development of local production and the augmentation of their export potential."[72] He concludes his work by urging the SCO to be careful so as not to end up as an instrument for "imported expansion"[73] from one member country to another—a diplomatic message that is clear to whoever knows how to read it. Speaking off the record, an Uzbek senior official claimed that China is in fact not solely responsible for Tashkent's failure to develop its industrial sector: the Uzbek policies of extreme protectionism have undermined the country's former role as a transit space, and massive corruption among customs officials serves to deter Chinese companies.[74]

In Kazakhstan, a more open expression of concerns about economic overspecialization has been permitted by greater freedom of speech and a larger number of economists and experts specializing in China. Dosym Satpayev, director of the Risk Assessment Group, considers that Astana has no choice other than to give up all its processing industry and instead specialize solely in hydrocarbons, uranium, electricity, cereals, and transit.[75] Konstantin Syroezhkin, for his part, is unequivocal on the matter, claiming, "China's economic successes objectively go against all Central Asian interests in the sector of industrial processing and to a certain extent in food processing."[76] In his view Kazakhstan has become so dependent on Chinese products that its economic sovereignty has been put in jeopardy: if these products were to vanish, then the country would suffer wide shortages of automobile spare parts, electronic goods, construction materials, clothing, and food, and a large part of the population, and not just that involved in the area of "shop-tourism," would lose its means of subsistence.[77]

Kazakh experts also criticize government attempts to conceal real bilateral trade figures. They claim these figures are calculated in such a way that Kazakh exports are overvalued and Chinese imports undervalued.[78] If some of these discrepancies are due to Astana's politically motivated desire to play down Chinese economic activity, nonetheless the Kazakh customs services are too corrupt to gauge the extent of this trade. According to Maria Disenova and Aitolkin Kurmanova, these uncontrolled flows of everyday consumer goods constitute a genuine stumbling block for the national economy.[79] Experts such as Alida Ashimbayeva, the head of the Institute for World Market, and Konstantin Syroezhkin point out that capital flight also poses significant financial risks, as Chinese investors established in Central Asia transfer money back to their home country,[80] and the development of shuttle trade reduces Kazakh liquidities.[81] China's "Far West development program" also attracts expert attention. Ablat Khodzhayev interprets Xinjiang's transformation into a zone of transit for commodities to Europe and Middle-East as a direct attempt to compete with comparable specializations in Central Asia.[82] Konstantin Syroezhkin considers that Xinjiang's development is in large part buoyed by Central Asian—and especially Kazakh—resources.[83] The idea of unfair competition in relation to the economic boom in Xinjiang, a region that was originally poorer than Central Asia, appears therefore to be a significant issue for Central Asian experts.

The probability of Kazakhstan joining the World Trade Organization has also raised concerns. Konstantin Syroezhkin suspects that Beijing is simply waiting for Astana's membership in the WTO before it invests more heavily in the Kazakh market, taking advantage of new, lower customs duties.[84] The IWEP-based scholar Gulnar Smailova criticizes Beijing for the protectionist measures which it employs in certain industrial sectors, but disallows to new members.[85] The prospect of transforming the SCO into a free-trade zone is viewed with skepticism.[86] On this issue, Tajik and Kyrgyz experts tend to support China's proposals, because they have everything to gain from a merger of the Eurasian Economic Community with China, whereas their Kazakh and Uzbek colleagues worry about the major repercussions this could have on their respective economies. Kazakh experts see it as being an economic risk for their country in view of the developmental differential with its neighbor.[87] According to Konstantin Syroezhkin, transformation of Russia and Central Asia into the providers of primary resources to China is liable to disturb the Russian-Chinese equilibrium within the SCO.[88] Only Maria Disenova and Aitolkin Kurmanova maintain that Kazakhstan would benefit from such a common economic zone, since this would enable it to have more control over the quality of Chinese products.[89]

An image problem: China's products, traders, and companies

Central Asian opinion harbors the widespread notion, skillfully manipulated in the media, that Chinese products are of bad quality. Experts take a more nuanced view. While most are of the opinion that Chinese products were of bad quality at the start of the 1990s, they argue that this is no longer strictly true. In any case, given the low standards of living of Kyrgyz, Tajik, and Uzbek households, the only affordable Chinese products will necessarily be of low quality. These specialists frame the question in another way by insisting on the responsibility of Central Asian businessmen, who purchase the cheapest Chinese goods in order to maximize their profits.[90] Numerous experts nonetheless call for the Central Asian and Chinese governments to deal seriously with this question, which may well have a long-term impact on the consumer choices of the middle classes, for whom quality remains synonymous with Russian, and even more so with Western or Japanese products.[91]

If Chinese products have a bad reputation, so do Chinese business people, at least according to public opinion which depicts them as rogues. However, Konstantin Syroezhkin and Dosym Satpayev note that the danger is not so much Chinese economic expansion as such, but the widespread massively corrupt environment in the whole of Central Asia.[92] The question of competition between Chinese and Central Asian traders has not been made the object of any detailed studies, but experts are well aware of the problem's long-term implications. Some Kyrgyz researchers maintain that it is potentially one of the country's destabilizing factor, and urge the government to engage in negotiations with Beijing in order to get it to exercise direct control over its own citizens abroad.[93] Others, like Akylbek Saliyev, have expressed the view that Chinese workers who come to work in the construction, mining, and metallurgical industries actually make up for the labor deficit resulting from the local population's refusal to work in these sectors.[94] In Tajikistan, the phenomenon of large Chinese bazaars is only in its infancy, and so conflicts with Tajik traders are rare, even if specialists like Guzel Maytdinova are wary of a possible rise in tensions.[95] As director of the Panorama Center in Dushanbe, Tatiana Bozrikova, has observed that Chinese migrants, who perform menial jobs, open restaurants, and work at bazaars, for the moment make up for the absence of a class of small- and medium-size Tajik entrepreneurs.[96]

In Uzbekistan, this first became an issue at the end of the 1990s but was settled by Tashkent's implementation of ultra-protectionist measures and the expulsion of Chinese businessmen. However, it will again become an important question when the country opens up its borders to foreign trade. As Ablat Khodzhayev and Farkhat Tolipov have pointed out, bazaar property has always been a particularly profitable financial manna for Uzbek mafia circles, and therefore competition with the Chinese will be harsh.[97] In Kazakhstan, the experts are more confident on this issue: there are far fewer feelings of competition since, with the exception of shop-tourism, Kazakh traders engage almost exclusively in big business and disregard the shuttle trade.[98] Konstantin

Syroezhkin even believes that Kazakh business circles are very much in favor of Chinese activity. They also feel more protected due to the fact that Astana has been much stricter than Bishkek in the granting of visas and working permits to Chinese citizens.[99] Moreover, menial and construction jobs are mostly done by Uzbek and Kyrgyz immigrant workers, who currently have a competitive edge (Russian language and cultural similarities), and this state of affairs is unlikely to change in favor of the Chinese.

Finally, the Chinese companies that have established in Central Asia have bad reputations. To begin with, in no country of the region does it seem possible to get reliable figures on their numbers. Konstantin Syroezhkin questions what their real activities are since the majority of companies with Chinese capital are classified as wholesale traders, but this is an imprecise term that could conceal many potential shadow activities.[100] In addition, nearly two thirds of Chinese companies registered in Kazakhstan either no longer provide information about themselves or quickly become idle, which is seen as confirming the suspicion that Chinese traders often seek to obtain a legal front and then disappear into the black market.[101] While some experts contend that this shadow economy can be explained by the Central Asian environment itself, Murat Auezov and Ablat Khodzhayev, for instance, consider the establishment of so many fictitious companies to be part of a Chinese strategy to set up indirectly in Central Asia. Auezov openly expresses his concern about China's staunch determination to establish itself on the shores of the Caspian Sea. "That will give China," he says, "an extraordinary chance to legalize its massive physical presence beginning with the western regions of Kazakhstan."[102]

* * *

In considerations of geopolitical balance, *Realpolitik* prevails in Central Asian expert opinion. All tend to share the conviction that the Central Asian states have to adapt to their Chinese neighbor, regardless of whether or not they view this presence positively. They doubt the SCO's capacity to impact upon the region's security, especially given Russia's predominance in strategic partnerships and the absence of binding supranational competencies in the organization. Nor do they entertain any illusions about the long-term solidity of the Sino-Russian partnership, which they think is doomed to fade in the years to come. A majority of them consider that China's advance into Central Asia presents significant risks in the medium term and cannot be seen as entirely positive for national interests. In one of his most widely distributed articles, Konstantin Syroezhkin sums up this majority opinion well by saying that

China remains a *challenge* for Central Asia, including on those issues that are presently regarded as having been resolved, such as border delimitation.[103]

In the economic domain, the most optimistic experts insist that China's proximity has to be taken as an opportunity to develop the local economies. Central Asian governments must resign themselves to accepting the disappearance of non-competitive sectors and adapt to a phenomenon that is not specific to Chinese influence but attributable to the process of globalization as a whole. They therefore urge the authorities to be pragmatic with regard to China and to elaborate adaptive strategies based on raw material exports and transit strategies. For their part, the pessimists believe that China does not want the Central Asian economies to acquire new technologies. As a result, they think that the region is doomed to remain in the inglorious stage of a producer of raw materials, and thus that it will remain exposed to the volatility of geopolitics and especially to the stranglehold of China. Many experts are indeed convinced that Beijing is trying to transform the economies of Central Asia to suit its own interests, weaken their potential for autonomy, and further establish their status as Chinese protectorates dependent on their neighbor for technological know-how. On this issue, distinctions can be made between Central Asian countries: on the one hand, both Tajikistan and Kyrgyzstan are clear-sighted about the state of their economies and resolute about taking advantage of the opportunities that China offers by becoming zones for the re-export of Chinese products; on the other, Kazakhstan and Uzbekistan, whose economic and particularly industrial ambitions have not faded, aim to develop competitive technological sectors not dependent on Chinese goodwill.

10

CULTURAL APPREHENSIONS

HISTORICAL LEGACIES AND DEMOGRAPHIC PHOBIAS

Following centuries of relatively little contact between the two zones, China has recently made an abrupt entry into the Central Asian imagination. The local identity landscape is still stamped by the old clichés of Soviet propaganda casting China as the historical enemy. In Soviet times, Moscow claimed that Chinese development had no future and that the PRC was basically a patriarchal society struggling hard to survive the consequences of the Cultural Revolution. In spite of the divergences in their opinion on China, Central Asian experts have all been schooled in the same Soviet culture, and a majority of them identify with the idea that they are part of a common "civilization" that includes Russia. In addition to this, there exists an old and this time specifically Central Asian tradition, handed down through centuries-old oral epics, which presents China as a distant but recurrent enemy of Turkic peoples and as an historical opponent of Islam. Still today, these key clichés are largely operative: aside from the theme of the "Yellow Peril," the ideas that Chinese power does not evolve historically, that it pursues atemporal objectives which stretch across several hundreds or even thousands of years, and that the Chinese authorities conceal their imperialist objectives as a matter of principle, are all very widespread.

The thorny border question: resolution or stalemate?

Central Asian and Chinese diplomats unanimously consider the border disputes to have been settled.[1] In all bilateral and multilateral conferences, there is a sense of satisfaction about the fact that these questions were peacefully dealt with—undoubtedly the first step toward strengthening cooperation. Nevertheless, Kazakh, Kyrgyz, and Tajik experts present more varied viewpoints in their texts and interviews than do their political leaders. Once again, whereas in Kyrgyzstan and Tajikistan opinion is balanced, in Kazakhstan it is much more critical. However, all the experts are in agreement on the importance of the principle of diplomatic reciprocity: Not to subscribe to the "One China" policy would mean that their border disputes with Beijing could be turned by the latter into instruments of coercion.

When it comes to interpreting the history of Sino-Soviet border disputes, all Central Asian experts adopt Russian-Soviet arguments: they accuse China of being the instigator of the 1969 confrontations by its incursions into Soviet territory, which thus gave Moscow no other option but to defend itself. All of them uphold the Soviet reading of the dispute. They recall that for many years China had seemed satisfied with the border situation before suddenly deciding to claim that various parcels situated in Soviet territory were "under dispute" while Moscow itself had never laid any claim to land on Chinese territory.[2] A book focusing on Kazakhstan's borders published in 2006 caused a stir when China was explicitly referred to as the sole perpetrator of the violence in 1969, and the majority of China's claims were presented as unfounded. The authors argue that despite a Soviet commission dispatched to the region in the 1970s, Moscow actually agreed to renegotiate with Beijing on the basis of China's claims and not its own observations.[3]

In Kyrgyzstan, some experts consider that the relatively quick settlement of border disputes has worked to consolidate the pragmatic atmosphere of Sino-Central Asian relations: although the territorial disputes were settled to Beijing's advantage, it is argued that these disputes are now a thing of the past, that China was above all concerned with stabilizing its north-west border which it has now achieved.[4] Others are nonetheless critical of the inequality of the land swap negotiated in 1999: while Bishkek obtained a large part of the Khan Tengri peak, a national symbol, it lost the Uzengi-Kuush agricultural zone. In Tajikistan, the majority of experts are likewise pleased that Beijing claimed much less land than it had originally wanted. Nonetheless, some of them have stated off the record that the border agreements signed in 2002 have deferred resolution to an unknown point in the future. They suspect that Emomali Rakhmon's regime has tried to appease China by secretly postponing the further cession of territories, only to leave it to a future government to manage the scandal.[5]

In Kazakhstan, many experts consider that Chinese threats to Soviet integrity were linked to the Cultural Revolution ideology. As that page of history has today been turned, they urge public opinion not to dwell on the lost territories.[6] Some of their colleagues nonetheless believe that Beijing did take advantage of the weakness of the newly formed independent states to procure a more favorable settlement.[7] They therefore reproach their leader for the fact that, while triumphantly professing to have succeeded in keeping 53 percent of the contested territories, he unilaterally ceded the remaining 47 percent. Objections were also raised about the official claims that these lands were of no strategic value: Kazakh border guards are now stationed in the valleys that are dominated by their Chinese counterparts, who have taken up position on the mountain ridges.[8] Konstantin Syroezhkin, for his part, quite rightly remarks that the refusal by the Kazakh, Kyrgyz and Tajik governments to publish the complete texts of the border agreement can only sow seeds of doubt in people's minds, leading them to surmise that certain aspects have been deliberately hidden.[9] The question of cross-border water resources alone constitutes a major stake of Sino-Kazakh relations. There is broad unanimity on this subject: all the experts consider that China's attitude is indicative of the low regard in which it holds Kazakhstan's legitimate concerns. Even the most Sinophile experts are convinced that the Kara Irtysh-Karamay canal is going to have a negative impact on Kazakhstan's economic and ecological situation.[10]

Xinjiang's intensive development also raises ecological issues: in addition to the fact that winds carry nuclear particles from the Lob Nor experimentation site to as far away as Central Asia, China is also having a negative impact on Kazakhstan's soil quality, not to mention on its water supplies and forests.[11] Experts with the most Sinophobe tendencies, like Murat Auezov, argue that the draining of water supplies is actually one of China's primary means to pressure Kazakhstan and limit its autonomy.[12] Those with more moderate views recognize that China is doing its utmost to modify the river flow in its favor, as well as to exclude Russia from the negotiating table in order to take the greatest possible advantage of its power differential with Kazakhstan.[13] Konstantin Syroezhkin formulated his point of view on the future of the cross-border river issue unambiguously: "China speaks as an equal only with those that are stronger than it, or with those from whom it wants concessions."[14] Kazakhstan's hopes of procuring an equitable share of water from the Ili and the Irtysh, then, would seem to be lost.

Is China a threat? Political pressure and the Uyghur question

On the political level, very few Central Asian experts hold the Chinese political system up as an example to emulate except for those very few individuals who label themselves as supporters of a single-party Communist system. Notwithstanding, many of them do acknowledge that they admire the way in which the current generation of Chinese leaders, lacking the legitimacy of the revolutionary past, is able to discuss publicly economic and social problems. Such an approach stands in stark contrast to the atmosphere of censorship and secrecy that prevails in Central Asia. Some of them also emphasize that the strengthening of ties between China and Central Asia was made possible by the compatibility of their respective political systems, in particular the refusal to comment on domestic situations.[15] Nevertheless, the political pressure that Beijing has exerted on the Central Asian authorities in regard to the Uyghur issue has raised doubts about the former's intentions. Most of the Central Asian experts believe that China coerces the governments by directly applying pressure at the highest levels of state and has the capacity to "buy off" the political elites, including the presidential families, especially given the high-level of corruption in the region.[16]

On the whole, experts from Central Asia consider that China constitutes risks for the region's social and political stability. The idea that, contrary to appearances, China remains a fragile country is very widespread.[17] Some experts claim that, even if the massive presence of the military in the political life is not a positive element in itself,[18] the single-party system is at present the best solution for ensuring the country's development, while others believe that the Chinese single party system will soon be undermined, and thus that China harbors the risk of political upheaval—which will be dangerous both for itself and for its neighbors.[19] Central Asian experts also regularly examine the economic risks that China presents. Many worry about the possibility that the PRC's economy will overheat, since this would affect Chinese investments in Central Asia.[20] Irrespective of the scenario, a majority of experts, in particular those from Kazakhstan, fear that instability in China and the possibility of social unrest among the Han population could give rise to a flow of migrants that would have a huge impact on Central Asia.[21]

Unsurprisingly, Xinjiang is a key element of Central Asian concerns, not because of a theoretical sympathy for the Uyghurs but because of pragmatic issues to do with Xinjiang's proximity. While some experts have adopted the "three evils" discourse, others express far more nuanced opinions. Kazakh researchers criticize the general marginalization to which the Uyghurs have been subjected on their ancestral territory. According to them, the "Far West development program" and the idea of redressing regional disparities in development are useful for the Han populations, enabling them to overcome land shortage problems by moving to the North West, but they have been detrimental to the indigenous populations of this autonomous region.[22] All the Central Asian experts draw attention to the fact that the national minorities remain confined to the sectors of least growth and are mostly unable to gain access to higher education, whereas the Han tend to occupy those sectors for which technical specializations are required.[23] The shortage of cadres is not being addressed in a way that benefits the national minorities. Instead, it is being solved by bringing in Han Chinese from eastern regions, thereby modifying Xinjiang's ethnic make-up to the detriment of Turkic peoples.[24] The closure of schools that teach in the national language is also perceived as proof of Beijing's policy of forced Hanicization.[25]

Like his colleagues, Konstantin Syroezhkin is extremely critical of Chinese policy in Xinjiang. He does not believe that the Uyghurs can achieve independence, since never before has the region had such a large population of Han Chinese, or a culture that was so Chinese-influenced, nor has it ever been so economically integrated into China's maritime trade. However, this observation does not suffice to resolve the problems. He believes that there are real risks of interethnic conflicts between the Han and the Uyghurs. He argues that because of Beijing's policy initiatives designed to facilitate the national minorities' entry into university, the emergence of an Uyghur elite is bound to create further interethnic competition between cadres.[26] Although many Central Asian scholars have discreetly raised the issue of the plight of China's Kazakhs, Syroezhkin is one of the few who have dealt at length with the issue of interethnic tensions between the Uyghurs and Kazakhs. He denounces the way that the Uyghurs conceive Xinjiang as being their own national territory, while neglecting the existence of other Central Asian minorities living there, and suggests that China's Kazakhs are losing out as much to the Hanicization of the region as they are to its "Uyghurization."[27]

The majority of Central Asian experts doubt that Uyghur Islamism presents any real risks and criticize Beijing's repression of Islam as being counter-productive.[28] Some of them maintain that the Chinese refusal to listen to any autonomist demands, even cultural ones, can only encourage radical separatism to take root. Beijing's abandonment of Uyghur rural youth and its favoring of urban student youth are pushing the former group into the swelling ranks of Islamists.[29] Konstantin Syroezhkin is even more critical and believes that Chinese policy is leading the Uyghurs to interpret Islam as an ideology of national liberation.[30] Notwithstanding, he claims that the Uyghur separatist movement has no future: the independentist groups are not large in number; they are heterogeneous in their demands and modes of action; they lack the backing of the Urumqi-based Uyghur intelligentsia; and so long as some of them remain affiliated with international radical islam they will never be able to obtain the aid of the international community.[31] Moreover, scattered Uyghur diasporic associations throughout the world have little influence on the ground and have failed to elaborate a well-structured ideology.[32]

China as empire: a culturally entrenched suspicion

This critical analysis of Chinese policy forms part of a broader background of suspicion about Beijing's real objectives in Central Asia. A prevailing misperception of China has allowed many phantasmagorical elements to color the picture. Central Asian experts in Kazakhstan and Kyrgyzstan regularly bemoan the media dissemination of caricatural information about their large neighbor, which is most often focused on the popular topic of the "Yellow Peril." Some Sinophile experts object that the information about China received by Central Asian societies is imported from foreign, and mainly Russian, sources, and this tends to distort the local view of China by superposing it with European fears.[33] However, several Sinologists have observed that, in contrast to Western Europe and Russia, Central Asian societies are not attracted to the kinds of Orientalized fashions that might actually work to promote a positive image of Chinese (and Japanese) culture.[34] Many note that, on the contrary, China's cultural visibility is significantly less even than that of the more distant India, which is comparatively well known amongst the former Soviet populations.[35]

Central Asian experts share with public opinion a dominant feeling of suspicion about Chinese ambitions. They all insist on the historical dimension of Chinese foreign policy and on its ancestral conceptions of its relations to others. Those who have studied history point to the fact that China's presence in Central Asia has always been that of a conqueror seeking expansion to the detriment of Turkic-Mongolian peoples. Ablat Khodzhayev took up this topic in the 1970s and began to specialize in ancient Chinese sources. Through the study of ancient ethnonyms, his aim has been to show that the Han Dynasty (200 BC–200 AD) had at one time recognized that Xinjiang lay outside its borders and was peopled by non-Han groups, an historical fact that would confirm the Turkic population's right to form states on its original territories despite being subsequently incorporated into the Chinese Empire.[36] Khodzhayev is one of the few to have voiced criticism of the Tsarist Empire, accusing it of having prevented the emergence of a Turkic state, including Xinjiang, by retroceding the Ili region to China and then allying itself with Beijing against the local populations.[37] In the conclusion to his book, he expresses his hope that contemporary Chinese leaders will not return to the conqueror-and-warrior model of the Qing dynasty, but expresses his doubts as to their good intentions.[38]

Klara Khafizova, for her part, contends that until the end of the Qing dynasty in 1911 the Chinese Empire actually structured its relations to "barbaric" neighboring peoples in accordance with their acceptance of Chinese values.[39] She has worked for many years on the Qing strategies in relation to Xinjiang and the Kazakh world, and many of her works have been translated into Chinese. Her analyses, however, are not uncritical of Chinese policies, which she qualifies as "Machiavellian."[40] As she notes, "In the second half of the nineteenth century, Qing China adopted active policies of aggression and violence against the peoples of Central Asia."[41] She argues, for example, that Qing China not only deliberately accentuated the divisions between the Kazakh Hordes, but also obstructed attempts at rapprochement between Central Asian peoples. In addition, it transformed Xinjiang into the launch pad for its conquest of Central Asia, refused to give the pasture lands taken from the Dzungars back to the Kazakh and Kyrgyz, developed trade policies prejudicial to the nomads, and even persisted with occasional military raids despite the collapse of Dzungaria. Klara Khafizova states that it was only after Russia's arrival in the area, which she describes as "progressive,"[42] that Chinese ambitions were effectively curbed and Central Asia was able to enter modernity.

According to Konstantin Syroezhkin, ethnocentrism is the very foundation of Chinese foreign policy. Contrary to what is written in Chinese sources, he asserts that the Han Chinese played no role in Eastern Turkestan ancient history, and moreover that Uyghur territory remained independent from China until the eighteenth century.[43] He blames the Qing for having transformed the process of Sinicization, which traditionally involved trying to entice the "barbarians" to adopt Chinese values, into a violent military conquest aiming at incorporating Eastern Turkestan into the Empire, whereas it could have preserved its autonomy as a buffer-zone. His emphasis on the negative historical role of the Qing is not unrelated to contemporary events. Indeed, according to Syroezhkin, a major social crisis would probably cause certain ancient cultural traits to resurface. In such an instance, he writes, the

"Chinese political mentality may well revert to the memory of its 'lost territories', which include some immense areas of Russia, Kazakhstan, and the Central Asian states, not to mention Mongolia."[44]

Many experts espouse the argument that Chinese diplomacy gets its results through long-term strategies, not via quick, sharp blows. Thus, if Beijing is careful not to offend the national feeling of the newly independent Central Asian states by claiming more territories, this does not mean that it will not return to the issue in future decades.[45] These persistent suspicions of its supposed ulterior motives have been bolstered by the prevailing nationalist mood in contemporary China, not to mention the aggravation of tensions with Japan over the interpretation of the past, and the rehabilitation of pre-Communist traditions. Many experts, for example, mention that an increasing number of Chinese publications present the Qing advances into Central Asia as having had a positive "unifying" effect. The launching, in 2008, of a large project on the history of the Qing dynasty allegedly confirms the determination of the Chinese government to revive its foreign policy traditions of widening its sphere of influence.[46] Lastly, the discovery that some Chinese school textbooks published in the 2000s displayed maps in which a large part of Central Asia (that is, the "historical" lands, which include all of Tajik Pamirs, all of Kyrgyzstan, and the Kazakh region of Semirechie as far as Lake Balkhash) is presented as belonging to the Chinese Empire also caused much dismay among Central Asian experts. For them, this is a sign that Beijing has not totally abandoned its territorial ambitions and may one day renege on its border treaty commitments.[47]

The Xinjiang Production and Construction Corps or Bingtuan, used by Beijing at once as its armed wing against Uyghur separatism and as a major component of its colonization of Xinjiang, is probably the most criticized Chinese institution in the whole Central Asia, the one that causes the most fear and that some imagine may well take root, in indirect forms, outside China's borders. Murat Auezov has expressed his concern about China's expansionist designs in his typically forthright manner: "I know Chinese culture. We ought not to listen to what Chinese politicians tell us. As a historian, I can tell you that the China of the nineteenth century, that of the twentieth century, and that of the twenty-first century are three different Chinas. But what unites them is the will to expand their territories."[48] In sum, experts who maintain, along with the Uzbek journalist of *The Voice of Russia*, Rakhimdzhon Sultanov, that China has taken its revenge on history and is no longer focused on this territorial issue;[49] those who assert, with Dosym Satpayev, that Beijing does not have an ideology of external domination;[50] and those who claim, with the former director of the KISI, Umerserik Kasenov, that China presents no territorial threat, are firmly in the minority.

The recurrent prism of the "Yellow Peril"

If Central Asian experts underscore the fundamental continuity of China's history, their views are also influenced by a more contemporary concern linked to the question of migration. The facts allegedly speak for themselves: whereas Central Asia as a whole has about 60 million inhabitants, an overpopulated China has a population of nearly one and a half billion. Each year the Chinese population increases by more than 15 million people, a number almost equivalent to the total population of Kazakhstan. Kazakh newspapers have taken this as an opportunity to denounce what they call China's "soft expansion" (*tikhaia ekspansiia*) into Central Asia. In so doing, they often deliberately confuse the number of migrants who are nationals of neighboring Central Asian states with the number of Chinese. They also attribute the increases in crime in urban zones to the Chinese and regularly exclaim their alarm at the emergence of Chinese ghettoes in large cities, in particular the Chinatowns in the capital cities. The tone of the articles is therefore explicitly alarmist: "The more that the question of migration is passed over in silence [by the government], the less chance we will have to prevent the appearance of Chinese provinces: our descendents will therefore be obliged to undertake a struggle of national liberation for the resurrection of Kazakhstan."[51]

The discourse of experts is far more nuanced, but it is not indifferent to the question of migration. As specialists on China, their chief concern is the social and political causes that might give rise to large waves of migration, such as China's abandoning of the one-child policy, which would see more people enter the workforce. Above all, however, they fear a possible deterioration in the Chinese domestic economic situation and a concomitant rise in unemployment.[52] Such an eventuality might cause the current migration flows from the central countryside toward the coast to redirect toward the less populated border zones of the North West. From this viewpoint, Xinjiang is almost systematically cast as the key example of the Chinese quest for a new *Lebensraum*, as the settlement of millions of Han constitutes the third phase of the "Far West development program."[53] Central Asian experts argue that Beijing plans to establish between 400 and 800 agricultural hamlets along the Chinese side of the Kazakh border, which are to be settled by millions of Han farmers: these highly militarized colonization brigades, part of the Bingtuan, would be under the direct control of Beijing and not of Urumqi, and would have the function, among others, of breaking the Turkic population continuum between the Central Asians and the Uyghurs.[54]

Central Asian experts are also interested in measuring the migration flows from China to Central Asia. They have to contend, however, with a persistent lack of figures, which only works to fuel polemics and open to every conceivable interpretation. Konstantin Syroezhkin openly denounces the Kazakh authorities' refusal to conduct precise studies on this topic, which he regards as the only way to put an end to the myth of the "Chinese invasion."[55] He condemns the Interior Ministry and the law enforcement agencies for their sponsoring of "fanciful" articles aimed at procuring additional funds for their fight against illegal migrants. One of the points at issue in this debate is whether the potential colonization of Central Asia is an explicit Chinese policy—a notion maintained by only the most Sinophobe experts—or whether migration flows are set to outstrip the Chinese authorities' capacity to control them, which seems to be a more realistic proposition. According to some experts, it is irrelevant to ask whether or not the Chinese diaspora in Central Asia forms a useful policy instrument for Beijing: Central Asia is not an attractive destination for Chinese migrants, the majority of whom aim to settle in Russia, Western Europe or the United States.[56] Others assert that the Chinese possess inassimilable cultural traits that dissuade them from settling in Central Asia for the long term. In Dushanbe Sukhrob Sharipov claims that the Chinese prefer not to settle in Muslim countries, where they find it difficult to integrate, but would rather head for the more open societies of Europe or Africa.[57]

Expert opinion on the migration issue can, then, be categorized by degree. Both Murat Auezov and Ablat Khodzhayev, for example, maintain that, with the Russian Far East, Xinjiang and Central Asia are the only possible corridors for Chinese expansion into the sparsely populated regions of Russia. As a result, Xinjiang and Central Asia, they claim, are destined to become submerged under waves of migrants searching for temporary or permanent homes further to the West.[58] Since the 1990s, Murat Auezov has unceasingly delivered warnings about the threat of Chinese expansionism. In his view, "What is happening in Xinjiang is the building of a platform for the next leap forward into the Central Asian and Kazakh territory."[59] Other experts are concerned about migrants because of the alleged social risks they pose: criminalization, money transfers, and monopolization of certain economic niches.[60] The KISI vice-director, Leila Muzaparova, also mentions that migrants could be carriers of epidemics, an idea that seems to be quite widespread in Central Asia. However, more pragmatic perspectives are also proposed. Dosym Satpayev contends, for instance, that Central Asia is likely to see arrivals of ecological migrants from China unless Beijing starts to take the environmental impact of its economic development into account.[61] Both Maria Disenova and Aitolkin Kurmanova, for their part, claim that this type of security discourse no longer has any relevance in an age of globalization, but nonetheless recognize that the Central Asian authorities would in any case be unable to repel any large-scale migratory flow from China.[62]

It is worth noting that Central Asian phobias in relation to the Chinese also apply to the Turkic minorities of Xinjiang. With the exception of a few individuals known for their Pan-Turkic sensibilities, such as Murat Auezov, or for their interest in the diasporic issue, such as Gulnara Mendikulova, from the Kazakh Institute of Oriental Studies, many Kazakh experts make no effort to hide their lack of sympathy for Chinese Uyghurs and Kazakhs. In their view, Astana's repatriation program is merely bound to complicate social relations by granting preferential treatment to poorly integrated populations. The Kazakh repatriates from China would pose the same risks as the Han Chinese to whom they have grown accustomed over the centuries.[63] Speaking on condition of anonymity, a Kazakh specialist claims that the Uyghurs and Kazakhs from China are a "fifth column" in the service of Beijing, ready to protect Chinese interests in the case of an outbreak of conflict with the Central Asian states.

The expert circles have proposed a wide range of solutions to the political authorities related to the so-called Chinese expansion. Both Murat Auezov and Bektas Mukhamedzhanov, for example, contend that Kazakhstan needs to implement a program to deal with domestic migration. This program should be designed to foster settlements of Kyrgyz and Uzbeks along the Chinese border, and to help compensate for the massive rural exodus of Kazakhs by supporting agriculture and preventing the depopulation of the border regions.[64] Some experts, such as Muratbek Imanaliyev in Bishkek, believe that friendly relations between the Central Asian and Chinese governments ought to suffice to compel Beijing to enforce strict control over its migration flows and prevent the uncertain consequences of interethnic conflict. Others, such as the Sharq vice-director in Dushanbe, Saodat Olimova, respond by saying that the good intentions of the Chinese authorities are in any case inadequate because the illegal migrants living in Central Asia are often the third or fourth children of Chinese families, that is, individuals officially considered non-existent and condemned to live clandestinely.[65] For the former deputy director of the Kazakhstan Institute for Development, Erlan Aben, the only chance the country has of reducing the risks of migration is to pass a law to restrict the employment of Chinese labor.[66] As for the IWEP, it has proposed not only that the government introduce quotas for migrant workers, but that it maintain its prohibition on the foreign acquisition of rental real estate and on the building of Chinese hotel complexes that would ghettoize the migrants.[67] Konstantin Syroezhkin argued that the Kazakh government should legalize the migration flows to prevent them from becoming monopolized by Chinese mafia networks specialized in the transportation and exploitation of illegal workers, as this is the case in the Russian Far East.[68]

The majority of Central Asian experts disagree with alarmist discourses about migration. However, they all confess that, although it is largely irrelevant to short-term concerns, the possibility of massive Chinese migration must be taken into account when considering long-term Central Asian interests.[69] Notwithstanding their differing stances, many experts speaking off the record admit to being worried about the future insofar as the impact on Central Asian societies of even a small-scale migratory flow from China would be massive. Their opinion of current developments in Xinjiang give away their pessimism. They steadfastly believe that present-day Xinjiang is tomorrow's Central Asia. Without loudly proclaiming it, many of them share the opinion expressed by Zhannur Ashigalide, at the Institute of Economic Strategies in Almaty, who bluntly states: "Analyze the relations of the Chinese authorities to its national minorities and you will see the future of the countries that neighbor China [...] Although Chinese diplomats display moderation and diplomacy towards the latter, in their domestic policy the Chinese occasionally show their 'true face' without worrying about the opinions of their neighbors."[70]

Central Asian specialists also share the vague sentiment that there exists a "civilizational difference" between China and Central Asia. Diverse arguments are used to justify the existence of this apparently unbridgeable cultural barrier. Some conceive of it in terms of Islam, others in terms of Russian-Soviet acculturation, and still others as involving a difference in national essences. Murat Auezov maintains, for instance, that the two regions are irreconcilable on the cultural level, in part because the Chinese consider the Central Asians to be "barbarians."[71] Basen Zhiger and Klara Khafizova lay stress on the sense of hierarchy embedded in Chinese tradition, which does not uphold equality between peoples.[72] According to Ablat Khodzhayev, ostensible differences in "ethnic mentality" between the Chinese and the Turkic populations have persisted across the centuries without having been abolished or modified.[73] In Dushanbe, Sukhrob Sharipov believes that Islam enables its populations to withstand assimilation into other cultures.[74] And according to Adil Kaukenov and Konstantin Syroezhkin, this "civilizational barrier," based on Russian-Soviet acculturation, ought to be maintained, since too much Sinophilia would endanger the future of the Central Asian peoples through cultural assimilation and interethnic marriage.[75]

* * *

In relation to cultural questions and the long-term outlook, Central Asian experts hold largely pessimistic views of China. All think that the states of the region will have inherent difficulties in trying to work the overall power differential with China to their advantage. They consider that the Chinese authorities' ultimate objective concerning Central Asia's independence is particularly unclear and that nothing prevents the currently fraternal status quo from one day being thrown into doubt—especially in relation to territorial and demographic matters. The suspicion that China still has imperial designs on Central Asia and merely wants to conceal or delay them is predominant. Even the most optimistic, who consider that Beijing's economic and geopolitical presence is a guarantee of stability for Central Asia, are by no means Sinophiles culturally speaking. All experts dismiss the notion that a Sinicization of Central Asian societies could take place by any means other than force. Moreover, the opinion is unanimous in regard to the importance of maintaining the "civilizational barrier" between Central Asia and China on the grounds that falling into the Chinese sphere of cultural influence would mean the ethnic disappearance of Central Asian nations.

CONCLUSION

Africa, Central Asia, or the globalization of Chinese presence

The deep transformations brought about by China's arrival in Central Asia are not unique, and can be viewed in parallel with similar processes happening, for instance, in sub-Saharan Africa.[1] The comparison seems pertinent on several levels: in both cases, China has been a relative and inexperienced latecomer, but it nonetheless has succeeded in establishing itself rapidly in energy, mining, and trade sectors, as well as becoming increasingly involved in agriculture and forest exploitation. As in Central Asia, China builds cheaply much of Africa's new infrastructure, sells goods that many Africans were previously unable to afford, and its aid is provided with no political conditions attached. In spite of this, there are contradictory tendencies in the modes of implantation: the Chinese state upholds the long-term economic sustainability of partner societies, but its state-owned enterprises pursue short-term financial gains and immediate exploitation to fill the need of the Chinese domestic market.[2]

African and Central Asian societies are both extremely diversified—the former more than the latter—and have differing degrees of contact with the Chinese world, which itself is just as variegated, ranging from the big state-run energy firms in Sudan or Angola to the private traders in Tanzania or Burkina Faso. In both cases, Chinese presence is embodied as much by the expatriates who work for large companies and are relatively well integrated in the host societies as by the workers who live at their work places, or by the private businessmen who have embarked on overseas trade, with or without their families. In everyday life, however, it is through the Chinese family shops that most Africans directly experience Chinese presence, just as the Central Asians do at the bazaars. China's impact on Central Asian and African societies' perception of the world is also comparable—which does not mean similar. For Central Asia, opening up to China has in part dethroned the dominance of Russia, as well as the more moderate dominance of Turkey, as its "natural" trading partners; for Africa, it has undermined the supremacy of former Western colonizers, such as France, for example, in its West African "backyard."[3]

In several African countries, governments have tended to foment a "Chinese problem" for domestic political purposes. In Central Asia, no ruling elites would dare to denounce the Chinese presence, but the latter can nonetheless be instrumentalized by both pro-Western and Islamist opposition, and also allows the public to express social and economic anxieties. China has therefore become part of the national narrative.[4] In Central Asia as well as in Africa, the dominant discourses revert to stereotypes about the effectiveness of Chinese workers compared to the wantonness of the natives, but also about China's lack of corporate transparency and the high degree of corruption of the national elites. If cross-cultural misunderstanding has heightened in some cases, in particular when business competition, labor relations, or environmental issues are at stake, the local narratives about Chinese presence nonetheless remain rather positive. Beijing is often thanked for the changes it induces in the everyday lives of populations through small-scale trade, while Europe and the United States are blamed for not backing up their grand words with action.[5] However, if the mechanisms of economic insertion are comparable, as is their social reception, Central Asia, in contrast to Africa, has to manage other complex components: geographical proximity with China; the presence of a Uyghur diaspora toward which suspicions are not likely to diminish; and reduced room for geopolitical and economic maneuver.

Central Asia: five states, five "Chinese Questions"

Each Central Asian state has a "Chinese question" that is specific to it. First, the three border countries of Kazakhstan, Kyrgyzstan, and Tajikistan have to be distinguished from the two non-border ones of Uzbekistan and Turkmenistan. While the former had to negotiate delicate border treaties and fear that one day they will have to transfer even more territory to their neighbor, the latter do not picture China as a power that could potentially undermine national unity. The former have experienced significant private enterprise trade flows and migrations from China, whereas the latter's economic relations with Beijing are limited to official agreements between large companies, and involve practically no private trade exchanges, and no back-and-forth cross-border migratory flows of Chinese, Uzbek, may be temporary: many Uzbek petty traders already travel to China or have stalls at Karasuu, therefore it is likely that Uzbekistan experience similar trade developments when the isolationist regime of Islam Karimov changes, peacefully or not, and the country re-engages with its historical vocation as a trade crossroads of Central Asia. For Turkmenistan, China will probably appear more slowly on the radar of everyday life, since neighboring Iran and close relations with Turkey will continue to be important. However, China's entry into the Iranian and Turkish markets in the coming decades will also serve to incorporate Turkmenistan into larger scale trade processes.

This division between China's border and non-border countries is heightened by a political divide: Kyrgyzstan, with its large public freedoms, remains a unique case in the region; Kazakhstan and Tajikistan are authoritarian states but allow a certain diversity of opinion to express itself provided it does not touch on sensitive issues such as the corruption of the presidential family; however, Uzbekistan and Turkmenistan are extremely repressive, and hence information on the impact and perception of China is rare.

Within the three border countries, further lines of division can be observed. The two poorest and most fragile countries, Kyrgyzstan and Tajikistan, understand the Chinese presence as a globally positive element, even if it also provokes anxieties. It is a guarantee of additional stability, since Beijing is the only great power to devote so many means to the development of transportation infrastructures, bank loans, etc. Belonging to the SCO is prestigious and has a positive connotation, even if they criticize it for having drifted from its initial security objectives. For these two countries, the question of China is often formulated in terms of having "no other choice," since the alternative candidates ready to invest in their economies are too few to enable them to benefit from competition. In the years to come, China's influence over Bishkek and Dushanbe risks becoming quasi-monopolistic, with political consequences that are hard to measure. On the other hand, Kazakhstan and Uzbekistan have more structured reservations about Chinese involvement, in particular in the economic domain. Both also harbor greater ambitions of regional autonomy vis-à-vis the great powers and want to have a certain freedom in their choice of partnerships.

In Kazakhstan and Kyrgyzstan, the "Chinese question" has been on the political agenda for more than a decade, longer than in the other three countries. For Uzbekistan and Turkmenistan the urgency of this question has not registered to the same extent, for the above-mentioned political reasons, while

Tajikistan was beset by civil war in the 1990s, with China not yet figuring on the radar. However, the situation is now changing rapidly and Dushanbe's relationship with China will almost certainly be modeled on that between Kyrgyzstan and China. Tajikistan can also be dissociated from the other Central Asian countries insofar as its own peculiar stance has been shaped by its ethno-linguistic specificities. Its fear of Pan-Turkism means that the Tajik elites do not express any reservations about China's handling of the Uyghur question; on the contrary, they are staunch supporters of the Chinese policy of fighting separatism, not to mention of the proliferation of Chinese texts on the pan-Turkist threat.

Lastly, it is possible to single out Kazakhstan from the rest of Central Asia on several points: it is the SCO's third largest power; its trade accounts for two-thirds of Central Asian trade with China; its economic dynamism has made it the driver of the whole region; and it is the only one to have performed a genuine analysis of its relation to China, involving a variety of specialists and lines of argumentation. It is also the most Sinophobe country, both economically and culturally, notably because its sparsely populated areas spark fears that this "void" might be "filled in" by waves of Chinese migrants. The disquieting irony for Beijing is that the Central Asian country most involved with China, and which knows it best, is also the most Sinophobe.

Sinophobe and Sinophile trends in the Central Asian societies

Sinophilia and Sinophobia go hand-in-hand in Central Asia: both can be present in the same person depending on the angle of view or the question being addressed. However, Sinophobia is taking the upper hand and might have long-term social consequences.

For the moment, the Sinophile circles have barely any institutional standing in Central Asia. Indeed, decision-making circles, the presidential families, the political elites, and the private sector oligarchs and directors of large public companies—often intricately linked through a variety of political, personal, regional, and corporatist allegiances—are already broadly oriented toward China: all have personal interests to protect, and have established direct contacts with Chinese decision-makers, whether embassies, businessmen or political leaders. China has no need therefore to finance institutional mediators to convey its viewpoints among decision-making circles. In addition, were an official pro-Chinese lobby to emerge, it might cause public opinion to react negatively and this might have the possible counter-effect of generating a more structured anti-Chinese lobby. The Sinophobe groups, in turn, are currently unable to acquire any institutional standing, as their criticisms of China would bear directly on the authorities' pro-Chinese policies, and therefore trigger mechanisms of repression against them. In addition, while pro-Chinese lobbies are liable to emerge as a part of the politico-economic establishment and thus be relatively unified, the anti-Chinese circles are divided by differing motivations and social affiliations. They comprise political opponents with pro-Western, nationalist or Islamic sensibilities, Uyghur associations, workers' unions, small businessmen and entrepreneurs, etc., all of whom would find it difficult to formulate common standpoint for the purpose of building genuine cooperation.

Among the Sinophobe political groups, worthy of note are those with Islamic convictions. Only Tajikistan has a recognized Islamic political party, although it is becoming increasingly marginalized. It may be assumed that Tajik elites with a pan-Islamic or pan-Iranian sensibility have particularly negative opinions of China, in which they see a new foreign cultural domination in the process of competing with or succeeding the more traditional domination of the West or Russia. In the other Central Asian states, Islamism as such—any political movement demanding the creation of an Islamic state in which *sharia* law would be applied—is prohibited, but in Kyrgyzstan or Kazakhstan well-known figures can express Islamic sensibilities in the sense of a wider religiosity or interaction with the umma. For them also, China is the new enemy of Central Asian societies, and its fight against Uyghur Islamism is one of the proofs. Central Asia is therefore bound to become part of a general movement which, in the decades to come, and depending on China's rise to power, will tend to see Islamic currents direct their criticisms at Beijing and not solely at the West.

Business people form what is probably the most complex group, prone to developing convitions that are both Sinophile and Sinophobe. All have gained from the boom in trade with China, but some fear Chinese competition. These feelings of competition are most developed in Kyrgyzstan where the bazaar economy has come to play a central role both in the country's functioning and in its instability; the business circles are at the very core of this process of state collapse and corruption, and thus comprise a politically and socially sensitive milieu which reacts fitfully to the Chinese presence. In Kazakhstan, the sense of competition with Chinese traders is less pronounced, because the latter have fewer rights to establish businesses, but also because they engage more in large-scale trade, which is better regulated, and because fewer Kazakhs work in the small retail trade. In Tajikistan the case is rather different: the high rates of emigration to Russia have enabled Chinese businessmen to invest in the market without provoking feelings of competition, at least for the moment. The local trade milieu here is less developed since the patterns of economic survival are tied to migrations. In neither Uzbekistan nor Turkmenistan do business circles come into direct contact with Chinese businessmen, although there appear to be tensions between Chinese and Uzbek traders at the Karasuu bazaar.

In the intellectual circles, the question of China does not give rise to as many debates as does the relationship to Russia, the West, or Turkey. China is not—yet—considered as bearing a choice of civilization—unless as a threat—which might carry Central Asia in a new direction. The admirers of the Chinese political system are extremely few in number, since the partisans of an authoritarian regime as the only solution to Islamism or to "democratic chaos" either endorse Russia or Belarus or advocate for a specific national model, but are not inspired by the Chinese-style single-party system, nor by the reference to Beijing's communism. Those who think themselves part of the "Soviet" or "Eurasianist" traditions are pleased about the Sino-Russian alliance against the West, but give their clear preference to the Russian model. Those with a Western, pan-Turkist or Islamic orientation view China negatively, believing that it hinders the evolution of their society in the desired direction. While there are pro-Western, nationalist, pan-Turkic or Russophile ideological traditions, nobody in Central Asia calls for a cultural choice in favor of China. Though Beijing may be thanked for its economic aid and anti-American geopolitical influence, when foregrounding questions of identity scarcely any experts can be classified as Sinophile.

It is almost impossible to draw up a precise map of public opinion in Central Asia. Even in Kazakhstan, Kyrgyzstan and Tajikistan, little information is available, while in Uzbekistan and Turkmenistan gauging trends in public opinion is virtually impossible. In contrast to Russia, which, for better or worse, is one of Central Asia's long-standing partners, and to the West, which is often mythologized, China still belongs to the domain of the unknown for Central Asian public opinion. The few available surveys reveal that the Soviet clichés have been replaced over the last two decades with criticisms of the poor quality of Chinese products and fears of the "Yellow Peril." However, local narratives also emphasize the incompetence of Central Asian workers in comparaison to their Chinese counterparts, who are admired for their reliability and great capacity for work.[6] A survey conducted in 2005 in Kazakhstan, Kyrgyzstan and Tajikistan revealed that Russia was still the country most trusted by 80 percent of those surveyed. The results for China reveal, by contrast, that it is trusted by 38 percent of those surveyed in Tajikistan, by 26 percent in Kyrgyzstan, and by only 19 percent in Kazakhstan—far behind Moscow but still well ahead of the United States. However, in terms of cultural affinities, Russia is squarely in front, while China only scores between 6 and 10 percent, lagging far behind Germany, Japan, and the United States. Finally, while in Tajikistan only 5 percent of people find China anxiety-provoking, this figure rises to 26 percent for Kyrgyzstan and 32 percent for Kazakhstan.[7]

Elena Sadovskaya carried out one of the only existing surveys on China in Kazakhstan. It demonstrates that awareness of China, its traditions and culture remains very weak. Public opinion actually displays much greater interest in the socio-demographic situation in China, and in questions of economic development and foreign policy, than in Chinese culture.[8] The survey also reveals significant anxiety about possible future tensions. Indeed, while the majority of respondents contend that immigration of Chinese citizens will increase in the coming years, almost 70 percent believe that this migration will have a negative impact, direct or indirect, on the domestic labor market. However, Sadovskaya's survey also shows that young people aged between 18 and 29 have the most tolerant attitudes toward China, and that the more familiar people are with the Chinese, the more highly they regard them.[9]

By contrast, public opinion in Tajikistan seems decidedly more Sinophile. More than three-quarters of people surveyed by the Sharq Analytical Center in 2008 have a positive view of China's presence in the country. They do not, however, necessarily consider it to be either a close ally of Dushanbe, or fated to overtake Russian and Iranian dominance, especially because, as Saodat Olimova remarks, Tajik public opinion is above all marked by its almost total ignorance of China, much more than by a consciously positive view of it.[10] The sparse information available in the whole region reveals some troubling tendencies. It seems that the more distant a country is from China, the more that country's vision of China is either very hazy (Uzbekistan and Turkmenistan) or positive (Tajikistan); at the same time, the two countries for which China has become an everyday reality, Kazakhstan and Kyrgyzstan, are those in which public opinion appears to be the most Sinophobe. The differences of opinion also vary depending on whether economic partnership is at issue, in which case China is often in second position behind Russia but ahead of the West, or cultural affinities are, in which case China is clearly behind the West.

Domestic order, strategic uncertainty, and the Chinese factor

What role does China play in the political and ideological orientation of the Central Asian regimes? The region's heads of state have often indicated that they consider China—but also Malaysia, Singapore, and sometimes South Korea—as possible models of development, but this has to be understood broadly as alluding to the combination of an authoritarian political regime with success in the transition to a globalized economy.[11] The democratic path in the Western sense has been devalorized, first because of the Gorbachev experience, identified as a failure, and also by independence, which saw the structuring of Islamist movements throughout the entire region, not to mention the civil war in Tajikistan, and Kyrgyzstan's decline into a failing state. China has undoubtedly contributed to reinforcing the authoritarian path of the Central Asian regimes: it supports them in the conflation made between political opposition and Islamism, has taken advantage, with them, of the discourse on the "War on Terror" to implement even more repressive policies, and does not hide its dissatisfaction at seeing the emergence of leaders with pro-democratic orientations, such as Roza Otunbayeva, who assumed the Kyrgyz presidency between April 2010 and December 2011.

However, the Central Asian elites are not "victims" of Moscow and Beijing, as if they were forced to be authoritarian and anti-Western. Although unambiguously closer to Putin's Russia than to the Chinese elites, they have had no need of any model per se to decide upon the trajectories of their regimes. They agreed to be slowly "socialized" by Beijing and even decided to borrow Chinese ideological narratives such as that of the "three evils". Their alliance with Beijing is above all an axis of convenience, a collective solidarity against regime change, but no political rapprochement whatsoever is envisaged: as Konstantin Syroezhkin has succinctly put it, the Sino-Central Asian alliance is "cold politically, and scorching economically."[12]

Central Asian anxieties about China are essentially tied to a feeling of uncertainty as to the future evolution of the country. This uncertainty expresses itself on many levels. On the political level, many in Central Asia are anxious about the rise of Chinese nationalism: in order to put a stop to increasing social tensions, the new ruling generations may well propose a distinctly nationalist program which would undermine the signed territorial treaties and the "good neighborhood" policy. Others picture a collapse of the single-party system and China's entry into a period of chaos. This would entail the loss of subsidies from Beijing, possible population movements across the borders, and the risk of unrest in Xinjiang. The Central Asians foresee themselves as losers as much from the regime's reinforcing of an official Han nationalism as well as from its collapse, especially as any population movement across Chinese borders would be proportionally immense for Central Asia.

The uncertainty is also strategic. Even if Sino-Central Asian military cooperation is limited for the moment and Russia still largely dominates, the situation is evolving: the Sino-Russian partnership in the military domain is being drastically curtailed and might be replaced, in the years to come, by their increasing competition on the world arms market. The modernization of the Chinese People's Liberation Army, investing in transformational offensive and defensive capabilities, will increase its ability to conduct missions in Xinjiang but also, at least potentially, outside of its borders.[13] Not only is the Chinese army rising in strength, further heightening the imbalance with the Central Asian armies, but the factors of destabilization have not reduced: the revival of the Uyghur question with the bomb attacks in 2008, the Urumqi riots in July 2009,[14] and the protests led by the Uyghur diaspora of Bishkek on this occasion,[15] are of major concern to the Central Asian elites, who would be unable to counter any punitive operations led by the Chinese army on their territory. In addition, the future of Kyrgyzstan and Tajikistan, and potentially also the Uzbek part of the Ferghana Valley, is uncertain, which heightens the feeling that China's currently non-interventionist stance could change if the Central Asian states fail to guarantee their own security. In 2009, provocative declarations by a senior Chinese military leader about the possibility of intervening in Central Asia in order to secure China's borders[16] were not officially commented on by the Central Asian capitals, but their conspicuous silence is revealing of local anxieties. These risks are taken very seriously by the Kazakh leading circles which are aware that, in case of destabilization of Kyrgyzstan or Tajikistan, an intervention by their own army, or by the CSTO forces, could be necessary to avoid the creation of a vacuum that Beijing might ask to fill.[17]

But do China's goals really extend beyond the preservation of the status quo in Central Asia and the conquest of new markets? Beijing has no interest in visibly ratcheting up its pressure on the Central Asian states, and prefers to defend the officially endorsed idea of a win-win partnership. The region has strategic value in Beijing's eyes due to its relationship with Xinjiang; any destabilization of the Central Asia-Afghanistan-Pakistan triangle could directly impact upon China's North West. But this issue aside, the Chinese authorities above all want to assure the status quo, which guarantees them allied regimes on their borders, a muzzled Uyghur diaspora, a total absence of support for Taiwan, and profitable investment and trade opportunities. The costs of dislodging Russian domination in Central Asia would be excessive in comparison to the modest advantages it would afford, and would compel Beijing unwillingly to become more involved in the domestic issues of Central Asian countries. The growing insecurity in the region, in particular in Kyrgyzstan and Tajikistan, confirms China in its view of Central Asia as a quagmire in which it is better to avoid establishing oneself too directly. Moreover, the Chinese authorities are aware of their limited ability to manage their own unstable national fringes and have no need to add external tensions to the domestic social problems that they already have to face.

Seen from the Chinese perspective, Central Asia's most plausible risk lies not in the reinforcement of Russian influence, in the ongoing American military presence, or even in India's possible rise to power, which remain remote and, despite everything, are minor elements of potential perturbation. Worse than having too much competition between the great powers in Central Asia would be their total lack of interest in it.[18] China has no interest in Moscow conceiving of Central Asia uniquely as a buffer zone, from which to keep at bay influences on its external borders without wanting to get involved in the domestic questions. Beijing's first objective is to avoid the dilemma of having to defend its domestic stability by intervening outside of its borders, and will do everything it can so that the question of intervention *manu militari* in Central Asia does not arise. To this end, the Chinese authorities are willing to accept influences that are contrary to their short-term interests, such as that of the United States, and even of India in the future. Thus, despite the power differential that plays in its favor, China has limited room for maneuver, as it seeks at all costs to avoid any unmanageable or unpredictable scenarios arising.

For the Central Asian states, too, the geopolitical choices are limited in what is a complex environment: so far Afghanistan is distinctly more a source of destabilization, in particular due to drug trafficking, than a dynamizing gateway to South Asia; the proximity of Iran, and therefore its potential, is thwarted by the international sanctions placed on the regime in Tehran; the European Union, Japan, and the United States are distant partners whose will and ability to really engage in the region in security terms can be doubted. As the "West" has caused much disillusionment in Central Asian societies in the 1990s and 2000s, the dominant mood is that a lack of credible alternatives has left the governments with no real choice other than to side with the two main continental neighbors, Moscow and Beijing.

But here again, the solutions are few. Strengthening of the Sino-Russian partnership in Central Asia, via the SCO or in a bilateral manner, would work to reduce further the foreign policy options of the Central Asian states, which are already struggling to make their differing viewpoints heard, and would heighten the sentiment that the Moscow-Beijing duo is more a form of control over them than a real partnership. A drastic change in the balance between Russia and China, over which the Central Asian elites would have no control, would be equally dangerous as it would force them to choose between Moscow and Beijing, a choice that no one in Central Asia hopes will be made, since it would provoke fierce tensions among the elites and create lines of division that undermine the current consensus. Any new actor that arrives to interfere in the Sino-Russian partnership is therefore welcome: the more players that are present on the Central Asian scene, the more the states can multiply flexible alliances, thus pursuing their historical balancing role between the great empires. China has nevertheless emerged as the measuring stick for the agency of other international actors in the region.

Self-representation, social changes, and the Chinese factor

The geopolitical future of the region is increasingly pointing to China: while it nonetheless remains the "south of Russia," Central Asia seems destined to become essentially the new "west of China." This situation concerns the Central Asian societies, which want at all costs to avoid a destiny that depends too much on the desiderata of a sole power. In addition, whereas Russia and the "West" are seen as societies shaped by immediate needs and desires, China is viewed as an atemporal state, able to project itself across a time span of several centuries; the underlying fear is, therefore, that it might one day try to recuperate what it considers to be its historical territories. The renegotiation of the SCO treaties in 2020, at a time when China will have become a superpower, at the expense of Russia, is thus seen as a sword of Damocles. Despite China's displays of engaging in multilateralism, being a globalized actor it has maximized its leverage: any deterioration of political or diplomatic relations would have an impact on the Chinese economic presence, and vice versa. China's soft hegemonism is therefore grounded on such a power asymmetry, so that although *soft*, it may have the same consequences as *hard* power: to oppose China head-on would almost assuredly kill off the independent states that were secured in 1991. However, the Chinese authorities prefer to play the card of soft power. Except for the questions tied to the Uyghur diaspora, they have no interest in forcefully coercing on the Central Asian states: the diplomatic instrument of the SCO, their "good neighborhood" policy, their massive investments in the main economic sectors, the trade boom, and their timid processes of intellectual and cultural cooptation, suffice to guarantee Chinese success, and reassure not only the Central Asian governments but also the Chinese authorities, who are mindful of the need to succeed in their peaceful rise.

For Beijing, the right balance of interests in Central Asia has probably been struck, but can it be maintained? While boasting about the "harmony" (*hexie*) promoted in its domestic and foreign policy, China risks one day having to face up to the contradictions that will emerge from the two opposite logics that it supports. With its massive economic aid, in particular in Kyrgyzstan and Tajikistan, it contributes significantly to defusing potential social and political conflicts, by offering employment and consumer opportunities to pauperized populations. In a similar vein to Russia as a destination country for migrants, which serves as a safety valve for the Central Asian societies and generates significant remittances, China is also transforming the social fabric, something that, for example, the United States or the EU is not doing. However, the political stability in Central Asia endorsed by Beijing as well as Moscow is a very short-term view: promoting the status quo that favors authoritarian regimes, even dictatorial ones, and corrupt presidents who have a predatory conception of their power will create a fertile hotbed for future destabilizations, on the model of the 2011 "Arab Spring," or indeed play into the hands of Islamist radicals. The region's insecurity will require tackling these questions, which China is eager to avoid in contrast to the European Union or the United States. China's impact on Central Asian societies is therefore contradictory, since it contributes to perpetuating political situations that have long-term destabilizing consequences while, at the same time, it establishes mechanisms of social development in a bid to promote the "harmonious" evolution of those societies.

Central Asians, for their part, keenly feel that they are stuck between a rock and a hard place, between escaping from Moscow's tutelage and being subsumed under a Chinese "protectorate": in Kazakhstan, where the international consortiums control two thirds of total hydrocarbon reserves, China's energy presence is overestimated. Many experts, often off the record, interpret Chinese purchases of hardly profitable deposits as a strategy for creating a complete network on Kazakh territory in order to legalize a Chinese right of inspection over Astana in case of political tensions. China is also perceived as a threat in ecological terms. Although studies on the impact of climate change on the fragile agricultural zones of Central Asia are alarmist and the local industries are all considered to be very polluting, Beijing is suspected of disregarding the issue, of not being prepared for the risks of climate refugees, of wanting to monopolize both the water of the Central Asian rivers and agricultural production. While industrial and consumer dependency on China can be accepted, dependency relating to food and health is seen as problematic, putting national sovereignty into question.

Central Asian societies are in large part exposed to the impact of globalization through China. Many of the criticisms directed against Beijing are not specific to Chinese influence but to the process of globalization as a whole. Indeed, Chinese trade domination is a worldwide phenomenon that is not limited to its immediate neighbors. Europe, and more so the United States, are also intrinsically connected to the "Made in China" phenomenon. However, the Central Asian societies, which have little available information about the rest of the world, have the impression that their situation is unique. Although the behavior of Chinese companies is symptomatic of contemporary global capital flows in general, Central Asia harbors more suspicion toward them than others. Similarly, China's role in the growing shadow economy can be explained by the Central Asian environment, not only by the practices of Chinese businessmen. In addition, Central Asia has no experience of free trade, and continues to be stamped by the principles of autarkic economic policies: better to produce at home than to buy from elsewhere. However, the local economies have no other wealth than their subsoil and their geography: the former implies creating mechanisms for the redistribution of the rent from extractive industries so that it benefits the mass of the population; the latter implies that the political and legislative environment is stabilized, open customs regimes created, controls over corruption established, improved transparency mechanisms implemented, and a service-centered economy promoted.

Central Asia's integration into a globalized world presumes the disappearance of a certain amount of local production—only products tied to agriculture remain a real question of national sovereignty—and the generating of ever greater commercial interactions. While the Central Asian elites, who are still trained in the Soviet mould, have been slow to wager on human capital and a service economy, the population, for its part, has been changing more rapidly. By creating new professional niches linked to the service economy, China has been dynamizing the Central Asian societies, and has the potential to provide for new modes of development. But does it have also the potential to become a cultural model?

The view that the Central Asian societies have of the world is in large part structured through fear of the loss of collective identity. The nation-states that came into being in 1991 are conceived as inviolable but ones whose futures are nonetheless fragile. For the population, if the future of states can be uncertain, that of ethnic groups must be preserved at all costs: while it is indeed possible to reacquire a state, the struggle for independence makes no sense if the "ethnic consciousness" has been lost. In this context, Beijing has to work hard to counter the apprehensions that it evokes in Central Asian societies, and therefore take this into account when making policy decisions. China has not yet managed to develop a cultural diplomacy, and currently lacks the symbolic means to compete with Moscow or the "West" for the conquest of Central Asian minds. Even if Russia is criticized for its barely disguised contempt for Central Asian societies, its past imperialist mentality, its historical inertia, and its inability to offer Central Asia a real long-term partnership,[19] it is acknowledged for having let the Central Asian peoples survive as national collectivities during the Tsarist colonization and the Soviet experiment, which gave rights to all Soviet peoples, forged national elites, and did not demographically drown the populations under its domination.

Beijing, by contrast, is suspected of aiming to destroy its national minorities by denying them cultural and linguistic rights, by preventing the structuring of national political and intellectual elites, and by demographically colonizing territories such as Xinjiang and Tibet to make any return to the past impossible. The most pragmatically-minded Central Asian experts argue therefore that a return of Russian domination would not have as negative an impact as Chinese domination: Moscow's control would be political, but not demographic or cultural, while Beijing imperils the very survival of the nation. Hence, when the debate is expressed in terms of "civilization," China continues to be perceived as the very embodiment of strangeness and foreignness, while Russia still belongs to the familiar and known world of Central Asia's everyday reality.

The relation to China, in its apparent contradiction—both Sinophobe and Sinophile—has to be deconstructed: it evolves according to the temporal scale one uses (rather positive in the short term, rather negative in the long term); it is relational (China relative to Russia is not China relative to the West, or China relative to Islamism); and it depends on the aim at issue, such as short-term political stability, the struggle against so-called non-traditional threats, long-term economic development, human security (food, environment, health, education), or survival of the nation as an imagined community. The

"Chinese question" therefore provides some catharsis for the Central Asians' collective and individual reflections about the changes that they have endured over the last two decades. In discovering neighboring China and interacting with it, the Central Asian societies have entered into the twenty-first century: like others all over the world, they have to manage the advantages and disadvantages afforded by the globalization of markets, to watch as sections of their economies collapse and others emerge, to undergo often painful transformations of the social fabric, to articulate their security and economic imperatives, to assess the long-term demographic and environmental stakes, and, last but not least, to project themselves as fully-fledged participants in global affairs, all the while preserving a collective identity founded on myth-making and everyday social intercourse.

NOTES

INTRODUCTION

1. The misconception of this notion has already been discussed in M. Laruelle, "Foreign Policy and Myth-Making: Great Game, Heartland, and Silk Roads," in M. Laruelle and S. Peyrouse (eds), *Mapping Central Asia: Indian Perceptions and Strategies* (Farnham: Ashgate, 2011), pp. 7–20.
2. R. Foot, "Chinese Strategies in a US-Hegemonic Global Order: Accommodating and Hedging," *International Affairs*, vol. 82, no. 1, 2006, pp. 77–94.
3. B. Gill, *Rising Star: China's New Security Diplomacy* (Washington, D.C.: Brookings Institution Press, 2007); Hongyi Lai, *The Domestic Sources of China's Foreign Policy: Regimes, Leadership, Priorities and Process* (London: Routledge, 2010); R. S. Ross and A. I. Johnston (eds), *New Directions in the Study of China's Foreign Policy* (Stanford: Stanford University Press, 2006).
4. For the Chinese point of view on Russia, see Iu. Galenovich, *Vzgliad na Rossii iz Kitaia. Proshloe i nastoiashchee Rossii i nashikh otnoshenii s Kitaem v traktovke kitaiskikh uchenykh* (Moscow: Vremia, 2010).
5. T. Kellner, "Le 'dragon' et la 'tulipe': les relations sino-afghanes dans la période post-11 septembre," *Asia Papers*, Brussels Institute of Contemporary China Studies, January 2009.
6. We shall not revisit either the positioning of India in Central Asia, already discussed in Laruelle and Peyrouse, *Mapping Central Asia: Indian Perceptions and Strategies*, or potential Indian-Chinese competition in the region, already studied in M. Laruelle, J.-F. Huchet, S. Peyrouse and B. Balci (eds), *China and India in Central Asia. A New "Great Game"?* (New York: Palgrave Macmillan, 2010).
7. See country information by the International Monetary Fund, http://www.imf.org/external/country/index.htm (January 12, 2011).
8. G. Kemp, *The East Moves West: India, China, and Asia's Growing Presence in the Middle East* (Washington, D.C.: Brookings Institution Press, 2010). See also A. Ter-Harutyunyan, "Turkey-China Interrelations," *Novarank.am*, November 29,

2010, http://www.noravank.am/eng/articles/detail.php?ELEMENT_ID=5165 (January 6, 2011); and Liu Jun, and Wu Lei, "Key Issues in China-Iran Relations," *Journal of Middle Eastern and Islamic Studies*, vol. 4, no. 1, 2010, pp. 40–57.

9. J. A. Millward, *Eurasian Crossroads: a History of Xinjiang* (New York: Columbia University Press, 2007). See also M. Dickens, *The Soviets in Xinjiang, 1911–1949*, http://www.oxuscom.com/sovinxj.htm (January 6, 2011).
10. On the migration flows between Xinjiang and Kazakhstan, see G. M. Mendikulova and B. Zh. Atanbaeva, *Istoriia migratsii mezhdu Kazakhstanom i Kitaem v 1860–1960-e gg.* (Almaty: Institut Vostokovedeniia, 2008).
11. On contemporary challenges in Xinjiang, see S. F. Starr (ed.), *Xinjiang: China's Muslim Borderland* (Armonk: M.E. Sharpe, 2004).
12. J. W. Garver, "Development of China's Overland Transportation Links with Central, South-West and South Asia," *The China Quarterly*, no. 185, 2006, pp. 1–22.
13. R. Ong, "China's Security Interests in Central Asia," *Central Asian Survey*, vol. 24, no. 4, 2005, pp. 425–39.
14. A. Goldstein, *Rising to the Challenge: China's Grand Strategy and International Security* (Stanford: Stanford University Press, 2005).
15. Statistics from the US-China Business Council, www.uschina.org (December 18, 2010).
16. C. Mackerras and M. Clarke (eds), *China, Xinjiang and Central Asia: History, transition and crossborder interaction into the 21st century* (New York: Routledge Contemporary China Series, 2009).
17. H. Zhao, "Central Asia in China's Diplomacy," in E. Rumer, D. Trenin, and H. Zhao, *Central Asia: Views from Washington, Moscow and Beijing* (New York: M.E. Sharpe, 2007), p. 137.
18. With some exceptions such as B. Gill and M. Oresman, *China's New Journey to the West: China's Emergence in Central Asia and Implications for US Interests* (Washington, D.C.: CSIS Press, 2003).
19. On this question see A. Khalid, *Islam after Communism: Religion and Politics in Central Asia* (Berkeley: University of California Press, 2007).
20. On migrations in Russia, see M. Laruelle (ed.), *Labor Migration and Social Upheaval as the Face of Globalization in Central Asia* (London: Brill, 2012).
21. M. Fumagalli, "The United States and Central Asia," in E. Kavalski (ed.), *The New Central Asia: The Regional Impact of International Actors* (New Jersey, London: World Scientific, 2010), pp. 177–90; M. Laruelle and S. Peyrouse, "The United States in Central Asia: Reassessing a Challenging Partnership," *Strategic Analysis*, vol. 35, no. 3, 2011, pp. 427–438.
22. The most detailed work on relations between Central Asia and China in the 1990s is T. Kellner, *L'Occident de la Chine: Pékin et la nouvelle Asie centrale (1991–2001)* (Paris: PUF, 2008).
23. To ease the reading of the text, we decided to use the adjectives Kazakh, Kyrgyz,

etc. rather than talking about Kazakhstani or Kyrgyzstani. The first term refers to the titular ethnic group, the second to civic belonging and therefore the state. Since this work is not devoted to issues of identity, we chose to use the former, while giving it a state-centric definition.

24. N. Swanström, "China and Central Asia: A New Great Game or Traditional Vassal Relations?," *Journal of Contemporary China*, vol. 14, no. 45, 2005, pp. 569–84.
25. M.T. Laumulin, "Na grani blefa i real'nosti," *Analytica*, June 13, 2006, http://www.analitika.org/article.php?story=20060613225246616 (January 4, 2012).
26. D. Zweig, "'Resource Diplomacy' Under Hegemony," Conference on "The Rise of China and Its Implications for Asia-Pacific," Academia Sinica, Taipei, August 25–26, 2006.
27. M.B. Olcott, "Is China a Reliable Stakeholder in Central Asia?," Testimony before the US-China Economic and Security Review Commission, August 4, 2006, http://www.carnegieendowment.org/publications/index.cfm?fa=view&id=18606&prog=zr (April 15, 2007).
28. On the regionalization issue, see Kavalski, *The New Central Asia: The Regional Impact of International Actors*.
29. A. Umarov, and D. Pashkhun, *Tensions in Sino-Central-Asian Relations and their Implications for Regional Security* (Swindon: Defence Academy of the United Kingdom, Conflict Studies Research Center, Central Asian Series, 06/02, 2006).
30. Russian remains the language of academic expression in the Central Asian states, in particular in contemporary disciplines related to international relations, political science, and sociology. Only studies of ancient history and literature are mainly offered in national languages.
31. We spent four months in Central Asia in 2008, one month in 2009 and two months in 2010; also four months in 2008 and two weeks in 2009, in China. In terms of published written sources from Central Asia, research has tried to be as comprehensive as possible. Interviews, open and unstructured, lasting on average between one and two hours, were conducted with some forty Central Asian academic experts and specialists on China. The largest number (about twenty) was in Kazakhstan, the others being divided almost equally between Kyrgyzstan, Tajikistan and Uzbekistan; in Turkmenistan, no researcher could be met. Some of the leading experts were interviewed on three occasions in 2008, 2009, and 2010. Fieldwork was also conducted at Chinese bazaars in Almaty, Bishkek, and Dushanbe, allowing for informal discussions with traders with links to China. More substantial ground was conducted with cross-border minorities, particularly Dungans. In China, we traveled in Xinjiang, Gansu, Shaanxi, Beijing, Shanghai, and Guangzhou, met with about twenty Chinese experts on Central Asia, visited the shopping places frequented by Central Asian traders, and organized interviews with Central Asian students in Chinese universities.

1. BORDERS AND DIASPORAS: SOLVING THE PROBLEMS ARISING FROM CENTRAL ASIAN INDEPENDENCE

1. B. N. Tsou, *China and International Law: The Boundary Disputes* (New York, London: Praeger, 1990).
2. G. Ginsburg and C. F. Pinkele, *The Sino-Soviet Territorial Dispute, 1949–64* (New York: Praeger, 1978); E. D. Stepanov, *Politika nachinaetsia s granitsy: Nekotorye voprosy pogranichnoi politiki KNR vtoroi poloviny XX v.* (Moscow: Institut Dal'nego Vostoka RAN, 2007).
3. Y.-H. Pi, "China's Boundary Issues with the former Soviet Union," *Issues and Studies*, vol. 28, no. 7, 1992, pp. 63–75.
4. More details in Kellner, *L'Occident de la Chine: Pékin et la nouvelle Asie centrale (1991–2001)*, op. cit., pp. 539–88.
5. N. Polat, *Boundary Issues in Central Asia* (Ardsley: Brill Transnational Publishers, 2002).
6. A. M. Aunasova and A.M. Suleimenov, "Iz istorii delimitatsii gosudarstvennykh granits Respubliki Kazakhstan," *EvraIuzh*, no. 4 (23), 2010, http://www.eurasialaw.ru/index.php?option=com_jcontentplus&view=article&id=652:2010-06-03-09-21-06&catid=99:2010-06-02-08-56-30&Itemid=196 (December 16, 2010); "Kazakhstan-Kitai," no date, http://karty.narod.ru/claim/kzcn/kzcn.html (December 16, 2010); V. Khliupin, *Geopoliticheskii treugol'nik. Kazakhstan-Kitai-Rossiia. Proshloe i nastoiashchee pogranichnoi problemy* (Moscow: Mezhdunarodnyi evraziiskii institut ekonomicheskikh i politicheskikh issledovanii, 1999), http://www.iicas.org/AIBOLIT/publ_VX_Tr.htm (March 23, 2008).
7. Z. A. Amanzholova, M. M. Atanov, and B. Sh. Turarbekov, *Pravda o gosudarstvennoi granitse respubliki Kazakhstan* (Almaty: Zhibek Zholy, 2006); K. L. Syroezhkin, *Kazakhstan-Kitai. Ot prigranichnoi torgovli k strategicheskomu partnerstvu* (Almaty: KISI, 2010), vol. 1, pp. 122–32.
8. C. Levinsson and I. Svanberg, "Kazakhstan-China Border Trade Thrives after Demarcation Treaty," *The Analyst*, February 16, 2000, pp. 63–75.
9. N. Kerimbekova and V. Galitskiy, "On the State Border between Kyrgyzstan and China," *Central Asia and the Caucasus*, no. 5, 2002, pp. 108–113.
10. More in S. K. Alamanov, *Kratkaia istoriia i opyt resheniia pogranichnykh problem Kyrgyzstana* (Bishkek: Friedrich Ebert Foundation, 2005).
11. E. Buldakova, "Conflicting Views on Land Issue between Kyrgyzstan and China," *CIMERA*, no. 24, May 2002, http://www.cimera.org/files/camel/en/24e/MICA24E-Buldakova2.pdf (January 4, 2012) (More details in chapter 6).
12. S. Smirnov, "Kitai otshchepil chast' Tadzhikistana," *Gazeta.ru*, January 12, 2011, http://www.gazeta.ru/politics/2011/01/12_kz_3489206.shtml (January 4, 2012).
13. J. A. Millward, *Eurasian Crossroads: a History of Xinjiang*, pp. 285–355.

14. "Xinjiang Oil Industry Development," Center for Energy and Global Development, http://www.wsichina.org/cs4_7.pdf (January 4, 2012). See also "China," *EIA Countries Analysis Briefs*, November 2010, http://www.eia.doe.gov/cabs/China/pdf.pdf (January 4, 2012).
15. G. Zholamanova, "Rol' ShOS v uregulirovanii transgranichnykh rek mezhdu Kazakhstanom i Kitaem," *Analytic*, no. 1, 2007, pp. 34–42, http://www.analitika.org/article.php?story=2007050701005068 (January 4, 2012).
16. B. Pannier and E. Magauin, "China discusses future of Irtysh River," *Asia Times*, June 5, 1999.
17. L. N. Kozlov and A. A. Beliakov, "Irtyshsko-obskaia glubokovodnaia magistral' ot Kitaia do severnogo morskogo puti v sostave transportno-energicheskoi vodnoi sistemy Evrazii," *Evraziiskaia ekonomicheskaia integratsiia*, no. 3 (4), 2009, pp. 132–43.
18. More in S. Peyrouse, "Flowing Downstream: The Sino-Kazakh Water Dispute," *China Brief*, vol. 7, no. 10, May 16, 2007, pp. 7–10, http://www.jamestown.org/single/?no_cache=1&tx_ttnews%5Btt_news%5D=4131 (January 4, 2012).
19. B. Temirbolat, "Mezhdu Kazakhstanom i Kitaem mozhet nachat'sia konflikt iz-za vody," *Saiasat*, no. 8, 2000, pp. 97–8.
20. S. Schafarenko, "Black Irtysh River endangered by Irrigation Channel," *European Rivers Network*, November 1999, http://www.rivernet.org/ob/irtysh.htm (April 20, 2012).
21. The Balkhash Lake has the peculiarity of being divided into two parts, the western part being made up of fresh water, the eastern part of salt water.
22. *Water Resources of Kazakhstan in the New Millennium* (Almaty: UNDP, 2004), p. 41.
23. E. W. Sievers, "Transboundary Jurisdiction and Watercourse Law: China, Kazakhstan, and the Irtysh," *Texas International Law Journal*, vol. 37, Winter 2002, p. 7.
24. "Murat Auezov rassuzhdaet ob ekologicheskikh problemakh, i ne tol'ko o nikh," *Megalopolis*, no. 3, November 22, 2000.
25. A. Mukhamberdiiarova, "Kazakhstan-Kitai: reshenie vodnoi problemy opiat' otkladyvaetsia," Institut Voiny i Mira, April 10, 2001, no longer available online.
26. A. D. Riabtsev, "Sushchestvuiushchii opyt vodnymi resursami na transgranichnykh rekakh," *Central Asian Water*, April 2006, http://www.cawater-info.net/library/rus/ryabtsev_rus.pdf (January 4, 2012).
27. "Conflict of interests has created water crisis," Eurodialogue, April 13, 2011, http://eurodialogue.org/Conflict-of-interests-has-created-water-crisis (January 4, 2012).
28. A. D. Riabtsev, *Ugrozy vodnoi bezopasnosti v Respublike Kazakhstan v transgranichnom kontekste i vozmozhnye puti ikh ustraneniia*, Interstate Commission for Water Coordination of Central Asia, 2008, http://www.icwc-aral.uz/workshop_march08/pdf/ryabtsev_ru.pdf (January 4, 2012).
29. D. Gladney, *Dislocating China: Reflections on Muslims, Minorities, and Other Subaltern Subjects* (Chicago: University of Chicago Press, 2004).

30. M. Clarke, "Xinjiang and China's Relations with Central Asia, 1991–2001: Across the 'Domestic–Foreign Frontier'?," *Asian Ethnicity*, vol. 4, no. 2, 2003, pp. 207–224.
31. D. Gladney, "Central Asia and China: Transnationalization, Islamization, and Ethnicization," in J. L. Esposito (ed.), *The Oxford History of Islam* (Oxford and New York: Oxford University Press, 2009), pp. 432–73; R. Castets, "Uyghur Islam: Caught between Foreign Influences and Domestic Constraints," in Laruelle, Huchet, Peyrouse, and Balci, *China and India in Central Asia: A New "Great Game?,"* op. cit., pp. 215–34.
32. Figures provided by Guzel Maitdinova, representative of the Uyghur community of Tajikistan, Dushanbe, March 27, 2008.
33. A. Kamalov, "Uighur Community in 1990s Central Asia: A Decade of Change," in T. Atabaki and S. Mehendale (eds), *Central Asia and the Caucasus: Transnationalism and Diaspora* (London: Routledge, 2005), pp. 148–68.
34. "Itogi perepisi naseleniia Respubliki Kazakhstan na 2009 g.," *Agentstvo Respubliki Kazakhstan po statistike*, February 4, 2010, http://www.stat.kz/news/Pages/pr_04_02_10.aspx (January 4, 2012).
35. W. Clarck and A. Kamalov, "Uighur Migration across Central Asian Frontiers," *Central Asian Survey*, vol. 23, no. 2, 2004, pp. 167–82.
36. For more details see A. Khamraeva-Aubert, "Migration, colonisation et formation d'une identité nationale chez les Ouïgours d'Asie centrale" (Masters Thesis, Paris: EHESS, 2005).
37. S. R. Roberts, "The Uighurs of the Kazakhstan Borderlands: Migration and the Nation," *Nationalities Papers*, vol. 26, no. 3, 1998, pp. 511–13.
38. Interview with Hamid Khamraev, member of the Association of Uyghur writers of Kazakhstan, Almaty, March 15, 2008.
39. See K. L. Syroezhkin, *Mify i real'nost' etnicheskogo separatizma v Kitae i bezopasnost' Tsentral'noi Azii* (Almaty: Daik-Press, 2003).
40. Anonymous interviews with members of the Uyghur community, Almaty, February-March 2008.
41. R. Castets, "Opposition politique, nationalisme et islam chez les Ouïghours du Xinjiang," *Les Etudes du CERI*, no. 110, 2004, p. 45.
42. Ibid.
43. Interview carried out at the Institute of Uyghur Studies (Institute of Oriental Studies, Academy of Sciences, Almaty), March 2008.
44. B. Bekturganova, *"Uigurskii ekstremizm" v Tsentral'noi Azii: mif ili real'nost'? (sotsiologicheskii analiz problem)* (Almaty: Kompleks, 2002).
45. N. Oka, "Transnationalism as a Threat to State Security? Case Studies on Uighurs and Uzbeks in Kazakhstan," in T. Uyama (ed.), *Empire, Islam, and Politics in Central Eurasia* (Sapporo: Slavic Research Center, Hokkaido University, 2007), pp. 351–68.

46. N. Maxwell, "How the Sino-Russian Boundary Conflict was Finally Settled: From Nerchinsk 1689 to Vladivostok 2005 via Zhenbao Island 1969," in A. Iwashita (ed.), *Eager Eyes Fixed on Eurasia* (Hokkaido: Slavic Research Center, Hokkaido University, 2007), pp. 47–73.
47. This, for example, was the case in January 2007 after the Chinese security forces attacked a would-be training camp of the East Turkestan Islamic Movement in the Tashkurgan region, situated about 25 kilometers from the Tajik-Chinese border; some 18 persons were killed and 17 others arrested. See "Kyrgyz Border Guards say China Tightening Security," *RFE/RL*, January 11, 2007, http://www.rferl.org/content/article/1073932.html (January 4, 2012).
48. Since independence, the Central Asian authorities have upheld the Chinese conception of "One China" and not established diplomatic relations with Taiwan. During the 1990s, however, Nursultan Nazarbayev met on several occasions with a Taiwanese teacher based at the Al-Farabi National University in Almaty. He served as a mediator for the first meetings between Kazakh and Taiwanese businessmen. Today, the few existing trade relations between Taiwan and the Central Asian states are discreetly approved beforehand by Beijing. Interviews with Jen-Kun Fu, Ching Yun University, Taiwan, October 25, 2008.

2. THE SHANGHAI COOPERATION ORGANIZATION: SUCCESSES AND CHALLENGES

1. S. Hanova, "Perspectives on the SCO: Images and Discourses," *The China and Eurasia Forum Quarterly*, vol. 7, no. 2, 2009, pp. 63–82.
2. B. F. Gonzalez, "Charting a New Silk Road? The Shanghai Cooperation Organization and Russian Foreign Policy" (Masters Thesis, University of Oregon, 2001).
3. More details in M. de Haas (ed.), *The Shanghai Cooperation Organisation: Towards a Full-Grown Security Alliance?* (Clingendael: Netherlands Institute of International Relations, 2007).
4. R. N. McDermott, "The Rising Dragon: SCO Peace Mission 2007," *Jamestown Occasional Paper*, October 2007.
5. Information provided by an observer of the Peace Mission 2010, Adil Kaukenov, former Director of the Center for Studies of Contemporary China at the Institute of Global Economics and Politics in Almaty, and today Editor-in-Chief of an analysis web portal, *Today.kz*, Almaty, September 28, 2010.
6. For more details, see S. Peyrouse, "Sino-Kazakh Relations: A Nascent Strategic Partnership," *China Brief*, November 7, 2008, http://www.jamestown.org/single/?no_cache=1&tx_ttnews%5Btt_news%5D=34142 (January 4, 2012).
7. More in de Haas, *The Shanghai Cooperation Organisation: Towards a Full-Grown Security Alliance?*, op. cit.
8. Interview with Irina Chernykh, and Rustam Burnashev, experts from the Institute for Policy Solutions, Almaty, September 27, 2010.

9. A. Cooley, *Great Games, Local Rules: The New Great Power Contest for Central Asia* (Oxford: Oxford University Press, 2012).
10. Anonymous interviews with several Central Asian experts with access to the ruling circles.
11. H. Zhao, *Kitai, Tsentral'naia Aziia i Shankhaiskaia Organizatsiia Sotrudnichestva* (Moscow: Carnegie Endowment for International Peace, 2005).
12. V. Shlapentokh, "China in the Russian Mind Today: Ambivalence and Defeatism," *Europe-Asia Studies*, vol. 59, no. 1, 2007, pp. 1–22.
13. E. Wishnik, *Russia, China, and the United States in Central Asia: Prospects for Great Power Competition and Cooperation in the Shadow of the Georgian Crisis* (Carlisle: US Army War College, 2009).
14. A. Tarzi, "Afghan Leader Talks About China Ties," *RFE/RL*, June 14, 2006, http://www.russian-news.com/msg04848.html (January 4, 2012).
15. "Moscow Special Conference on Afghanistan," permanent mission of Afghanistan in the United Nations, March 30, 2009, http://www.afghanistan-un.org/2009/03/moscow-special-conference-on-afghanistan/ (January 4, 2012).
16. M. Singh Roy, "Shanghai Cooperation Organisation and Afghanistan: Scope and Limitation," *Strategic Analysis*, vol. 34, no. 4, 2010, pp. 545–61.
17. M. Laruelle, "Beyond the Afghan Trauma: Russia's Return to Afghanistan," *Jamestown Occasional Paper*, August 2009.
18. K. Katzman, "Afghanistan: Post-Taliban Governance, Security, and US Policy," Congressional Research Service, April 20, 2010; A. Kuhn, "China becomes a Player in Afghanistan's Future," NPR, October 21, 2009, http://www.npr.org/templates/story/story.php?storyid=113967842 (January 4, 2012).
19. N. Bordiuzha, "ODKB gotova k sotrudnichestvu s Afganistanom," *Afghanistan.ru*, November 19, 2008, http://www.afghanistan.ru/doc/13412.html (January 4, 2012).
20. A. Kuchins, T. Sanderson, and D. Gordon, *The Northern Distribution Network and the Modern Silk Road* (Washington, D.C.: CSIS, December 2009).
21. O. G. Mirutina, "Perspektivy razvitiia sotrudnichestva Kitaia i Kazakhstana i ego znachenie dlia Rossii" (Masters Thesis, Omsk University, 2003).
22. Peyrouse, "Sino-Kazakh Relations: A Nascent Strategic Partnership," art. cit.
23. R. N. McDermott, "Kazakhstan's Emerging Security Ties with China," *Central Asia and Caucasus Analyst*, May 9, 2007, http://www.cacianalyst.org/?q=node/4684 (January 4, 2012).
24. A. Paramonov and O. Stolpovskii, *Kitai i Tsentral'naia Aziia: sotrudnichestvo v sfere bezopasnosti, CEASIA*, July 31, 2007, http://www.ceasia.ru/bezopasnost/kitay-i-tsentralnaya-aziya-sotrudnichestvo-v-sfere-bezopasnosti.html (January 4, 2012); see also *French Embassy in Turkmenistan News Digest*, January 22, 2009.
25. R. N. McDermott, "China Quietly Increases Military Links with Tajikistan," *Eurasia Daily Monitor*, vol. 2, no. 176, September 21, 2005, http://www.jamestown.org/single/?no_cache=1&tx_ttnews%5Btt_news%5D=30885 (January 4, 2012).

26. "Kitai i Tadzhikistan rasshiriat voennoe sotrudnichestvo," *Ni-hao.ru*, May 15, 2008, http://www.ni-hao.ru/news/china/1916 (January 4, 2012).
27. "Kitai okazal Kyrgyzstanu voenno-tekhnicheskuiu pomoshch' v razmere 4 mln iuanei," *Novosti Kyrgyzstana*, August 13, 2008, http://www.for.kg/ru/news/69727/ (January 4, 2012); and Paramonov, and Stolpovskii, *Kitai i Tsentral'naia Aziia: sotrudnichestvo v sfere bezopasnosti.*
28. "Voennoe sotrudnichestvo Uzbekistana i Kitaia," *China Embassy in Uzbekistan*, (no date), http://chinaembassy.uz/rus/dtxw/voennoe-sotrudnichestvo-uzbekistana-i-kitaya.htm (January 4, 2012).
29. "Kitai i Kazakhstan dostigli vysokogo urovnia vzaimoponimaniia—ministr oborony Kazakhstana," *Trends Kazakhstan*, December 25, 2009, http://ru.trend.az/news/politics/foreign/1607560.html (January 4, 2012); "Podgotovka kazakhstanskikh voennosluzhashchikh v voenno-uchebnykh zavedeniiakh Kitaia," *Atyrau*, January 26, 2009, http://atyrauobl.kz/podgotovka-kazaxstanskix-voennosluzhashhix-v-voenno-uchebnyx-zavedeniyax-kitaya/5950 (January 4, 2012).
30. H. Zhao, "The Shanghai Cooperation Organization at 5: Achievements and Challenges Ahead," *The China and Eurasia Forum Quarterly*, vol. 4, no. 3, 2006, pp. 105–123.
31. "Nazarbayev calls on countries to adopt universal declaration on nuclear-free world," *Interfax*, August 26, 2010, http://www.interfax.com/newsinf.asp?id=185218 (January 4, 2012); "Kazakhstan calls on OSCE states to adopt declaration on nuclear-free world," *RIA Novosti*, December 1, 2010, en.rian.ru/world/20101201/161573340.html (January 4, 2012).
32. V. Paramonov and A. Strokov, *Ekonomicheskoe prisutstvie Rossii i Kitaia v Tsentral'noi Azii* (Swindon: Defence Academy of the United Kingdom, Conflict Studies Research Center, Central Asian Series, 07/12, 2007).
33. On developments in Uzbek foreign policy in 2007–2008, see J. Nichol, "Uzbekistan: Recent Developments and US Interests," *Congressional Research Service*, August 27, 2008.
34. M. Laumulin, *The Shanghai Cooperation Organization as Geopolitical Bluff? A View from Astana* (Paris: IFRI, Series *Russie. NEI. Vision* no. 36, 2006).
35. S. Peyrouse, "Russia-Central Asia: Advances and Shortcomings of the Military Partnership," in S. Blank (ed.), *Central Asian Security Trends: Views from Europe and Russia* (Carlisle: Strategic Studies Institute, US Army War College, 2011), pp. 1–34.
36. R. N. McDermott, "United States and NATO Military Cooperation with Kazakhstan: The Need for a New Approach," *Journal of Slavic Military Studies*, vol. 21, no. 4, 2008, pp. 615–41.
37. On this point, see E. Madiev, "Perspektivy internatsionalizatsii kitaiskogo iuania v ramkakh ShOS," *Kazakhstan v global'nykh protsessakh*, no. 2, 2010, pp. 124–129.

38. G. Gleason, "The Uzbek Expulsion of US Forces and Realignment in Central Asia," *Problems of Post-Communism*, vol. 53, no. 2, 2006, p. 49–60.
39. In a cable released by Wikileaks, the United States is allegedly able to prove that China offered the Kyrgyz authorities US$3 billion to close down the US base at Manas. See D. Trilling, "China Gives US Base Advice," *Eurasianet*, November 29, 2010, http://www.eurasianet.org/node/62454 (January 4, 2012).
40. T. Ambrosio, "Catching the Shanghai Spirit: How the Shanghai Cooperation Organization Promotes Authoritarian Norms in Central Asia," *Europe-Asia Studies*, vol. 60, no. 8, 2008, pp. 1321–44.
41. S. Peyrouse, "Le tournant ouzbek de 2005. Éléments d'interprétation de l'insurrection d'Andijan," *La Revue Internationale et Stratégique*, no. 64, 2006, pp. 78–87; N. Megoran, "Framing Andijon, Narrating the Nation: Islam Karimov's Account of the Events of 13 May 2005," *Central Asian Survey*, vol. 27, no. 1, 2008, pp. 15–31.
42. M. Katz, "Russia and the Shanghai Cooperation Organization: Moscow's Lonely Road from Bishkek to Dushanbe," *Asian Perspective*, vol. 32, no. 3, 2008, pp. 183–7; S. Peyrouse, "Facing the Challenge of Separatism: The EU, Central Asia and the Uyghur Issue," *EUCAM Policy Brief*, no. 4, January 2009, http://www.eucentralasia.eu/fileadmin/user_upload/PDF/Policy_Briefs/Policy-Brief-4.Peyrouse.pdf (January 4, 2012).
43. A. Iwashita, "The Shanghai Cooperation Organization and its Implications for Eurasian Security: A New Dimension of 'Partnership' after the Post-Cold War Period," *Slavic Eurasia's Integration into the World Economy and Community* (Hokkaido: Slavic Research Center, Hokkaido University, 2004), pp. 259–81.
44. K. L. Syroezhkin, *Problemy sovremennogo Kitaia i bezopasnost' v Tsentral'noi Azii* (Almaty: KISI, 2006).
45. A. J. K. Bailes, P. Dunay, P. Guang, and M. Troitskiy, "The Shanghai Cooperation Organization," *SIPRI Policy Paper*, no. 17, May 2007.
46. See the Declaration of the Tenth Meeting of the Council of the Heads of the Member States of the Shanghai Cooperation Organization, June 11, 2010, http://www.sectsco.org/EN/show.asp?id=225 (January 4, 2012).
47. See their respective viewpoints in R. Zeb, "Pakistan and the Shanghai Cooperation Organization," *The China and Eurasia Forum Quarterly*, vol. 4, no. 4, 2006, pp. 51–60; "India keen to become member of SCO," *The Times of India*, June 1, 2010, http://timesofindia.indiatimes.com/india/India-keen-to-become-member-of-SCO/articleshow/5995619.cms (January 4, 2012).
48. See the Iranian viewpoint in A.U. Noi, "Iran and the Shanghai Cooperation Organization: Is it Possible for Iran to Become Full Member of the SCO under Pressure of Nuclear Issue?," *Perceptions*, Autumn-Winter 2006, pp. 79–104.
49. A. A. Pikayev, "Enlarging the Shanghai Cooperation Organization. Is Iran a Viable Member?" *PONARS Eurasia Policy Memo*, no. 15, August 2008.

50. Interviews conducted at the main Chinese think tanks and research centers working on the former Soviet Union in Shanghai, Beijing, Lanzhou and Xi'an, September-December 2008.
51. V. Paramonov and A. Strokov, *Russian-Chinese Relations: Past, Present, Future* (Swindon: Defence Academy of the United Kingdom, Russian Series, September 2006); B. Lo, "China and Russia. Common Interests, Contrasting Perceptions," *CLSA Asian Geopolitics* (London: Chatham House, May 2006).
52. B. Lo, "China and Russia: Common Interests, Contrasting Perceptions," art. cit., p. 4.
53. M. Laruelle, "Russia Facing China and India in Central Asia: Cooperation, Competition, and Hesitations," in Laruelle, Huchet, Peyrouse, and Balci (eds), *China and India in Central Asia: A New "Great Game?,"* op. cit., pp. 9–24.
54. B. Lo, *Axis of Convenience: Moscow, Beijing, and the New Geopolitics* (Washington, D.C., London: Brookings Institution Press and Chatham House, 2008).
55. A. Frost, "The Collective Security Treaty Organization, the Shanghai Cooperation Organization, and Russia's Strategic Goals in Central Asia," *The China and Eurasia Forum Quarterly*, vol. 7, no. 3, 2009, pp. 83–102.
56. A. Cooley, "The Stagnation of the SCO: Competing Agendas and Divergent Interests in Central Asia," *PONARS Eurasia Policy Memo*, no. 85, September 2009.
57. Also called the three extremisms (*sange jiduanzhuyi)*. This ideological drive is sometimes called the "Shanghai spirit." See, for example, M. Oresman, "Catching the Shanghai Spirit," *Journal of Social Sciences* (Shanghai), no. 12, December 2003, republished on http://www.foreignpolicy.com/articles/2004/05/01/catching_the_shanghai_spirit (January 4, 2012).

3. CHINESE ECONOMIC INROADS IN LANDLOCKED CENTRAL ASIA

1. V. Krivonogov, "Kazakhstansko-kitaiskie torgovo-ekonomicheskie i nauchnye-tekhnicheskie otnosheniia," *Kazakhstan i sovremennyi mir*, no. 1, 2003, pp. 24–41.
2. The Kyrgyz populations in the Murghab region confirm that they traded with the Kyrgyz in the PRC and in Afghanistan during the Soviet era and have episodically organized barter trade through family networks. Field research undertaken by the authors in June 2004, Karakul, Pamir.
3. E. Sadovskaia, "Kitaiskaia migratsiia v Kazakhstane: sovremennye tendentsii i perspektivy," *Analytic*, no. 6, 2007, pp. 33–44.
4. Paramonov and Strokov, *Ekonomicheskoe prisutstvie Rossii i Kitaia v Tsentral'noi Azii*, op. cit., p. 2.
5. Ibid.
6. G. Raballand and A. Andrésy, "Why should Trade between Central Asia and China Continue to Expand?" *Asia Europe Journal*, vol. 5, no. 2, 2007, pp. 235–52.
7. G. Raballand and B. Kaminski, "La Déferlante économique chinoise et ses conséquences en Asie centrale," *Monde Chinois*, no. 11, 2007, pp. 129–34.

8. See the European Union's statistics, October 2009, http://ec.europa.eu/trade/trade-statistics/ (January 4, 2012).
9. The 2011 European Commission's statistics, http://ec.europa.eu/trade/creating-opportunities/bilateral-relations/countries-and-regions/ (October 22, 2011). For 2010 the euro-dollar official exchange rate is 0.785.
10. H. Hu, "Dal'neishee usilenie ekonomicheskogo sotrudnichestva mezhdu SUAR KNR i Kazakhstanom v ramkakh ShOS," in *Problemy ekonomicheskogo i finansovogo sotrudnichestva v ramkakh ShOS* (Almaty: KISI, 2006), pp. 146–52.
11. K. L. Syroezhkin, "Bol'shaia igra v tsentral'no-aziatskom regione," *Ekonomicheskie strategii—Tsentral'naia Aziia*, no. 5, 2007, pp. 48–55.
12. S. Rakhimbaev, "Kazakhstan—Kitai. Pliusy i minusy vzaimodeistviia," *Smi.ru*, April 10, 2010, http://smi.kg/kazahstan/4389–2010–04–10–07–17–35 (May 2, 2010).
13. See European statistics, October 2011, http://ec.europa.eu/trade/creating-opportunities/bilateral-relations/statistics/ (January 4, 2012).
14. Syroezhkin, *Problemy sovremennogo Kitaia i bezopasnost' v Tsentral'noi Azii*, op. cit., p. 129.
15. "Sdacha v ekspluatatsiiu kitaisko-kazakhstanskogo mezhdunarodnogo tsentra prigranichnogo sotrudnichestva," *China-Hong Kong Business.ru*, August 5, 2008, http://www.china-hongkong-business.ru/index.php?option=com_content&task=view&id=4142&Itemid=2 (January 27, 2009).
16. In 2008, Xinjiang's volume of foreign trade reached US$22.217 billion, ranking twelfth in China. See "White Paper on Development and Progress in Xinjiang," *China Daily*, September 21, 2009, http://www.chinadaily.com.cn/ethnic/2009–09/21/content_8717461_3.htm (January 4, 2012).
17. Sh. Nadyrov, "Sin'tszian-uigurskii avtonomnyi raion v dinamike ekonomicheskikh i politicheskikh otnoshenii RK i KNR," *Kazakhstan-Spektr*, no. 1, 2006, pp. 14–25.
18. G. Raballand and B. Kaminski, "Entrepôt for Chinese Consumer Goods in Central Asia: The Puzzle of Re-exports through Kyrgyz Bazaars," *Eurasian Geography and Economics*, vol. 50, no. 5, 2009, pp. 581–90.
19. Interviews with experts in Chinese business, Bishkek, February 2008, Almaty, September 2010.
20. A. Beshimov, O. Abdykaimov, B. Radzhapov, and N. Tashbekov, *Prigranichnaia torgovlia. Otsenka perecheniia granits mezhdu Kyrgyzstanom i Uzbekistanom* (Bishkek: OSCE-Central Asian Free Market Institute, 2011).
21. "V 2010 g. vneshnii dolg Tadzhikistana sostavil dva milliarda dollarov," *Vesti.kz*, January 24, 2011, http://vesti.kz/asia/75511/ (January 4, 2012).
22. See S. Peyrouse, *Turkmenistan: Strategies of Power, Dilemmas of Development* (Armonk: M.E. Sharpe, 2011).
23. 2011 European Commission's statistics, http://ec.europa.eu/trade/trade-statistics/ http://ec.europa.eu/trade/creating-opportunities/bilateral-relations/countries-and-regions/ (October 22, 2011).

24. V. Shevchenko, "Sindrom Khorgosa?," *Kazakhstanskaia pravda*, May 27, 2005, http://www.nomad.su/?a=13-200605290119 (January 4, 2012).
25. R. Orange, "Kazakhstan: Russia Pressing for Clean-up at China Border Crossing," *Eurasianet*, May 5, 2011, http://www.eurasianet.org/node/63427 (January 4, 2012).
26. "MinProm o razvitii ekonomicheskikh otnoshenii mezhdu Kyrgyzstanom i Kitaem," *AKI-Press*, June 23, 2006, http://www.akipress.org/news/29316 (January 4, 2012).
27. Only Turkmenistan has yet to make an application. Kyrgyzstan entered the WTO in 1998.
28. Raballand and Andrésy, "Why should Trade between Central Asia and China Continue to Expand?," art. cit., p. 237.
29. R. Pomfret, "Turkmenistan's Foreign Policy," *The China and Eurasia Forum Quarterly*, vol. 6, no. 4, 2008, p. 29.
30. "China loans 10 bln dlrs to Kazakhstan," *Energy Daily*, April 17, 2009, http://www.energy-daily.com/reports/China_loans_10_bln_dlrs_to_Kazakhstan_state_media_999.html (January 4, 2012).
31. N. Kassenova, *Aide au développement: la percée chinoise au Tadjikistan et au Kirghizstan* (Paris: IFRI, Series *Russie. NEI. Vision*, no. 36, 2009), p. 10.
32. Ibid., p. 11.
33. For a breakdown by product, see H.-L. Wu and C.-H. Chen, "The Prospects for Regional Economic Integration between China and the Five Central Asian Countries," *Europe-Asia Studies*, vol. 56, no. 7, 2004, pp. 1069–70.
34. Paramonov and Strokov, *Economic Involvement of Russia and China in Central Asia*, p. 6.
35. More in Wu and Chen, "The Prospects for Regional Economic Integration between China and the Five Central Asian Countries," art. cit., pp. 1059–80.
36. M. Myant and J. Drahokoupil, "International Integration and the Structure of Exports in Central Asian Republics," *Eurasian Geography and Economics*, vol. 49, no. 5, 2009, pp. 604–22.
37. Interview with Sukhrob Sharipov, Center for Strategic Studies, Dushanbe, March 26, 2008.
38. Authors' interview at the main Chinese bazaars in Khujand and Istaravshan, June 2010.
39. On bazaar politics in Kazakhstan see R. Spector, "Bazaar Politics. The Fate of Market places in Kazakhstan," *Problems of Post-Communism*, vol. 55, no. 6, 2008, pp. 42–53.
40. Interview with Adil Kaukenov, Almaty, September 28, 2010.
41. More in S. Peyrouse, "The Growing Trade Stakes Of The Chinese-Kyrgyz-Uzbek Railway Project," *Central Asia-Caucasus Analyst*, March 11, 2009, http://www.cacianalyst.org/?q=node/5058 (January 4, 2012).

42. Authors's interviews with Kazakh experts on transport, Almaty, September 2010.
43. More in S. Peyrouse, "The New 'Aerial Silk Road' Between Central Asia and China," *Central Asia-Caucasus Analyst*, October 1, 2008, http://www.cacianalyst.org/?q=node/4948 (January 4, 2012).
44. More in PRC State Council, *White Paper on Development and Progress in Xinjiang* (Beijing: Beijing Language Press, 2009). See also K. Warikoo, "The Xinjiang Issue: Indian Perspectives on Chinese Strategies in the Far West," in Laruelle and Peyrouse, *Mapping Central Asia: Indian Perceptions and Strategies*, op. cit., pp. 217–40.
45. S. Peyrouse, "The New 'Aerial Silk Road' Between Central Asia and China," art. cit.
46. More in S. Peyrouse, "The Economic Aspects of the Chinese-Central-Asia Rapprochement," *Silk Road Papers*, September 2007, http://www.isdp.eu/images/stories/isdp-main-pdf/2007_peyrouse_economic-aspects-of-the-chinese-central-asia-rapprochement.pdf (January 23, 2011). See also *Free Trade Zone and Port Hinterland Development* (New York: ESCAP, 2005).
47. Fieldwork observations and interviews, Kashgar, September 2008.
48. Fieldwork observations and interviews, Urumqi, September 2008.
49. *Precursor Control on Central Asia's Border with China* (United Nations, Office on Drugs and Crime, Regional Office for Central Asia, no date), p. 9.
50. S. Bel'gibaev, "Otkrytie zonovoi dyry: SEZ na granitse s Kitaem mogut stat' 'vostochnymi vorotami' dlia deshevoi rabochei sily," *Gazeta.kz*, no. 42, March 14, 2006.
51. N. Swanström, N. Norling, and Zhang Li, "China," in S.F. Starr (ed.) *The New Silk Roads. Transport and Trade in Greater Central Asia* (Washington, D.C.: The Central Asia-Caucasus Institute, 2007), p. 406.
52. "Prem'er Kazakhstana odobril programmu razvitiia pogranichnogo perekhoda Dostyk na granitse s Kitaem i zheleznodorozhnogo uchastka Aktogai-Dostyk na 2006–20011 g.," *ITLS web site*, April 18, 2004, http://www.itls.kz/index.php?p=news_more&id=11 (January 4, 2012).
53. "Gruzoperevozki cherez stantsiiu Dostyk na granitse Kazakhstana s KNR v 2009 g. vyrosli na 18,7%," *RZD Partners.ru*, February 03, 2010, http://www.rzd-partner.ru/news/2010/02/03/350404.html (January 4, 2012).
54. More in E. Vinokurov and M. Emerson, "Optimisation of Central Asian and Eurasian Trans-Continental Land Transport Corridors," *EUCAM Working Paper*, no. 7, December 2009.
55. "Kazakhstan drives two new transit routes from China to Europe," International Information Center of the Republic of Kazakhstan, December 5, 2007, http://www.kazakhstanlive.com/2.aspx?ProdID=623d97b1-e4a1–4493–9425–613d36f1dcbc&CatID=9f9f8034–6dd6–4f7e-adcf-0f6a7c0406d9&sr=100&page=2 (January 4, 2012). See the Trans-Asian Trunk Railway website, http://www.unescap.org/ttdw/index.asp?MenuName=TheTrans-AsianRailway (January 4, 2012).

56. More in *Cross-Border Trade within the Central Asia Regional Economic Cooperation* (Washington, D.C.: World Bank, 2007).
57. "Work on free trade zone on the agenda," *People's Daily*, November 2, 2004, http://english.peopledaily.com.cn/200411/02/eng20041102_162447.html (March 6, 2007).
58. Authors' interviews with shuttle traders at Khorgos, Almaty, September 26, 2011.
59. "Masimov oznakomilsia s khodom stroitel'stva Khorgosa," *Nur.kz*, October 31, 2011, http://news.nur.kz/199682.html (January 7, 2012).
60. "Kazakhstan, China Plan Additional Border Railroad-Link in 2009," *Almaty Region web site*, May 28, 2007, http://www.almaty-reg.kz/almaty/investeng.phtml (January 4, 2012).
61. M. Junussova, *Global Market Needs New Cities or Development of Border Trade Ports of Kazakhstan* (Vienna: REAL CORP 007 Proceedings, May 20–23, 2007).
62. "Customs Union offers marginal benefits to Central Asia," Oxford Analytica, July 28, 2011.
63. "Stroitel'stvo i rekonstruktsiia avtodorogi Aksai-Chundzha-Kolzhat nachalis' v Almatinskoi oblasti," *Professional*, no. 121, April 24, 2006, http://www.professional.kz/?mod=text&tx=067075 (January 4, 2012).
64. "China Boosts Trade Ties with Kazakhstan," *Washington Profile*, February 2, 2006, http://www.washprofile.org/en/node/4593 (January 4, 2012).
65. More in *Cross-Border trade within the Central Asia Regional Economic Cooperation*, op. cit.
66. Authors' interviews with Kyrgyz drivers working with China, Dordoy, June 7, 2010.
67. Ibid.
68. V. Dubovitsky, "The Tajik-Chinese relations: the period of wariness over, the era of cooperation begins," *Ferghana.ru*, January 30, 2007, http://enews.ferghana.ru/article.php?id=1810 (January 4, 2012).
69. Fieldwork in the GBAO region, June 2004 and June 2010.
70. Interview with Sukhrob Sharipov, Center for Strategic Studies, Dushanbe, March 26, 2008.
71. *CAREC Transport and Trade Facilitation: Partnership for Prosperity* (Manila: Asian Development Bank, 2009).
72. E. Vinokurov, M. Jadraliyev, and Y. Shcherbanin, *The EURASEC transport corridor* (Astana: Eurasian Development Bank, March 2009); M. Denison, "The EU and Central Asia: Commercialising the Energy Relationship," *EUCAM Working Paper*, no. 2, 2009.
73. J.-F. Arvis, G. Raballand, and J.-F. Marteau, "The Cost of Being Landlocked: Logistics Costs and Supply Chain Reliability," *World Bank Working Paper*, June 2007.
74. Ibid., p. 34.
75. CAREC was set up in 1997. The program gathers the five post-Soviet states,

Afghanistan, Mongolia and Azerbaijan, as well as six international institutions, the Asian Development Bank, the European Bank for Reconstruction and Development, the International Monetary Fund, the Islamic Development Bank, the World Bank and the UNDP.

76. *CAREC transport and trade facilitation: partnership for prosperity*, op. cit., p. 12.

4. ENERGY-THIRSTY CHINA'S RESOURCE DIPLOMACY

1. T. Kellner, "La politique pétrolière de la RPC: stratégies et conséquences internationales," *Puissance Chine? Outre-terre. Revue de Géopolitique*, no. 15, 2006, pp. 425–69.
2. Sh. Shuja, "China's Energy Needs and Central Asia," *National Observer*, Council for the National Interest, Melbourne, no. 67, 2006, pp. 56–65.
3. P. Andrews-Speed and S. Vinogradov, "China's Involvement in Central Asian Petroleum: Convergent or Divergent Interests?," *Asian Survey*, vol. 40, no. 2, 2000, pp. 377–97.
4. Shuja, "China's Energy Needs and Central Asia," op. cit.
5. D. L. O. Hayward, "China's Oil Supply Dependence," *The Journal of Energy Security*, June 18, 2009, http://www.ensec.org/index.php?option=com_content&view=article&id=197:chinas-oil-supply-dependence&catid=96:content&Itemid=345 (January 4, 2012).
6. *British Petroleum's Statistical Review of World Energy 2010*, p. 6, http://www.bp.com/liveassets/bp_internet/globalbp/globalbp_uk_english/reports_and_publications/statistical_energy_review_2008/STAGING/local_assets/2010_downloads/statistical_review_of_world_energy_full_report_2010.pdf (January 4, 2012).
7. X. Xu, "The Oil and Gas links between Central Asia and China: a Geopolitical Perspective," *OPEC Review*, March 1999, pp. 33–54.
8. *Xinjiang Oil Industry Development*, Center for Energy and Global Development, Urumqi, 2009, http://www.wsichina.org/cs4_7.pdf (January 4, 2012); "Xinjiang becomes China's second largest crude oil producer," *Sina English*, January 1, 2009, http://english.sina.com/business/2009/0102/208741.html (January 4, 2012).
9. J. Jiang and J. Sinton, "Overseas investments by Chinese national oil companies. Assessing the drivers and impacts," *IEA Information Paper*, February 2011.
10. M. Kielmas, "China's Foreign Energy Asset Acquisitions: From Shopping Spree to Fire Sale?," *The China and Eurasian Forum Quarterly*, vol. 3, no. 3, 2005, pp. 27–30.
11. B..M. Frolic and G..T. Chin, "The Challenge of Energy Security in Northeast Asia: China's Rising Energy Needs and Northeast Asian Cooperation," *North Pacific Region Advanced Research Center Publications*, 2000, http://www.norpac.or.jp/main2/follow/1999–4.pdf (May 10, 2007).

12. B. Pannier, "Chinese-Central Asian Relationship Requires Delicate Balancing Act," *RFE/RL*, April 4, 2010, http://www.rferl.org/content/ChineseCentral_Asian_Relationship_Requires_Delicate_Balancing_Act/2002215.html (January 4, 2012).
13. C. E. Ziegler, "The Energy Factor in China's Foreign Policy," *Journal of Chinese Political Science*, vol. 11, no. 1, 2006, pp. 1–23.
14. *BP Statistical Review of World Energy*, June 2010, p. 6.
15. "Caspian Energy and Transport Issues Expand into Military-Political Confrontation," *Nezavisimoe voennoe obozrenie*, May 18, 2007.
16. "Gaffney, Cline & Associates confirms Turkmenistan possesses giant natural gas reserve," *Central Asian News*, October 16, 2008.
17. S. M. S. Yenikeyeff, *Kazakhstan's Gas: Export Markets and Export Routes* (Oxford: Oxford Institute for Energy Studies, November 2008), p. 19.
18. "KazMunaiGas to buy new assets, invest in output," *Kazworld*, October 21, 2011, http://kazworld.info/?p=17254 (October 4, 2011).
19. G. Raballand and R. Gente, "Oil in the Caspian Basin: Facts and Figures," in B. Najman, G. Raballand, and R. Pomfret (eds), *The Economics and Politics of Oil in the Caspian Basin. The Redistribution of Oil Revenues in Azerbaijan and Kazakhstan* (London: Routledge, 2007), pp. 9–29.
20. *Perspectives on Caspian Oil and Gas Development* (International Energy Agency Working Paper Series, December 2008), pp. 7–8.
21. "Kazakhstan Country Analysis Brief," *Energy Information Brief*, February 2008, p. 5.
22. *Perspectives on Caspian Oil and Gas Development*, op. cit., p. 12.
23. *BP Statistical Review of World Energy 2011*, p. 24.
24. Pomfret, "Turkmenistan's Foreign Policy," art. cit., pp. 19–34.
25. "Kazakhstan Country Analysis Brief," art. cit.
26. P. Jones Luong, and E. Weinthal, *Oil is not a Curse. Ownership Structure and Institutions in Soviet Successor States* (Cambridge: Cambridge University Press, 2010).
27. X. Xu, "Oil and Gas Linkages between Central Asia and China," James A. Baker Institute for Public Policy, July 18, 2000, http://riceinfo.rice.edu/projects/baker/publications/xuchina/xuchina.html (January 4, 2012).
28. A. Chebotarev, "Kazakhstan: Priority Oil Routes," *Central Asia and the Caucasus*, vol. 9, no. 3, 2001, pp. 29–30.
29. "Kazakhstan: Major Oil and Natural Gas Projects," *US Energy Information Administration*, http://www.eia.doe.gov/emeu/cabs/Kazakhstan/kazaproj.html (January 4, 2012).
30. P. Wonacott, "Western consortium shuts CNOOC out of oil project," *The Asian Wall Street Journal*, May 12, 2003.
31. F. W. Engdahl, "China lays down gauntlet in energy war," *Asia Times*, December 21, 2005, http://www.atimes.com/atimes/China/GL21Ad01.html (January 4, 2012).

32. E. Watkins, "CNPC becomes sole owner of Kazakh-Chinese development JV," *Oil and Gas Journal Online*, June 6, 2003.
33. "CNPC-Aktobemunaigas plans to maintain oil production at 2009 level," *Interfax-Kazakhstan*, April 2, 2010, http://goliath.ecnext.com/coms2/gi_0199-13068833/CNPC-Aktobemunaigas-plans-to-maintain.html (January 4, 2012).
34. E. Butyrina, "Portret Kompanii AO CNPC-Aktobemunaigaz," *Panorama*, October 8, 2010, http://panorama.kz/index.php?option=com_content&task=view&id=10319 (December 10, 2011).
35. V. Socor, "Implications of China's Takeover of Petrokazakhstan," *Eurasia Daily Monitor*, vol. 2, no. 165, 2005, http://www.jamestown.org/edm/article.php?article_id=2370186 (January 4, 2012).
36. "Kaz Munai Gaz, CNPC to Jointly Develop Darkhan Field," *Interfax Information Services*, October 5, 2005, http://www.uofaweb.ualberta.ca/chinainstitute/nav03.cfm?nav03=44401&nav02=43876&nav01=43092 (January 4, 2012).
37. "CITIC to buy Kazakhstan oil assets," *Beijing Invest*, October 2006, http://www.bjinvest.gov.cn/english/bn/200610/t141833.htm (January 4, 2012).
38. "KazMunayGas and CNPC E&D close deal for purchase of 100% stake in Mangistau Munay Gas," *Visor Capital*, November 25, 2009.
39. M. Yakovleva, "China Thirsts for Kazakh Oil," *Russian Petroleum Investor*, June 2005, http://www.wtexecutive.com/cms/content.jsp?id=com.tms.cms.article.Article_rpi_article_1 (January 4, 2012).
40. P. L. Dash, "Scramble for Caspian Energy: can Big Power Competition sidestep China and India?," in Laruelle, Huchet, Peyrouse, and Balci (eds), *China and India in Central Asia: A New "Great Game?,"* op. cit., pp. 141–53.
41. More in Peyrouse, "The Economic Aspects of the Chinese-Central-Asia Rapprochement," art. cit.
42. "Kazakhstan-China oil pipeline opens to commercial operation," *People's Daily Online*, July 12, 2006, http://english.people.com.cn/200607/12/eng20060712_282194.html (January 4, 2012).
43. T. Kaukenova, "Vliianie krizisa na politiku KNR v energeticheskom sektore Kazahstana," *East Time*, May 5, 2009, http://www.easttime.ru/analitic/1/3/627.html
44. Ibid.
45. R. Demytrie, "Struggle for Central Asian Energy Riches," *BBC News*, June 3, 2010, http://www.bbc.co.uk/news/10175847 (January 4, 2012).
46. See "Briefing on West-East Gas Pipeline," *US-China Oil and Gas Energy Forum*, no date, http://www.uschinaogf.org/Forum5/5XieGeguo_eng.pdf (January 4, 2012).
47. T. Kellner, *La Chine et la nouvelle Asie centrale* (Brussels: GRIP, 2002), p. 26.
48. "China launches massive gas pipeline campaign," *Oil and Gas Journal Online*, June 5, 2000.
49. K. J. Hancock, "Escaping Russia, Looking to China: Turkmenistan Pins Hopes

on China's Thirst for Natural Gas," *The China and Eurasia Forum Quarterly*, vol. 4, no. 3, 2006, pp. 67–87.

50. Pomfret, "Turkmenistan's Foreign Policy," art. cit., p. 29.
51. "Turkmenistan: gas pipeline to China is ready," *Asia News*, August 22, 2006, http://www.asianews.it/index.php?l=en&art=6997 (January 4, 2012).
52. V. S. Flolenkov, *Sovremennye torgovo-ekonomicheskie otnosheniia KNR s tsentral'noaziatskimi stranami-chlenami ShOS i Turkmenistanom* (Moscow: Institut Dal'nego Vostoka RAN, 2009).
53. See the CNPC website http://www.cnpc.com.cn/eng/cnpcworldwide/euro-asia/Turkmenistan/ (January 4, 2012).
54. "Turkmenistan: CNPC and Petrofac win gas field contract," Energy-pedia, January 3, 2010, http://www.energy-pedia.com/article.aspx?articleid=138419 (January 4, 2012).
55. Ia. Khummedov, "Kitai pokupaet Turkmenistan," *Gundogar*, July 19, 2010, http://www.gundogar.org/?0130497090000000000011000000 (January 4, 2012).
56. R. M. Cutler, "Turkmenistan to boost gas exports to China," *Asia Times*, December 1, 2011, http://www.atimes.com/atimes/Central_Asia/ML01Ag01.html (October 4, 2011).
57. "Difficulties Remain for a Turkmen-China Energy Deal," *Eurasianet*, March 9, 2011, http://www.eurasianet.org/node/63037 (April 27, 2011).
58. Z. Wan, "CNPC inks deal with Uzbekistan," *China Daily*, June 11, 2010, http://www.chinadaily.com.cn/business/2010–06/11/content_9964779.htm (January 4, 2012).
59. Z. Wan, "China agrees new gas pipeline," *China Daily*, June 14, 2010, http://www.chinadaily.com.cn/business/2010–06/14/content_9976316.htm (January 4, 2012).
60. "Kazakhstan and China sign gas, nuclear energy deals," *Daily Times*, June 13, 2010, http://www.dailytimes.com.pk/default.asp?page=2010%5C06%5C13%5Cstory_13–6–2010_pg20_2 (January 4, 2012).
61. T. Niazi, "The Ecology of Strategic Interests: China's Quest for Energy Security from the Indian Ocean and the South China Sea to the Caspian Sea Basin," *The China and Eurasia Forum Quarterly*, vol. 4, no. 4, 2006, pp. 97–116.
62. "CNPC to Tap Oil and Natural Gas in Uzbekistan," *Xinhua News Agency*, September 3, 2006, http://www.china.org.cn/english/2006/Sep/179963.htm (January 4, 2012).
63. "CNPC to Develop Uzbekistan's Mingbulak Oilfield," *King.com*, January 15, 2009, https://www.xing.com/net/eurasiabiz/recent-news-273931/cnpc-to-develop-uzbekistan-s-mingbulak-oilfield-17310424/ (January 4, 2012).
64. B. Pannier, "Tajikistan On Road to Energy Self-Sufficiency, Dicier Relations With Tashkent," *RFE/RL*, December 20, 2011, http://www.rferl.org/content/tajikistan_gas_uzbekistan/2253993.html (October 4, 2011).

65. P. Ipek, "The Role of Oil and Gas in Kazakhstan's Foreign Policy: Looking East or West?," *Europe-Asia Studies*, vol. 59, no. 7, 2007, pp. 1179–99.

5. CHINA'S BRAND: INVESTMENTS IN INFRASTRUCTURES

1. "V khode gosudarstvennogo vizita prezidenta Kazakhstana N. Nazarbaev v Kitai zakliucheny milliardnye kontrakty," *Ferghana.ru*, February 24, 2011, http://www.fergananews.com/news.php?id=16417&mode=snews (January 4, 2012).
2. More details in *2009 Minerals Yearbook* (Reston: U.S. Geological Survey, 2011).
3. R. M. Levine and G. J. Wallace, "The Mineral Industries of the Commonwealth of Independent States," in *2005 Minerals Yearbook* (Washington, D.C.: US Department of the Interior, US Geological Survey, December 2007).
4. McDonals, "Nuclear Power Global Status," *IAEA*, 2011, http://www.iaea.org/Publications/Magazines/Bulletin/Bull492/49204734548.html (December 9, 2011).
5. M. Laruelle, "Kazakhstan as a Uranium Power: Forthcoming Successes and Challenges," *Central Asia-Caucasus Analyst*, March 31, 2010, http://www.cacianalyst.org/?q=node/5296 (January 4, 2012).
6. "Kazatomprom vedet peregovory o prodazhe Kitaiu urana," *BusinessPress*, August 24, 2001, http://www.businesspress.ru/newspaper/article_mId_21960_aId_80147.html (January 4, 2012).
7. "Ul'binskii metallurgicheskii zavod zaregistriroval predpriiatie v Kitae," *Infogeo.ru*, August 30, 2004, http://www.infogeo.ru/metalls/news/?act=show&news=5432 (January 4, 2012).
8. A. Shmidke, "Atomnaia promyshlennost' Kazakhstana: sovremennoe sostoianie i perspektivy razvitiia," *PIR Center*, 2006, http://www.pircenter.org/data/publications/06–05–31Shmidke_Article.pdf (January 4, 2012).
9. T. Tashimov, "Kazatomprom propishetsia na kitaiskom rynke," *Ekspert Kazakhstan*, no. 21, 2007, http://www.expert.ru/printissues/kazakhstan/2007/21/atomnaya_energetika/ (January 4, 2012).
10. Syroezhkin, *Kazakhstan-Kitai. Ot prigranichnoi torgovli k strategicheskomu partnerstvu* (Almaty: KISI, 2010), vol. 2, pp. 178–181.
11. "Kazatomprom ventures into nuclear build," *World Nuclear News*, April 29, 2009, http://www.world-nuclear-news.org/C_Kazatomprom_ventures_into_nuclear_build_2804092.html (January 4, 2012).
12. "Kazakhstan and China sign gas, nuclear energy deals," *Daily Times*, June 13, 2010, http://www.dailytimes.com.pk/default.asp?page=2010%5C06%5C13%5Cstory_13–6–2010_pg20_2 (January 4, 2012).
13. B. Pannier, "Kazakh President Energized After China Trip," *RFE/RL*, February 23, 2011, http://www.rferl.org/content/kazakh_president_energized_china_trip/2318634.html (January 4, 2012).

14. Levine and Wallace, "The Mineral Industries of the Commonwealth of Independent States," art. cit.
15. "Kitaiskaia i kazakhstanskaia kompanii sozdali SP po dobyche zolota v Kazakhstane," *RosInvest*, September 7, 2005, http://www.rosinvest.com/news/126039/ (April 15, 2007).
16. "Kitai gotov investirovat' 900 millionov dollarov v Kyrgyzstane v obmen na resursy i stroitel'stvo zh.d." *CentrAsia*, January 29, 2005, http://www.centrasia.ru/newsA.php4?st=1106979480 (March 6, 2007).
17. "China Offers Assets-for-Investment Deal," *IWPR*, November 13, 2006, http://iwpr.net/?p=bkg&s=b&o=325357&apc_state=henbbkgdate200611 (March 5, 2007).
18. "Almazek Atambaev izbran predsedatelem Soveta direktorov ZAO Sarydzhaz Energo," *Tatar.kg*, July 6, 2006, http://www.tazar.kg/news.php?i=1230 (April 19, 2007).
19. "Tadzhikistan i Kitai sozdaiut novye sovmestnye predpriiatiia po razrabotke mestorozhdenii zolota," *Mineral.ru*, December 2005, http://www.mineral.ru/Chapters/News/20700.html (March 24, 2007).
20. V. Dubovitsky, "The Tajik-Chinese relations: the period of wariness over, the era of cooperation begins," art. cit.
21. M. Hasanova, "Talco and its foreign partners to build 11 large enterprises," *Asia Plus*, January 19, 2009, http://asiaplus.tj/en/news/31/45510.html (January 4, 2012).
22. J. C. K. Daly, "Kazakhstan's hydroelectric potential attracts foreign investment," *Upi.com*, March 27, 2009, http://www.upi.com/Energy_Resources/2009/03/27/Analysis-Kazakhstans-hydroelectric-potential-attracts-foreign-investment/UPI-86451238190422/ (January 4, 2012).
23. V. A. Dukhovny, and J. De Schutter, *Water in Central Asia. Past, Present, Future* (London: CRC Press, 2011).
24. T. Dadabaev, "Water Politics and Management of Trans-Boundary Water Resources in Post-Soviet Central Asia," in B. Schlyter (ed.), *Prospects for Democracy in Central Asia* (Istanbul: Swedish Research Institute in Istanbul, 2005), pp. 169–84.
25. *Electricity Sectors in CAREC Countries: A Diagnostic Review of Regulatory Approaches and Challenges* (Manila: Asian Development Bank, 2005).
26. For the Kyrgyz case see E. Marat, "Corruption in the Hydro-Energy Sector Becomes Clearer in Kyrgyzstan," *Eurasia Daily Monitor*, vol. 5, no. 184, September 25, 2008, http://www.jamestown.org/single/?no_cache=1&tx_ttnews%5Btt_news%5D=33970 (May 24, 2010).
27. R. Dwivedi, "China's Central Asia Policy in Recent Times," *The China and Eurasia Forum Quarterly*, vol. 4, no. 4, 2006, p. 158.
28. More in S. Peyrouse, "The Hydroelectric Sector in Central Asia and the Growing Role of China," *The China and Eurasia Forum Quarterly*, vol. 5, no. 2, 2007, pp. 131–48.

29. "Prisutstvie Kitaia v Kazakhstane: 'Dostizheniia' i 'perspektivy'," *Post Back USSR*, February 10, 2006, http://www.pbussr.ru/index.php?razdel=5&condition=show_news&id=8992 (January 4, 2012).
30. "Joint-Stock Company 'Stantsiya Ekibastuz GRES-2' is preparing for large-scale measures aimed at boosting and upgrading the plant's performance," *RAO UES*, http://www.interrao.ru/eng/news/group/52/ (August 26, 2008).
31. "Kazakhstan, China to jointly build large-scale power plant," *People's Daily Online*, April 1, 2006 http://english.people.com.cn/200604/01/eng20060401_255104.html (May 25, 2007).
32. More in S. Peyrouse, "Chinese Economic Presence in Kazakhstan: China's Resolve and Central Asia's Apprehension," *China Perspectives*, no. 3, 2008, pp. 55–75.
33. "Kazakhstano-kitaiskuiu granitsu razmyvaet. Na Khorgose budut stroit' damby," *CentrAsia*, August 11, 2003, http://www.centrasia.ru/newsA.php4?st=1060553880 (March 5, 2007).
34. G. D. Bessarabov and A. D. Sobianin, "Vodnye problemy KNR: kazakhskii i rossiiskii aspekty," *China databases website*, http://www.chinadata.ru/china_water.htm (May 3, 2007).
35. G. Feller, "Central Asian Power Rapid Development of Coal and Hydroelectric Power for Export—Financed by Russia, Iran & China," *Eco World*, September 25, 2006, http://www.ecoworld.com/home/articles2.cfm?tid=403 (May 3, 2007).
36. "Po itogam peregovorov liderov Kazakhstana i Kitaia v Shankhae podpisan riad dvukhstoronnikh soglashenii," *KazKommertsbank News*, June 14, 2006, http://news.kkb.kz/news/show.asp?no=447469 (March 15, 2007).
37. G. Petrov, "Tajikistan's Hydropower Resources," *Central Asia and the Caucasus*, vol. 21, no. 3, 2003, pp. 153–61.
38. "Chinese to Build Tajik Hydroelectric Plant," *RFE/RL*, January 18, 2007, http://www.rferl.org/featuresarticle/2007/01/C7ECA5D9-67F9-4659-88F9-696875AC873E.html (April 25, 2007).
39. Kassenova, *L'Aide au développement: la percée chinoise au Tadjikistan et au Kirghizstan*, op. cit., p. 19.
40. Iu. Sigov, "Kuda povernet Dushanbe?," *Aziia Inform*, November 27, 2009, http://asia-a.ru/content/view/4406/5/ (January 4, 2012).
41. "South-North electric main to be key link in Tajikistan's electric system, says President Rahmonov," *The Times of Central Asia*, September 18, 2006.
42. *Energy Information Administration, Kyrgyzstan Energy Sector*, May 2002, www.eia.doe.gov/emeu/cabs/kyrgyz.html (January 4, 2012).
43. T. Kellner, "La République populaire de Chine et l'Asie centrale post-soviétique: étude de politique étrangère" (Geneva: IUHEI, 2004), p. 462.
44. Interviews at the factory, Kyzyl-Kiia, June 2010.
45. Fieldwork in the Rasht Valley, June 2010.
46. *Proposed Loan, Asian Development Fund Grants, and Technical Assistance Grant.*

Kyrgyz Republic and Republic of Tajikistan: CAREC Regional Road Corridor Improvement Project (Manila: Asian Development Bank, October 2007).

47. Fieldwork in the GBAO, June 2010.
48. B. Kaminski and S. Mitra, *Skeins of Silk: Borderless Bazaars and Border Trade in Central Asia* (Washington, D.C.: The World Bank, 2009), pp. 92–4.
49. B. B. Uulu, "Zheleznodorozhnyi tupik," *Analitika Aki Press*, July 19, 2010, http://analitika.akipress.org/analytics/news:261 (January 15, 2011).
50. E. Vinokurov (ed.), *Mezhdunarodnye transportnye korridory EvrAzES* [International corridors for transport in the Eurasian Economic Community] (Astana: EABD, 2009), p. 42.
51. "Kitai osnachshaet Turkmeniiu novymi passazhirskimi vagonami i teplovozami," *CentrAsia*, August 11, 2006, http://www.centrasia.ru/newsA.php4?st=1155278340 (April 15, 2007). See also Peyrouse, *Turkmenistan*, pp. 182–4.
52. "Po itogam peregovorov liderov Kazakhstana i Kitaia v Shankhae podpisan riad dvukhstoronnykh soglashenii," op. cit.
53. "Kazakhstan rassmatrivaet vozmozhnost' priobreteniia 38 passazhirskikh vagonov u kitaiskoi kompanii," *Kazakhstan Today*, January 14, 2006, http://www.gazeta.kz/art.asp?aid=69950 (March 6, 2007).
54. K. Dodikhudoev and V. Niyatbekov, "The Chinese Vector in Tajikistan's Foreign Policy," *Central Asia and the Caucasus*, no. 2, 2009, p. 125.
55. D. Tynan, "International Telecoms Eye Central Asian Mobile Market," *Eurasianet*, January 17, 2008, http://www.eurasianet.org/departments/insight/articles/eav011808.shtml; *Central Asia Telecom Industry Report, 2008–2009*, Research in China, February 2009, http://www.researchinchina.com/FreeReport/PdfFile/633891259009885000.pdf (January 4, 2012).
56. See *Kazakhstan and Central Asia Telecommunications Report*, April 2011, by the Business Monitor International.
57. "Rostelekom prinial uchastie vo vstreche operatorov stran ShOS Regional Carrier Meeting," *Rostelecom*, August 25, 2005, http://www.rt.ru/press/news/detail.php?ID=35207 (March 24, 2007).
58. "Kazakhstan zakupaet deshevyi Internet v Kitae," *Netoscope*, January 8, 2001, http://www.netoscope.ru/news/2001/08/01/3052.html (March 6, 2007).
59. "ZTE budet vypuskat' apparaturu CDMA-450 v Kazakhstane," *Onliner*, June 21, 2004, http://www.onliner.ru/news/21.05.2004/20.25n/ (March 6, 2007).
60. "V TUIT otkroetsia uchebnyi tsentr Huawei Technologies," *Security.uz*, June 15, 2005, http://www.security.uz/news/default.asp?id=10667&do=print (April 15, 2007).
61. "Huawei Technologies i Perfectum Mobile uspeshno zapustili set' CDMA v Uzbekistane," *HTCom.ru*, June 27, 2006, http://www.htcom.ru/news-pc/newsd-19193/ (April 15, 2007).
62. "Kompaniia ZTE namerena vlozhit' v kommunikatsii Tadzhikistana eshche 70 mil-

lionov dollarov," *SNG News*, June 20, 2006, http://www.sngnews.ru/archive/2006/06/20/64820.html (April 15, 2007).

63. "V Pekine Prezident Kurmanbek Bakiev oznakomilsia s rabotoi krupnoi kompanii Huawei Technologies," *Kyrgyz Presidential Administration website*, June 10, 2006, www.president.kg/press/news/1222/ (April 17, 2007).
64. "ZTE nadvigaetsia," *ComNews.ru*, December 21, 2003, www.comnews.ru/index.cfm?id=9119&caid=print (March 24, 2007).
65. "Kompanii iz Germanii i Kitaia pomogut Turkmenistanu modernizirovat' sistemy sviazi," *Turkmenistan.ru*, July 6, 2004, www.turkmenistan.ru/?page_id=3&lang_id=ru&elem_id=2993&type=event&layout=pri (March 5, 2007).
66. "Kitai predostavil Turkmenistanu l'gotnyi kredit v razmere 200 millionov iuanei na razvitie sviazi i telekommunikatsii," *Market.ru*, December 17, 2006, http://www.finmarket.ru/z/nws/news.asp?id=555517&rid=1 (April 11, 2007).

6. DISCUSSING CHINA: SINOPHILIA AND SINOPHOBIA IN KAZAKHSTAN AND KYRGYZSTAN

1. K. Dzhusaev, "Perspektivy sotrudnichestva stran Tsentral'noi Azii s Kitaem," *Tsentral'naia Aziia i kul'tura mira*, no. 1, 1998, http://www.freenet.kg/jornal/n4/JRNAL407.htm (October 20, 2009).
2. N. Nazarbaev, "Poslanie k narodu Kazakhstana," *Akorda.kz*, March 2007, http://www.akorda.kz/www/www_akorda_kz.nsf/sections?OpenForm&id_doc=BC3DF7C6FB65732E46257291002A9331&lang=ru&L1=L2&L2=L2–22 (April 18, 2007).
3. "V Kyrgyzstane utverzhdena Kontseptsiia vneshnei politiki," *Kazakhstan Segodnia*, January 13, 2007, http://www.gazeta.kz/art.asp?aid=85637 (July 11, 2008).
4. Dodikhudoev and Niyatbekov, "The Chinese Vector in Tajikistan's Foreign Policy," art. cit.
5. M. Laruelle and S. Peyrouse, *Asie centrale, la dérive autoritaire. Cinq républiques entre héritage soviétique, dictature et islam* (Paris: Autrement/CERI, 2006).
6. Interview with Dosym Satpaev, Almaty, March 6, 2008, and with Nikolai Kuz'min, Almaty, June 7, 2008.
7. M. Brazhnikov, "Eksport kazakhstanskoi nefti: Tengiz-Novorossiisk, dalee vezde?," *Kontinent*, no. 7, April 11–24, 2001, p. 11.
8. "Shpionskii skandal v Kazakhstane," *Muslim Uzbekistan*, April 18, 2007, http://muslimuzbekistan.net/ru/centralasia/headlines/news.php?ID=10213 (December 18, 2009).
9. R. Orange, "Kazakhstan: Russia Pressing for Clean-Up at China Border Crossing," art. cit.
10. A. Zhaparov, "The Chinese Migrants Issue in Kyrgyzstan," *The China and Eurasia Forum Quarterly*, vol. 7, no. 1, 2009, p. 88.

11. K. L. Syroezhkin, "Social Perceptions of China and the Chinese: A View from Kazakhstan," *The China and Eurasia Forum Quarterly*, vol. 7, no. 1, 2009, p. 32.
12. See the many disclosed cases in S. Ibraimov, "China-Central Asia Trade Relations: Economic and Social Patterns," *The China and Eurasia Forum Quarterly*, vol. 7, no. 1, 2009, pp. 47–59.
13. "Kitaiskie gruppy vliianiia v Rossii," *Informatsionno-analiticheskii Biulleten'*, no. 13, 2006.
14. E. V. Savkovich, "Uigurskaia problema v ramkakh ShOS (Kazakhstan i Kitai, 1990-nachalo 2000kh gg.)," *Analytica*, January 11, 2006, www.analitika.org/article.php?story=20060111220552543 (April 18, 2008).
15. Interview with Hamid Khamraev, Almaty, March 15, 2008.
16. Mukhtar Auezov is regarded as one of the greatest Kazakh writers of the twentieth century. His most famous book, *The Path of Abay*, published in the 1950s, rehabilitated Abay's work (1845–1904) as part of the national patrimony. This earned Auezov prominence in the Soviet literary world.
17. Interview with Murat Auezov, Almaty, March 10, 2008.
18. Ibid.
19. Comments reported in *Narodnyi Kongress*, no. 5, June 1993, cited by A. Grozin, "Kazakhstan: problemy natsional'noi bezopasnosti," *Tsentral'naia Aziia i Kavkaz*, no. 4, 1999, http://www.ca-c.org/journal/cac-04–1999/st_11_grosin.shtml (September 12, 2008).
20. On the political life of the Russian minority in Kazakhstan, see M. Laruelle and S. Peyrouse, *Les Russes du Kazakhstan. Identités nationales et nouveaux États dans l'espace post-soviétique* (Paris: Maisonneuve & Larose/IFEAC, 2004).
21. V. Khliupin, *Geopoliticheskii treugol'nik*, op. cit.
22. A. M. Kazhegeldin, "Vremia razbrasyvat' i sobirat' kamni," *Tsentral'noaziatskii Biulleten'*, no. 4, 1999, pp. 14–15.
23. See, for example, "Murat Auezov rassuzhdaet ob ekologicheskikh problemakh, i ne tol'ko o nikh," *Megalopolis*, no. 3, November 22, 2000.
24. Interview with Murat Auezov, Almaty, March 10, 2008.
25. "V Parlamente Kazakhstana sformirovana novaia deputatskaia gruppa Enbek/Trud," *CentrAsia*, November 27, 2004, www.centrasia.ru/newsA.php?st=1101557580 (March 19, 2008).
26. "Posol Kitaia vstretilsia v Mazhilise s liderami bloka AIST i gruppy Enbek," *Kazakhstan Today*, December 15, 2004, http://www.inform.kz/showarticle.php?lang=rus&id=104411 (October 17, 2010).
27. Interview with Bektas Mukhamedzhanov, Almaty, March 5, 2008.
28. Interview with Murat Auezov, Almaty, March 10, 2008.
29. Zh. Zholamanova, "O nekotorykh aspektakh kazakhstansko-kitaiskogo ekonomicheskogo sotrudnichestva v ramkakh ShOS: Politologicheskii analiz," *Analytic*, no. 1, 2008, pp. 27–37.

30. For example, see the site of the Communist-leaning Revolutionary Party of Kazakhstan: http://www.revkom.com/index.htm?/za_rubezom/rabochie_v_mire/2007 1024Kazahstan.htm (December 20, 2010).
31. "Kitaiskie ekspluatatory kazakhskogo naroda," *Delo no. 0001*, August 14, 2007, http://www.delo001.ru/kz/399.htm (May 25, 2010).
32. "Prisutstvie Kitaia v Kazakhstane: 'dostizheniia' i 'perspektivy'," art. cit.
33. L. Khudova, cited in "Kitaiskaia ekspansiia v Sredniuiu Aziiu. Igra na operezhenie ili nastuplenie (mnenie ekspertov)," *CentrAsia*, August 8, 2007, www.centrasia.ru/newsA.php?st=1186517400 (May 21, 2008).
34. A. Ashimbaeva, "Starye problemy novoi ekonomiki Kazakhstana," *Kapital.kz*, no. 21 (108), May 31, 2007, republished in *CentrAsia*, June 2, 2007, www.centrasia.ru/newsA.php?st=1180737420 (June 5, 2008).
35. "Kitaem vedetsia bol'shaia rabota po priobreteniiu riada neftianykh kompanii, rabotaiushchikh v Kazakhstane," *Nomad*, November 2, 2006, http://www.nomad.su/?a=3–200611020217 (November 18, 2008).
36. More in Laruelle (ed.), *Labor Migration and Social Upheaval as the Face of Globalization in Central Asia* (London: Brill, 2012).
37. E. Eshamanova, "Tendentsii i puti sotrudnichestva Kazakhstana i Rossii v reshenii problem trudovoi migratsii iz stran Tsentral'noi Azii," *Informatsionno-analiticheskii tsentr izucheniia obshchestvennykh politicheskikh protsessov na postsovetskom prostranstve*, March 5, 2008, http://www.ia-centr.ru/expert/578/ (March 26, 2008).
38. "Kazakhstanskii deputat ob initsiative Kirgizii: Migratsiiu nuzhno regulirovat', ni v koem sluchae ne otkryvaia granitsy EvrazES," *UpMonitor*, April 18, 2007, http://www.upmonitor.ru/news/russia/100730a/0/print/ (November 29, 2008).
39. See chapter 10.
40. "Kitaitsy reshili osvaivat' zemli v Kazakhstane," *Altaiskaia pravda*, January 30, 2004, http://www.ap.altairegion.ru/023–04/14.html (December 17, 2005).
41. J. Lillis, "Kazakhstan: China Looking to Lease Land for Agricultural Purposes," *Eurasianet*, April 2, 2010, http://www.eurasianet.org/departments/insight/articles/eav020410.shtml (May 19, 2010).
42. B. Pannier, "Prospect of Chinese Farmers Brings Controversy to Kazakh Soil," *RFE/RL*, December 19, 2009, http://www.rferl.org/content/Prospect_Of_Chinese_Farmers_Brings_Controversy_To_Kazakh_Soil/1906896.html (October 20, 2010).
43. See the open letter that Akim Gadil'bek, President of youth movement Aibat, addressed to the President of the Republic, *Informatsionno-analiticheskii tsentr izucheniia obshchestvenno-politicheskikh protsessov na postsovetskom prostranstve*, December 12, 2006, http://www.ia-centr.ru/archive/public_details76b3.html?id=256 (March 16, 2008).
44. Iuri Zakharov, cited in "Kitaiskaia ekspansiia s Sredniuiu Aziiu," art. cit.

45. "Vernite nashu zemliu! Kirgiziiu zakhlestnyl antikitaiskii protest. Beknazarov prisoedinilsia k golodovke," *CentrAsia*, May 14, 2002, http://www.centrasia.ru/newsA.php?st=1021355040 (February 11, 2006).
46. A. Dubnov, "Kirgizskie palki v kitaiskie kolesa," *Vremia*, June 22, 2001, http://www.vremya.ru/2001/108/5/11015.html (February 11, 2006).
47. V. Volkov, "Kirgiziia: sud'by spornykh territorii dolzhen reshat' referendum," *Info House*, December 22, 2002, http://www.ricnews.com/map/vgw.html (March 17, 2007).
48. By "administrative resources" is to be understood the use by the established bureaucratic apparatus of multiple state and private resources (state- or municipality-funded publicity campaigns, public companies putting large financial means at the disposal of the authorities, etc.) to prevent political opponents from reaching public opinion.
49. "Kyrgyzgeit. Deputat A. Beknazarov nachal protiv prezidenta A. Akaeva protseduru impichmenta," *CentrAsia*, May 18, 2002, http://www.centrasia.ru/newsA.php4?st=1020802560 (June 07, 2007).
50. D. Usenbaev, "Roman vo imia...," *Oasis*, no. 16, August 2007, http://www.ca-oasis.info/oasis/?jrn=61&id=469 (December 17, 2010).
51. "Kitaiskie migranty prodolzhaiut ugrozhat' Kirgizii (anonimnoe pis'mo v redaktsiiu)," *CentrAsia*, July 26, 2004, http://www.centrasia.ru/newsA.php?st=109 0786200 (March 10, 2007).
52. S. Radnitz, "Networks, Localism and Mobilization in Aksy, Kyrgyzstan," *Central Asian Survey*, vol. 24, no. 4, 2005, pp. 405–24.
53. "RSE-RS novosti ot Kyrgyzstana," *Ferghana.ru*, May 7, 2002, http://www.ferghana.ru/article.php?id=288 (October 19, 2006).
54. "Kirgiziia ratifitsirovala pogranichnoe soglashenie s Kitaem," *Prima-News*, May 17, 2002, http://www.prima-news.ru/news/news/2002/5/17/10315.html (June 17, 2006).
55. A. Shukenov, "Novaia vlast': zemli svoei ne otdadim ni piadi," *Oasis*, no. 12, August 2005, http://www.ca-oasis.info/oasis/?jrn=13&id=86 (March 19, 2010).
56. E. Abdyldaev, "Kitaiskii vektor vneshnei politiki Kurmanbeka Bakieva," *Analytica*, June 2006, www.analitika.org/article.php?story=20060621024111739 (May 21, 2007).
57. On the functioning of Kyrgyz markets, see R. A. Spector, "Securing Property in Contemporary Kyrgyzstan," *Post-Soviet Affairs*, vol. 24, no. 2, 2008, pp. 149–76.
58. For more details about this law, its motivations, and its impact see M. Laruelle, "Russian Policy on Central Asia and the Role of Russian Nationalism," *Silk Road Papers*, April 2008, http://www.isdp.eu/files/publications/srp/08/ml08russia-central.pdf (January 28, 2011).
59. D. Karimov, "Pravitel'stvo Kyrgyzstana otmenilo postanovlenie, zapreshchaiushchee inostrannym grazhdanam rabotat' na mestnykh rynkakh," *24.kg*, March 3,

2007, http://www.24.kg/community/2007/03/03/46216.html (March 27, 2007).

60. "Pravitel'stvo Kyrgyzstana v blizhaishee vremia uporiadochit deiatel'nost' inostrannykh predprinimatelei na rynkakh strany," *For.kg*, January 12, 2007, http://www.for.kg/goid.php?id=21677 (March 17, 2007).
61. "Biudzhet poluchal mizer ot prisutstviia inostrannykh torgovtsev na rynkakh Kyrgyzstana," *For.kg*, February 6, 2007, http://www.for.kg/goid.php?id=24646 (March 17, 2007).
62. "Aigul' Ryskulova poiasnila kitaitsam Postanovlenie Pravitel'stva o doliakh inostrannykh grazhdan na rynkakh," *For.kg*, February 17, 2007, http://www.for.kg/goid.php?id=26232 (March 27, 2007).
63. "Mestnye prodavtsy Karasuuiskogo rynka trebuiut ochistit' rynok ot inostrannykh torgovtsev," *AkiPress*, January 2007, http://business.akipress.org/news/1510 (March 17, 2007).
64. "V Oshe obsudili ispolnenie pravitel'stvennogo postanovleniia o kvotirovanii inostrannoi rabochei sily," *For.kg*, February 5, 2007, http://www.for.kg/goid.php?id= 24501 (March 12, 2007).
65. "Kommentarii i mneniia o postanovlenii pravitel'stva KP o kvotakh dlia inostrannykh grazhdan, osushchestvliaiushchikh torgovliu v Kyrgyzstane," *Tazar*, February 23, 2007, http://www.tazar.kg/news.php?i=3335 (March 10, 2009).
66. T. Popova, "Postanovlenie no. 13: eshche raz ob ugrozakh i riskakh," *Slovo Kyrgyzstana*, February 28, 2007, p. 1.
67. Authors' observations, Osh, June 2010.
68. Syroezhkin, *Kazakhstan-Kitai. Ot prigranichnoi torgovli k strategicheskomu partnerstvu*, vol. 2, pp. 212–22.

7. THE NEW MEDIATORS: DIASPORAS, TRADERS, MIGRANTS, AND YOUTH

1. This repatriation program was implemented with the aim of modifying the country's demographic balance to the detriment of the Slavic populations. About 4.5 million persons living outside of Kazakhstan are regarded as Kazakhs. Each year the state program announces the quota of persons that are permitted to obtain the status of "returning Kazakhs" or Oralmans. They receive some thousands of dollars enabling them to buy housing in a rural zone, are reimbursed for their transport costs, are exempted from military service, and receive Kazakh citizenship. In 2006, Bishkek set up a similar repatriation program for ethnic Kyrgyz from abroad, referred to as Kairylmans, but made very little finance available.
2. C. Mackerras, *China's Ethnic Minorities and Globalisation* (London, New York: Routledge Curzon, 2003).
3. S. R. Roberts, "Uyghur Neighborhoods and Nationalisms in the Former Sino-Soviet

Borderland. An Historical Ethnography of a Stateless Nation on the Margins of Modernity" (PhD, Los Angeles: University of Southern California, 2003), p. 287.

4. Ibid., pp. 289–90.
5. Khliupin, *Geopoliticheskii treugol'nik*, op. cit.
6. J. Dautcher, "Folklore and Identity in an Uyghur Community in the 1990s Xinjiang China" (PhD: Berkeley, University of California, 1999), pp. 22–9.
7. D. Gladney, *Muslim Chinese: Ethnic Nationalism in the People's Republic* (Cambridge, Mass.: Harvard University Press, 1991, 1996). See also O. Chuah, "Muslims in China: the Social and Economic Situation of the Hui Chinese," *Journal of Muslim Minority Affairs*, vol. 24, no. 1, 2004, pp. 155–62.
8. E. Allès, "The Chinese-speaking Muslims (Dungans) of Central Asia: A Case of Multiple Identities in a Changing Context," *Asian Ethnicity*, vol. 6, no. 2, 2005, pp. 121–34.
9. Interview with Nurik Ma, representative of the Dungan Association of Kazakhstan at Xi'an, Xi'an, October 11, 2008.
10. Ibid.
11. Zhaparov, "The Issue of Chinese Migrants in Kyrgyzstan," art. cit., p. 86.
12. Interview with Husei Daurov, Almaty, June 6, 2008.
13. Interview with a Dungan businessman who runs a company that transports Chinese goods to Western Europe, Astana, March 13, 2008.
14. Interviews conducted with researchers and businessmen from the Association for Friendship with Foreign Countries of the Gansu province, Lanzhou, October 3, 2008.
15. *Xinjiang Statistical Yearbook 2007* (Urumqi, 2007) pp. 74–9.
16. Anonymous interviews conducted in Kashgar, Urumqi, Turfan, September 2008.
17. Fieldwork observations, Tashkorgan, September 2008.
18. Interview with researchers and businessmen of the Association for Friendship with Foreign Countries of the Gansu province, Lanzhou, October 3, 2008.
19. "U strakha glaza neveliki. Deputaty mazhilisa napugany rostom migratsii v Kazakhstan grazhdan KNR," *Liter*, http://www.liter.kz/site.php?lan=russian&id=151&pub=9324 (November 11, 2008).
20. A. Ikonnikov, "Mesto pod solntsem," *Kontinent*, no. 3 (188), February 27, 2007, http://www.continent.kz/2007/03/12.htm (September 24, 2008).
21. "Nashli delo po dushe," *Kazakhstanskaia pravda*, October 30, 2004, http://www.kazpravda.kz/index.php?uin=1152853640&chapter=1099106461&act=archive_date&day=30&month=10&year=2004 (December 9, 2008).
22. "I dym otechestva im sladok i priiaten?," *Liter*, no date, http://www.liter.kz/site.php?lan=russian&id=165&pub=1685 (December 10, 2008).
23. "Oralmanam postsovetskogo perioda otvetstvennye posty ne dostaiutsia," *Zona.kz*, May 28, 2008, http://www.zonakz.net/articles/22102 (December 6, 2008).
24. S. Olimova, "The Multifaceted Chinese Presence in Central Asia," *The China and Eurasia Forum Quarterly*, vol. 7, no. 1, 2008, pp. 61–77.

25. Ibraimov, "China-Central Asia Trade Relations: Economic and Social Patterns," art. cit., p. 55.
26. V. Babak, "Astana v treugol'nike Moskva, Vashington, Pekin. Kazakhstansko-kitaiskie otnosheniia," *Tsentral'naia Aziia i Kavkaz*, no. 1, 2000, http://www.ca-c.org/journal/cac-07–2000/19.babak.shtml (August 25, 2008).
27. Ibid.
28. Syroezhkin, *Problemy sovremennogo Kitaia i bezopasnost' v Tsentral'noi Azii*, op. cit., p. 134.
29. Paramonov and Strokov, "Ekonomicheskoe prisutstvie Rossii i Kitaia v Tsentral'noi Azii," art. cit., p. 10.
30. Zhaparov, "The Issue of Chinese Migrants in Kyrgyzstan," art. cit., pp. 79–91.
31. Interview with Central Asians in the main commercial malls devoted to post-Soviet traders in Kashgar, Urumqi, and Beijing, May and September 2008.
32. Fieldwork among tourist agencies for post-Soviet citizens in Urumqi, September 2008.
33. Interviews with Central Asian "shop-tourists" in Beijing, Urumqi and Guangzhou, May, September and November 2008.
34. Interviews with Akylbek Saliev, Bishkek, June 29, 2010, and Amantur Zhaparov, Bishkek, July 1, 2010.
35. Interview with Konstantin Syroezhkin, Almaty, September 29, 2010.
36. See for instance K. Borishpolets and A. Babadzhanov, "Migratsionnye riski stran Tsentral'noi Azii," *Analiticheskie zapiski MGIMO*, no. 2, 2007, pp. 9–19; and V.A. Korsun, *Vneshniaia politika Kitaia na poroge XXI veka* (Moscow: MGIMO, 2002), p. 50.
37. S. Kozhirova, "Vnutrennie i vneshnie aspekty sovremennoi kitaiskoi migratsii," *Analytic*, no. 6, 2007, p. 51.
38. E. Sadovskaia, "Sovremennaia kitaiskaia migratsiia v Kazakhstane: osnovnye tendentsii, problemy i perspektivy," in B. Sultanov and M. Laruelle (eds), *Tsentral'naia Aziia i Kitai: sostoianie i perspektivy sotrudnichestva* (Almaty: KISI, 2008), pp. 130–56.
39. "V Kyrgyzstane nakhoditsia bolee 60,000 grazhdan Kitaia," *24.kg*, January 30, 2008, www.24.kg/community/2008/01/30/75133.html (September 30, 2008).
40. *Report of the Deputy Head of Migration Service of the Ministry of Interior prepared for the Seminar on Labor Migration*, Dushanbe, June 19, 2008.
41. K. L. Syroezhkin, "Kitaiskaia migratsiia v Kazakhstane: voobrazhaemye i real'nye ugrozy i vyzovy," *Mezhdunarodnye issledovaniia*, no. 1, 2009, p. 122.
42. Interview with Muratbek Imanaliyev, Bishkek, February 14, 2008.
43. Raballand and Andrésy, "Why should Trade between Central Asia and China Continue to Expand?," art. cit.
44. See S. B. Kozhirova's current sociological study on Chinese expatriates and migrants. Interview with Svetlana Kozhirova, Astana, March 14, 2008, and Almaty, September 29, 2010.

45. E. Sadovskaia, "Chinese Migration to Kazakhstan: A Silk Road for Cooperation or a Thorny Road of Prejudice?," *The China and Eurasia Forum Quarterly*, vol. 5, no. 4, 2007, pp. 147–70.
46. As demonstrated in S. Kozhirova's still unpublished work.
47. M. Laruelle, "Kazakhstan, the new Migration Crossroads in Central Asia," in Laruelle, *Labor Migration and Social Upheaval as the Face of Globalization in Central Asia*, op. cit.
48. Zhaparov, "Chinese Migrants in Kyrgyzstan," art. cit., p. 83; and R. M. Rakhimov, "Rynok Dordoi i torgovtsy iz Kitaia," in Sultanov, and Laruelle, *Tsentral'naia Aziia i Kitai: sostoianie i perspektivy sotrudnichestva*, op. cit., pp. 193–200.
49. Fieldwork at the Dordoi bazaar, February 2008 and June 2010, and the Karasuu bazaar in June 2010.
50. Rakhimov, "Rynok Dordoi i torgovtsy iz Kitaia," art. cit.
51. "Assotsiatsiia kitaiskikh biznesmenov s ponimaniem otneslas' k meram po ogranicheniiu prisutstviia inostrannykh torgovtsev na rynkakh Kyrgyzstana," *For.kg*, February 16, 2007, http://www.for.kg/goid.php?id=26104 (March 28, 2008).
52. "Kitaitsy gotovy osvaivat' bednye regiony," *Moia stolitsa*, February 16, 2007, http://www.msn.kg/page.shtml?option=item&year=7&mon=2&id=17313 (March 28, 2008).
53. More in S. Olimova, "The Multifaceted Chinese Presence in Central Asia," art. cit.
54. Kassenova, *Aide au développement: la percée chinoise au Tadjikistan et au Kirghizstan*, op. cit., p. 17.
55. S. Kozhirova, "Sotsiologicheskii portret kitaiskoi migratsii v Kazakhstane," in Sultanov, and Laruelle, *Tsentral'naia Aziia i Kitai: sostoianie i perspektivy sotrudnichestva*, op. cit., pp. 170–84.
56. Interview with Saodat Olimova, Dushanbe, March 28, 2008.
57. Sadovskaia, "Kitaiskaia migratsiia v Kazakhstane: sovremennye tendentsii i perspektivy," art. cit.
58. Personal observation in Bishkek and Almaty, June and September 2010.
59. Russian is not considered to be a foreign language: the Constitution of Kyrgyzstan recognizes Russian-Kyrgyz bilinguism. In Kazakhstan, Kazakh has the status of national language, and Russian that of the language of interethnic communication.
60. Iu. Iakusheva, "Kitaiski iazyk—delo gosudarstvennoi vazhnosti," *Informatsionno-analiticheskii tsentr izucheniia obshchestvenno-politicheskikh protsessov v post-sovetskom prostranstve*, November 13, 2007, http://www.ia-centr.ru/archive/public_detailsc1ca.html?id=983 (December 16, 2010).
61. Interviews with Chinese teachers at Confucius Institutes in Bishkek, Almaty and Astana, February-March 2008.
62. Fieldwork surveys conducted in the Departments of Chinese in Almaty, Astana, and Bishkek, February-March 2008.

63. G. Kamzieva, "Vsled za Kyrgyzstanom kitaiskoe televidenie poiavilos' i v Kazakhstane," *Zakon.kz*, June 12, 2006, http://www.zakon.kz/72825-vsled-za-kyrgyzstanom-kitajjskoe.html (June 15, 2008).
64. Interview with Murat Auezov, Almaty, March 10, 2008.
65. Interviews conducted in learning institutions in Xinjiang, Urumqi, September 2008.
66. Information given by the Central Asian embassies in China, May 2008, updated by interviews in 2010.
67. "CNPC in Kazakhstan," *CNPC website*, http://www.cnpc.com.cn/eng/cnpcworldwide/euro-asia/Kazakhstan/ (December 18, 2010).
68. More on the Bolashak program http://www.edu-cip.kz/eng/index.php?option=com_content&task=view&id=167&Itemid=290 (December 18, 2010).
69. "Programmu Bolashak ozhidaiut izmeneniia," *Almanews.kz*, January 16, 2011, http://www.almanews.kz/news/programmu-bolashak-ozhidayut-izmeneniya_14072.html (January 28, 2011).
70. Interviews with Chinese experts having organized university exchanges with Central Asia in Lanzhou, Xi'an, Beijing and Shanghai, September-December 2008.
71. Interview with the headhunter, Beijing, May 11, 2008.
72. Interview with the Bolashak representative at the Kazakhstan Consulate in Shanghai, November 24, 2008.
73. This section is built on our interviews with Central Asian students in Urumqi, Lanzhou, Xi'an, Beijing, and Shanghai, September-November 2008.
74. Fieldwork observations in Urumqi and Xi'an, September-October 2008.
75. Fieldwork observations, Kazakhstan, February-March 2008.

8. CHINA AS AN OBJECT OF ACADEMIC KNOWLEDGE: STRUCTURING NATIONAL SINOLOGY

1. N. L. Mamaev, *Obraz Kitaia v sovremennoi Rossii* (Moscow: Institut Dal'nego Vostoka RAN, 2007).
2. Interview with Ablat Khodzhaev, Tashkent, March 22, 2008, and with Klara Khafizova, Almaty, June 6, 2008.
3. Interview with Risamet Karimova, the Director of the section of Uyghur Studies at the Institute of Oriental Studies of the Academy of Sciences, Almaty, February 25, 2008.
4. Interview with Zhon Ali, a researcher in the section of Dungan Studies at the Academy of Sciences, Bishkek, February 22, 2008.
5. Interviews with Ablat Khodzhaev, Tashkent, March 22, 2008, and Almaty, June 5, 2008.
6. For a biography of Sergei Tikhvinsky, see "Sergei Tikhvinskii, akademik RAN, byvshii rektor Diplomaticheskoi akademii MID RF," Ministerstvo inostrannykh

del Rossiiskoi Federatsii, http://www.dipacademy.ru/tixvinskyi_doc.shtml (December 17, 2008).

7. K. Khafizova, *Kazakhskaia strategiia tsinskoi imperii* (Almaty: Institut Ekonomicheskikh Strategii—Tsentral'naia Aziia, 2007).
8. Peyrouse, *Turkmenistan*, op. cit., pp. 97–9.
9. Interview with Zhon Ali, Bishkek, February 22, 2008.
10. Interview with Risamet Karimova, and with Ablet Kamalov, Institute of Oriental Studies at the Academy of Sciences, Almaty, March 4, 2008.
11. Interview with Ablat Khodzhaev, Tashkent, March 22, 2008.
12. Interview with Gulnara Mendikulova, Director of the Department of Complex Questions of International Relations at the Institute of Oriental Studies at the Academy of Sciences, Almaty, March 4, 2008.
13. Interview with Bakhyt Enzhenkhanuly, Director of the Far East Department at the Institute of Oriental Studies at the Academy of Sciences, and with Gul'zhakhan Khadzhieva, a researcher on Sino-Kazakh economic relations in the same department, Almaty, February 26, 2008.
14. Interview with Klara Khafizova, Almaty, March 12, 2008.
15. Interview with Meruert Abuseitova, Director of the Institute of Oriental Studies at the Academy of Sciences, Almaty, March 2, 2008.
16. Interview with Guzel Maitdinova, Director of the Center for Geopolitical Studies, Dushanbe, March 27, 2008.
17. Interview with Viktor Dubovitsky, Vice-Director of the Center for Geopolitical Studies, Dushanbe, March 20, 2008. For more on Eurasianism, see M. Laruelle, *Russian Eurasianism: An Ideology of Empire* (Washington, D.C.: Woodrow Wilson Press/Johns Hopkins University Press, 2008).
18. G. Shukurov, "Tashkentskii gosudarstvennyi institut vostokovedeniia zakrepliaet sviazi s KNR," *MFA.uz*, November 23, 2007, http://mfa.uz/rus/pressa_i_media_servis/231107r_8.mgr (November 23, 2010).
19. Interview with Duken Masimkhan, head of the Sinology Chair of the Lev Gumilev Eurasian University, Astana, March 27, 2008.
20. Interviews with these three individuals were held on February 14, 2008 at Bishkek, on March 10, 2008 at Almaty, and on March 22, 2008 at Tashkent respectively.
21. See the Institute's web site, www.kisi.kz (Jauary 24, 2011).
22. Interview with Bektas Mukhamedzhanov, Almaty, March 5, 2008. Also, see the Institute's website: www.iimp.kz (December 1, 2008).
23. See the website http://www.chinacenter.kz/ (December 1, 2008).
24. The MISI has no website but there is a quick presentation of it on the website of Valentin Bogatyrev's Analytic Consortium Perspektiva, http://www.perspect.org/about/?misi (December 1, 2008).
25. Consult the Center's website, http://www.src.gov.tj/ (December 1, 2008).

26. Interviews with Sukhrob Sharipov and Saifullo Safarov, Center for Strategic Studies, Dushanbe, March 26, 2008.
27. The website of the Institute for Strategic and Transregional Studies, www.uzstrateg.info, is no longer accessible.
28. Information provided by many Chinese scholars working on Central Asia. Interviews in Beijing, Shanghai, Lanzhou and Xi'an, September-December 2008.
29. For the Foundation for Regional Policy, see http://www.polit.uz/, and for The Center for Political Studies, http://www.cps.uz/ (November 15, 2010).
30. Interviews with Fakhrat Tolipov, National University of Uzbekistan, Tashkent, March 14, 2008 and Almaty, June 5, 2008.
31. Interviews conducted in Ashgabat in early April 2008.
32. See the website http://www.risk.kz (November 15, 2010).
33. See the website http://www.inesnet.kz/ (November 15, 2010).
34. See the website http://www.ipp. kg/ (November 15, 2010).
35. See the website http://www.knyazev.org/ (November 15, 2010).
36. Interview with Ainura Asamidinova, convener of the Social Research Center at the American University of Central Asia, Bishkek, February 21, 2008.
37. Interview with Akylbek Saliev, Bishkek, February 19, 2008.
38. http://www.easttime.ru (November 15, 2010).
39. A. Esenbekova, "Spetsialisty nedootsenivaiut perspektivy islamskoi radikalizatsii Kirgizii," *CentrAsia*, January 23, 2007, www.centrasia.ru/newsA.php?st=1169550660 (March 17, 2008).
40. See the website http://www.sange.kz/ (November 15, 2010).
41. See the website http://www.cessi.kz/ (November 15, 2010).
42. See the website http://www.perspect.org (November 15, 2010).
43. Interview with Saodat Olimova, Vice-Director of the Sharq Analytical Center, Dushanbe, March 28, 2008, and June 16, 2010.
44. See the website http://www.zerkalo.tj/ (November 15, 2010).

9. SECURITY AND ECONOMIC CONCERNS AS THE MATRIX OF CENTRAL ASIAN EXPERTISE

1. I. Karsakov, "Osobennosti politiki SShA v Tsentral'noi Azii 'Great Game,'" *Analytic*, no. 5, 2006, p. 15.
2. M. Imanaliev, "Tsentral'naia Aziia i vneshnii mir," *Institute for Public Policy*, February 2, 2007, www.ipp. kg/ru/analysis/foreign_policy/ (March 18, 2010).
3. Interview with Sukhrob Sharipov, Dushanbe, March 26, 2008.
4. A. Iskandarov, "ShOS: k voprosu o rasshirenii," *Analytic*, no. 1, 2007, http://www.analitika.org/article.php?story=20070514234555267 (April 14, 2008).
5. Anonymous interview, Bishkek, February 2008.
6. T. Kokchekeev, cited in "Kitaiskaia ekspansiia v Sredniuiu Aziiu," art. cit.

7. Syroezhkin, *Problemy sovremennogo Kitaia i bezopasnost' v Tsentral'noi Azii*, p. 199.
8. S. K. Kushkumbaev, "ShOS i bezopasnost' Tsentral'noi Azii," *Kazakhstan-Spektr*, no. 4, 2006, p. 19.
9. V. F. Galiamova and A. S. Kaukenov, "Aktual'nye voprosy razvitiia kazakhstansko-kitaiskikh otnoshenii," *Kazakhstan v global'nykh protsessakh*, no. 1, 2006, p. 107.
10. A. Abdrakhmanov and A. Kaukenov, "Otnosheniia Kitaia i stran Tsentral'noi Azii glazami kazakhstanskikh ekspertov," *Kazakhstan v global'nykh protsessakh*, no. 3, 2007, p. 123.
11. For instance A. Retivykh, *Voina za mirovoe gospodstvo* (Almaty: Galym, 2006).
12. Interview with Muratbek Imanaliyev, Bishkek, February 14, 2008.
13. E. Aben, "Kazakhstansko-rossiiskie otnosheniia: faktory 'za' i 'protiv'," *Tsentral'naia Aziia i Kavkaz*, no. 3, 2000, www.ca-c.org/journal/cac-09–2000/03.Aben.shtml (March 19, 2007).
14. Abdrakhmanov and Kaukenov, "Otnosheniia Kitaia i stran Tsentral'noi Azii glazami kazakhstanskikh ekspertov," art. cit.
15. Ibid., p. 121.
16. Galiamova and Kaukenov, "Aktual'nye voprosy razvitiia kazakhstansko-kitaiskikh otnoshenii," art. cit., p. 117.
17. Interview with Adil Kaukenov, Almaty, February 29, 2008, and September 28, 2010.
18. M. Suiunbaev, "Vneshniaia politika Kyrgyzstana: nelegkii vybor," *Analytica*, December 16, 2006, www.analitika.org/article.php?story=20061219232722382 (November 17, 2008).
19. T. Zhukeev and N. Kasenova, "Prioritety vneshnepoliticheskoi orientatsii Kazakhstana," *Analytica*, January 14, 2007, www.analitika.org/article.php?story=2007 0114214001106 (November 17, 2008).
20. For safety reasons, remarks made about this question have been kept anonymous.
21. Galiamova and Kaukenov, "Aktual'nye voprosy razvitiia kazakhstansko-kitaiskikh otnoshenii," art. cit., p. 115.
22. Iskandarov, "ShOS: k voprosu o rasshirenii," art. cit.
23. Abdrakhmanov and Kaukenov, "Otnosheniia Kitaia i stran Tsentral'noi Azii glazami kazakhstanskikh ekspertov," art. cit. pp. 119–29.
24. K. B. Sher'iazdanova, "ShOS v Tsentral'noi Azii," in *ShOS v poiskakh novogo ponimaniia bezopasnosti* (Almaty: IIMP, KISI, IWEP, 2008), p. 60; E.N. Orazalin, *ShOS: osnovy formirovaniia, problemy i perspektivy. Puti sovershenstvovaniia mekhanizmov sotrudnichestva* (Almaty: IWEP, 2007), pp. 93–106.
25. Zholamanova, "Rol' ShOS v uregulirovanii transgranichnykh rek mezhdu Kazakhstanom i Kitaem," art. cit.
26. K. L. Syroezhkin, "Rossiia i Kazakhstan v ShOS: problemy i perspektivy," *Analytica*, December 18, 2006, www.analitika.org/article.php?story=2006121823222 9163 (March 20, 2007).

27. K. L. Syroezhkin, "Sammit ShOS: ozhidaniia i real'nost'," *Analytic*, no. 5, 2007, pp. 9–19.
28. M. A. Olimov, "Ispol'zovanie vodnykh resursov v Tsentral'noi Azii: problemy i ugrozy," in *ShOS v poiskakh novogo ponimaniia bezopasnosti*, op. cit., pp. 73–4.
29. Interview with Sanat Kushkumbayev, researcher at Kazakhstan's Institute for Strategic Studies, Almaty, October 1, 2010; and with Guzel Maitdinova, the Director of the Chair of International Relations at the Slavic-Russian-Tajik University and a specialist on China, Dushanbe, June 26, 2010.
30. Criticisms expressed by the Central Asian participants to the ninth Conference of Central Asian & Shanghai Cooperation Organization, Shanghai International Culture Association, Shanghai Center for International Studies and the Center of SCO Studies at the Shanghai Academy of Social Sciences, Shanghai, July 17–19, 2009.
31. Interview with Konstantin Syroezhkin, Almaty, September 29, 2010.
32. Interviews with Murat Suiunbaev, Bishkek, July 3, 2010, and Iskander Firouz, Dushanbe, June 14, 2010.
33. A. Kniazev, "Afganskaia voenno-politicheskaia real'nost' i potentsial ShOS," in *ShOS v poiskakh novogo ponimaniia bezopasnosti*, p. 154; A. Kniazev, "Nuzhen li Shankhaiskoi Organizatsii Sotrudnichestva Afganistan?," *Knyazev.org*, January 23, 2009.
34. Interview with Viktor Dubovitsky, Dushanbe, June 26, 2010.
35. Paramonov, and Stolpovskii, *Kitai i Tsentral'naia Aziia: sotrudnichestvo v sfere bezopasnosti*, op. cit.
36. Debate between Parviz Mullojanov and Faredoun Khopizoi, Dushanbe, June 23, 2010.
37. Interview with Nurbek Omuraliev, Bishkek, February 22, 2008.
38. Iskandarov, "ShOS: k voprosu o rasshirenii," art. cit.
39. N. Omarov, "Tsentral'naia Aziia: vmeste ili porozn'? Pliusy i minusy regional'noi integratsii," *CentrAsia*, March 19, 2007, http://www.centrasia.ru/newsA.php?st=1174283340 (April 10, 2008).
40. F. Tolipov, "The SCO from the Central Asian Perspective," in Sultanov and Laruelle, *Tsentral'naia Aziia i Kitai: sostoianie i perspektivy sotrudnichestva*, op. cit., pp. 71–82.
41. V. F. Galiamova, "Politika i interesy Kitaia," in Sultanov, *Politika i interesy mirovykh derzhav v Kazakhstane*, op. cit., p. 133.
42. Anonymous interview, Tashkent, March 2008.
43. Syroezhkin, "Rossiia i Kazakhstan v ShOS: problemy i perspektivy," art. cit.
44. M. T. Laumulin, "Geopoliticheskoe polozhenie Tsentral'noi Azii i Kazakhstana na sovremennom etape (2005–2006 gg.)," in *Kontseptsii i podkhody k regional'noi bezopasnosti: opyt, problemy i perspektivy vzaimodeistviia v Tsentral'noi Azii* (Almaty: KISI, 2007), www.analitika.org/article.php?story=20061225010119387 (January 19, 2008).

45. Disenova and Kurmanova, cited in "Kitaiskaia ekspansiia v Sredniuiu Aziiu."
46. E. Usubaliev, "Kyrgyzsko-rossiiskie otnosheniia—k voprosu ob otvetstvennosti v mezhdunarodnykh otnosheniiakh," *Analytica*, June 4, 2007, www.analitika.org/article.php?story=2007060407235456 (April 29, 2008).
47. For example, B. Zhiger and K. Khafizova, "Kazakhstan i Kitai v XXI veke: strategiia sosedstva," *Analytica*, June 21, 2007, www.analitika.org/article.php?story=20070615050207340 (November 1, 2008); and interview with Viktor Dubovitsky, Dushanbe, March 27, 2008.
48. F. Khamraev, "ShOS v formirovanii sistemy regional'noi i global'noi bezopasnosti," *Kazakhstan v global'nykh protsessakh*, no. 1, 2005, p. 75.
49. E. Orazaliev, "Perspektivy ShOS v kontekste sotrudnichestva v oblasti regional'noi bezopasnosti," *Analytic*, no. 4, 2006, p. 27.
50. A. Khodzhaev, *Kitaiskii faktor v Tsentral'noi Azii* (Tashkent: FAN, 2007), p. 54.
51. A. E. Dzhorobekova, "Tsentral'naia Aziia na perekrestke strategicheskikh interesov Kitaia i Rossii," *Voprosy istorii Kyrgyzstana*, no. 4, 2007, pp. 38–41; M. Asanbaev, "Politika Kitaia i Rossii v Tsentral'noi Azii v ramkakh deiatel'nosti ShOS," *Analytic*, no. 2, 2007, pp. 32–42.
52. Syroezhkin, *Problemy sovremennogo Kitaia i bezopasnost' v Tsentral'noi Azii*, op. cit., p. 278. See also K. L. Syroezhkin, "Rossiia i Tsentral'naia Aziia: problemnye uzly," in *Kazakhstan i Rossiia: perspektivy strategicheskogo partnerstva* (Almaty: KISI, 2007), www.analitika.org/article.php?story=20070218084842792 (April 10, 2008).
53. Interview with Bektas Mukhamedzhanov, Almaty, March 5, 2008.
54. K. L. Syroezhkin, "Novaia arkhitektura bezopasnosti v Tsentral'noi Azii," in Sultanov and Laruelle, *Tsentral'naia Aziia i Kitai: sostoianie i perspektivy sotrudnichestva*, op. cit., pp. 55–62.
55. Interview with Leonid Skakovsky, Astana, October 5, 2010, and with Viktor Dubovitsky, Dushanbe, June 24, 2010.
56. Interview with Nurbek Omuraliev, Bishkek, February 22, 2008.
57. M. T. Laumulin, "Tsentral'naia Aziia, Rossiia i Zapad v usloviiakh rosta vliianiia Kitaia v regione," in Sultanov and Laruelle, *Tsentral'naia Aziia i Kitai: sostoianie i perspektivy sotrudnichestva*, op. cit., pp. 41–54.
58. K. L. Syroezhkin, "Rossiia i Kazakhstan v ShOS: problemy i perspektivy," art. cit.
59. Interview with Abdunabi Sattorov, Director of the Department for Foreign Affairs at the Center for Strategic Studies, Dushanbe, June 24, 2010.
60. Interview with Akylbek Saliev, Bishkek, February 19, 2008. This possibility was mentioned by A. Iskandarov, "ShOS: k voprosu o rasshirenii," by Sukhrob Sharipov during the interview, Dushanbe, March 26, 2008, and by Z. Chulanova, "Kitaiskaia model' vneshneekonomicheskogo razvitiia," *Kazakhstan v global'nykh protsessakh*, no. 4, 2007, pp. 30–43.
61. Interview with Sukhrob Sharipov, Dushanbe, March 26, 2008.

62. Interview with Viktor Dubovitsky, Dushanbe, March 27, 2008.
63. M. Imanaliev and E. Abdylbaev, "Vyzovy globalizatsii v Tsentral'noi Azii i nekotorye aspekty politiki KNR v regione," *Tsentral'naia Aziia i Kavkaz*, vol. 51, no. 3, 2007, www.ca-c.org/journal/2007–03-rus/08.shtml (March 7, 2008).
64. Zhukeev and Kasenova, "Prioritety vneshnepoliticheskoi orientatsii Kazakhstana," art. cit.
65. A. Ashimbaeva, "Starye problemy novoi ekonomiki Kazakhstana," art. cit.
66. Interview with Bektas Mukhamedzhanov, Almaty, March 5, 2008; G.U. Khadzhieva, "Kazakhstan i Kitai: strategicheskie podkhody k ekonomicheskomu sotrudnichestvu," in Sultanov, and Laruelle, *Tsentral'naia Aziia i Kitai: sostoianie i perspektivy sotrudnichestva*, op. cit., pp. 120–29.
67. A. S. Kaukenov, "Problemy sovremennogo ekonomicheskogo razvitiia Kitaia," *Kazakhstan v global'nykh protsessakh*, no. 2, 2005, pp. 97–108; Z. Chulanova, "Nekotorye aspekty spetsifiki rynochnoi ekonomiki Kitaia," *Kazakhstan v global'nykh protsessakh*, no. 1, 2006, pp. 76–86.
68. Interview with Muratbek Imanaliyev, Bishkek, February 14, 2008.
69. Interviews with Sukhrob Sharipov and Saifullo Safarov, Dushanbe, March 26, 2008.
70. K. U. Umarov, "O nekotorykh problemakh ekonomicheskikh otnoshenii mezhdu KNR i RT na sovremennom etape," *Tadzhikistan i sovremennyi mir*, no. 3, 2006, pp. 23–34.
71. Khodzhaev, *Kitaiskii faktor v Tsentral'noi Azii*, op. cit., p. 73.
72. Ibid., p. 78.
73. Ibid., pp. 157–8.
74. Anonymous interview, Tashkent, March 2008.
75. Interview with Dosym Satpaev, Almaty, March 6, 2008.
76. Syroezhkin, *Problemy sovremennogo Kitaia i bezopasnost' v Tsentral'noi Azii*, op. cit., p. 272.
77. Syroezhkin, "Kitaiskii vektor vo vneshnei politike Respubliki Kazakhstan," art. cit., p. 29.
78. Ibid.
79. Disenova and Kurmanova, "Neft' i gaz Kazakhstana—miagkaia natsionalizatsiia ili smena partnerov?," *Oasis*, July 30, 2007, www.ca-oasis.info/news/?c=1&id=19422 (November 18, 2008).
80. Ashimbaeva, "Starye problemy novoi ekonomiki Kazakhstana," art. cit.
81. Syroezhkin, *Problemy sovremennogo Kitaia i bezopasnost' v Tsentral'noi Azii*, op. cit., p. 134.
82. Interview with Ablat Khodzhaev, Tashkent, March 22, 2008.
83. For more details, see K. L. Syroezhkin, "Kitai i Tsentral'naia Aziia: politicheskie otnosheniia i torgovo-ekonomicheskoe partnerstvo," *Kazakhstan-Spektr*, no. 1–2, 1997, pp. 61–7.

84. Syroezhkin, *Problemy sovremennogo Kitaia i bezopasnost' v Tsentral'noi Azii*, op. cit., p. 185. But he has a more positive vision of the Chinese WTO experience in another article: K. L. Syroezhkin, "Kitai i VTO: uroki dlia Kazakhstana," *Analytic*, no. 3, 2008, http://www.kisi.kz/site.html?en=0 (April 9, 2010).
85. G. Smailova, "Vstuplenie Kitaia v VTO: usloviia, posledstviia i perspektivy," *Kazakhstan v global'nykh protsessakh*, no. 1, 2006, pp. 87–96.
86. Even if some are aware of the possibilities it could open for trading in a globalized world. See for instance A.T. Ashimbaeva, *Kitai v mirovoi ekonomike* (Almaty: Turan, 2008).
87. S. K. Kushkumbaev, "ShOS i bezopasnost' Tsentral'noi Azii," art. cit., pp. 20–21.
88. Syroezhkin, "Rossiia i Kazakhstan v ShOS: problemy i perspektivy," art. cit.
89. Disenova and Kurmanova, cited in "Kitaiskaia ekspansiia v Sredniuiu Aziiu."
90. Interview with Akylbek Saliev, Bishkek, February 19, 2008.
91. Interview with Viktor Dubovitsky, Dushanbe, March 27, 2008.
92. Interview with Dosym Satpaev, Almaty, March 6, 2008.
93. Interviews in Bishkek with Muratbek Imanaliyev, February 14, 2008; with Orozbek Moldaliev, February 15, 2008; and with Nurbek Omuraliev, February 22, 2008.
94. Interview with Akylbek Saliev, Bishkek, February 19, 2008.
95. Interview with Guzel Maitdinova, Dushanbe, March 27, 2008.
96. Interview with Tatiana Bozrikova, Dushanbe, March 25, 2008.
97. Interviews with Farkhat Tolipov, Tashkent, March 16, 2008, and with Ablat Khodzhaev, March 22, 2008.
98. Interview with Dosym Satpaev, Almaty, March 6, 2008.
99. Interview with Adil Kaukenov, Almaty, February 29, 2008.
100. Syroezhkin, *Problemy sovremennogo Kitaia i bezopasnost' v Tsentral'noi Azii*, op. cit., p. 182.
101. Ibid.
102. Murat Auezov, "Ia znaiu kitaiskuiu kul'turu," *Zona.kz*, November 29, 2004, http://zonakz.net/articles/7560 (November 3, 2008).
103. K.L. Syroezhkin, "Kitaiskii faktor v kontekste bezopasnosti v Tsentral'noi Azii," *Kazakhstan-Spektr*, no. 4, 2006, pp. 25–30.

10. CULTURAL APPREHENSIONS: HISTORICAL LEGACIES AND DEMOGRAPHIC PHOBIAS

1. See for example B. K. Sultanov and L. M. Muzaparova (eds), *Stanovlenie vneshnei politiki Kazakhstana. Istoriia, dostizheniia, vzgliad na budushchee* (Almaty: IWEP, 2005); M. Imanaliev, *Ocherki o vneshnei politike Kyrgyzstana* (Bishkek: Sabyr, 2002). See also S. Parham, *Narrating the Border: The Discourse of Control over China's North-West Frontier* (Berne: Institut für Ethnologie at Berne University, 2004).

2. K. L. Syroezhkin, "Central Asia between the Gravitational Poles of Russia and China," in B. Rumer (ed.), *Central Asia. A Gathering Storm?* (Armonk: M.E. Sharpe, 2002), p. 182; Khodzhaev, *Kitaiskii faktor v Tsentral'noi Azii*, op. cit., pp. 133–4.
3. Amanzholova, Atanov, and Turarbekov, *Pravda o gosudarstvennoi granitse respubliki Kazakhstan*, op. cit., pp. 40–4.
4. Interview with Orozbek Moldaliev, Bishkek, February 15, 2008.
5. Off-the-record interviews, Dushanbe, March 2008.
6. Zhiger and Khafizova, "Kazakhstan i Kitai v XXI veke: strategiia sosedstva," art. cit.
7. Syroezhkin, *Problemy sovremennogo Kitaia i bezopasnost' v Tsentral'noi Azii*, op. cit., p. 204.
8. "Murat Auezov o vremeni i o sebe," *Ekspress K.*, no. 161, September 8, 2000.
9. Interview with Konstantin Syroezhkin, Almaty, March 4, 2008.
10. Zhiger and Khafizova, "Kazakhstan i Kitai v XXI veke: strategiia sosedstva," art. cit.
11. K. T. Talipov, "Prirodnye resursy Sin'tszian-uigurskogo avtonomnogo raiona Kitaia: problemy na fone optimisticheskikh prognozov," *Shygyz*, no. 1, 2005, pp. 95–100.
12. M. Auezov, "Istoriia i sovremennost' v kitaisko-kazakhstanskikh otnosheniiakh," *Tsentral'naia Aziia i Kavkaz*, no. 4, 1999, www.ca-c.org/journal/cac-04–1999/st_20_auezov.shtml (March 10, 2008).
13. G. Zholamanova, "Rol' ShOS v uregulirovanii transgranichnykh rek mezhdu Kazakhstanom i Kitaem."
14. Syroezhkin, "Central Asia between the Gravitational Poles of Russia and China," art. cit., p. 196.
15. B. K. Sultanov, "Politika Rossii, KNR i SShA v Srednei Azii v novykh geopoliticheskikh realiiakh," in *Kazakhstansko-kitaiskoe sotrudnichestvo: sostoianie i perspektivy* (Almaty: KISI, 2007), www.analitika.org/article.php?story=2007 0130002921374 (November 13, 2008).
16. For safety reasons, remarks made about the corruption among the presidential families have been kept anonymous.
17. Interview with Dosym Satpaev, Almaty, March 6, 2008.
18. A. Kaukenov, "Vooruzhennye sily KNR i ikh rol' v politicheskoi zhizni strany," *IWEP website*, www.iwep.kz/index.php?option=com_content&task=view&id=750&Itemid (March 17, 2009).
19. Interview with Ablat Khodzhaev, Tashkent, March 22, 2008.
20. Maria Disenova, cited in "Kitaiskaia ekspansiia v Sredniuiu Aziiu."
21. Zhiger and Khafizova, "Kazakhstan i Kitai v XXI veke: strategiia sosedstva," art. cit.
22. G. U. Khadzhieva and V. M. Krivonogov, "Ekonomicheskaia modernizatsiia zapadnykh regionov Kitaia: zadachi i perspektivy," *Shygyz*, no. 1, 2005, pp. 90–95; G.U. Khadzhieva, "Problema regional'nogo razvitiia Kitaia i strategicheskie podkhody k ee resheniiu," *Shygyz*, no. 1, 2004, pp. 88–93.

23. Syroezhkin, *Problemy sovremennogo Kitaia i bezopasnost' v Tsentral'noi Azii*, op. cit., p. 141.
24. G. U. Khadzhieva, "Zapadnye raiony KNR v kontekste gosudarstvennoi strategicheskoi programme," in *Uigurovedenie v Kazakhstane: traditsiia i novatsiia* (Almaty: Nash Mir, 2007), pp. 164–71.
25. Interview with Murat Auezov, Almaty, March 10, 2008.
26. K. L. Syroezhkin, "Strategiia 'bol'shogo osvoeniia zapada' i problemy bezopasnosti Tsentral'noi Azii," *Analytic*, no. 2, 2007, pp. 22–32.
27. Syroezhkin, *Mify i real'nost' etnicheskogo separatizma v Kitae i bezopasnost' Tsentral'noi Azii*, op. cit., pp. 271 and 536.
28. Many experts see a parallel between the Chinese pressures on Islam and those in effect in Central Asian states, which are also criticized for fueling rather than of stopping extremism. On this matter, we protect the identity of those experts interviewed.
29. V. F. Galiamova, "Etnicheskii separatizm v Sin'tsziane: sostoianie problemy i perspektivy," *Kazakhstan-Spektr*, no. 1, 2004, pp. 9–15.
30. Syroezhkin, *Mify i real'nost' etnicheskogo separatizma v Kitae i bezopasnost' Tsentral'noi Azii*, op. cit., p. 299.
31. Ibid., p. 358.
32. Ibid., p. 522.
33. Interview with Muratbek Imanaliyev, Bishkek, February 14, 2008.
34. Interview with Adil Kaukenov, Almaty, February 29, 2008.
35. Interviews with Murat Auezov, Almaty, March 10, 2008, and Dosym Satpaev, Almaty, March 6, 2008.
36. Khodzhaev, *Kitaiskii faktor v Tsentral'noi Azii*, op. cit., pp. 24–5. Ethnogenetic theories are common currency in Central Asia and especially in Uzbekistan, where the theme of the millenary existence of the Turkic peoples on their present territory is a part of official dogma.
37. Ibid., p. 40.
38. Ibid., p. 165.
39. Zhiger and Khafizova, "Kazakhstan i Kitai v XXI veke: strategiia sosedstva," art. cit.
40. Khafizova, *Kazakhskaia strategiia tsinskoi imperii*, op. cit., p. 51.
41. Ibid., p. 41.
42. Ibid., p. 91.
43. Syroezhkin, *Mify i real'nost' etnicheskogo separatizma v Kitae i bezopasnost' Tsentral'noi Azii*, op. cit., p. 82.
44. Ibid., p. 214.
45. Interview with Murat Auezov, Almaty, March 10, 2008.
46. E. Usubaliev, "Kitaiskaia 'kolonizatsiia' Afriki," *Analytica*, February 12, 2007, http://www.analitika.org/article.php?story=20070212052315456 (April 16, 2008).

47. B. Zhumalieva, "Kazakhstan i Kitai: vzaimovliianie i sotrudnichestvo," *Ekonomicheskie strategii—Tsentral'naia Aziia*, no. 5, 2007, p. 43.
48. M. Auezov, "Ia znaiu kitaiskuiu kul'turu," *Zona.kz*, November 29, 2004, http://zonakz.net/articles/7560 (October 17, 2007).
49. Rakhimdzhon Sultanov, cited in "Kitaiskaia ekspansiia v Sredniuiu Aziiu."
50. Interview with Dosym Satpaev, Almaty, March 6, 2008.
51. B. Bekturganova, "Pochemu uezzhaiut liudi iz Kazakhstana? Monitoring ot ASiP 15 maia 2001 gg.," *Zona.kz*, May 15, 2001, http://zonakz.net/oldnavi/articles/asip150501a.shtml (June 20, 2008).
52. G. U. Khadzhieva, "Vnutrenniaia migratsiia v Kitae: podkhody k izucheniiu i osobennosti kitaiskoi statistiki," *Kazakhstan Spektr*, no. 2, 2010, pp. 20–25.
53. Muzaparova (ed.), *Sovremennyi Kitai. Ekonomika, demografiia, vneshniaia politika*, op. cit., p. 383.
54. Interviews with Bektas Mukhamedzhanov, Almaty, March 5, 2008, and Murat Auezov, Almaty, March 10, 2008.
55. Interview with Konstantin Syroezhkin, Almaty, September 29, 2010.
56. Syroezhkin, *Problemy sovremennogo Kitaia i bezopasnost' v Tsentral'noi Azii*, op. cit., p. 156.
57. Interview with Sukhrob Sharipov, Dushanbe, March 26, 2008.
58. Interview with Murat Auezov, Almaty, March 10, 2008.
59. "Murat Auezov: Nachalos' velikoe pereselenie!," *Postskriptum*, no. 38, 2005, http://www.gorno-altaisk.ru/archive/2005/38/003.htm (January 17, 2007).
60. Muzaparova (ed.), *Sovremennyi Kitai. Ekonomika, demografiia, vneshniaia politika*, op. cit., p. 408.
61. Interview with Dosym Satpaev, Almaty, March 6, 2008.
62. Interview with Sukhrob Sharipov, Dushanbe, March 26, 2008.
63. Muzaparova, *Sovremennyi Kitai. Ekonomika, demografiia, vneshniaia politika*, op. cit., p. 406.
64. Interview with Bektas Mukhamedzhanov, Almaty, March 5, 2008.
65. Interview with Saodat Olimova, Dushanbe, March 28, 2008.
66. Aben, "Kazakhstansko-rossiiskie otnosheniia: faktory 'za' i 'protiv'," art. cit.
67. Muzaparova, *Sovremennyi Kitai. Ekonomika, demografiia, vneshniaia politika*, op. cit., p. 409.
68. Syroezhkin, *Problemy sovremennogo Kitaia i bezopasnost' v Tsentral'noi Azii*, op. cit., p. 185.
69. A. S. Kaukenov (ed.), *Kitai v XXI veke. Aktual'nye tendentsii razvitiia kliuchevykh sfer zhizni* (Almaty: IMEM, 2008), vol. 2, pp. 47–55.
70. Z. Ashigalide, "Malye narody KNR: neizvestnyi Kitai," *Ekonomicheskie strategii—Tsentral'naia Aziia*, no. 5, 2007, pp. 78–9.
71. Interview with Murat Auezov, Almaty, March 10, 2008.
72. Zhiger and Khafizova, "Kazakhstan i Kitai v XXI veke: strategiia sosedstva," art. cit.

73. Interview with Ablat Khodzhaev, Tashkent, March 22, 2008.
74. Interview with Sukhrob Sharipov, Dushanbe, March 26, 2008.
75. Interview with Konstantin Syroezhkin, Almaty, March 4, 2008.

CONCLUSION

1. H. G. Broadman, *Africa's Silk Road: China and India's New Economic Frontier* (Washington, D.C.: World Bank Publications, 2007).
2. See J. C. Strauss, and M. Saavedra, "Introduction: China, Africa and Internationalization," *The China Quarterly*, no. 199, 2009, pp. 551–62, and the whole special issue on China-Africa.
3. C. M. Dent (ed.), *China and Africa Development Relations* (London: Routledge, 2010).
4. F. Manji and S. Marks (eds), *African Perspectives on China in Africa* (Nairobi, Oxford: Fahamu, 2007).
5. B. Sautman and Y. Hairong, "African Perspectives on China–Africa Links," *The China Quarterly*, no. 199, 2009, pp. 729–60.
6. Syroezhkin, "Kitaiskaia migratsiia v Kazakhstane: voobrazhaemye i real'nye ugrozy i vyzovy," art. cit., pp. 117–28.
7. E. Gel'bras, "ShOS na fonde obshchestvennykh nastroenii naseleniia Rossii, Kazakhstana, Kirgizii, Tadzhikistana i Kitaia," in M. Ashimbaev, and G. Chufrin (eds), *ShOS: stanovlenie i perspektivy razvitiia* (Almaty: IWEP, 2005), p. 186.
8. E. Sadovskaia, "Kitaiskie migranty v Kazakhstane: otnosheniia kazakhstanskikh grazhdan (po resul'tatam sotsiologicheskogo issledovaniia)," *Analytic*, no. 5, 2007, pp. 20–9.
9. Ibid., pp. 23–4.
10. More details in Olimova, "The Multifaceted Chinese Presence in Tajikistan," art. cit.
11. Syroezhkin, *Problemy sovremennogo Kitaia i bezopasnost' v Tsentral'noi Azii*, op. cit., p. 199.
12. Syroezhkin, "V politike—kholodno, v ekonomike—goriacho," *Kazakhstan-Kitai. Ot prigranichnoi torgovli k strategicheskomu partnerstvu*, vol. 2, p. 154.
13. S. J. Blank, *China's Military Power: Shadow over Central Asia* (Arlington: Lexington Institute, 2006); K.L. Syroezhkin, *Kitai: voennaia bezopasnost'* (Almaty: KISI, 2008).
14. On the Urumqi riots and the media handling of the event by a self-confident China, see Sh. Wei and Ch. Gang, "The Urumqi Riots and China's Ethnic Policy in Xinjiang," *East Asian Policy*, vol. 1, no. 3, 2009, pp. 14–22; Y. Li, "Notes on the Chinese Government's Handling of the Urumqi Riot in Xinjiang," *The China and Eurasia Forum Quarterly*, vol. 7, no. 4, 2009, pp. 11–15; K. L. Syroezhkin, "Sobytiia 5ogo iulia v Urumchi: prichiny i uroki," *Kazakhstan v global'nykh protsessakh*, no. 3, 2009, pp. 98–110; *Repression in China: Roots and Repercussions of the*

Urumqi Unrest (The Hague: Unrepresented Nations and Peoples Organization, November 2009); and the World Uyghur Congress website, http://www.uyghur-congress.org/en/

15. In July 2009, about 500 activists from the Uyghur associations of Kyrgyzstan protested in front of the Chinese Embassy in Bishkek against the violent repressions orchestrated by Beijing. The chairman of the Uyghur Association Ittipak, Dilmurat Akbarov, has been arrested by the Kyrgyz authorities, who were mindful of showing Beijing that they have the ability to control any potential anti-Chinese movement.
16. *Ta Kung Pao* [Hong Kong], September 24, 2009.
17. Confidential information from circles of the security services of Kazakhstan.
18. C. Hawkins and R. R. Love (eds), *The New Great Game: Chinese Views on Central Asia* (Leavenworth: Foreign Military Studies Office, 2006).
19. All the arguments advanced in relation to Russia emerged in interviews conducted with Central Asian experts in the framework of this research.

BIBLIOGRAPHY

2009 Minerals Yearbook (Reston: U.S. Geological Survey, 2011).

Abdrakhmanov A. and Kaukenov A., "Otnosheniia Kitaia i stran Tsentral'noi Azii glazami kazakhstanskikh ekspertov" [The View of Kazakh Experts on the Relations between China and the Countries of Central Asia], *Kazakhstan v global'nykh protsessakh*, no. 3, 2007, pp. 119–28.

Abdyldaev E., "Kitaiskii vektor vneshnei politiki Kurmanbeka Bakieva" [The Chinese Vector of Kurmanbek Bakiyev's Foreign Policy], *Analytica*, June 2006, www.analitika.org/article.php?story=20060621024111739 (May 21, 2007).

Aben E., "Kazakhstansko-rossiiskie otnosheniia: faktory 'za' i 'protiv'" [Kazakhstan-Russia Relations: Pro and Contra], *Tsentral'naia Aziia i Kavkaz*, no. 3, 2000, http://www.ca-c.org/journal/cac-09–2000/03.Aben.shtml (March 19, 2007).

Alamanov S. K., *Kratkaia istoriia i opyt resheniia pogranichnykh problem Kyrgyzstana* [A Short History of Solving Border Issues in Kyrgyzstan] (Bishkek: Friedrich Ebert Foundation, 2005).

Allès E., "The Chinese-speaking Muslims (Dungans) of Central Asia: A Case of Multiple Identities in a Changing Context," *Asian Ethnicity*, vol. 6, no. 2, 2005, pp. 121–34.

Amanzholova Z. A., Atanov M. M. and Turarbekov B. Sh., *Pravda o gosudarstvennoi granitse respubliki Kazakhstan* [The Truth about the State Borders of the Republic of Kazakhstan] (Almaty: Zhibek Zholy, 2006).

Ambrosio, T., "Catching the Shanghai Spirit: how the Shanghai Cooperation Organization Promotes Authoritarian Norms in Central Asia," *Europe-Asia Studies*, vol. 60, no. 8, 2008, pp. 1321–44.

Andrews-Speed P. and Vinogradov S., "China's Involvement in Central Asian Petroleum: Convergent or Divergent Interests?," *Asian Survey*, vol. 40, no. 2, 2000, pp. 377–97.

Arvis J.-F., Raballand G. and Marteau J.-F., "The Cost of Being Landlocked: Logistics Costs and Supply Chain Reliability," *World Bank Working Paper*, June 2007.

Asanbaev M., "Politika Kitaia i Rossii v Tsentral'noi Azii v ramkakh deiatel'nosti ShOS" [Chinese and Russian Policy in Central Asia in the Context of SCO Activities], *Analytic*, no. 2, 2007, pp. 32–42.

Ashigalide Z., "Malye narody KNR: neizvestnyi Kitai" [The Small Peoples of the PRC: An Unknown China], *Ekonomicheskie strategii—Tsentral'naia Aziia*, no. 5, 2007, pp. 72–9.

Ashimbaev M. and Chufrin G. (eds), *ShOS: stanovlenie i perspektivy razvitiia* [Formation and Perspectives for Development of the SCO] (Almaty: IWEP, 2005).

Ashimbaeva A. T., *Kitai v mirovoi ekonomike* [China in the World Economy] (Almaty: Turan, 2008).

Atabaki T. and Mehendale S. (eds), *Central Asia and the Caucasus: Transnationalism and Diaspora* (London: Routledge, 2005), pp. 148–68.

Aunasova A. M. and Suleimenov A. M., "Iz istorii delimitatsii gosudarstvennykh granits Respubliki Kazakhstan" [On the History of the State Border Delimitation of the Republic of Kazakhstan], *EvraIuzh*, no. 4 (23), 2010, http://www.eurasialaw.ru/index.php?option=com_jcontentplus&view=article&id=652:2010-06-03-09-21-06&catid=99:2010-06-02-08-56-30&Itemid=196 (December 16, 2010).

Bailes A. J. K., Dunay P., Guang P. and Troitskiy M., "The Shanghai Cooperation Organization," *SIPRI Policy Paper*, no. 17, May 2007.

Bekturganova B., *"Uigurskii ekstremizm" v Tsentral'noi Azii: mif ili real'nost'? (sotsiologicheskii analiz problem)* [The "Uyghur Extremism" in Central Asia: Myth or Reality? (A Sociological Analysis of the Problem)] (Almaty: Kompleks, 2002).

Beshimov A., Abdykaimov O., Radzhapov B. and Tashbekov N., *Prigranichnaia torgovlia. Otsenka perecheniia granits mezhdu Kyrgyzstanom i Uzbekistanom* [Border trade. An assessment of border crossing between Kyrgyzstan and Uzbekistan] (Bishkek: OSCE-Central Asian Free Market Institute, 2011).

Blank S. J., *China's Military Power: Shadow over Central Asia* (Arlington: Lexington Institute, 2006).

Borishpolets K. and Babadzhanov A., "Migratsionnye riski stran Tsentral'noi Azii" [Migratory Risks for Central Asian Countries], *Analiticheskie zapiski MGIMO*, no. 2, 2007, pp. 9–19.

Broadman H. G., *Africa's Silk Road: China and India's New Economic Frontier* (Washington, D.C.: World Bank Publications, 2007).

Buldakova E., "Conflicting Views on Land Issue between Kyrgyzstan and China," *CIMERA*, no. 24, May 2002, http://www.cimera.org/files/camel/en/24e/MICA24E-Buldakova2.pdf (December 16, 2010).

CAREC Transport and Trade Facilitation: Partnership for Prosperity (Manila: Asian Development Bank, 2009).

Castets R., "Opposition politique, nationalisme et islam chez les Ouïghours du Xinjiang," *Les Etudes du CERI*, no. 110, 2004.

Chebotarev A., "Kazakhstan: Priority Oil Routes," *Central Asia and the Caucasus*, vol. 9, no. 3, 2001, pp. 29–30.

Chuah O., "Muslims in China: the Social and Economic Situation of the Hui Chinese," *Journal of Muslim Minority Affairs*, vol. 24, no. 1, 2004, pp. 155–62.

Chulanova Z., "Kitaiskaia model' vneshneekonomicheskogo razvitiia" [The Chinese Model of Foreign Economic Development], *Kazakhstan v global'nykh protsessakh*, no. 4, 2007, pp. 30–43.

——— "Nekotorye aspekty spetsifiki rynochnoi ekonomiki Kitaia" [Some Specific Aspects of the Market Economy in China], *Kazakhstan v global'nykh protsessakh*, no. 1, 2006, pp. 76–86.

Clarck W. and Kamalov A., "Uighur Migration across Central Asian Frontiers," *Central Asian Survey*, vol. 23, no. 2, 2004, pp. 167–82.

Clarke M., "Xinjiang and China's Relations with Central Asia, 1991–2001: Across the 'Domestic–Foreign Frontier'?," *Asian Ethnicity*, vol. 4, no. 2, 2003, pp. 207–24.

Cooley A., *Great Games, Local Rules: The New Great Power Contest for Central Asia* (Oxford: Oxford University Press, 2012).

——— "The Stagnation of the SCO. Competing Agendas and Divergent Interests in Central Asia," *PONARS Eurasia Memo* no. 85, September 2009.

Cross-Border Trade within the Central Asia Regional Economic Cooperation (Washington, D.C.: World Bank, 2007).

Dautcher J., "Folklore and Identity in an Uyghur Community in the 1990s Xinjiang China" (PhD: Berkeley, University of California, 1999).

De Haas M. (ed.), *The Shanghai Cooperation Organisation. Towards a Full-Grown Security Alliance?* (Clingendael: Netherlands Institute of International Relations, 2007).

Denison M., "The EU and Central Asia: Commercialising the Energy Relationship," *EUCAM Working Paper*, no. 2, 2009.

Dent C. M. (ed.), *China and Africa Development Relations* (London: Routledge, 2010).

Dickens M., *The Soviets in Xinjiang, 1911–1949*, http://www.oxuscom.com/sovinxj.htm (January 6, 2011).

Dodikhudoev K. and Niyatbekov V., "The Chinese Vector in Tajikistan's Foreign Policy," *Central Asia and the Caucasus*, no. 2, 2009, pp. 119–29.

Dukhovny V. A. and De Schutter J., *Water in Central Asia. Past, Present, Future* (London: CRC Press, 2011).

Dwivedi R., "China's Central Asia Policy in Recent Times," *The China and Eurasia Forum Quarterly*, vol. 4, no. 4, 2006, pp. 139–59.

Dzhorobekova A. E., "Tsentral'naia Aziia na perekrestke strategicheskikh interesov Kitaia i Rossii" [Central Asia at the Crossroads of Russia's and China's Strategic Interests], *Voprosy istorii Kyrgyzstana*, no. 4, 2007, pp. 38–41.

Electricity Sectors in CAREC Countries: A Diagnostic Review of Regulatory Approaches and Challenges (Manila: Asian Development Bank, 2005).

Esposito J. L. (ed.), *The Oxford History of Islam* (Oxford and New York: Oxford University Press, 2009).

Flolenkov V. S., *Sovremennye torgovo-ekonomicheskie otnosheniia KNR s tsentral'noaziatskimi stranami-chlenami ShOS i Turkmenistanom* [China's Contemporary Trade and Economic Relations with Central Asian SCO members and Turkmenistan] (Moscow: Institut Dal'nego Vostoka RAN, 2009).

Foot R., "Chinese Strategies in a US-Hegemonic Global Order: Accomodating and Hedging," *International Affairs*, vol. 82, no. 1, 2006, pp. 77–94.

Free Trade Zone and Port Hinterland Development (New York: ESCAP, 2005).

Frolic B. M. and Chin G. T., "The Challenge of Energy Security in Northeast Asia: China's Rising Energy Needs and Northeast Asian Cooperation," *North Pacific Region Advanced Research Center Publications*, 2000, http://www.norpac.or.jp/main2/follow/1999–4.pdf (May 10, 2007).

Frost A., "The Collective Security Treaty Organization, the Shanghai Cooperation Organization, and Russia's Strategic Goals in Central Asia," *The China and Eurasia Forum Quarterly*, vol. 7, no. 3, 2009, pp. 83–102.

Galenovich Iu., *Vzgliad na Rossii iz Kitaia. Proshloe i nastoiashchee Rossii i nashikh otnoshenii s Kitaem v traktovke kitaiskikh uchenykh* [Looking on Russia from China. The Past and the Present of Russia and of our Relations to China in Chinese Academic Works] (Moscow: Vremia, 2010).

Galiamova V. F., "Etnicheskii separatizm v Sin'tsziane: sostoianie problemy i perspektivy" [Ethnic Separatism in Xinjiang: State of the Problem and Outlook], *Kazakhstan-Spektr*, no. 1, 2004, pp. 9–15.

Galiamova V. F. and Kaukenov A. S., "Aktual'nye voprosy razvitiia kazakhstansko-kitaiskikh otnoshenii" [Current Questions concerning the Development of Sino-Kazakh Relations], *Kazakhstan v global'nykh protsessakh*, no. 1, 2006, pp. 106–120.

Garver J. W., "Development of China's Overland Transportation Links with Central, South-West and South Asia," *The China Quarterly*, no. 185, 2006, pp. 1–22.

Gill B., *Rising Star. China's New Security Diplomacy* (Washington, D.C.: Brookings Institution Press, 2007).

Gill B. and Oresman M., *China's New Journey to the West: China's Emergence in Central Asia and Implications for US Interests* (Washington, D.C.: CSIS Press, 2003).

Ginsburg G. and Pinkele C.F., *The Sino-Soviet Territorial Dispute, 1949–64* (New York: Praeger, 1978).

Gladney D., *Dislocating China: Reflections on Muslims, Minorities, and Other Subaltern Subjects* (Chicago: University of Chicago Press, 2004).

——— *Muslim Chinese. Ethnic Nationalism in the People's Republic* (Cambridge, Mass.: Harvard University Press, 1991, second edition 1996).

Gleason G., "The Uzbek Expulsion of US Forces and Realignment in Central Asia," *Problems of Post-Communism*, vol. 53, no. 2, 2006, pp. 49–60.

Goldstein A., *Rising to the Challenge: China's Grand Strategy and International Security* (Stanford: Stanford University Press, 2005).

Gonzalez B. F., "Charting a New Silk Road? The Shanghai Cooperation Organization and Russian Foreign Policy" (Master Thesis, University of Oregon, 2001).

Hancock K. J., "Escaping Russia, Looking to China: Turkmenistan Pins Hopes on China's Thirst for Natural Gas," *The China and Eurasia Forum Quarterly*, vol. 4, no. 3, 2006, pp. 67–87.

Hanova S., "Perspectives on the SCO: Images and Discourses," *The China and Eurasia Forum Quarterly*, vol. 7, no. 2, 2009, pp. 63–82.

Hawkins C. and Love R. R. (eds), *The New Great Game. Chinese Views on Central Asia* (Leavenworth: Foreign Military Studies Office, 2006).

Hu H., "Dal'neishee usilenie ekonomicheskogo sotrudnichestva mezhdu SUAR KNR i Kazakhstanom v ramkakh ShOS" [The Forthcoming Reinforcement of Economic Cooperation between Chinese Xinjiang and Kazakhstan in the SCO Framework], in *Problemy ekonomicheskogo i finansovogo sotrudnichestva v ramkakh ShOS* [Problems of Economic and Financial Cooperation in the SCO Framework] (Almaty: KISI, 2006), pp. 146–52.

Ibraimov S., "China-Central Asia Trade Relations: Economic and Social Patterns," *The China and Eurasia Forum Quarterly*, vol. 7, no. 1, 2009, pp. 47–59.

Imanaliev M., *Ocherki o vneshnei politike Kyrgyzstana* [Essays on the Foreign Policy of Kyrgyzstan] (Bishkek: Sabyr, 2002).

Imanaliev M. and Abdylbaev E., "Vyzovy globalizatsii v Tsentral'noi Azii i nekotorye aspekty politiki KNR v regione" [Challenges of Globalization in Central Asia and Several Aspects of PRC Policy in the Region], *Tsentral'naia Aziia i Kavkaz*, vol. 51, no. 3, 2007, www.ca-c.org/journal/2007–03-rus/08.shtml (December 16, 2010).

Ipek P., "The Role of Oil and Gas in Kazakhstan's Foreign Policy: Looking East or West?," *Europe-Asia Studies*, vol. 59, no. 7, 2007, pp. 1179–99.

Iskandarov A., "ShOS: k voprosu o rasshirenii" [SCO: the Issue of Enlargement], *Analytic*, no. 1, 2007, http://www.analitika.org/article.php?story=20070514234555267 (April 14, 2008).

Iwashita A. (ed.), *Eager Eyes Fixed on Eurasia* (Hokkaido: Slavic Research Center, Hokkaido University, 2007).

——— "The Shanghai Cooperation Organization and Its Implications for Eurasian Security: A New Dimension of 'Partnership' after the post-Cold War Period," *Slavic Eurasia's Integration into the World Economy and Community* (Hokkaido: Slavic Research Center, Hokkaido University, 2004), pp. 259–81.

Jiang J. and Sinton J., "Overseas investments by Chinese national oil companies. Assessing the drivers and impacts," *IEA Information Paper*, February 2011.

Jones Luong P. and Weinthal E., *Oil is not a Curse. Ownership Structure and Institutions in Soviet Successor States* (Cambridge: Cambridge University Press, 2010).

Junussova M., *Global Market Needs New Cities or Development of Border Trade Ports of Kazakhstan* (Vienna: REAL CORP 007 Proceedings, May 20–23, 2007).

Kaminski B. and Mitra S., *Skeins of Silk: Borderless Bazaars and Border Trade in Central Asia* (Washington, D.C.: World Bank, 2009).

Karsakov I., "Osobennosti politiki SShA v Tsentral'noi Azii 'Great Game'" [The Particularities of US Policy in the "Great Game" in Central Asia], *Analytic*, no. 5, 2006, pp. 14–7.

Kassenova N., *Aide au développement: la percée chinoise au Tadjikistan et au Kirghizstan* (Paris: IFRI, Series *Russie. NEI. Vision*, no. 36, 2009).

Katz M., "Russia and the Shanghai Cooperation Organization: Moscow's Lonely Road from Bishkek to Dushanbe," *Asian Perspective*, vol. 32, no. 3, 2008, pp. 183–7.

Katzman K., "Afghanistan: Post-Taliban Governance, Security, and US Policy," *Congressional Research Service*, April 20, 2010.

Kaukenov A. S. (ed.), *Kitai v XXI veke. Aktual'nye tendentsii razvitiia kliuchevykh sfer zhizni* [China in the Twenty-First Century: Current Tendencies in the Development of Key Life Sectors] (Almaty: IMEP, 2008).

——— "Problemy sovremennogo ekonomicheskogo razvitiia Kitaia" [Problems Associated with China's Current Economic Development], *Kazakhstan v global'nykh protsessakh*, no. 2, 2005, pp. 97–108.

Kavalski E. (ed.), *The New Central Asia. The Regional Impact of International Actors* (New Jersey, London: World Scientific, 2010).

Kazakhstan i Rossiia: perspektivy strategicheskogo partnerstva [Kazakhstan and Russia: Prospects for a Strategic Partnership] (Almaty: KISI, 2007).

Kazakhstansko-kitaiskoe sotrudnichestvo: sostoianie i perspektivy [Sino-Kazakh Cooperation: Its Current State and Outlook] (Almaty: KISI, 2007).

Kazhegeldin A. M., "Vremia razbrasyvat' i sobirat' kamni," [It is time to disseminate and collect stones], *Tsentral'noaziatskii biulleten'*, no. 4, 1999, pp. 14–5.

Kellner T., *La Chine et la nouvelle Asie centrale* (Brussels: GRIP, 2002).

——— "Le 'Dragon' et la 'tulipe': les relations sino-afghanes dans la période post-11 septembre," *Asia Papers*, Brussels Institute of Contemporary China Studies, January 2009.

——— *L'Occident de la Chine. Pékin et la nouvelle Asie centrale (1991–2001)* (Paris: PUF, 2008).

——— "La politique pétrolière de la RPC: stratégies et conséquences internationales," *Puissance Chine? Outre-terre. Revue de Géopolitique*, no. 15, 2006, pp. 425–69.

Kemp G., *The East Moves West: India, China, and Asia's Growing Presence in the Middle East* (Washington, D.C.: Brookings Institution Press, 2010).

Kerimbekova N. and Galitskiy V., "On the State Border between Kyrgyzstan and China," *Central Asia and the Caucasus*, no. 5, 2002, pp. 108–13.

Khadzhieva G. U., "Problema regional'nogo razvitiia Kitaia i strategicheskie podkhody k ee resheniiu" [Problems of China's Regional Development and Strategic Approaches to Resolve them], *Shygyz*, no. 1, 2004, pp. 88–93.

——— "Vnutrenniaia migratsiia v Kitae: podkhody k izucheniiu i osobennosti kitaiskoi statistiki" [Internal Migrations in China: Approaches to the Study and Particularities of Chinese Statistics], *Kazakhstan Spektr*, no. 2, 2010, pp. 20–5.

Khadzhieva G. U. and Krivonogov V. M., "Ekonomicheskaia modernizatsiia zapadnykh regionov Kitaia: zadachi i perspektivy" [Economic Modernization of the Western Regions of China: Objectives and Outlook], *Shygyz*, no. 1, 2005, pp. 90–5.

Khafizova K., *Kazakhskaia strategiia tsinskoi imperii* [The Qing Empire's Kazakh Strategy] (Almaty: Institut Ekonomicheskikh Strategii—Tsentral'naia Aziia, 2007).

Khalid A., *Islam after Communism: Religion and Politics in Central Asia* (Berkeley: University of California Press, 2007).

Khamraev F., "ShOS v formirovanii sistemy regional'noi i global'noi bezopasnosti" [The SCO's Role in the Formation of a System of Regional and Global Security], *Kazakhstan v global'nykh protsessakh*, no. 1, 2005, pp. 73–88.

Khamraeva-Aubert A., "Migration, colonisation et formation d'une identité nationale chez les Ouïgours d'Asie centrale" (Master Thesis, Paris: EHESS, 2005).

Khliupin V., *Geopoliticheskii treugol'nik. Kazakhstan-Kitai-Rossiia. Proshloe i nastoiashchee pogranichnoi problemy* [The Geopolitical Triangle of Kazakhstan-China-Russia: Past and Present of the Border Disputes] (Moscow: Mezhdunarodnyi Evraziiskii Institut Ekonomicheskikh i Politicheskikh Issledovanii, 1999), http://www.iicas.org/AIBOLIT/publ_VX_Tr.htm (March 23, 2008).

Khodzhaev A., *Kitaiskii faktor v Tsentral'noi Azii* [The Chinese Factor in Central Asia] (Tashkent: FAN, 2007).

Kielmas M., "China's Foreign Energy Asset Acquisitions: From Shopping Spree to Fire Sale?," *The China and Eurasian Forum Quarterly*, vol. 3, no. 3, 2005, pp. 27–30.

Kontseptsii i podkhody k regional'noi bezopasnosti: opyt, problemy i perspektivy vzaimodeistviia v Tsentral'noi Azii [Conceptions and Approaches toward Regional Security: Experiences, Problems and Outlooks for Cooperation in Central Asia] (Almaty: KISI, 2007).

Korsun V. A., *Vneshniaia politika Kitaia na poroge XXI veka* [China's Foreign Policy on the Threshold of the Twenty-first Century] (Moscow: MGIMO, 2002).

Kozhirova S., "Vnutrennie i vneshnie aspekty sovremennoi kitaiskoi migratsii" [Domestic and Foreign Aspects of Contemporary Chinese Migration], *Analytic*, no. 6, 2007, pp. 45–52.

Kozlov L. N. and Beliakov A. A., "Irtyshsko-obskaia glubokovodnaia magistral' ot Kitaia do severnogo morskogo puti v sostave transportno-energicheskoi vodnoi sistemy Evrazii" [The Irtysh-Ob Road from China to the Northern Sea, as part of the Hydro-System of Transport and Energy in Eurasia], *Evraziiskaia ekonomicheskaia integratsiia*, no. 3 (4), 2009, pp. 132–43.

Krivonogov V., "Kazakhstansko-kitaiskie torgovo-ekonomicheskie i nauchnye-tekhnicheskie otnosheniia" [Kazakhstan-China Trade, Economic, Scientific and Technical Relations], *Kazakhstan i sovremennyi mir*, no. 1, 2003, pp. 24–41.

Kuchins A., Sanderson T. and Gordon D., *The Northern Distribution Network and the Modern Silk Road* (Washington, D.C.: CSIS, December 2009).

Kushkumbaev S. K., "ShOS i bezopasnost' Tsentral'noi Azii" [The SCO and Security in Central Asia], *Kazakhstan-Spektr*, no. 4, 2006, pp. 18–21.

Lai H., *The Domestic Sources of China's Foreign Policy: Regimes, Leadership, Priorities and Process* (London: Routledge, 2010).

Laruelle M., "Beyond the Afghan Trauma: Russia's Return to Afghanistan," *Jamestown Occasional Paper*, August 2009.

——— *Labor Migration and Social Upheaval as the Face of Globalization in Central Asia* (London: Brill, 2012).

——— "Russian Policy on Central Asia and the Role of Russian Nationalism," *Silk Road Papers*, April 2008, http://www.isdp.eu/files/publications/srp/08/ml08russiacentral.pdf (January 28, 2011).

Laruelle M., Huchet J.-F., Peyrouse S. and Balci B. (eds), *China and India in Central Asia: A New "Great Game"?* (New York: Palgrave Macmillan, 2010).

Laruelle M. and Peyrouse S., *Asie centrale, la dérive autoritaire. Cinq républiques entre héritage soviétique, dictature et islam* (Paris: Autrement/CERI, 2006).

——— (eds) *Mapping Central Asia: Indian Perceptions and Strategies* (Farnham: Ashgate, 2011).

——— *Les Russes du Kazakhstan. Identités nationales et nouveaux États dans l'espace post-soviétique* (Paris: Maisonneuve & Larose/IFEAC, 2004).

——— "The United States in Central Asia: Reassessing a Challenging Partnership," *Strategic Analysis*, vol. 35, no. 3, 2011, pp. 427–38.

Laumulin M., *The Shanghai Cooperation Organization as Geopolitical Bluff? A View from Astana* (Paris: IFRI, Series *Russie. NEI. Vision*, no. 36, 2006).

Levinsson C. and Svanberg I., "Kazakhstan-China Border Trade thrives after Demarcation Treaty," *The Analyst*, February 16, 2000, pp. 63–75.

Li Y., "Notes on the Chinese Government's Handling of the Urumqi Riot in Xinjiang," *The China and Eurasia Forum Quarterly*, vol. 7, no. 4, 2009, pp. 11–5.

Liu Jun and Wu Lei, "Key Issues in China-Iran Relations," *Journal of Middle Eastern and Islamic Studies*, vol. 4, no. 1, 2010, pp. 40–57.

Lo B., *Axis of Convenience. Moscow, Beijing, and the New Geopolitics* (Washington, D.C., London: Brookings Institution Press and Chatham House, 2008).

——— "China and Russia. Common Interests, Contrasting Perceptions," *CLSA Asian Geopolitics* (London: Chatham House, May 2006).

Mackerras C., *China's Ethnic Minorities and Globalisation* (London, New York: Routledge, Curzon, 2003).

Mackerras C. and Clarke M. (eds), *China, Xinjiang and Central Asia: History, Transition and Crossborder Interaction into the 21st Century* (New York: Routledge Contemporary China Series, 2009).

Madiev E., "Perspektivy internatsionalizatsii kitaiskogo iuania v ramkakh ShOS" [Perspectives for Internationalizing the Chinese Yuan in the Framework of the SCO], *Kazakhstan v global'nykh protsessakh*, no. 2, 2010, pp. 124–9.

Mamaev N. L., *Obraz Kitaia v sovremennoi Rossii* [The Image of China in Contemporary Russia] (Moscow: Institut Dal'nego Vostoka RAN, 2007).

Manji F. and Marks S. (eds), *African Perspectives on China in Africa* (Nairobi and Oxford: Fahamu, 2007).

McDermott R. N., "The Rising Dragon. SCO Peace Mission 2007," *Jamestown Occasional Paper*, October 2007.

——— "United States and NATO Military Cooperation with Kazakhstan: The Need for a New Approach," *The Journal of Slavic Military Studies*, vol. 21, no. 4, 2008, pp. 615–41.

Megoran N., "Framing Andijon, Narrating the Nation: Islam Karimov's Account of the Events of 13 May 2005," *Central Asian Survey*, vol. 27, no. 1, 2008, pp. 15–31.

Mendikulova G. M. and Atanbaeva B. Zh., *Istoriia migratsii mezhdu Kazakhstanom i Kitaem v 1860–1960-e gg.* [History of Migration between Kazakhstan and China, 1860–1960] (Almaty: Institut Vostokovedeniia, 2008).

Millward J. A., *Eurasian Crossroads: a History of Xinjiang* (New York: Columbia University Press, 2007).

Mirutina O. G., "Perspektivy razvitiia sotrudnichestva Kitaia i Kazakhstana i ego znachenie dlia Rossii" [Perspectives of Developing Cooperation between China and Kazakhstan and its Significance for Russia] (Master Thesis, Omsk University, 2003).

Myant M. and Drahokoupil J., "International Integration and the Structure of Exports in Central Asian Republics," *Eurasian Geography and Economics*, vol. 49, no. 5, 2009, pp. 604–22.

Nadyrov Sh., "Sin'tszian-uigurskii avtonomnyi raion v dinamike ekonomicheskikh i politicheskikh otnoshenii RK i KNR" [The Xinjiang-Uygur Autonomous Region in the Dynamic of Economic and Political Relations between Kazakhstan and China], *Kazakhstan-Spektr*, no. 1, 2006, pp. 14–25.

Najman B., Raballand G. and Pomfret R. (eds), *The Economics and Politics of Oil in the Caspian Basin. The Redistribution of Oil Revenues in Azerbaijan and Kazakhstan* (London: Routledge, 2007).

Niazi T., "The Ecology of Strategic Interests: China's Quest for Energy Security from the Indian Ocean and the South China Sea to the Caspian Sea Basin," *The China and Eurasia Forum Quarterly*, vol. 4, no. 4, 2006, pp. 97–116.

Nichol J., "Uzbekistan: Recent Developments and US Interests," *Congressional Research Service*, August 27, 2008.

Noi A. U., "Iran and the Shanghai Cooperation Organization: Is it Possible for Iran to Become Full Member of the SCO under Pressure of Nuclear Issue?," *Perceptions*, Autumn-Winter 2006, pp. 79–104.

Olcott M. B., "Is China A Reliable Stakeholder in Central Asia?" Testimony before the US-China Economic and Security Review Commission, August 4, 2006, http://www.carnegieendowment.org/publications/index.cfm?fa=view&id=18606&prog=zr (April 15, 2007).

Olimova S., "The Multifaceted Chinese Presence in Central Asia," *The China and Eurasia Forum Quarterly*, vol. 7, no. 1, 2008, pp. 61–77.

Ong R., "China's Security Interests in Central Asia," *Central Asian Survey*, vol. 24, no. 4, 2005, pp. 425–39.

Orazaliev E., "Perspektivy ShOS v kontekste sotrudnichestva v oblasti regional'noi bezopasnosti" [Outlook for the SCO in the Context of Cooperation on Regional Security], *Analytic*, no. 4, 2006, pp. 26–8.

Orazalin E. N., *ShOS: osnovy formirovaniia, problemy i perspektivy. Puti sovershenstvovaniia mekhanizmov sotrudnichestva* [The SCO: Formation, Problems, and Prospects. The Paths for Advancing the Cooperation Mechanisms] (Almaty: IWEP, 2007).

Paramonov V. and Strokov A., *Ekonomicheskoe prisutstvie Rossii i Kitaia v Tsentral'noi Azii* [The Economic Presence of Russia and China in Central Asia] (Swindon: Defence Academy of the United Kingdom, Conflict Studies Research Center, Central Asian Series, 07/12, 2007).

——— *Russian-Chinese Relations: Past, Present, Future* (Swindon: Defence Academy of the United Kingdom, Russian Series, September 2006).

Parham S., *Narrating the Border. The Discourse of Control over China's North-West Frontier* (Berne: Institut für Ethnologie at Berne University, 2004).

Perspectives on Caspian Oil and Gas Development (International Energy Agency Working Paper Series, December 2008).

Petrov G., "Tajikistan's Hydropower Resources," *Central Asia and the Caucasus*, vol. 21, no. 3, 2003, pp. 153–61.

Peyrouse S., "Chinese Economic Presence in Kazakhstan: China's Resolve and Central Asia's Apprehension," *China Perspectives*, no. 3, 2008, pp. 55–75.

——— "The Economic Aspects of the Chinese-Central-Asia Rapprochement," *Silk Road Papers*, September 2007, http://www.isdp.eu/images/stories/isdp-main-pdf/2007_peyrouse_economic-aspects-of-the-chinese-central-asia-rapprochement.pdf (January 23, 2011).

——— "Facing the Challenge of Separatism: The EU, Central Asia and the Uyghur Issue," *EUCAM Brief Paper*, no. 4, January 2009, http://www.eucentralasia.eu/fileadmin/user_upload/PDF/Policy_Briefs/Policy-Brief-4.Peyrouse.pdf (January 23, 2011).

——— "Flowing Downstream: The Sino-Kazakh Water Dispute," *China Brief*, vol. 7, no. 10, May 16, 2007, pp. 7–10, http://www.jamestown.org/single/?no_cache=1&tx_ttnews%5Btt_news%5D=4131 (January 23, 2011).

——— "The Hydroelectric Sector in Central Asia and the Growing Role of China," *The China and Eurasia Forum Quarterly*, vol. 5, no. 2, 2007, pp. 131–48.

——— "Russia-Central Asia: Advances and Shortcomings of the Military Partnership," in S. Blank (ed.), *Central Asian Security Trends: Views from Europe and Russia* (Carlisle: Strategic Studies Institute, US Army War College, 2011), pp. 1–34.

——— "Sino-Kazakh Relations: A Nascent Strategic Partnership," *China Brief*, November 7, 2008, http://www.jamestown.org/single/?no_cache=1&tx_ttnews%5Btt_news%5D=34142 (January 23, 2011).

——— "Le tournant ouzbek de 2005. Éléments d'interprétation de l'insurrection d'Andijan," *La Revue internationale et stratégique*, no. 64, 2006, pp. 78–87.

——— *Turkmenistan. Strategies of Power, Dilemmas of Development* (Armonk: M.E. Sharpe, 2011).

Pi Y.-H., "China's Boundary Issues with the former Soviet Union," *Issues and Studies*, vol. 28, no. 7, 1992, pp. 63–75.

Pikayev A. A., "Enlarging the Shanghai Cooperation Organization. Is Iran a Viable Member?," *PONARS Eurasia Policy Memo*, no. 15, August 2008.

Polat N., *Boundary Issues in Central Asia* (Ardsley: Brill Transnational Publishers, 2002).

Pomfret R., "Turkmenistan's Foreign Policy," *The China and Eurasia Forum Quarterly*, vol. 6, no. 4, 2008, pp. 19–34.

Proposed Loan, Asian Development Fund Grants, and Technical Assistance Grant. Kyrgyz Republic and Republic of Tajikistan: CAREC Regional Road Corridor Improvement Project (Manila: Asian Development Bank, October 2007).

Raballand G. and Andrésy A., "Why should Trade between Central Asia and China Continue to Expand?," *Asia Europe Journal*, vol. 5, no. 2, 2007, pp. 235–52.

Raballand G. and Kaminski B., "La Déferlante économique chinoise et ses conséquences en Asie centrale," *Monde Chinois*, no. 11, 2007, pp. 129–34.

——— "Entrepôt for Chinese Consumer Goods in Central Asia: The Puzzle of Re-exports through Kyrgyz Bazaars," *Eurasian Geography and Economics*, vol. 50, no. 5, 2009, pp. 581–90.

Radnitz S., "Networks, Localism and Mobilization in Aksy, Kyrgyzstan," *Central Asian Survey*, vol. 24, no. 4, 2005, pp. 405–24.

Report of the Deputy Head of Migration Service of the Ministry of Interior prepared for the Seminar on Labor Migration, Dushanbe, June 19, 2008.

Repression in China: Roots and Repercussions of the Urumqi Unrest (The Hague: Unrepresented Nations and Peoples Organization, November 2009).

Retivykh A., *Voina za mirovoe gospodstvo* [The War for World Domination] (Almaty: Galym, 2006).

Riabtsev A. D., *Ugrozy vodnoi bezopasnosti v Respublike Kazakhstan v transgranichnom kontekste i vozmozhnye puti ikh ustraneniia* [Threats to the Water Security of the Republic of Kazakhstan in the Crossborder Context and Possible Ways of Solving them], Interstate Commission for Water Coordination of Central Asia, 2008, http://www.icwc-aral.uz/workshop_march08/pdf/ryabtsev_ru.pdf (September 27, 2009).

Roberts S. R., "The Uighurs of the Kazakhstan Borderlands: Migration and the Nation," *Nationalities Papers*, vol. 26, no. 3, 1998, pp. 511–3.

——— "Uyghur Neighborhoods and Nationalisms in the Former Sino-Soviet Borderland. An Historical Ethnography of a Stateless Nation on the Margins of Modernity" (PhD, Los Angeles: University of Southern California, 2003).

Ross R. S. and Johnston A. I. (eds), *New Directions in the Study of China's Foreign Policy* (Stanford: Stanford University Press, 2006).

Rumer B. (ed.), *Central Asia: A Gathering Storm?* (Armonk: M.E. Sharpe, 2002).

Rumer E., Trenin D. and Zhao H., *Central Asia: Views from Washington, Moscow and Beijing* (Armonk: M. E. Sharpe, 2007).

Sadovskaia E., "Chinese Migration to Kazakhstan: A Silk Road for Cooperation or a Thorny Road of Prejudice?," *The China and Eurasia Forum Quarterly*, vol. 5, no. 4, 2007, pp. 147–70.

——— "Kitaiskaia migratsiia v Kazakhstane: sovremennye tendentsii i perspektivy" [The Chinese Migration in Kazakhstan: Contemporary Tendencies and Perspectives], *Analytic*, no. 6, 2007, pp. 33–44.

——— "Kitaiskie migranty v Kazakhstane: otnosheniia kazakhstanskikh grazhdan (po resul'tatam sotsiologicheskogo issledovaniia)" [Chinese Migrants in Kazakhstan: the Attitudes of Kazakhstan's Citizens (Results of a Sociological Survey)], *Analytic*, no. 5, 2007, pp. 20–9.

Sautman B. and Hairong Y., "African Perspectives on China-Africa Links," *The China Quarterly*, no. 199, 2009, pp. 729–60.

Schlyter B. (ed.), *Prospects for Democracy in Central Asia* (Istanbul: Swedish Research Institute in Istanbul, 2005).

Shlapentokh V., "China in the Russian Mind Today: Ambivalence and Defeatism," *Europe-Asia Studies*, vol. 59, no. 1, 2007, pp. 1–22.

ShOS v poiskakh novogo ponimaniia bezopasnosti [The SCO on the Search for a New Conception of Security] (Almaty: IIMP, KISI, IWEP, 2008).

Shuja Sh., "China's Energy Needs and Central Asia," *National Observer*, Council for the National Interest, Melbourne, no. 67, 2006, pp. 56–65.

Singh Roy M., "Shanghai Cooperation Organisation and Afghanistan: Scope and Limitation," *Strategic Analysis*, vol. 34, no. 4, 2010, pp. 545–61.

Smailova G., "Vstuplenie Kitaia v VTO: usloviia, posledstviia i perspektivy" [China's Membership in the WTO: Conditions, Consequences and Prospects], *Kazakhstan v global'nykh protsessakh*, no. 1, 2006, pp. 87–96.

Spector R. A., "Bazaar Politics. The Fate of Marketplaces in Kazakhstan," *Problems of Post-Communism*, vol. 55, no. 6, 2008, pp. 42–53.

——— "Securing Property in Contemporary Kyrgyzstan," *Post-Soviet Affairs*, vol. 24, no. 2, 2008, pp. 149–76.

Starr S. F. (ed.), *The New Silk Roads. Transport and Trade in Greater Central Asia* (Washington, D.C.: The Central Asia-Caucasus Institute, 2007).

——— *Xinjiang: China's Muslim Borderland* (Armonk: M.E. Sharpe, 2004).

Stepanov E. D., *Politika nachinaetsia s granitsy. Nekotorye voprosy pogranichnoi politiki KNR vtoroi poloviny XX v.* [Politics begin with Borders. Some Questions about the

PRC's Border Policy in the Second Half of the Twentieth Century] (Moscow: Institut Dal'nego Vostoka RAN, 2007).

Strauss J. C. and Saavedra M., "Introduction: China, Africa and Internationalization," *The China Quarterly*, no. 199, 2009, pp. 551–62.

Sultanov B. K. (ed.), *Politika i interesy mirovykh derzhav v Kazakhstane* [Policies and interests of world powers in Kazakhstan] (Almaty: Friedrich Ebert Stiftung, 2002).

Sultanov B. and Laruelle M. (eds), *Tsentral'naia Aziia i Kitai: sostoianie i perspektivy sotrudnichestva* [Central Asia-China: Current Status and Prospects for Cooperation] (Almaty: KISI, 2008).

Sultanov B. K. and Muzaparova L. M. (eds), *Stanovlenie vneshnei politiki Kazakhstana. Istoriia, dostizheniia, vzgliad na budushchee* [The Establishment of Kazakhstan's Foreign Policy. History, Successes, Vision for the Future] (Almaty: IWEP, 2005).

Swanström N., "China and Central Asia: A New Great Game or Traditional Vassal Relations?," *Journal of Contemporary China*, vol. 14, no. 45, 2005, pp. 569–84.

Syroezhkin K. L., "Bol'shaia igra v tsentral'no-aziatskom regione" [The Great Game in the Central Asian Region], *Ekonomicheskie strategii—Tsentral'naia Aziia*, no. 5, 2007, pp. 48–55.

——— *Kazakhstan-Kitai. Ot prigranichnoi torgovli k strategicheskomu partnerstvu* [Kazakhstan-China. From Border Trade to Strategic Partnership] (Almaty: KISI, 2010, 2 vol.).

——— *Kitai: voennaia bezopasnost'* [China: Military Security] (Almaty: KISI, 2008).

——— "Kitai i Tsentral'naia Aziia: politicheskie otnosheniia i torgovo-ekonomicheskoe partnerstvo" [China and Central Asia: Political Relations and Economic and Trade Partnership], *Kazakhstan-Spektr*, no. 1–2, 1997, pp. 61–7.

——— "Kitaiskaia migratsiia v Kazakhstane: voobrazhaemye i real'nye ugrozy i vyzovy" [Chinese Migrations to Kazakhstan: Imagined and Real Threats and Challenges], *Mezhdunarodnye issledovaniia*, no. 1, 2009, pp. 117–27.

——— "Kitaiskii faktor v kontekste bezopasnosti v Tsentral'noi Azii" [The Chinese Factor in the Context of Security in Central Asia], *Kazakhstan-Spektr*, no. 4, 2006, pp. 25–30.

——— *Mify i real'nost' etnicheskogo separatizma v Kitae i bezopasnost' Tsentral'noi Azii* [Myths and Realities of Ethnic Separatism in China and Security in Central Asia] (Almaty: Dajk-Press, 2003).

——— *Problemy sovremennogo Kitaia i bezopasnost' v Tsentral'noi Azii* [Problems of Contemporary China and Security in Central Asia] (Almaty: KISI, 2006).

——— "Sammit ShOS: ozhidaniia i real'nost'" [The SCO Summit: Hopes and Realities], *Analytic*, no. 5, 2007, pp. 9–19.

——— "Sobytiia 5ogo iulia v Urumchi: prichiny i uroki" [The Events of July 5 in Urumqi. Causes and lessons], *Kazakhstan v global'nykh protsessakh*, no. 3, 2009, pp. 98–110.

——— "Social Perceptions of China and the Chinese: A View from Kazakhstan," *The China and Eurasia Forum Quarterly*, vol. 7, no. 1, 2009, pp. 29–46.

——— "Strategiia 'bol'shogo osvoeniia zapada' i problemy bezopasnosti Tsentral'noi Azii" [The Strategy for the Development of the "Far West" and the Security Problems for Central Asia], *Analytic*, no. 2, 2007, pp. 22–32.

Talipov K. T., "Prirodnye resursy Sin'tszian-uigurskogo avtonomnogo raiona Kitaia: problemy na fone optimisticheskikh prognozov" [The Natural Resources of the Uyghur Autonomous Region of Xinjiang in China: Problems on a Background of Optimistic Forecasts], *Shygyz*, no. 1, 2005, pp. 95–100.

Temirbolat B., "Mezhdu Kazakhstanom i Kitaem mozhet nachat'sia konflikt iz-za vody" [A Water-related Conflict might Occur between Kazakhstan and China], *Saiasat*, no. 8, 2000, pp. 97–8.

Tsou B. N., *China and International Law. The Boundary Disputes* (New York, London: Praeger, 1990).

Uigurovedenie v Kazakhstane: traditsiia i novatsiia [Uyghur Studies in Kazakhstan: Traditions and Innovations] (Almaty: Nash Mir, 2007).

Umarov A. and Pashkhun D., *Tensions in Sino-Central-Asian Relations and their Implications for Regional Security* (Swindon: Defence Academy of the United Kingdom, Conflict Studies Research Center, Central Asian Series, 06/02, 2006).

Umarov K. U., "O nekotorykh problemakh ekonomicheskikh otnoshenii mezhdu KNR i RT na sovremennom etape" [Some Current Problems in the Economic Relations between the PRC and Tajikistan], *Tadzhikistan i sovremennyi mir*, no. 3, 2006, pp. 23–34.

Uyama T. (ed.), *Empire, Islam, and Politics in Central Eurasia* (Sapporo: Slavic Research Center, Hokkaido University, 2007).

Vinokurov E. and Emerson M., "Optimisation of Central Asian and Eurasian Trans-Continental Land Transport Corridors," *EUCAM Working Paper*, no. 7, December 2009.

Vinokurov E., Jadraliyev M. and Shcherbanin Y., *The EURASEC Transport Corridor* (Astana: Eurasian Development Bank, March 2009). In Russian: *Mezhdunarodnye transportnye korridory EvrAzES* (Astana: EABD, 2009).

Water Resources of Kazakhstan in the New Millennium (Almaty: UNDP, 2004).

Wei S. and Gang C., "The Urumqi Riots and China's Ethnic Policy in Xinjiang," *East Asian Policy*, vol. 1, no. 3, 2009, pp. 14–22.

Wishnik E., *Russia, China, and the United States in Central Asia: Prospects for Great Power Competition and Cooperation in the Shadow of the Georgian Crisis* (Carlisle: U.S. Army War College, 2009).

Wu H.-L. and Chen C.-H., "The Prospects for Regional Economic Integration between China and the Five Central Asian Countries," *Europe-Asia Studies*, vol. 56, no. 7, 2004, pp. 1069–70.

"Xinjiang Oil Industry Development," Center for Energy and Global Development, http://www.wsichina.org/cs4_7.pdf (January 4, 2012).

Xu X., "The Oil and Gas links between Central Asia and China: a Geopolitical Perspective," *OPEC Review*, March 1999, pp. 33–54.

Yenikeyeff S. M. S., *Kazakhstan's Gas: Export Markets and Export Routes* (Oxford: Oxford Institute for Energy Studies, November 2008).

Zeb R., "Pakistan and the Shanghai Cooperation Organization," *The China and Eurasia Forum Quarterly*, vol. 4, no. 4, 2006, pp. 51–60.

Zhao H., *Kitai, Tsentral'naia Aziia i Shankhaiskaia Organizatsiia Sotrudnichestva* [China, Central Asia and the SCO] (Moscow: Carnegie Endowment for International Peace, 2005).

——— "The Shanghai Cooperation Organization at 5: Achievements and Challenges Ahead," *The China and Eurasia Forum Quarterly*, vol. 4, no. 3, 2006, pp. 105–23.

Zhaparov A., "The Chinese Migrants Issue in Kyrgyzstan," *The China and Eurasia Forum Quarterly*, vol. 7, no. 1, 2009, pp. 79–91.

Zhiger B. and Khafizova K., "Kazakhstan i Kitai v XXI veke: strategiia sosedstva"[Kazakhstan and China in the 21st Century: Neighborhood Strategy], *Analytica*, June 21, 2007, www.analitika.org/article.php?story=20070615050207340 (November 1, 2008).

Zholamanova G., "Rol' ShOS v uregulirovanii transgranichnykh rek mezhdu Kazakhstanom i Kitaem" [The Role of the SCO in the Regulation of Crossborder Rivers between Kazakhstan and China], *Analytic*, no. 1, 2007, pp. 34–42.

Zholamanova Zh., "O nekotorykh aspektakh kazakhstansko-kitaiskogo ekonomicheskogo sotrudnichestva v ramkakh ShOS: Politologicheskii analiz" [On Several Aspects of Kazakhstan-China Economic Cooperation in the SCO Framework: A Political Analysis], *Analytic*, no. 1, 2008, pp. 27–37.

Zhumalieva B., "Kazakhstan i Kitai: vzaimovliianie i sotrudnichestvo" [Kazakhstan and China: Interaction and Cooperation], *Ekonomicheskie strategii—Tsentral'naia Aziia*, no. 5, 2007, pp. 42–7.

Ziegler C. E., "The Energy Factor in China's Foreign Policy," *Journal of Chinese Political Science*, vol. 11, no. 1, 2006, pp. 1–23.

Zweig D., "'Resource Diplomacy' Under Hegemony," Conference on "The Rise of China and Its Implications for Asia-Pacific," Academia Sinica, Taipei, August 25–26, 2006.

INDEX